CAXTON'S *GOLDEN LEGEND*

EARLY ENGLISH TEXT SOCIETY
O.S. 357
2021

auenture / he slewe Cayn / For Cayn was alway aferde and hid hym emong busshes / and breres / and the child that lad lameth had supposed it had ben som wild beest & directed lameth to shote ther at / and so wenyng to shote at a beest / slewe Cayn / And whan he knewe that he had slayn Cayn he with his bowe slewe the chyld / and thus he slewe them bothe / to his dampnacion / therfor as the synne of Cayn was punysshyd vij sythes / so was the synne of lameth seuenty sythes and vij / that is to saye lxxvij sowles that cam of lameth were perysshyd in the deluuye and noes flode also his wif dyde hym moche sorowe / & euyl entreted hym / And he beyng wroth said that he suffred that for his double homycide and manslaughter / yet neuertheles he fered hym by payne sayeng / Why wil ye sle me / he shal be more and sorer punysshed that sleeth me / than he that slewe Cayn / After that abel was slayn strabus saith that Adam auowed nomore to haue to doo with his wif / but by an angel he brake the vowe / by cause a sone shold be born to god / yet neuertheles Josephus said that whan abel was slayn And Cayn fled alway Adam thought of procreacion of chyldren / And so whan he was Cxxx yere old he engendrid seth lyke to his simylitude / & he to the ymage of god / This seth was a good man / & he gate Enos and Enos Caynam / And Cynam begate Malael / and Malael Jareth / And Jareth Enoch / and Enoch Matussale / And matussale Lamech / And Lamech Noe / And lyke as in the generacion of Cayn the seuenth was the werst / so in the generacion of Seth the seuenth was the beste / that was Enoch whom god toke and brought hym in to paradys vnto the tyme that he shal come with hely for to conuerte the hertes of the faders in to the sones / And adam lyued after that he had begoten Seth viij C yere and engendrid sones and doughtres Somme hold opinyon xxx sones and xxx doughtres and some .l. of that one / and .l. of that other / we fynde no certeynte of thys in the bible / But alle the dayes of adam lyuyng here in erthe amounte to the somme of ix Cxxx yere / And in thende of his lyf whan he shold dye / it is said but of none auctoryte / that he sente Seth his sone in to paradys for to fetche the oyle of mercy / where he receyued certayn graynes of the fruyt of the tree of mercy by an angel / And whan he come agayn / he fonde his fader adam yet alyue and told hym what he had don And thenne Adam lawhed first / and thenne deyed / and thenne he leyd the graynes or kernellis vnder his faders tonge and buryed hym / in the vale of ebron / and out of his mouth grewe thre trees of the thre graynes / of whiche the crosse that our lord suffred his passion on / was made by vertue of whiche he gate very mercy and was brought out of derknes in to veray lyght of heuen / to the whiche he brynge vs that lyueth and regneth god world with oute ende /

Here endeth the lyf of Adam /

Here begynneth the hystorye of Noe the first sonday in Sexagesme /

After that Adam was deed deyd Eue / and was buryed by hym At the begynnyg in the first age the peple lyuyd longe / Adam lyuyd ix C xxx yere / And Matussale lyued ix C lxix yere / Seynt Jherom said that he deyde the same yere the flood was / ¶ Thenne Noe was the tenthe

Woodcut of Noah in the Ark with creatures. [Caxton's *Golden Legend*] (Westminster: William Caxton, [1483–4]). Cambridge University Library, Inc.2.J.1.1 [3781], f. 39r (sig. e7r). Reproduced by permission of the Syndics of Cambridge University Library

CAXTON'S *GOLDEN LEGEND*

VOLUME II

THE OLD TESTAMENT LEGENDS

EDITED BY

MAYUMI TAGUCHI

JOHN SCAHILL

AND

SATOKO TOKUNAGA

Published for

THE EARLY ENGLISH TEXT SOCIETY

by the

OXFORD UNIVERSITY PRESS

2021

OXFORD
UNIVERSITY PRESS

Great Clarendon Street, Oxford, OX2 6DP,
United Kingdom

Oxford University Press is a department of the University of Oxford.
It furthers the University's objective of excellence in research, scholarship,
and education by publishing worldwide. Oxford is a registered trade mark of
Oxford University Press in the UK and in certain other countries

First edition published in 2021
Impression: 1

British Library Cataloguing in Publication Data
Data available

ISBN 9780192847676

Typeset by Alan Bennett, Oxford
Printed in Great Britain
on acid-free paper by
TJ Books Limited, Padstow, Cornwall

CONTENTS

VOLUME II

LIST OF ILLUSTRATIONS

PLATES

LIST OF SIGLA

Sigla of Extant Copies

C	Cambridge, Cambridge University Library, Inc.2.J.1.1[3781] (base copy)
Cc	Cambridge, Corpus Christi College, Parker Library, EP.H.7
Ch	Chantilly, Bibliothèque du Musée Condé, XXI-(1)-C-006
H	Hereford, Hereford Cathedral Library, K.5.6
L	London, British Library, C.11.d.8
M_1	Manchester, the Special Collections of University of Manchester Library (formerly the John Rylands Library), 12018.1–2
S_1	San Marino, California, Huntington Library, 69797

ABBREVIATIONS

AL	Anglo-Latin
Bh	*Bible historiale*
BL	British Library
Cm	*Cursor mundi*
D-L	*La Légende dorée*, ed. Brenda Dunn-Lardeau, Textes de la Renaissance, 19 (Paris, 1997)
EV	Early Version (of the Wycliffite Bible)
GiL	*Gilte Legende*
GoL	William Caxton, *The Golden Legend* ([1483–4])
Hodnett	Edward Hodnett, *English Woodcuts 1480–1535* (Oxford, 1935; rev. 1973)
HP	*The Historye of the Patriarks*
Hs	Petrus Comestor, *Historia scholastica*
JA	Flavius Josephus, *Jewish Antiquities*
LgA	*Legenda aurea*
LgD	*Légende dorée*
LV	Later Version (of the Wycliffite Bible)
MED	*Middle English Dictionary* ⟨https://quod.lib.umich.edu/m/middle-english-dictionary/dictionary⟩
OE	Old English
OED	*Oxford English Dictionary* ⟨https://www.oed.com⟩
OF	Old French
OT	Old Testament
om.	omitted
STC	*A Short-Title Catalogue of Books Printed in England, Scotland and Ireland, and of English Books Printed Abroad 1475–1640*, first compiled by A. W. Pollard and G. R. Redgrave, 2nd edn., rev. and enlarged, begun by W. A. Jackson and F. S. Ferguson, completed by K. F. Pantzer, 3 vols. (London, 1976–91)
WB	Wycliffite Bible
{}	enclose letters that are indistinct in C, but can be confirmed from other copies

[]	enclose letters added or interchanged editorially
/	indicates a virgule in MSS and incunabula
|	indicates a column/page break
–	indicates a printed hyphen in *GoL* (in the apparatus)
\	indicates a line-break in *GoL* (in the apparatus)
C+	indicates that the reading is shared by C and one or more of the other copies collated

ADDITIONS TO BIBLIOGRAPHY

Blake, N. F., 'St. Ursula and the Eleven Thousand Virgins', edited in *Selections from William Caxton*, with an introduction, notes, and glossary by N. F. Blake, Clarendon Medieval and Tudor Series (Oxford, 1973).

Calmette, Joseph, 'Dom Pedro, roi des Catalans et la cour de Bourgogne', *Annales de Bourgogne*, 18 (1946), 7–15.

Ford, Judy Ann, *English Readers of Catholic Saints: The Printing History of William Caxton's Golden Legend* (London, 2020).

Murdoch, Brian, *The Apocryphal Adam and Eve in Medieval Europe: Vernacular Translations and Adaptations of the Vita Adae et Evae* (Oxford, 2009).

Patterson, Jeanette, 'Interpreting Job's Silence in the *Bible historiale*', *Modern Language Notes*, 127/5 (2012), S217–S242.

Sutton, Anne F., 'Caxton was a Mercer: His Social Milieu and Friends', in Nicholas Rogers (ed.), *England in the Fifteenth Century: Proceedings of the 1992 Harlaxton Symposium* (Stamford, Conn., 1994), 118–48.

ADDITIONAL NOTES TO VOLUME I

p. lxx: A digital facsimile of W_1 is now available at https://hdl.loc.gov/loc.rbc/Rosenwald.0566.

p. 200: While the standard version of *LgA*, as in the editions of Häuptli and Maggioni, does not include a legend for Corpus Christi, there is one among the additional legends at the end of Graesse's edition (Cap. CCXXIII, pp. 935–6). The first few sentences of this correspond to lines 64–71 and 76–93 in *GoL* and its source in *LgD*(c); the two phrases added in *GoL* (see notes to lines 80–1 and 91) have no equivalent in the Latin. Otherwise the Latin and vernacular legends appear to be unrelated.

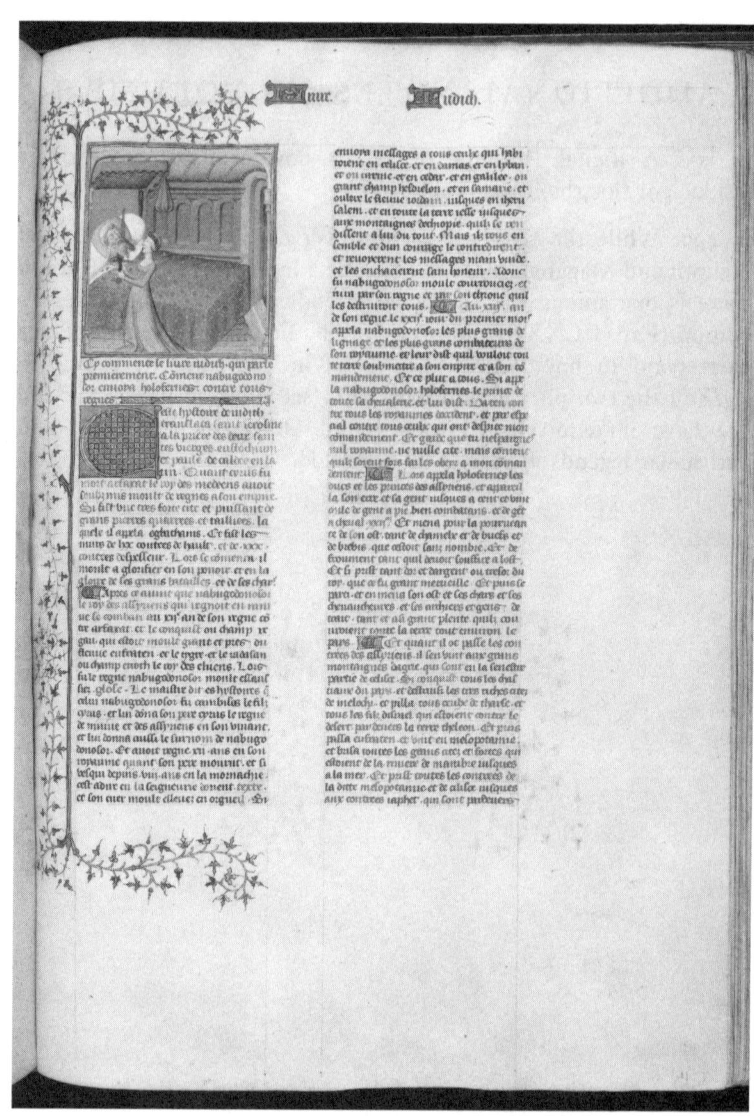

Pl. 1. Judith killing Holofernes in his bed. *Bible historiale*. London, British Library, Royal 19. D. iii, f. 227r

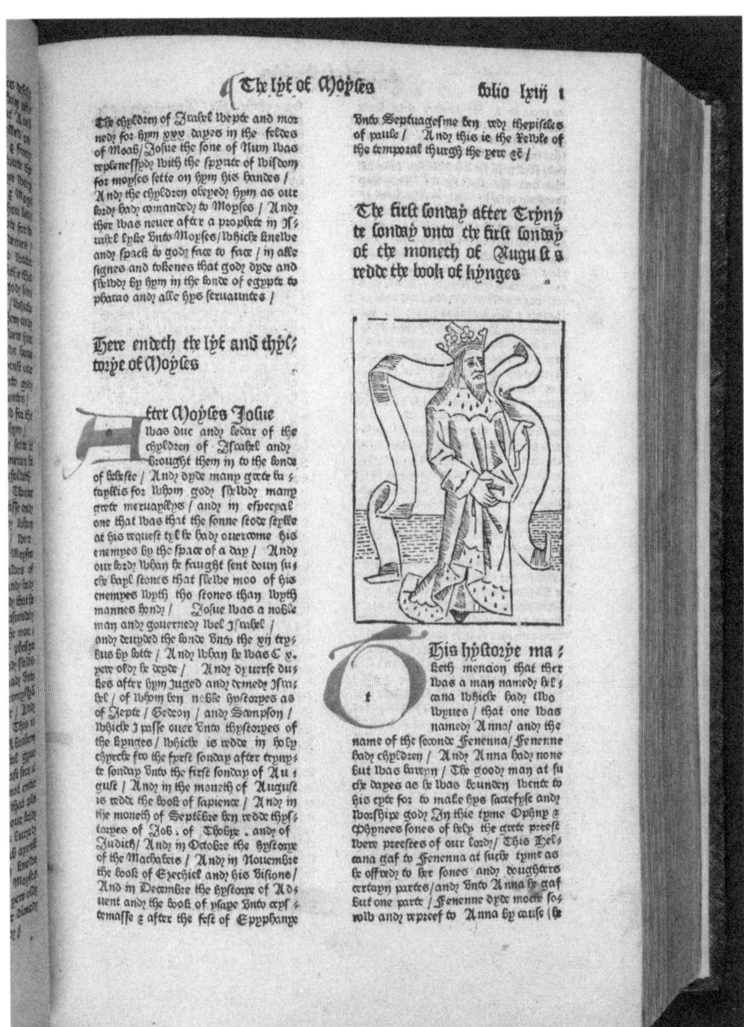

The lyf of Moyses folio lxiij

The chyldren of Israel wepte and morned for hym xxx dayes in the feldes
of Moab/ Josue the sone of Num was
replenesshyd with the spyrite of wisdom
for moyses sette on hym his handes /
And the chyldren obeyed hym as our
lord had comanded to Moyses / And
ther was neuer after a prophete in Israel lyke vnto Moyses / which knewe
and spack to god face to face / in alle
signes and tokenes that god dyde and
shewd by hym in the londe of egypte to
pharao and alle hys seruauntes /

Here endeth the lyf and thystorye of Moyses

After Moyses Josue
was duc and leder of the
chyldren of Israhel and
brought them in to the londe
of beheste / And dyde many grete bataylles for whom god shewd many
grete meruayllys / and in especyal
one that was that the sonne stode stylle
at his requeste tyl he had ouercome his
enemyes by the space of a day / And
our lord whan he faught sent doun suche hayl stones that slewe moo of his
enemyes wyth tho stones than wyth
mannes hond / Josue was a noble
man and gouerned wel Israhel /
and deuyded the londe vnto the xij trybus by lotte / And whan he was C x.
yere old he deyde / And dyuerse dukes after hym juged and demed Israhel / of whom ben noble hystoryes as
of Jepte / Gedeon / and Sampson /
which I passe ouer vnto thystoryes of
the kynges / which is redde in holy
chyrche fro the fyrst sonday after trynyte sonday vnto the first sonday of August / And in the moneth of August
is redde the book of sapience / And in
the moneth of Septembre ben redde thystoryes of Job. of Thobye. and of
Judith/ And in Octobre the hystorye
of the Machabeis / And in Nouembre
the book of Ezechiel and his visions/
And in Decembre the hystorye of Ad-
uent and the book of ysaye vnto cryst-
emasse & after the fest of Epyphanye
vnto Septuagesme ben red thepistles
of paule / And this is the rewle of
the temporal thurgh the yere &c /

The first sonday after Trynyte
sonday vnto the first sonday
of the moneth of August is
redde the book of kynges

This hystorye ma-
keth mencion that ther
was a man named hel-
cana which had two
wyues / that one was
named Anna/ and the
name of the seconde Fenenna/ Fenenne
had chyldren / And Anna had none
but was barayn / The good man at suche dayes as he was bounden wente to
his cyte for to make hys sacrefyse and
worshipe god In this tyme Ophny &
Phynees sones of hely the grete preest
were preestes of our lord/ This Helcana gaf to Fenenna at suche tyme as
he offred to her sones and doughters
certayn partes/ and vnto Anna he gaf
but one parte / Fenenne dyde moche sorowe and repreef to Anna by cause she

Pl. 2. [Caxton's *Golden Legend*]: the end of *Ten Commandments*, the entirety of *Joshua*, and the beginning of *Saul* (with the continuing running head for *Moses*) (Westminster: William Caxton, [1483–4]). London, British Library, C.11.d.8, f. 63[r] (sig. h7[r])

[1. ADAM]

Here folowen the storyes of the Byble [f. 36vb1 / sig. e4]

The Sonday of Septuagesme begynneth the storye of the Byble, in [f. 36va2] whiche is redde the legende and storye of Adam whiche foloweth.

In the begynnyng God made and created heuen and erthe. The erthe was ydle and voyde and couerd with derknes. And the spyrite of God was born on the | watres. And God said: 'Be made lyght.' And anon [f. 36vb2] lyght was made. And God sawe that lyght was good, and dyuyded the lyght fro derknes, and called the lyght day and derknes nyght. And thus was made lyght with heuen and erthe fyrst, and euen and mornyng was made one day.

The seconde day he made the firmamente, and dyuyded the watres that were vnder the firmament fro them that were aboue, and called the firmament heuen. The thyrde day were made on the erthe herbes and fruytes in theyr kynde. The fourth day God made the sonne and mone and | sterres *etc*. The fyfth day he made the fisshes in the water [f. 37ra / sig. [e5]] and byrdes in th'ayer. The sixthe day God made the beestis on the erthe, eueryche in his kynde and gendre. And God sawe that all thyse werkes were good and said: *Faciamus hominem etc.*: 'Make we man vnto our similitude and ymage.' Here spack the Fader to the Sone and Holy Ghooste, or ellis as it were the comune voys of thre persones, whan it was sayd 'Make we' and 'to oure' in plurel nombre. Man was made to the ymage of God in his sowle. Here is to be noted that he made not only the sowle without the body but he made both body and sowle. As to the body, he made male and female. God gaf to man the lordship and power vpon alle lyuyng beestis. Whan God had made man, it is not wreton *Et vidit quod esset bonum quia in proximo sciebat eum lapsurum*, for yet he was not parfyght til the woman was made, and therfore it is red: 'It is not good the man to be allone.' Thus in sixe dayes was heuen and erthe made and alle the ornacion of them. And thenne he made the vij day in whiche he rested, not for that he was wery, but cessyd of hys operacion, and shewd the vij day whiche he blessyd. Thus ben shortly shewd the generacions of heuen and erth. For here ben determynat the werkis of the vj dayes; and the seuenth day he sanctefyed and made holy.

3 In] I *five-line capital supplied by hand in red*

God had planted in the begynnyng Paradyse, a place of desyre and delyces, and man was made in þe felde of Damaske. He was made of the slyme of the erthe. Paradyse was made the thyrde day of creacion and was bysette with herbes, plantes and trees, and is a place of most myrthe and ioye. In the myddes wherof ben sette two trees, that is the tree of lyf, and that other the tree of knowyng good and euyll.

And ther is a welle, whiche casteth out water for to watre the treeis and herbes of Paradys. This welle is the moder of alle watres, whiche welle is deuyded into iiij partyes. One parte is called Phison; this goeth aboute Ynde. The second is called Gyon, otherwyse called Nilus, and that renneth aboute Ethiope. The other two ben called Tigris and Eufrates. Tigris renneth toward Assiryens. And Eufrates is
f. 37rb | called fruytful, whiche renneth in Chaldee. Thise iiij flodes comen and spryngen out of the same welle, and departe, and yet in somme place somme of them mete agayn.

Thenne God toke man from the place of his creacion and brought hym into Paradys for to werke there, not to laboure nedely, but in delytyng and recreacyng hym and that he shold kepe Paradys, for lyke as Paradys shold refresshe hym, so shold he laboure to serue God. And ther God gaf hym a comandement. Euery comandement standeth in two thyngis, in doyng or forbedyng. In doyng he comanded hym to ete of all the trees of Paradys; in forbedyng, he comanded that he shold not ete of the tree of the knowleche of good and euyll. This comandement was gyuen to the man, and by the man it wente to the woman, for whan the woman was made, it was comanded to them bothe. And herto he setted a payne, sayeng: 'Whatsomeuer daye thou etest therof, thou shalt dye by deth.'

God said: 'It is not good a man to be allone. Make we to hym an helper lyke to hymselfe for to brynge forth children.' Adam supposed that somme helpar to hym had ben emong the beestis whiche had ben lyke to hym. Therfore God brought to Adam alle lyuyng beestis of the erthe and ayer, in whic[h]e ben vnderstande them of the water also; whiche with one comandement alle cam tofore hym. They were brought for two causes. One was bycause man shold gyue to eche of them a name, by whiche they shold knowe that he shold domyne ouer them; and the second cause was bycause Adam shold knowe that there was none of them lyke to hym. And he named hem in Hebrews tonge, whiche was only the langage and none other atte begynnyng. And so,

65 whiche] whicle

none beyng founde lyke vnto hym, God sente in Adam a luste to slepe, whiche was no dreme but as is supposed in a extasi or in a traunse, in whiche was shewd to hym the celestial courte. Wherfore, whan he awoke, he prophecyed of the coniunction of Crist to his Chirche, and of the flode that was to come; and of the dome and destruction of the world by fyre he knewe, whiche afterward he told to his chyldren.

Whiles that Adam slepte, God toke {on}e | of his ribbes, both f. 37va flesshe and bone, and made that a woman, and sette her tofore Adam, whiche thenne saide: 'This is now a bone of my bones and flessh of my flessh.' And Adam gaf here a name lyke as her lord, and said she shal be called *Virago*, whiche is as moche to saye as 'made of a man', and is a name taken of a man. And anon the name gyuyng, he prophecied, sayeng: 'Bycause she is taken of the syde of a man, therfor a man shall forsake and leue fader and moder, and abyde and be adherent vnto his wif, and they shal be two in one flesshe.' And thaugh they be two persone, yet in matrymony and wedlok they be but one flesshe, and in other thyngis tweyne, for-why neyther of them hath power of his owne fless[h]e. They were bothe naked and were not asshamed; they felte nothyng of meuyng of theyr flessh ne to refrayne them as we now doo, for they stode bothe in the state of innocensye.

Thenne the serpente, whiche was hotter than ony beste of th'erthe and naturelly deceyuable, for he was ful of the deuyll, Lucifer, whiche was deiecte and caste out of heuen, had grete enuye to man that was bodyly in Paradys, and knewe wel yf he myght make hym to trespace and breke Gods conmandement that he shold be cast out also. Yet he was aferd to be taken or espied of the man; he wente to the woman, not so prudent and more prone to slyde and bowe, and in the forme of the serpente, for thenne the serpente was erecte as a man. Bede saith that he chace a serpente hauyng a maydens chere, for lyke ofte aplye to lyke, and spake by the tonge of the serpente to Eue and said: 'Why commanded you God that ye shold not ete of alle the trees of Paradys?' This he said to fynde occasyon to saye that he was come fore. Thenne the woman answerde and said: *Ne forte moriamur*, 'Leste happely we dye', whiche she saide doubtyng, for lightly she was flexible to euery parte. Whervnto anon he answerd: 'Nay, in no wyse ye shal dye, but God wold not that ye shold be lyke hym in science; and knowyng that whan ye ete of this tre, ye shal be as goddes,

81 is] is \ is   90 flesshe] flessle   99 and[1]] & \ and

knowyng good and euyll, he, as enuyous, forbade you.' And anon the woman, elate in pryde, | (f. 37vb) willyng be lyke to God, accorded therto and byleuyd hym.

The woman sawe that the tree was fayr to loke on, and clene and swete of sauour, toke and ete therof, and gaf vnto Adam of the same, happyly desiryng hym by fayr wordes. But Adam anon agreed, for whan he sawe the woman not deed, he supposed that God hath said that they shold dye to fere hem with, and thenne ete of the fruyt forboden. And anon theyr sight was opened that they sawe theyr nakydnes. And thenne anon they vnderstode that they had trespaced, for anon their flesshe began to meue and stire to concupiscence; for tofore that they had eten of the forboden fruyt, tho meuynges were repressed and closed as in yong children, and thenne after they had synned, they were opend lyke spryngys of water and began to meue, and then they were experte and knewe them. And lyke as they were inobedyent to theyr superyor, ryght soo theyr membres began to meue ayenst theyr superior, whiche is reson, and they felte theyr first meuyng in theyr preuy membres, and therof they were asshamed. And thus they knewe then that they were naked, and they toke figge leuis and sewed them togyder for to couere theyr membres in maner of brechis.

And anon after, they herde the voys of Our Lord God walkyng, and anon they hyd them. Our Lord called the man and said: 'Adam, where art thou?', callyng hym in blamyng hym, and not as not knowyng where he was, but as who said: 'Adam, see in what myserye thou art.' Whiche answerd: 'I haue hydde me, Lorde, for I am naked.' Our Lord said: 'Who tolde the that thou were naked, but that thou hast eten of the tree forboden?' He thenne not mekely confessyng his trespas but leyde the fawte in his wyf, and in hym as gyuer of the woman to hym, and saide: 'The woman whom thou gauyst to me as a felawe gaf to me of the tree, and I ete therof.' And thenne Our Lord s[a]id to the woman: 'Why dydyst thou soo?' Neyther she accused herself but leyd the synne on the serpente, and pryuely she leyd the faute in the maker of hym. The serpente was not demanded, for he dyde it not of hymself but the deuyl by hym.

(f. 38ra / sig. [e6]) And Our Lord, cursyng them, | began at the serpente, kepyng an ordre and congrue nombre of curses. The serpente was the first and synned most, for he synned in iij thyngis. The woman next, and

140 said] soid

synned lesse than he but more than the man, for she synned in two thyngis. The man synned last and leest, for he synned but in one. The serpente had enuye, he lyed and deceyued; for thyse thre, he had thre curses. Bycause he had enuye at th'excellence of man, it was sayd to hym: 'Thou shalt goo and crepe on thy breste'; bycause he lyed, he is punysshid in his mouth whan it was said: 'Thou shalt ete erthe alle the dayes of thy lyf'; also he toke away his voys and put venym in hys mouth; and bycause he deceyued, it was said: 'I shal put enemyte bytweyne the and woman, and thy seed and her seed. She shal breke thy heede *etc.*'

In two thyngis the woman synned: in pryde and etyng the fruyte. Bycause she synnyd in pryde, he meked her, seyeng: 'Thou shalt be vnder the power of man. And I shal haue lordship ouer the and I shal put the to affliction.' Now is she subiecte to a man by condicion and drede, whiche tofore was but subiecte by loue. And bycause she synned in the fruyt, she is punysshed in her fruyt, whan it was said to her: 'Thou shalt brynge forth children in sorowe.' In the payne of sorow standeth the curs, but in bryngyng forth of chyldren is a blessyng. And so in punysshyng, God forgate not to haue mercy, whiche is to be noted *etc.*

And bycause Adam synned but only in etyng of the fruyt, therfore he was punysshed in sechyng his mete, as it is said to hym: 'Acursed be the erthe in thy werke', that is to saye: 'For thy werke of thy synne, for whiche is made that the erthe, that brought forth good and holsom fruytes plentyuously, fro hensforth shal brynge forth but seld and also none without mannes laboure; and also somtyme wedes, breres and thornes shal growe.' And he added therto: 'Thou shalst ete herbes of the erthe', as wo saith: 'Thou shalt be lyke a beeste or iumente.' He cursyd the erthe bycause the trespaas was of the fruyt of the erthe and not of the water. He added therto to hym of labour: 'In the swete of thy chere, thou | shalt ete thy brede vnto the tyme thou retorne agayn f. 38rb
into th'erthe', that is to saye: 'Til thou dye, for thou art erthe, and into erthe thou shal goo agayn.' Thenne Adam, wayllyng and sorowyng the myserye that was to come of his posteryte, named his wyf Eue, whiche is to saye, 'moder of all lyuyng folke'.

Thenne God made to Adam and Eue two letheren cotes of the skynnes of dede bestes, to th'ende that they bere with them the signe of mortalite, and sayde: 'Loo, Adam is made as one of vs, knowyng good and euyl. Now leste he put his hande and take of the tree of lyf and lyue euer', as who saith: 'Beware and caste hym out lest he take and ete of the tre of lyf.' And so he was cast out of Paradys and sette in the felde of Damask, whereas he was made and taken fro, for to werke and laboure there. And Our Lord sette cherubin to kepe Paradys of delyte with a brennyng swerde and plyaunt, to th'ende that none shold entre there ne come to the tre of lyf.

After thenne that Adam was caste out of Paradys and sette in the world, he knewe his wyf and engendryd Cayn, the xv yere after he was made, and his suster Calmana. They cam out of Paradys virgynes, as Methodius saith; and whan Adam was made, he was made a parfyght man as a man of xxx yere of age whan he was but one day old, and he myght wel haue goten many chyldren tofore Cayn, but after other xv yere was Abel born, and his sister Delbora. Whan Adam was an C xxx yere of age, Cayn slewe Abel his brother.

Trouthe it is, after many dayes, Cayn and Abel offrid sacrefyse and yeftes vnto God; it is to be byleuyd that Adam taught his sonnes to offre to God theyr tythes and first fruytes. Cayn offrid fruytes, for he was a ploughman and teliar of erthe. And Abel offrid mylke and the first of the lambes – Moyses saith, of the fattest of the flocke. And God behelde the yeeftes of Abel, for he and his sacrefyses were acceptable to Our Lord. And as to Cayn and his sacrefyses, God behelde hem not, for they were not to hym acceptable; he offryd wethes and thornes. And as somme doctours saye, fyre cam from heuen and
f. 38va lyghted the sacrefyse of Abel, and | the yeftes of Cayn plesed not Our Lord, for the sacrefyse wold not belight ne brenne clere in the light of God.

Wherof Cayn had grete envye vnto his brother Abel, wiche roose ayenst hym and slewe hym. And Our Lord said to hym: 'Where is Abel thy brother?' He answerd and said: 'I wote neuer. Am I kepar of my brother?' Thenne Our Lord said: 'What hast thou doo? The voys of the blood of thy brother cryeth to me fro th'erthe. Wherfore thou art cursyd, and acursyd be th'erthe that receyued the blode of thy broder by his mouth, of thyn hondes. Whan thou shalt werke and laboure th'erthe, it shal brynge forth no fruyt, but thou shal be fugytyf, vacabunde and voyde on th'erthe.' This Cayn deseruyd wel to be cursyd, knowyng the payne of the fyrst trespaas of Adam. Yet he added therto murdre and slaughter of his brother. Thenne Cayn, dredyng that beestis shold deuoure hym, or yf he wente forth, he shold be slayn of the men, or yf he dwelled with hem, they wold sle hym for his synne, dampned hymself and in despayer sayd: 'My wyckednesse is more than I can deserue to haue foryefnes. Whoso fynde me shal sle me.’ This he saide of drede or ellis wesshyng, as who said: ‘Wold God he wold slee me!’ Thenne Our Lord saide: ‘Nay, not so. Thou shalt dye but not sone. For whosomeuer sleeth Cayn shal be punysshed vij sythes more, for he shold delyure hym fro drede, fro labour and myserye’, and added that he shold be punysshed personaly vij-fold more. This punicion shal endure to hym in payne vnto the seuenth, Lameth. Whosomeuer shal sle Cayn shal loose vij vengeancis. Some holde that his payne endured vnto the vij generacion, for he comysed vij synnes: he departed not truly; he had envye to his broder; he wrought gylefully; he slew his broder fa[l]sely; he denyed it; he despayred; and dampned, he dyd no penaunce.

And after he wente into the eest, fugytyf and vacabunde, Cayn knewe his wyf, which bare Enoch; and he made a cyte, and named it Enoch after the name of his sone Enoch. Here it sheweth wel that this tyme were many men thaugh their generacion be not said, whom Cayn called to his cyte, by whos helpe he made | it, whom he enduced f. 38vb
to thefte and roberye. He was the fyrst that walled or made cytees, dredyng them that he hurted, for seurete brought his peple into the townes.

Thenne Enoch gate Irath. And Irath Mauahel, and he gate Matusale; and Matusale, Lameth, whiche was the seuenth fro Adam and werst, for he brought in fyrst bygamye, and by hym was comysid first aduoultrye ayenst the lawe of God and of nature, and agayn the decree of God.

This Lameth toke two wyues, Ada and Sella. Of Ada he gate Iabel, whiche fonde first the crafte to make foldes for shepherdes and to chaunge their pasture, and ordeyned flo[c]kes of sheep and departed the sheep fro the gheet after the qualite; the lambes by themself, and the older by themself, and vnderstode the fedyng of hem after the seeason of the yere.

The name of his broder was Iubal, fader of syngers in the harpe and organes; not of th’ynstrumentis, for they were founde longe after, but he was the fyndar of musyke, that is to saye, of consonantes of acorde suche as shepherdes vse in their delyces and sportes. And for as moche as he herde Adam prophecye of two iugementis by the fyre and water that all thyng shold be destroyed therby, and that his crafte newe founde shold not perisshe, he dyde doo wryte it in two pilers or colompnes, one of marble and another of claye of th’erthe, to th’ende

237 falsely] fasely   244 roberye] ro \ roberye   254 flockes] floekes

that one shold endure ayenst the water and that other ayenst the fyre. Iosephus saith that the piler of marble is yet in the lande of Siriac.

Of Sella he begate Tubalcain whiche fonde first the crafte of smytherye and werkyng of yron and made thynges for warre and sculptures and grauynges in metal to the playsir of the eyen; whiche he so werkyng, Iubal, tofore said, had delyte in the sowne of his hamers, of whiche he made the consonantes and tunes of acorde in his songe. Noema, suster of Tubalcain, fonde first the crafte of dyuerse texture.

Lameth was a shoter and vsed to shote at wild beestis, for none vse of the mete of them but only for to haue the skynnes for their clothyng. And lyuyd so longe that he was blynde, and had a chylde to f. 39ra / sig. [e7] lede hym. And on a tyme, by | auenture, he slewe Cayn, for Cayn was alway aferde and hid hym emong busshes and breres, and the child that lad Lameth had supposed it had ben som wild beest and directed Lameth to shote therat; and so wenyng to shote at a beest, s[l]ewe Cayn. And whan he knewe that he had slayn Cayn, he with his bowe slewe the chyld, and thus he slewe them bothe to his dampnacion. Therfor as the synne of Cayn was punysshyd vij sythes, so was the synne of Lameth seuenty sythes and vij, that is to saye lxxvij sowles that cam of Lameth were perysshyd in the deluuye and Noes flode. Also his wif dyde hym moche sorowe and euyl entreted hym. And he, beyng wroth, said that he suffred that for his double homycide and manslaughter. Yet neuertheles he fered hym by payne, sayeng: 'Why wil ye sle me? He shal be more and sorer punysshed that sleeth me than he that slewe Cayn.'

After that Abel was slayn, Strabus saith that Adam auowed no more to haue to doo with his wif, but by an angel he brake the vowe bycause a sone shold be born to God. Yet neuertheles, Iosephus said that whan Abel was slayn and Cayn fled away, Adam thought of procreacion of chyldren. And so whan he was C xxx yere old, he engendrid Seth lyke to his simylitude, and he to the ymage of God. This Seth was a good man, and he gate Enos, and Enos Caynam. And C[a]ynam begate Malael, and Malael Iareth. And Iareth Enoch, and Enoch Matussale. And Matussale Lamech, and Lamech Noe. And lyke as in the generacion of Cayn, the seuenth was the werst, so in the generacion of Seth, the seuenth was the beste, þat was Enoch, whom God toke and brought hym into Paradys vnto the tyme that he shal come with Hely for to conuerte the hertes of the faders into the sones.

280 slewe] sbewe 297 Caynam] Cynam

And Adam lyuyd after that he had begoten Seth viij C yere and engendrid sones and doughtres. Somme hold opinyon xxx sones and xxx dou[gh]tres, and some l of that one and l of that other. We fynde no certenyte of them in the Bible. But alle th[e] dayes of Adam lyuyng here in erthe amounte to the somme of ix C xxx yere. And in th'ende of his lyf whan he shold dye, it is said, but of none auctoryte, that he | sente Seth his sone into Paradys for to fetche the oyle of mercy, where f. 39rb he receyuyd certayn graynes of the fruyt of th[e] tree of mercy by an angel, and whan he come agayn, he fonde his fader Adam yet alyue and told hym what he had don, and thenne Adam lawhed first, and thenne deyed, and thenne he leyd the greynes or kernellis vnder his faders tonge and buryed hym in the vale of Ebron; and out of his mouth grewe thre trees of the thre graynes, of whiche the crosse that Our Lord suffred his passion on was made; by vertue of whiche he gate very mercy and was brought out of derknes into veray lyght of heuen, to the whiche he brynge vs that lyueth and regneth, God, world withoute ende.

Here endeth the lyf of Adam.

[2. NOAH]

H[e]re begynneth the hystorye of Noe. The first Sonday in Sexa̍gesme

After that Adam was deed, deyd Eue and was buryed by hym. At the begynny[n]g in the first age, the peple lyuyd longe. Adam lyuyd ixC xxx yere and Matussale lyued ixC lxix yere. Seynt Iherom said that he deyde the same yere the flood was. Thenne Noe was the tenthe | fro Adam in the generacion of Seth, in whom the first age was f. 39va ended. The lxx Interpreters saye that this first age dured ijM ijC xliiij yere. Seynt Iherom saith not fully ijM, and Methodius full ijM *etc.*

Noe thenne was a man perfight and rightwys, and kept Goddes comandement. And whan he was vC yere old, he gate Sem, Cham and Iafeth. This tyme men began to multeplye on th'erthe, and the chyldren of God, that is to saye of Seth, as religious, sawe the doghters of men, that is to saye of Cayn, and were ouercome by concupiscence and toke them to theyr wyues. This tyme was so moche

306 doughtres] douhgtres 307 the] th– \ 308 amounte] amoūe \ te
311 the] th– \
1 Here] Hre 3 After] A *five-line capital supplied by hand in red*
4 begynnyng] begynnyg

synne on th'erthe in the synne of lecherye whiche was mysused agayn nature. Wherfore God was displesid, and determyned in his prescience to destroye man that he had made, and said: 'I shal put man away that I haue made, and my spiryte shal not abide in man for euer, for he is flessh.' As who saide: 'I shal not punyssh man perpetuelly as I doo the deuyll, for man is frayll. And yet er I shal destroye hym, I shal gyue hym space and tyme of repentance, and t'amende hym, yf he wil. The tyme of repentance shal be C xx yere.'

Thenne Noe, rightwys and perfyght, walked with God, that is in his lawes, and the erthe was corrupt by synne and fyllyd. Whan God sawe th'erthe to be corrupte and that euery man was corrupte by synne vpon th'erthe, he said to Noe: 'The ende of all peple is come tofore me exepte them that shal be sauyd, and the erthe is replenesshyd with theyr wickednesse. I shal destroye them with th'erthe'; *id est*, wyth the fertilite of th'erthe. 'Make to the an arcke of tree, hewen, polysshyd and squared, and make ther dyuerse places, and lyme it with cleye and pitche within and without', that is to wete, with glewe whiche is so feruente that the tymbre may not be losed. 'And thou shal make it iijC cubytes of lengthe, fyfty in brede and xxx of heyghte, and make therin dyuerce distynctions of places and chambres, and of warderops.' And the arcke hath a dore for to entre in and come out; and a wyndow was made theron, whiche þat, the Hebrews saye, was of crystall. This arcke was on makyng, fro the begynnyng that God f. 39vb comanded first | to make it, C xx yere. In whiche tyme Noe ofte desired the peple to leue their synne, and [told] how he had spoken with God and that he was comanded to make the shippe, for God shold destroye hem for their synne but yf they left it. And they mocked hym and said that he raued and was a foole, and gaf no faith to his sayeng, and contynued in theyr synne and wickednes.

Thenne whan the arcke was parfyghtly maad, God bad hym to take into it of all the beestis of th'erthe, and also of the fowles of th'ayer, of eche two, male and female, 'that they may lyue, and also of all the metes of th'erthe that ben comestible, that they may serue and fede the and them'. And Noe dyde all that Our Lord commanded hym. Thenne said Our Lord to Noe: 'Entre thou and all thy houshold into the arke', that is to saye, thou and thy wyf, and thy thre sones and theyr thre wiuys. 'I haue seen that thou art rightful in this generacion. Of all beestis that ben clene thou shalt take seuen, and of vnclene

40 told] *om.*   44 synne] synnne

beestis but only two; and of the byrdes seuen and seuen, male and female, that they may be saued on the face of th'erthe. Yet after vij dayes, I shal rayne vpon th'erthe xl dayes and xl nyghtis, and shal destroye all the substance that I made on the erthe.'

And Noe dyde all thyng that Our Lord comanded hym. He was vjC yere old whan the flod began on the erthe. And thenne Noe entryd in and his sones, his wyf and the wyues of his sones, all into the arke t'eschewe the watres of the flood. Of all the beestis and the fowles, and of all that meuyd and had lyf on erthe, male and female, Noe toke in to hym as Our Lord had boden. And seuen dayes after they were entred, the water began t'encrece, the welles of the abysmes were broken and the cataractes of heuen were opened, that is to saye the clowdes, and it rayned on th'erthe xl dayes and xl nyghtes. And the arke was eleuate and born vpon the watres on height aboue the montaynes and hylles. For the water was growen hyer, xv cubites aboue all the montaynes, that it shold purge and wasshe the fylthe of th'ayer. Thenne was consumed all that was on th'erthe lyuyng, man, woman and beest and byrdes, and | f. 40ra / sig. [e8] alle that euer bare lyf, so that nothyng abode vpon th'erthe, for the water was xv cubytes [a]boue the hyest montayne of th'erthe. And whan Noe was entrid, he shitte the dore fast withoutforth and lymed it with glewe. And so the wat[r]es abode, eleuate in highte, an C l dayes fro the daye that Noe entred in. And Our Lord thenne remembred Noe and all them that were in the arke with hym, and also on the beestis and fowles, and cessed the watres. And the welles and catharactes were closid, and the raynes were prohybyted and forboden to rayne no more. The vij moneth, the xxvij day of the moneth, the arke rested on the hylles of Armenye.

The x moneth, the first day of the moneth, the toppes of the hylles appiered first. After thise xl dayes after the lassyng of the watres, Noe opened the wyndowe and desired sore to haue tydynges of cessyng of the flood and sente out a rauen for to haue tydynges. And whan she was goon, retorned no more agayn, for parauentu[re] she fonde somme dede carayne of a beest swymmyng on the water, and lighted theron to fede her and was lefte there. After this he sente out a douue, whiche flewhe out, and whan she coude fynde no place to reste ne sette her foot on, she retorned vnto Noe, and he toke her in. Yet thenne were not the toppes of the hillis bare? And vij dayes after he sente here out agayn, whiche at euen retorned, beryng a braunche of an olyue tree,

72 aboue] oboue   74 watres] watees   85 parauenture] parauentu– \

burgyng, in her mouth. And after other vij dayes, he sente her agayn, whiche cam no more agayne. Thenne in the yere of Noe vjC j, the first day of the moneth, Noe opened the coueryng of the arke and sawe that the erthe was drye, but he durst not goo out but abode the commandement of Our Lord.

The second moneth, the xxvij day of the moneth, Our Lord said to Noe: 'Goo oute of the arke, thou and thy wyf, thy sones and the wyues of thy sones.' He commanded them to goo coniunctly out whiche disiunctly entred. 'And late goo out with the, alle the beestis and fowles lyuyng and all the reptyle, euerich after his kynde and gendre.' To whom Our Lord saide: 'Growe ye and multiplye vpon th'erthe.' Thenne Noe yssued out, and his wyf and his sones with their wyues, |
f. 40rb and all the beestis, the same day a yere after they entryd in, euerich after his gendre.

Noe thenne edefyeed an awter to Our Lord, and toke of all the beestis that were clene and offrid sacrefise vnto Our Lord. And Our Lord smellyd the swetenes of the sacrefise, and said to Noe: 'From hensforth, I shal not curse the erthe for man, for he is prone and redy to fall fro the begynnyng of his yongthe. I shal no more destroye man by suche vengeance.' And thenne Our Lord blessid hem, and said: 'Growe ye and multeplye the erthe, and be ye lordes of all the beestis of th'erthe, of the fowles of th'ayer and of the fisshes. I haue gyuen alle thynges to you, but ete not flessh with the blood. I commande you to slee no man ne to shede no mans blood. I haue made man after myn ymage. Whosomeuer shedeth his broders blood, his blood shal be shedde. Go ye forth, and growe and multeplye and fylle the erthe.' This said Our Lord to Noe and his sones: 'Lo, I haue made a couenaunt with yow, and with them that shal come after yow, that I shal no more brynge suche a flood to slee alle peple. And in token therof, I haue sette my raynebowe in the clowdes of heuen. For who that trespaceth, I shal doo iustice otherwyse on hym.'

Noe lyuyd after the flood iijC l yere. Fro the tyme of Adam vnto after Noes flood, the tyme and season was alleway grene and tempryd. And alle that tyme, men ete no flesshe, for th'erbes and fruytes were thenne of grete strengthe and effecte. They were pure and norisshyng. But after the flood, the erthe was weyker and broght not forth so good fruyte, wherfore flesshe was ordeyned to be eten. And thenne Noe began t[o] laboure for his lyfelode with his sones and began to tyllye

129 to] te

th'erthe, destroye breris and thornys and to plante vignes. And so on a tyme Noe had dronke so moche of the wyne that he was dronke and laye and slepte and his prevy membres laye bare and open. Cham his myddelest sone espied it, and lowhe and s[c]ornyd his fader, and called his brethern to see, whiche cam [b]ackward for to couure her fader and wold not loke on hit, and rebuked Cham of his folye and synne. And whan Noe was couured with the mantel, anon he awoke, and whan | he vnderstode how Cham his sone had scorned hym, he f. 40va
cursid hym and also his sone Canaan, and blessyd Sem and Iaphet bycause they couerd hym.

Alle the dayes of Noe were ixC l yere, and thenne deyed. And after his deth, his sones deled alle the world bytwene hem. Sem had all Asye, Cham Affryke and Iaphet all Europe. Thus was it departed. Asye is the best part, and is as moche as the other two, and that is in the eest. Affryke is the south part, and therin is Cartage and many ryche contre. Therin ben blew and black men. Cham had that to his parte, Affrica. The thyrde parte is Europe, whiche is in the north and weste. Therin is Grece, Rome and Germanye. In Europe regneth now moste the Crysten lawe and faith; wherin is many ryche royame. And so was the world departed to the iij sones of Noe.

Thus endeth the lyf of Noe.

[3. ABRAHAM]

Here foloweth the lyf of Abraham.

The Sonday called Quinquagesme, is redde in the chirche th'ys-torye of the holy patriarke Abraham, whiche was sone of Thare. This Thare was the tenthe fro Noe in the ge|neracion of Sem. Iaphet had f. 40vb
vij sones, and Cham four sones. Out of the generacion of Cham, Nembroth cam, whiche was a wicked man and cursid in his werkis, and began to make the tour of Babylone, whiche was grete and hye. And at the makyng of this tour, God chaunged the langages in suche wyse that no man vnderstode other. For tofore the byldyng of that tour was but one maner speche in all the world. And ther were made lxxij speches. The tour was grete: it was x myle aboute and vM lxxxiiij steppes of height. This Nembroth was the first man that founde mawmetryee and ydolatrye, whiche endured long and yet doth.

Thenne I torne agayne to Thare, whiche had thre sones, whiche

133 scornyd] stornyd 134 backward] hackward
2 The] T *five-line capital supplied by hand in red*

was Abram, Nacor and Aram. Of Nacor cam Vs, Bus and Batuel. Of Vs cam Iob, of Bus cam Balam; and of Batuel, Rebecca and Laban. Of Aram cam Loth and ij doughtres, Melcha and Sara. Now I shal speke of Abram, of whom Our Blessid Lady come. He weddyd Sara, doughter of his broder Aram. Abram was euer faithful and trewe. He was lxv yere old whan his fader deyde, for whom he morned tyl Our Lord comforted hym, whiche said to Abram: 'Abram, make the redy and goo out of thy lande and kynrede, and also fro the hows of thy fader, and come into the lande that I shal shewe to the. I shal make the growe into moche peple. I shal blesse the and shal magnefye thy name, and thou shalt be blessyd. And I shall blesse them that blesse the, and curse them that curse the. And in the shal be blessyd alle the kynredes of the erthe.'

Abram was lxx yere olde whan he departed from the lond of Aram, and he toke with hym Sara his wyf and Loth the sone of his broder and their meyne and his catell and substaunce, and cam into the londe of Canaan, and cam into the vale of Sichem, in whiche were ylle peple, whiche were the peple of Canaan. And Our Lord saide to Abram: 'I shal gyue to the this lande and to thyn eyres.' Thenne Abram did reyse an aulter, on whiche he dide sacrefise. And blessid and thankyd Our Lord. Abram beheld all the londe toward the south and sawe the beawte therof, and fonde hit lyke as Our Lord told hym.

f. 41ra / sig. f1 But he | had not be longe in the lande but that ther fylle grete hungre therin. Wherfore he lefte that contre and wente into Egypte, and toke with hym Sara his wyf. And as they wente by the way, Abram said to his wif: 'I fere and drede sore that whan we come to this peple, which ben lawles, that they shal take the for thy beaute, and sle me bycause they wold vse the. Wherfore saye that thou art my suster, and I thy brother.' And she agreed therto. And whan they were comen into that contre, the peple sawe that she was so fayr; anon they told the kynge. Whiche anon commanded that she shold be brought vnto his presence. And whan she was come, God of his good grace so pourueyed for her that no man had power to vse ony lecherye wyth her ne to doo her vylanye. Wherfore the kynge was ferd that God wold haue taken vengeaunce on hym for her, and sende for Abram, and said to hym that he shold take his wyf and that he had euyl don to saye that she was his suster, and so delyuerd her agayn and gaf hym gold and siluer and bad that men shold worshyp hym in al his londe, and he shold frely at his playsyr departe with all his goodes.

Thenne after this, Abram toke his wyf Sara and wente home agayn;

and cam into Bethel and sette there an aulter of stone, and there he adoured and worshipped the name of God. His store and beestis began to multeplye. And Loth with his meyne was also there, and theyr beestis began so sore to encrece and multeplye that vnnethe the contre myght suffyse to theyr pasture, in so moche that rumour and grutchyng began to sourde and ryse bytwene the herdmen of Abram and the herdmen of Loth. Thenne Abram said to Loth: 'Lo, this cont[r]e is grete and wyde. I praye the to chese on whiche hande thou wilt goo and take it for thy meyne and thy beestis, and late no strif be bytwene me and the, ne bytwene my herdmen ne thy herdmen. Lo, beholde all the contrey is tofore the. Take whiche thou wilt. Yf thou goo on the right side, I shal goo on the lyft side. And yf thou take the lyft, I will goo on the right side.' Thenne Loth byhelde the contrey and sawe a fair playn toward | flom Iordan, whiche was playsaunt, and (f. 41rb) the flode ran toward Sodom and Gomor, whiche was lyke a paradys, and toke that parte for hym. And Abram toke toward the weste, whiche was beside the peple of Canaan at the foot of Mount Mambre. And Loth dwellid in Sodomys; the peple of Sodom were worst of all peple.

Our Lord said to Abram: 'Lyfte vp thyn eyen and see directly fro the place that thou art now in, fro the north to the south and fro the eest to the weste. Alle this londe that thou seest, I shal gyue the, and to thy seed for euermore. I shal make thy seed as pouldre or dust of th'erthe; who that may nombre the dust of the erthe shal nombre thy seed. Arise therfore and walke the londe in lengthe and in brede, for I shal gyue it to the.' Abram meuyd th[e]nne his tabernacle and dwellyd in the valey of Mambre, whiche is in Ebron, and sette there his tabernacle.

It happed sone after that ther was a werre in that lande that foure kynges warred agayn other fyue kynges, whiche were of Sodom, Gomor and other. And the iiij kynges ouerthrewe the fyue and slewe them, and spoylled and toke alle the substaunce of the contre, and toke also with hem Loth and alle his good. And a man gate away fro them and cam to Abram and told hym how that Loth was taken and lad away. And thenne anon Abram dyde do gadre his peple togydre the nombre of iijC xviij, and folowyd after, and departed his peple into two partyes bycause they shold not escape. And Abram smote in emonge them and slewe the kynges and rescowed Loth and all his

62 contre] contee   80 thenne] thnne

goodis, and delyuerd the men of Sodom that were taken and the women.

And they of Sodom cam agayn hym. And Melchisedech cam and mette with hym and offrid to hym brede and wyn. This Melchisedech was kynge and preest of Iherusalem and all the contree, and blessid Abram. And there Abram gaf to hym the tythes of all that he had. And the kynge of Sodom wold þat Abram shold haue had suche pray as he toke, but he wold not haue as moche as þe lachet of a shoo. And thus gate Abram moche loue of all þe peple.

After this Our Lord apperid to Abram in a vision and saide:
f. 41va 'Abram, drede the nothyng. I am thy protector, | and thy reward and mede shal be grete.' Abram answerd: 'Lord God, what wylt thou gyue me? Thou wotest welle I haue no children, and sith I haue non, I wil wel that Eleazar the sone of my baily be myn heyr.' 'Nay,' said Our Lord, 'he shal not be thyn heir, but he that shal yssue and come of thy seed shal be thyn heyr.' Our Lord ledde hym out and bad hym: 'Beholde the heuen and nombre the sterres yf thou mayst', and said to hym: 'So shal thy ofspryngyng and seed be.' And Abram byleuyd it and gaf faith to Our Lordes wordes, and it was reputed to hym to iustice. And Our Lord said to hym: 'I am the Lord that ladde þe out of the londe of Hur of the Chaldeeis for to gyue to the this londe into thy possession.' And Abram said: 'Lord, how shal I knowe that I shal possede it?' A voys said to Abram: 'Thy seed after the shal be exiled into Egipte by the space of iiijC yere, and shal be there in seruitude; and after I shal brynge them hether agayn in the fourthe generacion. Thou shalt abyde here vnto thy good age and shal be buryed here and goo with thy faders in pees.'

Sara was yet without childe. She had an handmayd named Agar, an Egypcian, and she on a day sayd to Abram her housbond: 'Thou seyst I may bere no chyld; wherfore I wold thou toke Agar my maide and lye by her that thou myght gete a chylde, whiche I myght kepe and holde as for myn.' And x yere after that Abraham had dwellid in that londe, he toke Agar and gate her with chylde. And anon as she felte herself with chylde, she despised her maistresse. Thenne Sara said to Abram: 'Thou dost euyl; I gaf the licence to lye with my seruant, and now syth she is conceyued by the, she hath me in despyte. God iuge this bytwene the and me!' To whom Abram answerd: 'Thyn handmaid is in thyn handes; chastise her as it pleseth þe.' After this Sara chastised Agar and put her to so grete affliction that she wente away. And as she wente, an aungel mette with her in the wildernes by a wel, and said: 'Agar, whens comest and whyther goost þou?' She answerd: 'I flee away fro the face of my lady Sara.' To whom the angele sayde: 'Retorne agayn and submytte the by humblenes vnto thy lady, and I shal multeplye thy seed, and so moche peple shal come of it that it can not by nombred for multytude.' And he said forthermore: 'Thou haste conceyued and shal bere a child and shalt | calle hym Ysmael. f. 41vb He shal be a fiers man; he shal be agayn alle men, and alle men agayn hym.' Thenne Agar retorned home and seruyd her lady, and sone after she was delyueryd of Ysmael. Abram was lxxxvj yere old whan Ismael was born.

Whan Abram was lxxxxix yere, Our Lord apperid to hym and saide: 'Abram, loo, I am the Lord Almyghty. Walke thou bifore me and be parfyght, and I shal kepe couenaunt bitwene me and the and shal multeplye thy seed gretly.' And Abram fyll doun lowtyng lowe to th'erthe and thanked hym. Thenne Our Lord said: 'I am; and my couenaunt I shal kepe to the. Thou shalt be fader of moche peple. Thou shalt no more be called Abram but Abraham, for I haue ordeyned the fader of moche peple. I shal make the t'encrece most habondantly; kynges and prynces shal come of the, and shal stablisshe my couenaunt bytwene me and the, and thy seed in thy generacions. I shal gyue to the and to thy seed after the the londe of thy pylgremage, all the londe of Canaan into their possession, and I shal be theyr God.' Yet said God to Abraham: 'And thou shalt kepe thy couenant to me, and thyn heyres after the in theyr generacions. And this shal be the couenaunt that ye shal kepe, and thyn heyres after the: euery man chyld and male shal [b]e circumsiced in his preuy membre that it be a token bytwene me and you; euery chyld masculyn that shal be born shal be circumcysed whan he is viij dayes old. And I wyl that this signe shal be in your flesshe. And see that the men in your generacion be circumcised. Begynne at thyself and thy chyldren and alle that dwelle in thy kynred. Who of yow that shal not be circumcised in his flesshe shal be caste and put out for euer fro my peple bycause he obeyeth not my statute and ordenaunce. And thy wyf Saray shal be callid no more Saray, but she shal be called Sara, and I shal blesse her and shal gyue to þe a sone of her, whom I shal blesse also. I shal hym encrece into nacions, and kynges of peples shal come of hym.' Abraham fyl doun, his face toward th'erthe, and lawhed, in his herte sayeng: 'May it be that a woman of lxxxx yere may conceyue

158 be] le

and bere a chyld! I beseche the, Lord, that Ismael may lyue tofore the!' Our Lord said to Abraham: 'Sara shal brynge forth a sone, whom f. 42ra / sig. f2 þou shalt name Ysaac, | and I shal kepe my couenaunt to hym for euermore, and to his heyres after hym. And I haue herd thy request for Ysmael also. I shal blesse hym and encrece, and shal multeplye his seed into moc[h]e peple: xij dukes shal come of hym. I shal kepe my couenaunt to Ysaac, whom Sara shal brynge forth the next yere.' Whan thise wordes were fynysshed, Abraham toke Ismael his sone, and all the men, smale and grete, straungers and other that were in his hows, and circumcised them. Ismael was xiij yere old whan he was circumcised, and Abraham was 99 yere whan he hymself was circumcised. And thus that same day, he and his sone Ismael and all the men in his hows, as wel straungers of what degre, they were receyuyd this newe lawe of circumcision, wherby they were knowen from other peple.

After this, on a tyme as Abraham satte beside his hous in þe vale of Mambre, in the hete of the day; and as he lifte vp his eyen, he sawe iij yong men comyng to hym, and anon as he sawe thise iij standyng by hym, he ran to them and worrshipped one allone. He sawe thre, and worshippid but one—that bytokeneth the Trynyte—and prayd them to be herberowed with hym, and toke water and wesshe their feet and prayd hem to tarye vnder the tree, and he wold brynge brede to them for to comforte hem; and they bad hym doo as he had said. He wente and bad Sara to make iij asshy cakes and sente his child for a tendre, fat calf, which was soden and boylled, and he seruid hem with butter and mylk and the calf, and sette it tofore them; he stode by them. Whan they had eten, they demanded hym: 'Where is Sara thy wyf?' And he said: 'Yonder in þe tabernacle.' And he said: 'I shal goo and come agayn, and Sara, thy wyf, shal haue a child.' And she stode byh[y]nde the dore and herd it and loughe, and seyde softly to herself: 'How may it be that my lord is so olde and I also that I shold bere a childe?' She thought it imp[o]ssible. Thenne said Our Lord to Abraham: 'Why lawheth Sara thy wyf, sayeng in scorne, "Shal I bere a ch[il]d?" But as I said to the tofore, I shal retorne and come agayn, and she shal haue a child in that tyme.' And he axid Sara why she smylyd in scorne, and she sayd she smylid ne lawhed not. And Our Lord said: 'It is not so, for thou lawhedest.'

176 moche] mocbe 200 byhynde] byhnde 202 impossible] imppssible 204 child] chlid

Whan they had restid, Abraham conueyed hem on the way. And Our Lord said to Abraham: 'I | shal not hyde fro the that I purpose to doo. The crye of Sodome and Gomor is multeplied, and theyr synne is moche greuous. I shal descende and see yf the synne be so grete; the stenche therof cometh to heuen. I shal take ve[n]geance and destroye them.' Thenne Abraham said: 'I hope, Lord, thou wilt not destroye the iuste and rightwis man with the wicked synnar. I beseche the, Lord, to spare them.' Our Lord said: 'Yf ther be fyfty good and rightwis men emong them, I shal spare them.' And Abraham saide: 'Good Lord, yf ther be found xl, I praye the to spare them.' Our Lord said: 'Yf ther be xl, I shal spare them.' And so fro xl to xxx, and fro xxx to xx, and fro xx to x, and Our Lord said: 'Yf ther be found x good men emong them, I shal not destroye them.' And thenne Our Lord wente fro Abraham, and he retorned home agayn. f. 42rb

That same euentyde, cam ij angels into Sodom, and Loth sat at his gate. And whan he sawe hem, he wente and worshippid them, and prayd them to come and reste in his hous and abyde there and 'wesshe your feet'. And they said: 'Nay, we shal abide here in the strete.' And Loth constrayned them and brought hem into his hous, and made a feest to them. But er they shold goo to bedde, þe synful and cursid peple of the toun, yong and old, bisette and enuyroned Loths hous, and called Loth and saide: 'Wher [b]en the men that thou tokest into thi hous this nyght? Brynge them forth that we may knowe and vse them.' And Loth anon shette the dore and stode byhynde and saide to them: 'O, ye my brethern, I beseche you þat ye wyll not doo ne commyse thise wicked synne on them. I haue ij doughtres, virgyns which yet neuer knewe man. I shal brynge them out to you, and vse ye them. But thise men I pray you to spare. They ben entrid vnder the shadowe of my protection.' They said agayn to hym: 'Goo forth and fetche them. Thou art entred emong vs as a straunger. Shalt thou rewle and iuge vs? We shal put the to more affliction than them.' Loth withstode them myghtily; they had almost broken vp the dores, but the men sette hand to and dide helpe Loth, and brought hym in and dyd shette fast the dore, and smote them that were without with blyndenes, þat they myght not see ne fynde the dore. Thenne said the angels to Loth: 'Yf þou haue here of thy kynred sones or douchtres, all them that longe to þe lede out of this cyte. We shal destroye this place, for the | crye therof is comen to Our Lord, whiche hath sente vs for to f. 42va

212 vengeance] vegeāce 229 ben] hen

destroye them.' Loth wente vnto his kynnesmen and saide: 'Aryse and take your chyldren and goo out of this cyte, for Our Lord shal destroye it.' And they supposed that they had raued or iaped.

And as sone as it was day, the angels said to Loth: 'Aryse and take thy wif and thy ij doughtres, and goo out of this toun, leste that ye perisshe with them.' Yet he dyssimylyng, they toke hym by the hand and his wif and ij doughtres, bycause that God shold spare hem, and ladde them out of the cyte. And there they said to hym: 'Saue thy sowle and loke not behynde the, lest thou perysshe also, but saue the in þe montayn.' Loth said to hem: 'I beseche the, my Lord, for as moche as thy seruaunt hath founde grace byfore the and that thou hast shewde thy mercy to me, and that perauenture I myght take harm on the hille, that I may goo into the lytyl cyte hereby and may be sauyd there.' He said to Loth: 'I haue herd thy prayers, and for thy sake, I s[h]al not subuerte this toun for whiche thou hast prayd. Hye the and saue thyself there, for I may do nothyng tyl thou be theryn.' Therfore that toun is called Segor. Soo Loth went into Segor, and the sonne aroos.

And Our Lord rayned fro heuen vpon Sodom and Gomor sulphur and fyre, and subuerted the cytees and all the dwellers of the townes aboute that region, and all that was there growyng and burgenyng. Lothis wif torned her and loked toward the cytees, and anon she was torned into a statue or ymage of salte, whiche abideth so into this day. Abraham arose in the mornyng erly, and loked toward the cytees and sawe the smoke ascendyng fro the places lyke as it had be the layte of a fornays. What tyme Our Lord subuerted thise cytees, he remembred Abraham, and delyueryd Loth fro the vengeaunce of the cytees in which he duellid.

Thenne Loth ascended from Segor and dwellid in the montayne, and his ij doughtres with hym. He dredde to abyde ony lenger in the toun, but dwellid in a caue, he and his ij doughtres with hym. Thenne the elder doughter said to þe yonger: 'Our fader is old, and ther is no man lefte on the erthe lyuyng that may doo haue adoo with vs after the maner of the world. Come and late vs make hym dronke, and late vs
f. 42vb slepe with hym, that we may haue som | seed of hym.' They gaf their fader wyne to d[ry]nke that nyght and made hym dronke. And the elder doughter wente to hym and conceyued of hym, he not knowyng of it. And the second nyght, in lyke wyse, conceyuyd the yonger

260 shal] sal   281 drynke] CcChLS$_1$, dyrnke C+

doughter; and Loth was not knowyng therof. They conceyuyd bothe of theyr fader. The more had a sone and callyd hym Moab; he is fader of the Moabites vnto this day. The yonger brought forth another sone and callid hym Amon; he is fader of the Amonytes vnto this day.

Abraham departed fro thens and wente southward, and dwellid bytwene Cades and Sur, and wente a pilgremage to Geraris. He said that his wif was his suster. Abymelech the kyng of Geraris sente for her and toke her. God cam to Abymelech in his slepe and said: 'Thou shal be deed for the woman that thou hast taken; she hath an husbonde.' Abymelech towched her not, and said: 'Lord, wilt thou sle a man ygnoraunt and rightful? She said that she was his suster. In the symplen{e}s of my herte and clennes of my handes I dyde this.' And God said to hym: 'I know{e} wel that with a symple herte thou dydest it, and therfore I haue kepte the fro hauyng to doo with her. Nowe yelde the woman to her husbond, and he shal pray for the—he is a prophete—and thou shalt lyue. And yf thou delyuer her not, thou shalt dye and all they that ben in thy hows.'

Abymelech aroos vp the same nyght and called all his seruauntes and told them all thise wordes. All they dredde sore. Also Abymelech called Abraham and said to hym: 'What hast thou don to vs, that we haue trespaced to the? Thou hast caused me and my royam to synne gretly. Thou hast don that thou sholdest not haue don. What sawest thou for to do so?' Abraham saide: 'I thought that þe drede of God was not in this place and that ye wold sle me for my wyf. And certaynly o{t}herwyse, she is also my suster, the doughter of my fader but not of my moder, and I haue wedded her. And after that I wente fro the hows of my fader, I saide to her: 'Wheresomeuer we goo, saye thou art my suster.' Thenne Abymelech toke sheep and oxen, and seruauntes and maydens, and gaf to Abraham, and delyuerid to hym Sara his wif, and said: 'Lo, the londe is here tofore the. Whersomeuer þou wilt, dwell and abyde.' And he said to Sara: 'Lo, I haue gyuen to thy brother a M peces of syluer. | This shal be to the a veylle of thyn f. 43ra /
eyen, and whersomeuer thou goo, remembre that thou were taken.' sig. f3
Abraham prayde for Abymelech and his meyne, and God heled hym, his wyf and all his seruauntes and conceyuyd; Our Lord had closed the place of engendr[y]ng of alle the hows of Abymelech for Sara the wyf of Abraham.

Our Lord thenne vysyted Sara and she conceyuyd and brought

319 engendryng] engendrng

forth a sone in her old age that same tyme that God had promysed. Abraham called his sone that she had born Ysaac; and whan he was viij dayes old, he circumcised hym as God had conmanded, and Abraham was thenne an honderd yere old. Thenne said Sara: 'Who wold haue supposed that I shold gyue souke to my chyld, beyng so olde? I lawhed whan I herd Our Lord saye soo. And all they that shal here of it may wel lawhe.' The chyld grewe and was wened fro the pappe, and Abraham made a grete feste at the day of hys wenyng.

After thys, on a day whan Sara sawe the sone of Agar her handmayde playe with her sone Ysaac, she said to Abraham: 'Caste out this handmayde and her sone. The sone of the handmayde shal not be her with my sone Ysaac.' Abraham toke this word hard and greuously for his sone. Thenne God said to hym: 'Late it not be harde to the for thy sone and handmayde. Whatsomeuer Sara saye to the, here her voys, for in Isaac shal thy seed be called. Yet shal I make the sone of the handmayd growe into grete peple, for he is of thy seed.' Abraham arose erly in the mornyng, and toke brede and a botell of water and leyd hyt on her sholdre, and gaf to her the chyld and lete her goo. Whiche, whan she was departed, erryd in the wyldrenes of Bersabee. And whan the water was consumed that was in the botel, she lefte the chyld vnder a tre that was there, and wente thens as ferre as a bowe shote and sette her doun, and said: 'I shal not see my sone dye'; and there she wepte. Our Lord herde the voys of the chyld. And an angele callyd Agar, sayeng: 'What doest thou, Agar? Be not aferd. Our Lord hath herde the voys of the chyld fro the place whiche he is now inne. Aryse and take the chyld, and holde hym by the honde, for I shal make hym t'encrece into moche p[e]ple.' God opened her eyen,
f. 43rb and she sawe a pytte of water, | and anon she wente and fylled the botell and gaf the chyld to drynke. And [God] abode with hym, which grewe and dwellid in the wildernes, and becam there a yong man and an archer, and dwellid also in the deserte of Pharam. And his moder toke to hym a wyf of the lond of Egypte.

That same tyme said Abymelech, and Phicol the prynce of his oost, vnto Abraham: 'Our Lord is with the in all thynges that thou doest. Swere thou by the Lord that thou greue not me ne them that shal come after me, ne my kynrede; but after the mercy that I haue shewd to the, so doo to me and my londe, in whiche thou hast dw[e]lled as a straunger. And Abraham said: 'I shal swere.' And he blamed

348 peple] paple   350 God] *om.*   358 dwelled] dwlled

Abymelech for the pytte of water, whiche his seruauntis had taken away by strengthe. Abymelech answerd: ‘I know not who hath don this thynge. And thou toldest me not therof, and I neuer herd therof tyl this day.’ And then after this, they made couenaunt togydre, and promysed eche to other to be frendes togydre.

After alle thyse thynges, God temptyd Abraham and said to hym: ‘Abraham, Abraham.’ He answerd and said: ‘I am here.’ And he said to hym: ‘Take thou thyn only sone, that thou louest, Ysaac, and goo into the londe of vysyon, and offre hym in sacrefyse to me vpon one of the hilles that I shal shewe to the.’ Thenne Abraham arose in the nyght, and made redy his asse, and toke with hym two yong men and Ysaac his sone. And whan they had hewen and gadred the wood togydre to make sacrefyse, they wente to the place that God commanded hym. The thyrde day after, he lyft vp his eyen and sawe fro ferre the place. And he said to his children: ‘Abyde ye here with the asse. I and my sone shal goo to yonder place, and whan we haue worshipped there, we shal retorne to you.’ Thenne he toke the wode of the sacrefise and leyd it on his sone Ysaac, and he bare in his hondes fyre and the swerd. And as they wente bothe togydre, Ysaac said to his fader: ‘Fader myn.’ ‘What wilt thou, my sone?’ said Abraham. And he said: ‘Loo, here is fyre and wode. Wher is the sacrefise þat shal be offred?’ Abraham answerd: ‘My sone, God shal prouide for hym a sacrefise wel ynough.’ They wente forth, and cam to the place þat God had ordeyned, and there made an awter, and leyd the wode theron, and | [f. 43va] toke Ysaac and sette hym on the wode on the awter, and toke his swerde and wold haue offred hym vp to God. And lo, the angele of God cryed to hym fro heuen, sayeng: ‘Abraham, Abraham’; whiche answerd: ‘I am here.’ And he said to hym: ‘Extende not thy hande vpon thy chyld, and do nothyng to hym. Now I knowe that thou dredest God, and hast not spared thyn only sone for me.’ Abraham loked behynde hym and sawe emonge the breres a ramme, faste by the hornes, whiche he toke, and offrid hym in sacrefyse for his sone. He called that place ‘The Lord seeth’. The angele called Abraham the second tyme, sayeng: ‘I haue sworn by myself’, saith the Lord, ‘bycause thou hast don this thing, and hast not spared thyn only sone for me. I shal blesse the and shal multeplye thy seed as the sterres of heuen, and lyke the grauel þat is on the see syde. Thy seed shal possede the yates of theyr enemyes. And in thy seed shal be blessyd all the peple of th’erthe, for thou obeydest to me.’ Abraham thenne retorned to his seruantes and wente vnto Bersabee, and dwellyd there.

Sara lyuyd an C xxvij yere, and deyed in the cyte of Arbee, whiche is Hebron in the londe of Canaan. For whom Abraham made sorow and wepte, and bought of the children of Heth a felde, and buryed her worshipfully in a dobble spelunke.

Abraham was an old man and God blessyd hym in all his thingis. He said to the eldest and vpperist seruaunt of all his hows: 'I charge and coniure the by the name of God of heuen and of erthe that thou suffre not my sone Ysaac to take no wyf of þe doughtres of Canaan, emonge whom I dwelle, but goo into the contre where my kynrede is, and take of them a wyf to my sone.' And the seruaunt answerd: 'Yf no woman there wil come with me into this contre, shal I brynge thy sone into that contre fro whens thou camest?' Abraham said: 'Beware that thou lede not my sone theder. The Lord of heuen and of erthe, that toke me fro the hows of my fader and fro the place of my natyuyte, hath said and sworn to me, sayeng: "To thy seed I shal gyue this londe." He shal sende his angele tofore the, and thou shalt take there a wyf for my sone. Yf no woman wil come with the, thou shalt not be
f. 43vb bounden by thyn oth, but in no wyse lede my | sone thyder.' His seruaunt thenne swore and promysyd to hym that he wold soo doo.

He toke x cameles of the flock of his lord, and of alle his goodes bare with hym and wente into Mesopotany vnto the toun of Nachor. And he made the cameles to tarye without the toun by a pytte syde at suche tyme as the women ben wonte to come out for to drawe water. And there he prayd Our Lord, sayeng: 'Lord, God of my lord Abraham, I beseche the to helpe me this day and do mercy vnto my lord Abraham. Lo, I stonde here nyhe by the welle of water, and the doughters of the dwellers of this toun come hether for to drawe water. Therfore the mayde to whom I saye: "Sette doun thy potte that I may drynke", and thenne she sette doun her potte and saye: "I will gyue to the drynke and to the camelis", that I may vnderstande therby that she be the mayde that thou hast ordeyned to thy seruaunt Ysaac, and thou shewest thy mercy to my lord Abraham.' He had not fully fynysshid these wordes within hymself, but that Rebecca doughter of Batuel, sone of Melche, wyf of Nachor, brother of Abraham, cam out of the toun, hauyng a potte on her sholder, whiche was a right faire mayde and moche beautevous, and vnknowen to the man. She wente doun to the welle and fylled her pot with water, and retorned. The seruaunt of Abraham ranne to her and saide: 'I praye the to gyue me a lytil of the water in thy potte for to drynke.' Whiche said: 'Drynke, my lord', and lyghtly toke the potte fro her sholdre and helde it, and gaf hym drynke; and whan he had dronke, she said yet: 'I shal gyue to thy camels drynke and drawe water for them tyl alle haue dronken.' And she poured out the water into a vessel that was there for beestis to drynke, and ran to the pytte and drewe water, that eueriche dranke his draughte. He thenne thought in hymself secretly that God had made hym to haue a prosperous iourney. After they had dronke, he gaf her ij rynges to hange on her eeris weyeng ij sycles and as many armyllis weyeng x sycles, and asked her whos doughter she was, and yf ther were ony rome in her faders hous to be lodged. And she answerd: 'I am doughter to Bathuel, Nachors sone, and in my faders hows is place ynough to lodge the and thy camels, and | plente of chaf and heye for them.' And the man enclyned doun to the grounde and worshipped God, sayeng: 'Blessid be the Lord God of my lord Abraham, which hath not take away his mercy ne hys trouthe fro my lord, and hath brought me in my iourney right into the hous of my lordes brother.' f. 44[ra] / sig. f4

The mayde Rebecca ran, and tolde at home alle that she had herd. Rebecca had a brother named Laban, whiche hastely wente out to the man, whereas he was. Whan he had seen the ryngis in his susters eeris and her poynettis or armylles on her handes, and had herd her saye alle that the man saide, he cam to the man that stode by the welle yet and said to hym: 'Come in, thou blessyd of God; why standest thou withoute? I haue made redy the hows for the, and haue ordeyned place for thy camels.' And brought hym in and strowed his cameles and gaf them chaf and heye, and water to wasshe the camels feet and the mens feet that cam with hym. And they sette forth brede tofore hym, whiche saide: 'I shal not ete tyl I haue don myn erande', and said: 'wherfor I am comen.' And it was answerd to hym: 'Saye on.' And he saide: 'I am seruaunt of Abraham. And God hath blessyd and magnefyed hym gretly, and hath gyuen to hym oxen and sheep, syluer and gold, seruauntes, men and wymen, cameles and asses. And Sara his wyf hath brought hym forth a sone in her olde age, and he hath gyuen to hym alle that he had. And my lord hath charged and adiured me, sayeng: "In no wyse late my sone Ysaac haue no wyf of the doughters of Canaan", in whos londe he dwelleth, "but goo vnto the hows of my fader and of my kynrede, and of them thou shalt take a wyf to my sone". Wherfore I am comen hether', and told alle how he prayd God of som token and how Rebecca dyde to hym, and in conclusion desired to haue Rebecca for his lord Ysaac, and yf he wold not, that he myght departe and goo into some other place on the right side or the lyft, to seke a wyf for his lordes sone.

Thenne Bathuel and Laban said to hym: 'This worde is comen of God. Agayn his wille, we may nothyng do. Lo, Rebecca standeth tofore the. Take her and goo forth that she may be wyf vnto the sone f. 44rb of thy lord, as Our Lord hath said.' Whiche wordes whan Abra|hams seruaunt had herde, fylle doun to the ground and thanked Our Lord, and anon toke forth syluer vessell and of gold and good clothis, and gaf them to Rebecca for a yefte. And to her brethern and moder he gaf also yeftes. And anon made a feste and ete, and were ioyeful togyder. On the morn betymes the seruaunt of Abraham aroos, and desyred to departe and take Rebecca with hym and goo to his lord. Thenne the moder and her brethern said: 'Late the mayde abyde with vs but only x dayes, and thenne take her and goo thy waye.' 'I pray you', said he, 'reteyne ne lette me not. Our Lord hath adressyd my way and achyeuyd my erand, wherfor late me goo to my lord.' And they saide: 'We shal calle the mayde and knowe her wille.' And whan she was demanded yf she wold goo with that man, she saide: 'Ye, I shal goo with hym.' Thenne they lete her goo, and her noryce wyth her. And so she departyd and they sayd to her: 'Thou art our suster. We pray God that thou may encrece into a thousand thousand, and that thy seed may possede the yates of theyr enemyes.' Thenne Rebecca and her maydens ascended vpon the cameles and folowed the seruaunt of Abraham, whiche hastely retorned vnto his lord.

That same tyme whan they come, Ysaac walked by the way without-forth, and loked vp and sawe the cameles comyng fro ferre. Rebecca espyed hym and demanded of the seruaunt who that he was that cam in the felde ayenst them. He answerd and saide: 'That is my lord Ysaac.' And anon she toke her palle or mantel, and couerd her. The seruaunt anon tolde vnto his lord Ysaac alle that he had doon, whiche resceyuyd her and lad her into the tabernacle of Sara his moder, and wedded her and toke her in to his wyf, and so moche louyd her that the loue attempered the sorow that he had for his moder.

Abraham after this wedded another wyf, by whom he had diuerse children. Abraham gaf to Ysaac alle his possessyons. And to his other chyldren he gaf meuable goodes, and departed the sones of his concubynes fro his sone Ysaac, whyles he yet lyued. And alle the dayes of the lyf of Abraham were C lxxv yere, and thenne deyed in good mynde and age. And Ysaac and Ismael buryed hym by his wyf Sara in a double spelunke.

[4. ISAAC]

Here begynneth the lyf of Ysaac with th'istorye of Esau and of Iacob, whiche is redde in the chirche the Second Sonday of Lente. f. 44[va]

Ysaac was xl yere olde whan he wedded Rebecca. And she bare hym no children, wherfore he besought Our Lord that she myght conceyue and brynge forth fruyt. Our Lord herd his pra[ye]r, that she conceyued of hym and had tweyne sones attones, whiche two er they were born fought ofte in their moders bely. For whiche cause she prayd God to counseylle her and to gyue her comfort, whiche apperid and said to her: 'Two maner peple ben in thy bely, and two maner folke shal be deuyded fro thy wombe. Peple shal ouercome peple, and the more shal serue the lasse.' Thus said Our Lord to her.

After this, whan tyme cam that she shold be delyuerd, ther were tweyne to be born. The first that yssued was rough fro the heed to the foot and he was named Esau. And forthwith folowed that other, holdyng the plante of his broders foot in his hond, and he was named Iacob. Ysaac the fader was lx yer old whan | thise children were born. f. 44[vb]

And after this, whan they were growen to resonable age, Esau becam a plowhman and a telyar of th'erthe and an hunter. And Iacob was symple and dwellyd at home with his moder. Ysaac the fader loued wel Esau bycause he ete ofte of the venyson that Esau toke. And Rebecca the moder loued Iacob.

Iacob on a tyme had made good potage. And Esau his broder had ben an huntyng al day, and cam home sore anhungrid and fonde Iacob hauyng good potage and prayd hym to gyue hym some, for he was wery and moche hungry. To whom Iacob said: 'Yf thou wyllt selle to me thy patrymony and heritage, I shal gyue the somme potage.' And Esau answerd: 'Lo, I dye for hungre. What shal auaylle me myn enheritaunce yf I dye, and what shal proufyte me my patrymonye? I am contente that thou take it for this potage.' Iacob thenne said: 'Swere that to me that thou shalt neuer clayme hit, and that thou art content that I shal enioye it.' And Esau sware it, and so sold away his patrymony, and toke the potage and ete it and wente his waye, settyng nothyng therby that he had sold his patremony. This aforsaid is for to brynge in my mater of th'ystorye that is redde. For now foloweth the legende as it is redd in the chirche.

Ysaac began to wexe olde and his eyen faylled and dymmed that he

3 Ysaac] Y *six-line capital supplied by hand in red* 5 prayer] praeyr

myght not clerly see. And on a tyme he called Esau his oldest sone and said to hym: 'Sone myne'; which answerde: 'Fader, I am here redy.' To whom the fader saide: 'Beholde that I wexe olde and knowe not the day that I shal dye and departe out of this world. Wherfore take thyn harneys, thy bowe and quyuer with takles and goo forth an huntyng. And whan thou hast taken ony venyson, make to me therof suche maner mete as thou knowest that I am woned to ete, and brynge it to me that I may ete it and that my sowle may blesse the or I dye.'

Whiche all thise wordis Rebecca herde. And Esau wente forth for t'accomplyssh the comandement of his fader; and she saide thenne to Iacob: 'I haue herde thy fader saye to Esau thy brother: "Brynge to me f. 45[ra] / sig. [f5] of thy venyson and make therof mete that I | may ete and that I may blesse the tofore Our Lord er I dye." Now my sone take hede to my conceyll, and goo forth to the flock and brynge to me two the beste kyddes that thou canst fynde, and I shal make of them mete suche as thy fader shal gladly ete, whiche whan thou hast brought to hym and hath eten, he may blesse the er he dye.' To whom Iacob answerd: 'Knowest thou not that my brother is rowhe and heery and I smothe? Yf my fader take me to hym and taste me and fele, I drede me that he shal thynke that I mocke hym and shal gyue me his curse for the blessyng.' The moder thenne seid to hym: 'In me', said she, 'be this curse, my sone. Neuertheles here me. Go to the flocke and doo that I haue said to the.'

He wente and fette the kyddes and delyuerd them to his moder. And she wente and ordeyned them into suche mete as she knewe wel that his fader louyd, and toke the beste clothes that Esau had and dyde hem on Iacob. And the skynnes of the kyddes she dyde aboute his necke and handes there as he was bare, and delyueryd to hym brede and the pulmente that she had boyled. And he wente to his fader and saide: 'Fader myn.' And he answerd: 'I here. Who art thou, my sone?' Iacob saide: 'I am Esau, thy fyrst begoten sone. I haue don as thou comaundest me. Aryse, sitte and ete of the venyson of myn huntyng, that thy soule may blesse me.' Thenne said Ysaac agayn to his sone: 'How myghtest thou', said he, 'so soone fynde and take it, my sone?' To whom he answerd: 'It was the wyll of God that suche thyng as I desired cam sone to my hande.' Ysaac said to hym: 'Come hether to me my sone, that I may touche and handle the, that I may preue whether thou be my sone Esau or not.' He cam to his fader; and whan he had felte hym, Ysaac saide: 'The voys truly is the voys of Iacob, but the handes ben the handes of Esau.' And he knewe hym not, for his handes expressyd the lyknes and symylitude of the more brother. Therfore, blessyng hym he said to hym: 'Thou art thenne my sone Esau.' He answerd and said: 'I am he.' Thenne said Ysaac: 'Brynge to me the mete of thyn huntyng, my sone, that my sowle may blesse the.' Whiche he offrid and gaf to his | fader, and also wyn. And whan he f. 45rb had eten and dronken a good draught of the wyn, he said to Iacob: 'Come hether to me my sone and kysse me.' And he wente to hym and kyssed hym. Anone, as he felte the swete sauour and smelle of his clothes, blessyng hym he said: 'Lo, the swete odour of my sone is as the odour of a felde ful of flowres, whom Our Lord blesse. God gyue to the of the dewe of heuen and of the fattenes of th'erthe, habundaunce of whete, wyne and oyle. And the peple serue the and the trybus worshipe the. Be thou lord of thy brethern; and the sones of thy moder shal bowe and knele to the. Whosomeuer curse the, be he accursed, and who that blessyth the, with blessynges be he fulfylled.'

Vnneth Ysaac had fulf[y]lled thyse wordes and Iacob gon out, whan that Esau cam with his mete that he had goten with huntyng, entred in and offred to his fader, sayeng: 'Aryse, fader myn, and ete of the venyson that thy sone hath ordeyned for the, that thy sowle may blesse me.' Ysaac said to hym: 'Who art thou?' To whom he answerd: 'I am thy fyrst begoten sone Esau.' Ysaac thenne was gretly abasshid and astoned, and meruaylled more than can be thought credyble. And thenne he was in a traunce, as the Mayster of Historyes saith, in whiche he had knowleche that God wold that Iacob shold haue the blessyng, and said to Esau: 'Who thenne was he that ryght now a lityl tofore thy comyng brought to m[e] venyson? And I haue eten of alle that he brought to me er thou camest. I haue blessyd hym and he shal be blessyd.' Whan Esau herde thise wordes of his fader, he cryed wyth a grete crye and was sore astonyed and saide: 'Fader, I praye the blesse me also.' To whom he said: 'Thy brother germayn is comen fraudelently and hath receyuyd thy blessyng.' Thenne said Esau: 'Certaynly and iustly may his name be called wel Iacob, for on another tyme tofore this he supplanted me of my patrymonye, and now secondly he hath vndernome fro me my blessyng.' And yet thenne he said to his fader: 'Hast thou not reseruyd to me one blessyng?' Ysaac answerd: 'I haue ordeyned hym to be thy lord. I haue subdued alle his brethern to his seruytude. | I haue stablysshed hym in whete, wyne f. 45va

93 fulfylled] fulflled   103 me] my

and oyle. And after this what shal I doo to the, my sone?' To whom Esau said: 'Hast thou not, fader, yet one blessyng? I beseche the to blesse me.' Thenne with a grete syghyng and wepyng, Ysaac, moued, said to hym: 'In the fattenes of th'erthe and in the dewe of heuen shal be thy blessyng. Thou shalt lyue in thy swerd and shalt serue thy brother.'

Thenne was Esau woo-begoon, and hated Iacob for supplanty[n]g of his blessyng that his fader had blessyd hym wyth; and seid in his herte: 'The dayes of sorowe shal come to my fader, for I shal slee my brother Iacob.' This was told to Rebecca, whiche anon sente for Iacob her sone and sayd to hym: 'Lo, Esau thy brother threteneth to slee the. Therfore now, my sone, here my voys and doo as I shal counseyl. Make the redy and goo to my brother in Aran. And dwelle ther with hym vnto the tyme that his angre and furye ben ouerpassed and his indignacion cessed and that he forgete suche thynges that thou hast don to hym; and thenne after that I shal sende for the and brynge the hether agayn.' And Rebecca wente to Ysaac her husbond and saide: 'I am wery of my lyf bycause of the doughters of Heth. Yf Iacob take to hym a wyf of that kynrede, I wyll no lenger lyue.'

Ysaac thenne callid Iacob and blessyd hym and comanded to hym, sayeng: 'I charge the in no wyse to take a wyfe of the kynred of Canaan, but goo and walke into Mesopotamye of Syrye vnto the hows of Bathuel, fader of thy moder. And take to the there a wyf of the doughtres of Laban thyn vncle. God Almyghty blesse the and make the growe and multeplye, that thou may be encreced into tourbes of peple; and gyue to the the blessynges of Abraham, and to thy seed after the, that thou may possesse and owe the londe of thy pylgremage, whiche he graunted to thy grauntsyre.' Whan Ysaac had thus said and gyuen hym leue to goo, he departed anon and wente into Mesopotamye of Sirye to Laban sone of Bathuel, brother of Rebekke his moder.

Esau, seeyng that his fader had blessid Iacob and sente hym in Mesopotamye of Syrie for to wedde a wyf there an[d] that after his
f. 45vb blessyng commanded to hym, sayeng: 'Take thou no | wif of the doughtres of Canaan', and he, obeyeng his fader, wente into Syrye, prouyng therby that his fader sawe not gladly the doughtres of Canaan, he wente to Ismael and toke hym a wyf, besyde them that he had taken tofore, that was Melech doughter of Ismael sone of Abraham.

121 supplantyng] supplantyg   147 and] Ans

Thenne Iacob departed fro Bersabee, wente forth on his iourney toward Aran. Whan he cam to a certayn place after goyng doun of the sonne and wolde reste there alle nyght, toke of the stones that were there and leyed vnder his heed and slepte in the same place. And there he sawe in his sleep a ladder standyng on th'erthe, and the vpper ende therof touched heuen, and angeles of God ascendyng and descendyng vpon it, and Our Lord in the myddys of the ladder, sayeng to hym: 'I am the Lord God of Abraham thy fader and of Ysaac. The londe on whiche thou slepest I shal gyue to the and to thy seed, and thy seed shal be as duste of th'erthe. Thou shalt sprede abrood vnto the eest and to the weste and north and south, and alle the trybus of th'erthe shalle be blessid in the and in thy seed. And I shal be thy keper whersomeuer thou shalt goo and shal brynge the agayn into this londe. And I shal not leue tyl I haue accomplysshyd alle that I haue said.'

Whan Iacob was awaked fro his sleep and dremyng, he said: 'Verely God is in this place, and I wist not of it.' And he said dredyngly: 'How terryble is this place! None other thynge is here but the hows of God and the yate of heuen.' Thenne Iacob arose erly and toke the stone that laye vnder his heed and reysed it for wytnes, pouryng oyle theron, and callid the name of the place Betel, whiche tofore was callid Luza. And there he made a vowe to Our Lord, sayeng: 'Yf God be wyth me and kepe me in the waye that I walke, and gyue me brede to ete and clothes to couer me, and may retorne prosperously into the hows of my fader, the Lord shal be my God and this stone that I haue reysed in wytnes, this shal be called the hows of God. And good of all thynges that thou gyuest to me, I shal offre to the the tythes and teenth part.'

Thenne Iacob wente forth into the eest and sawe a pytte | in a felde f. 46ra /
and thre flockes of sheep lyeng by it; for of that pytte were the beestis sig. [f6]
watred. And the mouth therof was shette and closed with a grete stone; for the custom was whan alle the sheep were gadred they rolled away the stone, and whan they had dronken they leyde the stone agayn at the pitte mouth. And thenne he saide to the shepherdes: 'Brethern, whens ar ye?' Whiche answerde: 'Of Aran.' Thenne he, askyng them, saide: 'Knowe ye not Laban sone of Nachor?' They saide: 'We knowe hym well.' 'How farith he?', said he, 'Is he al hool?' 'He farith wel', saide they, 'and loo, Rachel his doughter cometh there with her flocke.' Thenne saide Iacob: 'It is yet fer to euen. It is yet tyme that the flockes be ledde to drynke and after be dryuen to pasture.' Whiche answerd: 'We may not so doo til alle the beestis be

gadred, and thenne we remeue the stone fro the mouth of the pitte and watre our beestis.'

And as they talked, Rachel cam with the flock of her fader, for she kepte that tyme the beestes. And whan Iacob sawe her and knewe that she was his emes doughter and that they were his emes sheep, he remeuyd the stone fro the pittes mouth. And whan her sheep had dronken, he kissed her, and wepyng he tolde her that he was brother to her fader and sone of Rebecca. Thenne she hyed her and told it to her fader, which, whan he vnderstode that Iacob his suster sone was come, he ran ayenst hym and enbracyng, kissed hym and lad hym into his hows. And whan he had herde the cause of his iourney, he said: 'Thou art my mouth and my flessh.' And whan he had ben there the space of a moneth, he demaunded Iacob yf he wold gladly serue hym bycause he was his cosyn, and what hyre and reward he wold haue.

He had two doughters. The more was named Lya and the lasse was called Rachel, but Lya was blereyed and Rachel was fair of visage and wel fauoured. Whom Iacob loued and saide: 'I shal serue the for Rachel thy yonger doughter vij yere.' Laban answerd: 'It is better that I gyue her to the than to a straunge man. Dwelle and abyde with me, and thou shalt haue her.' And so Iacob seruyd hym for Rachel vij yere, and hym thought it but a lytil while bycause of the grete loue that he | f. 46rb had to her. And at th'ende of vij yere Iacob said to Laban: 'Gyue to me my wyf, for the tyme is come that I shold haue her.' Thenne Laban callid all his frendes and made a feste for the weddyng, and at nyght he brought in Lya the more doughter, and delyuered to her an handmayde named Zelpha. Thenne [Iacob, wenyng] that it had ben Rachel, wente to her as the maner is; and whan the morny[n]g cam and sawe that it was Lya, he said to Laban her fader: 'What haste thou don? Haue I not seruid the for Rachel? Why hast thou brought Lya to me?' Laban answerd: 'Hit is not the vsage ne custome of our contre to gyue the yonger first to be wedded, but fulfylle and make an ende of this coplement and maryage this weke, and thenne shal I gyue to the Rachel my doughther for other vij yer that thou shalt yet serue to me.' Iacob agreed gladly, and whan that weke was passed, he wedded Rachel to his wyf, to whom Laban her fader gaf an handmayde named Bala. Neuertheles whan the weddyng of the yonger was fynysshyd, bycause of the grete loue that he had to her, hym thought that the other vij yere were but shorte.

218 Iacob, wenyng] wenyng Iacob 219 mornyng] mornyg

Our Lord sawe that he despysed Lya. He lete Lya conceyue, and Rachel her suster abode bareyne. Whiche thenne Lya bare a sone and named hym Ruben, sayeng: ‘Our Lord God hath beholden myn humylite and mekenes. Now shal myn husbonde loue me.’ She conceyued yet and bare another sone and saide: ‘Bycause Our Lord sawe me despysed, he hath gyuen to me this sone.’ And she called hym Symeon. She conceyuyd the thyrd and brought forth another sone and said: ‘Now shal my husbonde be coupled to me bycause I haue born to hym thre sones.’ And she called his name Leuy. She conceyuyd the fourth sone and was delyueryd of hym and saide: ‘Now I shal knowleche me to Our Lord.’ And therfor she named hym Iudas. And thenne she cessed of beryng of chyldren.

Rachel, s{ee}yng herself bareyn, had enuye to her suster, and said to Iacob her husbond: ‘Make me with child or ellys I shal deye.’ To whom Iacob was wroth and answerde: ‘What, wenest thou that I were God and hath pryued fro the the fruyt of thy bely?’ Thenne she said: ‘I haue my seruaunt Bala. | Goo vnto h{e}r and late her conceyue of f. 46[va] the on my knees, that I may haue of her somme sones.’ She gaf Bala vnto her husbond to knowe her, whiche whan Iacob had knowen, she conceyued and bare a sone. Thenne sayde Rachel: ‘Our Lord hath herde my peticion, gyvyng to me a sonne’, and she named hym Dan. After that Bala conceyued agayn and bare another sone, for whom Rachel saide: ‘Our Lord hath compared me to my suster and [I] haue avayled’, and she named hym Neptalim. Then[n]e Lya, felyng that she conceyued no more, she gaf Zelpha her handmaide to her husbonde, whiche conceyued and bare a sone, whom Lya named Gad. After, Zelpha conceyved another sone, for whom Lya sayde: ‘This is for my blessidnes, and certaynly alle generations shal saye that I am blessyd.’ Therfor she called hym Aser.

Hit happed that Ruben wente out in harvest tyme into the felde, and toke there a mandrake, whiche he brought and gaf to his moder. Thenne Rachel said to her suster Lya: ‘Gyue me somme parte of the mandrake of thy sone.’ Lya answerd: ‘Is it not ynough t[o] take fro me my husbonde, but that also thou wilt haue pa{r}te of the mandrake of my sone?’ Thenne said Rachel: ‘He shal slepe with the this nyght for the mandrake of thy sone.’ At euen, whan Iacob cam home fro the felde, Lya wente ayenst hym and said to hym: ‘Thou shalt this nyght slepe with me, for I haue bought the for the mede of the mandrake of

253 I] *om.* 254 Thenne] Then \ de 263 to] ta

my sone.' He slepte with her that nyght. And Our Lord herde her prayers: she conceyuyd and brought forth the fyfthe sone, and she said: 'God hath rewarded me bycause I gaf my handmayde to my husbond.' She called his name Ysachar. Yet Lya conceyuyd and bare the sixthe sone, and said: 'God hath endowed m[e] with a good dower; yet shal my husbond abyde with me bycause I haue born to hym vj sones.' And she called his name Zabulon. After this she conceyuyd and bare a doughter named Dyna. Thenne Our Lord remembryd Rachel and herde her and opende the place of concepcion, whiche conceyuyd and bare a sone, sayeng: 'Our Lord hath taken away myn obprobrye and shame', and named his name Ioseph, sayeng: 'I praye God to sende me another.'

f. 46vb Whan | Ioseph was born, Iacob saide to Laban his wyuys fader: 'Gyue me leue to departe, that I may goo into my contre and my londe. Gyue to me my wyuys and chyldren, for whom I haue seruyd the, that I may goo hens. Thou knowest what seruyse I haue seruyd the.' Laban said to hym: 'I haue founden grace in thy sight. I knowe it by experience that God hath blessyd me for the. I haue ordeyned the reward that I shal gyue to the.' Thenne Iacob answerd: 'Thou knowest how I haue serued the and how moche thy possession was in my handes. Thou haddest but lytyl whan I cam to the, and now thou art ryche. God hath blessyd the at myn entre. Hit i[s] now right that I prouyde somwhat toward myn hows.' Laban saide: 'What shal I gyue to the?' Iacob answerd: 'I wyll nothyng but that thou doo that I demaunde. I shal yet fede and kepe thy beestes, and departe asondre all the sheep of dyuerse colour. And alle that euer that shal be of dyuerse colours and spotty, as wel in sheep as in gheet, late me haue them for my reward and mede.' And Laban graunted therto.

Thenne Iacob toke roddes grene and toke part of the rynde away and made tho roddes to be of ij colours and sette them tofore the sheep and beestis whan they shold engendre, and the bestes conceyuyd seeyng the roddes of varyable colour. In lyke wyse all the lambes that cam forth that yere were whyte and black, and of dyuerse colour. Thenne Laban sawe that Iacob hath the most parte, and chaunged the couenaunt the next yere and wold haue all them of variable colour, and Iacob shold haue all them that were of one colour. And Iacob thenne sette roddes of one colour afore them whan the sheep and beestis conceyuyd. Thenne atte tyme of departyng Laban

273 me] my 290 is] it

toke them of two colours and Iacob them that were of one colour. Thus was Iacob made moche ryche ou[t] of mesure and had many flockes, seruauntes bothe men and wymen, camels and asses.

After that Iacob had herde Laban[s] sones saye: 'Iacob hath taken all that was our faders from hym and of his faculte is made ryche', he was abasshed and vnderstode wel by Labans lokyng that he was not so frendly to hym ward as he | had ben tofore. And also Our Lord said to hym that he shold retorne into the londe of his faders and to his generacion, and that he wold be with hym. He thenne called Rachel and Lya into the felde whereas he fedde his flockes, and said to them: 'I see wel by youre faders visage þat he is not toward me as he was yesterday or þat other day. Forsothe the God of my fader was with me, and ye knowe wel how I haue seruyd your fader with alle my myght and strength. But he hath deceyued me, and hath chaunged myn hyre and mede x tymes. And yet Our Lord hath not suffred hym to greue me. Whan he said the beestis of party colour shold be myn, thenne alle the ewes brought forth lambes of variable colours. And whan he said the contrarye, they brought forth all whyte. God hath taken the substaunce of your fader and hath gyuen it to me. And now God hath comaunded me to departe, wherfore make you redy and late vs departe hens.'

f. 47ra / sig. [f7]

Thenne answerd Rachel and Lya: 'Shal we haue nothyng ellis of our faders faculte and of th'eritage of his hows? Shal he repute vs as straungers, and he hath eten and sold our good? Sith God hath taken the goodes of our fader and hath gyuen it to vs and to our chyldren, wherfor all that God comandeth to the, doo it.' Iacob aroose and sette his children and his wyues vpon his camels and wente his waye, and toke all his substaunce and flockes and alle that he had goten in Mesopotamye, and wente toward his fader Ysaac into the londe of Canaan.

That tyme was Laban goon to shere his sheep, and Rachel stale away the ydollis of her fader. Iacob wold not lete Laban knowe of his departyng. Whan he was departed with all that longed to hym of right, he cam to the mount of Galaad. It was told to Laban the thirde day after that Iacob was fled and goon, who anon toke his brethern and poursiewed hym by the space of vij dayes and ouertoke hym in the Mount of Galaad. He sawe Our Lord in his sleep sayeng to hym: 'Beware that thou speke not angerly ne hard wordes to Iacob.' That

308 out] ouf   310 Labans] laban

tyme Iacob had sette his tabernacle in the hylle, and whan he cam theder with his brothern, he said to Iacob: 'Why hast thou don thus | f. 47rb to me, to take away my doughters as prysoners taken by swerd? Why fleddest fro me and woldest not lete me haue knowleche therof? Thou hast not suffred me to kysse my sones and doughtres. Thou hast don folyly. Now may I doo the harm and euyll, but the God of thy fader said to me yesterday: "Beware that thou speke no hard wordes ayenst Iacob." Thou desirest to goo to the hows of thy fader; why hast thou stolen my goddes?' Iacob answerd that: 'I departed, the not knowyng; I dredde that vyolently thou woldest haue taken fro me thy doughters. And where thou repreuest me of thefte, whosomeuer haue stolen thy goddes, late hym be slayn tofore our brethern. Seche, and what thou fyndest that is thyn, take with the.' He, sayeng this, knew not that Rachel had stolen her faders goddes.

Thenne Laban entred the tabernacle of Iacob and Lya, and soughte and fonde nothyng. And whan he cam into the tabernacle of Rachel, she hyed her and hydde the idollis vnder the lytter of the camel and satte vpon it. And he soughte, and fond nought. Thenne said Rachel: 'Late not my lord be wroth for I may not aryse to the, for now suche sekenes as wymen ben wonte to haue is fallen to me.' And so she deceyuyd her fader. Thenne Iacob, beyng angry and grutchyng, said to Laban: 'What is my trespaas and what haue I synned to the, that thou thus hast pursiewed me and hast serched euerithyng? What hast thou nowe founden of all the substaunce of thy hous? Leye it forth tofor my brethern and thy brethern, that they iuge bitwene me and the. I haue seruyd the xx yere and haue ben with the. Thy sheep and thy gheet were neuer barreyn. I haue eten no wethers of thy flock, ner beste hath destroyed none. I shal make alle good what was stolen. I prayd therfore day and nyght. I laboured bothe in hete and in colde. Slepe fled from myn eyen. Thus I seruyd the in thy hows xx yere, xiiij for thy doughters and sixe for thy flockes. Thou hast chaunged myn hyre and reward x tymes. But yf God of my fader Abraham and the drede of Ysaac had ben with me, happely thou woldest now haue lefte me naked. Our Lord God hath beholden myn affliction and the labour f. 47va of | myn handes, and repreuyd the yesterday.'

Laban answerd to hym: 'My doughters and sones, and thy flockes and all that thou beholdest ar thyn. What may I doo to my sones and neu{e}ws? Late vs now be frendes and make we a faste leghe and

361 the[3]] the \ the

confedersy togydre.' Thenne Iacob reysed a stone and reysed it in token of frendship and pees, and so they ete togydre in frendship and sware eche to other to abide in loue euer after. And after this Laban rose in the nyght and kyssyd his doughtres and sones and blessyd them and retorned into his contre.

Iacob wente forth in his iourney that he had taken. Angels of God mette hym, which whan he sawe he saide: 'Thyse ben the castellis of God', and called that place Manaym. He sente messagers tofore hym to Esau his brother in the londe of Seir in the londe of Edom, and bad them saye thus to Esau: 'This said thy broder Iacob: "I haue dwellid with Laban vnto this day. I haue oxen ande asses, seruauntes bothe men and wymen. I sende now a legacion vnto my lord that I may fynde grace in his sight."' Thise messagers retorned to Iacob and saide: 'We cam to Esau thy brother. And lo, he cometh for to mete with the with iiijC men.' Iacob was sore aferde thenne, and deuyded his companye into tweyne turmes, sayeng: 'Yf Esau come to that one and destroye that, that other shal yet be saued.' Thenne said Iacob: 'O God of my fader Abraham and God of my fader Ysaac, O Lord that saydest to me: "Retorne into thy londe and place of thy natyuyte", and saidest: "I shal do wel to the", I am the leste in all thy mercyes, and in thy trouth that hast graunted to thy seruaunt. With my staf I haue goon this ryuer of Iordan. And now I retorne with ij turmes. I beseche the, Lord, kepe me fro the hondes of my brother Esau, for I fere hym gretly, leste he come and smyte doun the moder with the sones. Thou hast sayde that thou sholdest do wel to me, and sholdest sprede my seed lyke vnto the grauel of the see and that it may not be nombred for multytude.'

Thenne, whan he had slept that nyght, he ordeyned yeftes for to sende to his brother: gootes ijC, kyddes xx, sheep ijC and rammes xx, xl kyen and xx bulles, xx asses and x fooles of them. | f. 47[vb] And he sente by his seruauntes all thise beestis, and bad them saye that Iacob his seruaunt sente to hym this presente and that he foloweth after. And Iacob thought to plese hym with yeftes.

The nyght folowyng, hym thought a man wrastlyd with hym all that nyght tyl the mornyng. And whan he sawe he myght not ouercome hym, he hurted the synewe of his thye, that he halted therof, and said to hym: 'Late me goo and leue me, for it is in the morny[n]g.' Thenne Iacob answerd: 'I shal not leue the but yf thou

420 mornyng] mornyg

blesse me.' He said to hym: 'What is thy name?' He answerd: 'Iacob.' Thenne he said: 'Nay,' said he, 'thy name shal no more be called Iacob, but Israhel. For yf thou hast ben stronge ayenst God, how moche more shalt thou preuaylle ayenst men?' Thenne Iacob said to hym: 'What is thy name? Telle me.' He answerd: 'Why demandest thou my name, whiche is meruayllous?' And he blessyd hym in the same place. Iacob called the name of that same place Phanuel, sayeng: 'I haue seen Our Lord face to face and my soule is made sauf.' And anon as he was passed Phanuel, the sonne aroos. He halted on his foot. Therfore the chyldren of Israhel ete noo synews, bycause it dryed in the thye of Iacob.

Thenne Iacob, lyftyng vp his eyen, saw Esau comyng and iiijC men with hym, and deuyded the sones of Lya and of Rachel and of bothe her handmaydens and sette eche handmaid and their children tofore in the first place, Lya and her sones in the seconde, and Rachel and Ioseph al behynde. And he, gooyng tofore, knelid doun to grounde, and worshippyng his brother, approched hym. Esau ran for to mete with his brother and enbraced hym, straynyng his necke, and wepyng kyssyd hym.

And he loked forth and sawe the wymen and theyr chyldren and said: 'What ben thyse and to whom longen they?' Iacob answerd: 'They ben chyldren whiche God hath gyuen to me thy seruaunt.' And his handmaydens and their children approched and kneled doun. And Lya with her chyldren also worshippid hym. And laste of alle Ioseph and Rachel worshippid hym. Thenne said Esau: 'Whos ben thise turmes that I haue mette?' Iacob answerd: 'I haue sente them to the, f. 48ra/sig. [f8] my | lord, vnto th'ende that I may stande in thy grace.' Esau said: 'I haue many myself. Kepe thyse and lete them be thyn.' 'Nay,' said Iacob, 'I praye the to take this yefte whiche God hath sent me, that I may fynd grace in thy sight. For me semeth I see thy vysage lyke the vysage of God, and therfore be thou to me mercyful and take this blessyng of me.' Vnneth, by compellyng, he takyng it saide: 'Late vs go on togyder. I shal accompanye the and be felawe of thy iourney.' Thenne said Iacob: 'Thou knowest wel, my lord, that I haue yong children and tendre, and sheep and oxen whiche, yf I ouerlaboured, shold deye alle in a daye. Wherfore plese it yow my lord to goo tofore, and I shal folowe as I may with my chyldren and beestis.' Esau answerd: 'I pray the thenne late my felaws abyde and accompanye the, whatsomeuer nede thou haue.' Iacob said: 'It is no nede. I nede no moo but one, that I may stonde in thy fauour, my lord.'

And Esau retorned thenne the same way and iourney that he cam, into Seir. And Iacob cam into Sochot and bylde there an hous. And fro thens he went into Salem, the toun of Sychymys, whiche is in the londe of Canaan, and bought there a parte of a felde, in whiche he fixed his tabernacles, of the sones of Emor fader of Sychem, for an hondred lambes. And there he reysed an awter and worshipped vpon it the strengest God of Israhel.

Hyt happed that Dyna, doughter of Lya, wente out for to see the wymen of that regyon, whiche whan Sychem, sone of Emor prynce of that londe, sawe, anon louyd and rauysshed and slepte wyth her, oppressyng her by strengthe, and was assotted on her in suche wyse as he wente to his fader Emor and said: 'Gyue me this damoyselle in maryage that she may be my wyf.' Whiche whan Iacob knewe and herde how his doughter was rauyssed, his sones thenne beyng absente in occupacion of fedyng of theyr beestis in the felde, he helde it secrete til they retorned.

Thenne Emor wente for to speke of this mater to Iacob, and that tyme his sones cam fro the felde and herde what was happend and don, and were passyng wroth and angry bycause he had so defowled theyr suster. Thenne said Emor to them: 'Sychem my sone louyth your doughter. Gyue her to hym in | [f. 48rb] maryage, and late vs alye eche wyth other. Late our doughters be gyuen to you and youris to vs, and duelle ye with vs. Alle the contre is in your power. Exercise and occupye it, bye and selle, and take ye it.' Thenne said Sichem to his [f]ader and brethern: 'Whatsomeuer ye ordeyne I wyl doo, and what ye demande, yeftes or dower, I shal gladly gyue it, so I may haue this damoyselle vnto my wif.'

Thenne answerd the sones of Iacob to Sichem and his fader in gyle, dissymilyng as they had not knowen the rauysshement of theyr suster: 'We may not doo that ye desyre, ne gyue our suster to a man incircumsiced. It is a thyng vnlauful and grete synne to vs. Yf ye wyl be circumsiced in euery man emong you and man child and be lyke as we be, we shal take your doughtres and ye ouris and shal dwelle togydre and ben one peple. Yf ye wyl not be circumsiced, we shal take our suster and goo hens.' This offre plesed t[o] Emor and Sychem his sone, and ther was no yong man but anon was agreed to that they asked. He loued so moche the damoyselle that anon he wente into the cyte and told al this to the peple, and that these men were

485 fader] sader   495 to] te

pesible peple and 'wille dwelle emong vs and that ther was no lette but that we be not circumsiced as they be'. To whiche they assented and forthwith were circumsiced.

And the thirde day after, whan the most payne of the woundes greued them, thenne tweyne of Iacobs sones, Symeon and Leui, brethern of Dyna, drewe out their swerdis and entred into the cyte hardely and slewe alle the men, both Emor and Sychem, and toke Dyna theyr suster with them fro Sychems hows. And this don, the other sones of Iacob fylle on the remenaunt and slewe all that they fond in auengyng the shame and rauysshement of theyr suster, wastyng oxen and sheep, asses and other beestis, and toke theyr wyues and chyldren into captyuyte.

Whiche thyngis thus don, Iacob saide to Symeon and Leui: 'Ye haue troubled me and haue made me hateful to the Cananees and Phereseis, dwellars in this contre. We ben but a fewe. They shal gadre them togydre and destroye me and my hows.' They answerd: 'Shold we suffre our suster to be holden as a comyn woman?'

f. 48va After this Our Lord apperid | to Iacob and said: 'Aryse and goo vp to Bethel, and dwelle there, and make there an awter to the Lord that apperid to the in the way whan þou fleddest fro thy broder Esau.' Iacob thenne called alle them of his hows and sayde: 'Caste away fro yow alle your straunge goddes that ben emonge yow, and make yow clene and change your clothes. Arise and late vs go into Bethel, and make we there an awter to Our Lord, that herde me in the day of my tribulacion, and was felaw of my iourney.' Thenne they gaf to hym alle their straunge goddes and the golde that henge on their eeris. And he dalfe a pit behynde the cyte of Sichem and threwe hem therin. And whan they departed, alle the contrees th[e]raboute were aferd and durste not pursiewe them. Thenne Iacob cam to a place called Luza, whiche is in the londe of Canaan, and all the peple with hym, whiche otherwise is called Bethel. He edefyed there an awter to Our Lord, and named that place the Hows of God; Our Lord apperid to hym in that place whan he fledde fro his broder Esau.

That same tyme deyde Delbora the noryce of Rebecca and was buryed at the rote of Bethel vnder an oke.

Our Lord apperid agayn to Iacob after that he was retorned fro Mesopotamye of Syrye and was come into Bethel, and blessyd hym, sayeng: 'Thou shalt no more be called Iacob, but Israhel shal be thy

509 sheep] sheeep 523 Thenne] Theeune 526 theraboute] thrr aboute

name', and called hym Israhel; and said to hym: 'I am God Almyghty. Growe and multeplye. Folkes and peples of nacion[s] shal come of the. Kynges shal come of thy lendes. The londe that I gaf to Abraham and Isaac I shal gyue to the and thy seed'; and vanysshed away fro hym. He thenne reysed a stone for a remembraunce in the place where God spack to hym, and enoynted it with oyle, callyng the name of the place Bethel.

He wente thens and cam in veer tyme vnto the londe that goth to Effratam, in which place Rachel trauaylled and began for cause of chyldyng to deye. The mydwyf said to her: 'Be not aferd, for thou shalt haue a sonne.' And the deth drawyng nere, she named hym Bennoni, whiche is as moche to saye as the sone of my sorowe. The fader called hym Beniamin, that is [to] saye the sone of the right hand. Ther Rachel deyde and was buryed in the way | toward Effratam, that f. 48vb
is Bethleem. Iacob reysid a tytle vpon her tombe. This is the tytle of the monumente of Rachel vnto this present day.

Iacob wente thens and cam to Ysaac his fader into Mambre, cyte of Arbee, that is Ebron, in whiche dwellyd Abraham and Ysaac. And all the dayes of Ysaac were complete, whiche were an honderd and foure score yere. And he, consumed, deyd in good mynde, and Esau and Iacob his sones beryed hym.

Thus endeth th'ystorye of Ysaac and his two sones Esau and Iacob.

[5. JOSEPH]

Hyer begynneth th'ystorye of Ioseph and his brethern, whiche is red the thirde Sonday in Lente.

Ioseph, whan he was xvj yere old, began to kepe and fede the flock with his brethern, he beyng yet a child; and was accompanyed with the sones of Bala and Zelpha, wyues of his fader. Ioseph complayned on his brethern and accused them to their fader of the most euylle synne. | Israhel louyd Ioseph aboue all his sones for as moche as he f. 49ra /
had goten hym in his old age, and made for hym a motley cote. His sig. g1
brethern thenne, seeyng that he was byloued of his fader more than they were, hated hym and myght not speke to hym a pesyble worde.

It happed on a tyme that Ioseph dremed and sawe a sweuene and told it to his brethern, whiche caused hem to hate hym þe more. Ioseph saide to his brethern: 'Here ye my dreme that I had. Me

538 nacions] nacion 549 to] *om.*
3 Ioseph] I *five-line capital supplied by hand in red*

thought that we bonde sheuys in the felde. And my sheef stoode vp, and youres stondyng rounde aboute [dyde] worshipe my sheef.' His brethern answerde: 'Shalt thou be our kyng? And shal we be subgette and obey thy comandement?' Therfor this cause of dremes and of thyse wordes mynystred the more fume of hate and enuye. Ioseph sawe another sweuene and told to his fader and brethern: 'Me thought I sawe in my sleep the sonne, the mone and xj sterres worshipe me.' Whiche whan his fader and his brothern had herd, the fader blamed hym and said: 'What may betokene this dreme that thou sawest? Trowest thou that I, thy moder and thy brethern shal worshipe the vpon th'erthe?' His brethern had grete enuye hereat. The fader thought and consydered a thynge secretly in hymself.

On a tyme whan hys brethern kepte theyr flockes of sheep in Sichem, Israhel said to Ioseph: 'Thy brethern fede their sheep in Sichem. Come, and I shal sende the to them.' Whiche answerd: 'I am redy.' And he saide: 'Goo and see yf all thynge be wel and prosperous at thy brethern and beestis, and come agayn and telle me what they doo.' He wente fro the vale of Ebron and cam vnto Sichem. There was a man fonde hym erryng in the felde, and axed hym what he sought. And he answerd: 'I seche my br[e]thern. Telle me were they fede their flockes.' The man said to hym: 'They ben departed fro this place. I herde them saye: "Late vs goo into Dothaim."' Whiche thenne, whan his brethern sawe hym come fro ferre, tofore he approched to them, they thoughte to slee hym and spack togydre, sayeng: 'Loo, see, the
f. 49rb dremer cometh. Come and lete vs slee hym, | and put hym into this olde cisterne. And we shal saye that som wilde euyl beest hath deuoured hym. And thenne shal appere what his dremes shalle proufyte hym.' Ruben, heeryng this, thought for to delyuer hym fro their handes and said: 'Late vs not sle hym ne shede his blood, but kepe your hondes vndefowled.' This he said, willyng to kepe hym fro theyr handes and rendre hym agayn to his fader. Anon thenne as he cam, they toke of his motley cote and sette hym into an olde cisterne that had no water.

As they satte for to ete brede, they sawe Ysmaelites come fro Galaad and theyr camels bryngyng spyces and reysyns into Egypte. Thenne said Iudas to his brethern: 'What shold it pr{ou}ffyte vs, yf we slewe our brother and shedde his blood? It is better that he be sold to Ismalytes, and our handes be not defow[l]ed; he is our brother and

15 dyde] & 33 brethern] brthern 51 defowled] defowhed

our flessh.' His brethern agreed to his wordes and drewe hym out of the cysterne, solde hym to the Madyanytes marchantes passyng forth by, to Ismalytes for xxx pecis of syluer, whiche lad hym into Egypte.

At this tyme whan he was sold, Ruben was not there but was in another felde with his beestis. And whan he retorned and cam vnto the cysterne and fonde not Ioseph, he tare his clothes for sorow and cam to his brethern and said: 'The chyld is not yonder. Whyther shal I goo to seche hym?' He had supposed his brethern had slayn hym in his absence. They told hym what they had don and toke his cote and besprenklid it wyth the blood of a kyd which they slowe, and sente it to their fader, sayeng: 'See whether this be the cote of thy sone or not. This we haue founden.' Whiche anon as the fader sawe it, saide: 'This is my sones cote. An euyl wylde beeste haue deuouryd hym; somme beste hath eten hym', and rente his clothis and dyde on hym a sackecloth, bewayllyng and sorowyng his sone a long tyme. Alle his sones gadred them togyder for to comforte their fader and aswage his sorowe, but he wold take no comforte but saide: | [f. 49va] 'I shal descende to my sone into helle for to bewaylle hym there.' And thus, he abydyng in sorow, the Madianytes caryed Ioseph into Egypte and solde hym to Putiphar, eunuche of Pharao, maister of his knyghtes.

Thus was Ioseph ledde into Egypte, and Putiphar prynce of the oost of Pharao, an Egypcian, bought hym of the handes of Ismaelites. Our Lord God was alway with Ioseph, and he was wyse, redy and prosperous in alle maner thynges. He dwellyd in hys lordes hous, and plesed so wel his lord that he stode in his grace, þat he made hym vpperist and aboue all other, and betoke hym þe rule and gouernaunce of alle his hows, which wel and wysely gouerned þe houshold and alle that he had charge of. Our Lord blessyd the hows of Egypte for Iosephs sake and multeplyed as wel in beestis as in feldes all his substaunce.

Ioseph was fair of vysage and wel fauoured. After many dayes þe lady, his maisters wyf, behelde and caste her eyen on Ioseph and said to Ioseph: 'Come and slepe with me.' Which anon refused that and wold not attende ne listen vnto her wordes, ne wold not consente to so synful a werke, and said to her: 'Lo, hath not my lord delyueryd to me all that he hath in his hous, and he knoweth not what he hath, and ther is nothyng therin but that it is in my power and at my commandement, exepte the, which art his wyf. How may I doo this euyl and synne to my lorde?' Suche maner or semblable wordes he saide dayly to her, and the woman was the more desirous and

greuous to the yong man, and he alway forsoke and refused the synne. Hit happed on a day that Ioseph entred into the chambre aboute certayn nedes that he had to doo, and she caught hym by hys mantel and helde it faste and said to hym: 'Come and lye with me.' Who anon wold not agree to her but fledde forth out of the doores, and lefte hys mantel behynde hym in her hande. And whan the lady sawe þat she was refused and his mantel in her hande, she cryed and called the men of the hous and said to hem: 'Loo, this Ebrewe is comen to my chambre and wold haue enforced and haue leyn by me; and whan I cryed, he fledde out of the chambre and lefte for hast his mantel that I helde behynde hym.' And into witnes of trouthe she
f. 49vb shewde to her hus|bond the mantel whan he cam home and saide: 'Thy seruaunt Hebrew whom thou hast brought into this hous is entred into my chambre for to haue leyn by me. And whan I cryde, he lefte his mantel that I held and fledde away.' Whan the lord herde this, anon he gaf faith and byleuyd hys wyf; and beyng sore wroth, sette Ioseph in pryson, whereas the prysoners of þe kyng were kept, and he was ther faste sette in.

Our Lord God was with Ioseph and had mercy on hym and made hym in the fauour and grace of the chief kepar of the pryson, in so moche þat he delyueryd to Ioseph the kepyng of all the prysoners. And what he dyde was doon, and þe chyef gayler was plesid with all. Our Lord was with hym and directed all his werkis.

After this it fylle so that ij offycers of the kynges trespaced vnto their lord. Wherfor he was wroth with hem and comanded them to the pryson whereas Ioseph was. That one of them was the boteler and that other the baker, and the kepar betoke them to Ioseph to kepe, and he seruyd them. After a whyle that they had ben in pryson, they bothe sawe on one nyght a dreme, of whiche they were astonyed and abasshed. And whan Ioseph was comen in to serue them and sawe them heuy, he demanded them why they were heuyer than they were woned to be. Which answerd: 'We haue dremed, and ther is none to interprete it to vs.' Ioseph said to them: 'Suppose ye þat God may not gyue me grace to interprete it? Tell to me what ye sawe in your slepe.' Thenne the boteler tolde first, and said: 'Me thought I sawe a vyne had iij branches and after they had flowred, þe grapes were rype. And thenne I toke the cuppe of Pharao in my hande and toke the grapes and wrange out of them wyn into the cuppe that I helde and presented it to Pharao to drynke.' Ioseph answerd: 'The iij braunches ben yet iij dayes, after which Pharao shal remembre thy seruyse and shal res[to]re the into thy formest offyce and gree, for to serue hym as thou were woned to doo. Thenne I pray the to remembre me when thou art at thyn aboue and be to me so mercyful to sue vnto Pharao that he take me out of this pryson, for I was stolen out of þe londe of Hebrews and am innocently sette here in pryson.' Thenne | the maister baker sawe [f. 50ra / sig. g2] that he had wysely interpreted the botelers dreme; he saide: 'Me thought that I had iij baskettes of mele vpon my heed and in that one baskette that was hiest me thought I bare all the mete of the bachows, and birdes came and ete of hit.' Ioseph answerd: 'This is th'ynterpretacion of the dreme: þe iij baskettis ben iij dayes yet to come, after which Pharao shal smyte of thy heed and shal hange the on the crosse, and the byrdes shal tere thy flessh.' And the thyrd day after this, Pharao made a grete feeste vnto his children and remembrid hym emong the meles on the maister boteler and the maister baker. He restored his boteler vnto his office, and to serue hym of the cuppe; and that other was hanged, that the trouth of the interpretour was byleuyd and proued. Notwithstondyng, the maister boteler in his welth forgate Ioseph his interpretour.

Two yere after, Pharao sawe in his slepe a dreme. Hym thought he stode vpon the ryuer, fro which he sawe vij oxen ascende to the lande, which were fair and right fatte and were fedde in a fatte pasture. He sawe other vij come out of the ryuer, poure and lene, and were fedde in places plenteuous and bourgenyng. Thise deuoured the other that were so fatte and fayr. Herewith he sterte out of his slepe, and after slepte agayn and sawe another dreme. He sawe seuen eeris of corn standyng on one stalke, ful and fayr of cornes, and as many other eeris voyde and smeton with drought, which deuoured the beaute of the first vij. In þe mornyng Pharao awoke and was gretly aferde of thyse dremes, and sente for all coniectours and dyuynours of Egypt and wyse men, and whan they were gadred he told to them his dreme, and ther was none that coude interprete it. Thenne at laste the maister boteler, remembryng Ioseph, said: 'I knowleche my synne. On a tyme the kyng, beyng wroth with his seruauntis, sente me and the maister of the bakers into pryson, where we in one nyght dremed bothe prodyges of thynges comyng. And ther was a chylde of th'Ebrewes, seruaunt to the gayler, to whom we tolde our dremes, and he expowned them to vs and said what shold happene: I am restored to myn offyce and that other was hanged on the crosse.'

132 restore] res– \ re 144 hym] hym \ hym

f. 50rb Anone by the kynges commandement Ioseph was taken out of pryson and shauen, bayned and chaunged his clothes, and brought tofore Pharao, to whom he saide: 'I sawe a dreme, which I haue shewd vnto wyse men, and ther is none þat can telle me th'interpretacion therof.' To whom Ioseph answerd: 'God shal answere by me thynges prosperous to Pharao.' Thenne Pharao told to hym his dremes, like as is tofore wreton, of the vij fatte oxen and vij lene and how the lene deuoured þe fatte, and in lyke wyse of the eeris. Ioseph answerde: 'The kyngis dreme [is] one thyng, wi[c]h God hath shewde to Pharao: the vij fatte oxen and þe vij eris fulle betokene vij yere to come, of grete plente and comodyous; and the vij lene oxen and the vij voyde eeris smeton with drought betokene vij yere after them, of grete hungre and scarcete. Loo, ther shal come first vij yere of grete fertilite and plente in all the londe of Egypt, after whom shal folow other vij yere of so grete sterilite bareyne and scarcete, that th'abundaunce of the first shal be al forgoten; the gret hungre of thyse latter yeres shal consume alle the plente of the first yeris. The latter dreme perteyneth to the same, bycause God wold that yt shold be fulfyllid. Now therfor late þe kynge prouyde for a man that is wyse and wytty, that may comande and ordeyne prouostis and officers in all places of the royame, that they gadre into garners and barnes the fyfthe part of all the corne and fruytes þat shal growe thyse first vij plenteuous yeres that ben to come; and that all this whete may be kepte in barnes and garners, in townes and villages, that it may be made redy ayenst the comyng of the vij scarse yeris that shal oppresse by hungre all Egypt, to th'ende þat the peple be not enfamyned.'

This counseil pleysid moche to Pharao and to all his mynystris. Thenne Pharao said to his seruantes: 'Where sholde we fynde suche a man as this is, which is fulfyllyd with the spirite of God?' And thenne he said to Ioseph: 'For as moch as God hath shewd to the all that thou hast spoken, trowest thou that we myght fynde ony wyser than thou or lyke to the? Thou shalt be vpperist of my hows, and to the commandement of thy mouth all peple shal obeye. I only shal goo f. 50va tofore the and sytte but one | sete aboue the.' Yet said Pharao to Ioseph: 'Lo, I haue ordeyned the aboue and maister vpon all the londe of Egypte.' He toke a rynge fro hys hande and gaf it into his hande, and cladde hym with a double stole furryd with byse, and a golden coler he put aboute his necke, and made hym to ascende vpon his

178 is] *om.* wich] with

chare, the second trompet cryeng that all men shold knele tofore hym and that they shold knowe hym vpperyst prouoste of alle the londe of Egypte. Thenne said þe kynge of Egypte to Ioseph: 'I am Pharao. Without thy comandement shal no man meue hande ne fote in all the lande of Egypte.'

He chaunged his name, and called hym in the tongue of Egypte the sauyour of the world. He gaf to hym a wyf named Assenech, doughter of Putiphar preest of Eliopoleos. Ioseph wente forth thenne into the londe of Egypte. Ioseph was xxx yere olde whan he stode in the fauour and grace of Pharao. And he wente round aboute all þe regyone of Egypte. The plenteuosnes and fertylyte of the vij yere cam; and sheues and shockes of corn were brought into the barnes. Alle the habundaunce of fruytes was leyde in euery toun. Ther was so grete plente of whete that it myght be compared to the grauel of the see, and the plente therof excedeth mesure.

Ioseph had ij sones by hys wyf er þe famyne and hungre cam, whiche Assenech the prestes doughter brought forth. Of whom he callid the name of þe first Manasses, sayeng: 'God hath made me to forgete alle my labours, and the hous of my fader hath forgoten me.' He callid the name of the second sone Effraim, sayeng: 'God hath made me to growe in the londe of my pouerte.'

Thenne passyd the vij yeris of plente and fertylyte that were in Egypte. And the vij yeris of scarcete and hungre began to come, which Ioseph had spoken of tofore. And hungre began to wexe and growe in the vnyuersal world. Also in alle the londe of Egipt was hungre and scarcete, and when the peple hungred, they cryed to Pharao, axyng mete. To whom he answerd: 'Goo ye to Ioseph, and whatsomeuer he saye to you, doo ye.' Dayly grewe and encresyd the hungre in all the londe. Thenne Ioseph openyd the barnes and garners and sold corn to th'Egipciens. For the hungre oppressid them sore, all prouynces cam
into | Egypte for to bye mete to them and t'eschewe the hungre. f. 50vb

Iacob, fader vnto Ioseph, herde telle that corn and vytayllis were sold in Egypte and saide to his sones: 'Why be ye necglygent? I haue herd saye that corn is sold in Egypte. Goo ye theder and bye for vs that is necessarye and behoefful, þat we may lyue and consume not for nede.' Thenne the x brethern of Ioseph descended into Egypte for to bye whete, and Beniamyn was left at home with the fader, bycause whatsomeuer happed to the brethern in her iourney. Thenne they entrid into the londe of Egypte, with other, for to bye corn. Ther was grete famyne in the londe of Canaan.

And Ioseph was prynce in þe londe of Egypte; also by his comandement whete was solde vnto þe peple. Thenne whan his brethern were comen and had adoured and worshiped hym, he anon knewe them, and spack to them as to strangers harde wordes, demandyng them, sayeng: 'Whens be ye?' Whiche answerd: 'Of the londe of Canaan, and come hether to bye that is necessarye for vs.' And though he knewe his brethern, yet was he vnknowen of them. He remembryd the dremes that he somtyme had seen and told them, and saide: 'Ye be spyes and be comen hether for t'espye the weykest places of this londe.' Whiche said to hym: 'It is not soo, lorde, but we thy seruauntes ben comen for to bye vytaylles. We ben alle sones to one man. We come pesybly; ne we thy seruauntes thynke ne ymagyne none euyll.' To whom he answerd: 'It is alle otherwyse. Ye be comen for to espye and considere the secretest places of this royame.' Thenne they saide: 'We were xij brethern, thy seruants, sones of one man in the londe of Canaan; the yongest is at home with our fader, and that other is deed.' 'That is', said he, 'that I saide: "Ye be spyes." Now I haue of you th'experyence. I swere to yow by th'elthe of Pharao, ye shal not departe tyl that your yongest brother come. Sende ye one of you for hym, for to brynge hym hether. Ye shal abyde in fethers in pryson, tyl the trouthe be prouyd wether tho thyngis that ye haue said be trewe or false. Els, by th'elthe of Pharao, ye be spyes.' And delyueryd them to be kepte thre dayes.

The third day they were brought out of pryson, to whom he sayde:
f. 51ra / | 'I drede God. Yf ye be pesible as ye saye, doo as Y haue said, and ye
sig. g3 shal lyue. Late one brother be bounden in pryson, and goo ye your waye and lede home the whete that ye haue bought into your houses, and brynge to me with you your yongest broder. Than I may preue your wordes, þat ye deye not.' They dyde as he saide, and spacken togydre: 'We ben worthy and haue wel deseruyd to suffre this, for we haue synned in our broder, seeyng his anguyssh whan he prayd vs and we herd hym not. Therfor this trybulation is fallen on vs.' Of whom Ruben saide: 'Sayde not I to you: "In no wyse synne not ye in the child"?; and ye wold not here me. Now his blood is wroken.' They knewe not that Ioseph vnderstode them, for as moche as he spack alway to them by an interpretour.

Thenne Ioseph torned hym a lytyl and wepte. After, he retorned to hem, and toke Symeon in their presence and bonde hym and sente

272 Y] ye

hym to pryson, and commanded to his mynystris to fil their sackis with whete and to put eche mans money in their sackis, and aboue that to gyue them mete to spende in their [way]; whiche dyde soo. And they toke theyr whete and leyde it on theyr asses and departed on theyr way. After, one of them on the way opened his sack for to gyue his beest mete, and fonde his money in the mouth of his sack and saide to his brethern: 'M[y] money is gyuen to m[e] agayn. Lo, I haue founde it in my sack.' And all they were astonyed: 'What is this that God hath don to vs?'

Thenne they cam hom to their fader into the londe of Canaan, and told to hym all thynges that was fallen to them, sayeng: 'The lord of the contre hath spoken harde to vs, and had supposed that we had ben spyes of that prouynce. To whom we answerd that we were pesible peple ne were no suche espyes, and that we were xij sones goten of one fader; one is deed, and the yongest is with our fader in þe londe of Canaan. Which thenne saide to vs: "Now shal I preue whether ye be pesible or no. Ye shal leue here one broder with me, and lede home that is necessarye for you and goo your waye, and see that ye brynge with yow your yongest broder, that I may knowe that ye be none espyes, and that ye maye r[e]sseyue this brother that I hold in pryson; and | thenne forthon what that ye wil bye, ye shal haue lycence."' f. 51rb And this said, eche of them poured oute the whete, and euery man fonde his money bounden in the mouth of euery sack. Thenne saide Iacob their fader: 'Ye haue made me without chyldren. Ioseph is goon and lost, Symeon is bounden in pryson, and Beniamyn ye wil take away fro me. In me comen all thyse euillis.' To whom Ruben answerd: 'Slee my two sones yf I brynge hym not agayn to the. Delyuer hym to me in my hande and I shal restore hym agayn to the.' The fader saide: 'My sone shal not goo with you. His brother is deed, and he is lefte now allone. Yf ony aduersyte shold happe to hym in the way that ye goo vnto, ye shal lede my olde heres with sorowe to helle.'

In the menewhile famyne and hungre oppressid alle the londe gretly. And whan the corn that they brought fro Egypte was consumed, Iacob said to his sones: 'Retorne ye into Egypte and bye for vs som mete that we may lyue.' Iudas answerde: 'That man said to vs vnder sweryng of grete othes that "Ye shal not see my face ne come to my presence but yf ye brynge your yongest brother with you." Therfor yf thou wil sende hym with vs, we shal goo togyder and shal

288 way] *om.* 292 My] me me] my 305 resseyue] Rsseyue

bye for vs that shal be necessarye; and yf thou wilt not, we shal not goo. The man saide as we ofte haue said to the, that yf we brynge hym not, we shal not see his visage.' Israhel said to them: 'This haue ye don into my myserye, that ye tolde to hym that ye had another brother.' And they answerde: 'The man demanded of vs by ordre our progenye, yf our fader lyued and yf we had ony brother. And we answerde hym consequently after that he demanded. We wiste not what he wold saye, ne þat he saide: "Brynge your broder with you."' 'Sende the child with vs that we may goo forth and lyue, and that we ne our chyldren deye not for hungre. I shal resseyue thy sone; and requyre hym of my hande. Yf I lede hym not thedre and brynge hym agayn, I shal be gylty to the of the synne euer after. Yf ther had ben no delaye of this, we had ben there and comen agayn by this tyme.'

Thenne Israhel their fader sayde to them: 'Yf it be so necessarie as
f. 51va ye | saye, doo ye as ye wyll, take with you of the best fruytes of this londe in your vessellis, and gyue ye and presente to that man yeftes, a lytyl reysyns and hony, storax, s[t]acten, therebinthe and dates, and bere with you double money and also the same money that ye fonde in your sackes lest ther by ony errour therfore, and take with you Beniamin your brother. My God that is almyghty make hym plaisaunt vnto you, and that ye may retorne in saefte with this, your brother, and hym also that he holdeth in pryson. I shal be as a man barayen therwhiles wythout chyldren.'

Thenne the brethern toke the yeftes and double money and Beniamyn, and wente forth into Egypte, and cam and stode tofore Ioseph. Whom whan he had seen, and Beniamyn, he commanded to þe steward of his hows that he shold do slee sheep and calues and make a feste, 'for thyse brethern shal dyne wyth me this day'. He dyde as he was commanded and brought the men into his lordes hous. Thenne were they all aferd and said softly togydre: 'Bycause of the money that we had in our sackis we be brought in, that he take vs with the defaulte, and shal by violence brynge vs and our asses into seruytude.' Wherfor they said to the steward of the hous in the yate of the hows er they entrid, sayeng: 'We praye the to here vs. The laste tyme that we cam to bye vitaille, whiche whan we had bought and departed and were on our way, for to gyue our beestis mete we openyd our sackes and we fonde in the mouth of our sackis our money that we had payd, whiche we now brynge agayn of the same weight. And we

340 stacten] scacten

haue more other for to bye to vs that shal be necessarye. It is not in oure conscience to haue it; we wete neuer who put it in our sackis.' He answerd to hym: 'Pees be emonge you. Fere ye nothyng. The God of your fader hath gyue to you þe tresour þat ye fonde in your sackes, for the money þat ye paid to me, I haue it redy.' And thenne he brought in Symeon to them, and brought them into the hous and wesshe their feet and gaf mete to their asses. They made redy and ordeyned theyr yeftes and presentes agayn the comyng of Ioseph. T[h]ey herd saye that they shold dyne and ete there.

Thenne Ioseph entrid into the hows, and they offred | f. 51vb to hym the yeftes, holdyng them in their handes, and worshiped hym, fallyng doun to the grounde. And he debonairly salewed them and demanded them, sayeng: 'Is your fader in good helth, of whom ye told me? Lyueth he yet?' They answerd: 'Thy seruaunt our fader is in good helth and lyueth yet', and kneled doun and worshipid hym. Thenne he, castyng his eyen on his brother Beniamyn, that was of one moder, and said: 'Is this your yonge brother, of whom ye told me?', and also said: 'God be mercyful to the, my sone.' He hyed hym fro them ward, for he was meuyd in all his spirites and wept on his broder and wente into his bedde chambre. After this he wesshe his vysage and cam out, makyng good contynaunce and comanded to set brede on þe borde. And after þat he set his brothern in ordre, eche after their age, and ete togydre. And Ioseph sat and ete with th'Egipciens, for it was not lauful to th'Egipciens to ete with th'Ebrewis. And eche of them were wel seruyd, but Beniamyn had the beste part. And they ete and dranke so moche that they were dronken.

Thenne Ioseph comanded the styward of his hous to fille their sackes with whete, as moche as they myght receyue, 'and the money of the whete, put it into euery mannes sack, and take my cuppe of siluer and the money of the yongest and put that in his sack'. And all this was doon.

And on the morn bytymes they were suffred to departe with their asses. And whan they were goon out of the toun and a lytyl on their way, thenne Ioseph said to his steward: 'Make the redy and ride after, and saye to them: "Why haue ye don euyl for good? The cuppe that my lord is acust[o]med to drynke in, ye haue stolen. Ye myght not doo a werse thyng."' He dide as Ioseph had comanded, and ouertoke them and said to them all by ordre like as he had charge. Which answerde:

369 They] Tey 397 acustomed] acustmed

'Why saith your lord so, and doth to vs his seruaunts suche lettyng? The money that we fonde in our sackes we brought agayn to þe fro the londe of Canaan. And how may it folowe þat we shold stele ony gold or siluer fro þe hous of thy lorde? Loke, at whom it be founde of vs alle thy seruants, late hym deye.' Whiche saide to them: 'Be it after your sentence. At whom that it euer be founden, he shal be my f. [52][ra] / sig. g4 seruaunt, and the other | shal goo free and be not gylty.' Thenne he hyed and sette doun all their sackes, begynnyng at th'oldest vnto the yongest, and at last fonde the cuppe in the mouth of the sack of Beniamin. Thenne they alle for sorowe cutte and rented their clothes and laded their asses agayn and retorned alle into the toun agayn. Thenne Iudas entrid first with his brethern vnto Ioseph. And alle they togydre fille doun platte to the grounde. To whom Ioseph saide: 'Why haue ye doo thus? Knowe not ye that there is no man lyke to me in the science of knowleche?' To whom Iudas answerd: 'What shal we answer to the my lord, or what shal we speke or rightfully desyre? God hath founden and remembrid th'iniquite of vs thy seruauntes, for we all be thy seruantes; ye, we and he, at whom the cuppe was founden.' Ioseph answerd: 'God forbede that I shold so doo. Whosomeuer stale the cuppe shal be my seruaunt. And go ye your waye, for ye shal be free and goo to your fader.'

Thenne Iudas approchyd ner hym and spack with a hardy chere to hym and saide: 'I beseche the, my lorde, to here me thy seruaunt that I may saye to thyn audyence a worde, and that thou wilt not be wroth to thy seruaunt. Thou art nexte to Pharao, my lord. Thou demandest first of vs thy seruauntes: "Haue ye a fader or brother?" And we answerd to the my lord: "Our fader is an old man, and we haue a brother a yonge childe, whiche was born to hym in his old age, whos brother of the same moder is deed, and he is an only sone, whom the fader loueth tenderly." Thou saidest to vs thy seruauntes: "Brynge hem hether to me, that I may see." We told to the my lord for trouthe: "Our fader may not forgoo the childe. Yf he forgoo hym, certaynly he shal deye." And thou saidest to vs thy seruants: "But yf ye brynge hym with you, ye shal no more see my vysage." Thenne when we cam to our fader and tolde hym all thyse thynges, and our fader bad vs to retorne and bye more corn. To whom we saide: "We may not go theder but yf our yongest brother goo with vs, for yf he be absente, we f. [52][rb] dar not approche ne come to the pre|sence of þe man." And he

406 f. 52] folio xlix   423 and] & \ and

answerd to vs: “Ye knowe well that my wyf brought to me forth but ij sones. That one wente out and ye said that wild beestis had deuoured hym, and yet I herd neuer of hym ne he apperid not. Yf now ye sholde take this my sone, and onythyng happend to hym in the waye, ye shold brynge myn hore here with sorowe to helle.” Therfor yf I shold come home to my fader and brynge not the child with me, sith the sowle and helth of my fader depende{t}h of this child, and see þat he is not come with vs, he shal deye. And we thy seruantes shold lede his old age with wayllyng and sorowe to helle. I myself shal be thy propre seruaunt, whiche haue receyuyd hym vpon my faith and haue promysed for hym, sayeng to my fader: “Yf I bryng hym not agayn, I shal be gylty of the synne to my fader euer after.” I shal abyde and contynue thy seruaunt for þe child, in the mynystery and seruyse of the my lord. I may not departe, the chyld beyng absente, leste I be witnes of the sorow that my fader shall take. Wherfore I beseche the to suffre this child to goo to his fader, and receyue me into thy seruyse.’ Thus said Iudas with moche more, as Iosephus *Antiquitatum* reherceth more pytously, and saith moreouer that the cause why he dide do hyde the cuppe in Beniamyns sacke was to knowe whether they louyd Beniamin or hated hym, as they dide hym what tyme they sold hym to th’Ismaelites.

Thenne, this requeste made, Ioseph my[gh]t no lenger forbere, but comanded them that stode by to withdrawe them, and whan all men were goon out sauf he and his brethern, he began to saye to them, wepyng: ‘I am Ioseph your brother. Lyueth yet my fader?’ The brethern were so aferd þat they coude not speke ne answere to hym. Thenne he debonairly saide to them: ‘Come hether to me.’ And whan they cam nere hym, he saide: ‘I am Ioseph your brother that ye sold into Egypte. Be ye not aferde, ne thynke not harde vnto you that ye solde me into thise regions. God hath sente me tofore you into Egypte for your helth. It is ij yere sith the famyne began and yet ben v yere to come, in which men may not ere, sowe ne repe. God hath sente me tofore you | that ye shold be reseruyd on th’erthe and that ye may f. [52]va
haue mete to lyue by. It is not by your counseyl that I was sente hether, but by the wyll of God, whiche hath ordeyned me fader of Pharao and lord of alle his hows and prynce in all the londe of Egypte. Hye you and goo to my fader, and saye ye to hym: “This worde sendeth to the thy sone Ioseph: God hath made me lord of the

459 myght] myhgt 470 you] you | you

vnyuersal londe of Egypte. Come to me lest thou deye, and thou shalt dwelle in the londe of Iessen. Thou shalt be next me, þou and thy sones, and the sones of thy sones; and I shal fede thy sheep, thy beestis and all that thou hast in possession. Yet resten fyue yere to come of famyne, therfore come lest thou perysshe, thy hows and all that þou owest." Lo, your eyen and the eyen of my brother Beniamyn see that my mouth speketh thyse wordes to you. Shewe ye to my fader alle my glorye and alle that ye haue seen in Egypte. Hye ye and brynge hym to me.' This said, he enbraced his brother Beniamyn aboute his necke and wepte; and he also wepte on hym. Ioseph thenne kyssed all his brethern and wepte vpon eche of them. After this they durste better speke to hym.

Anon it was tolde and knowen alle aboute in the kynges halle that Iosephs brethern were comen. And Pharao was ioyeful and glad therof, and alle his housholde. And Pharao said to Ioseph that he shold saye to his brethern: 'Lade ye [y]our beestis and goo into the londe of Canaan, and brynge fro thens your fader and kynred and come to me. And I shal gyue you alle the goodes of Egypte, that ye may ete the mary of th'erthe. Comande also that they take cariage of this londe of Egypte for the cariage of their chyldren and wyues, and saye to them: "Take your fader and come as sone as ye may and leue nothyng behynd you. For alle the beste thynges shal be youris."'

The sones of Israhel dyde as they were commanded. To whom Ioseph gaf caryage after the commandement of Pharao, and mete to ete by the way. He comanded to gyue to euerich two garmentis. To Beniamyn he gaf iijC pieces of siluer with fyue garmentis of the beste, f. [52]vb and also | he sente clothyng to his fader, addyng to them ten asses which were laden all wyth richesses of Egypte, and as many asses laden and beryng brede and vytayll to spende by the way. And thus he lete his brethern departe fro hym, sayeng: 'Be ye not wroth in the waye.' Thenne they, thus departyng, cam into the londe of Canaan to theyr fader, and shewde al this to their fader and saide: 'Ioseph thy sone lyueth and he lordeth in alle the londe of Egypte.' Whan Iacob herde this, he awoke as a man had ben awaked sodenly out of his slepe, yet neuertheles he byleuyd them not. And they tolde to hym al the ordre of the mater. Whan he sawe the caryage and alle that he had sente, his spyrite reuyued and saide: 'It suffyseth to me yf Ioseph my sone yet lyue. I shal goo and see hym er I dye.'

491 your] our

Thenne Israhel wente forth with alle that he had, and cam to the pytte where tofore he had sworn to God, and slewe there beestis to make sacrefises to þe God of Ysaac his fader. He herde God by a vysion that same nyght, sayeng to hym: 'Iacob, Iacob.' To whom he answerd: 'I am here al redy.' God said to hym: 'I am strengest God of thy fader Ysaac. Drede the not, but descende doun into Egypte. I shal make the to growe there into grete peple. I shal descende with the theder, and I shal brynge the agayn whan thou retornest. Ioseph sothly shal putte his handes vpon thyn eyen.'

Iacob thenne aroos on the morn erly. And his sones toke hym with their children and wyues, and sette them on the caryages that Pharao had sente to brynge hym and alle that he had in the londe of Canaan. And so cam into Egypte with all his progenye, sones and children *etc*. Thyse ben the names of the sones of Israhel that entrid with hym into Egypt. The first begoten, Ruben, with his children foure; Symeon with his vij sones; Leuy wyth his iij sones; Iudas and his sones iij; Ysachar and his iiij sones; Zabulon and his sones iij. Thyse were sones of Lya that Iacob gate in Mesopotamye and Dyna his doughter. Alle thyse sones and doughtres were xxxiij. Gad also entred with his chyldren vij; Aser | with his children v, and of his childis children ij. f. [53][ra] / sig. [g5] Thise were sones of Zelphe, in nombre xvj. The sones of Rachel were Ioseph and Beniamyn. Ioseph had two sones in the londe of Egipte by his wyf Assenech: Manasses and Effraim. The sones of Beniamyn were x. Alle thyse chyldren that cam of Rachel were in nombre xiiij. Dan entrid with one sone, and Neptalim with iiij sones. Thise were the children of Bala; they were in nombre vij. Alle the sowles that were yssued of his seed that entrid into Egipte with hym, withoute the wyues of his sones, were lxvj. The sones of Ioseph that were born in Egypte, tweyne. Summa of all the sowles of the hows of Iacob that entrid into Egypte were in all lxx.

Iacob sente thenne tofore hym Iudas vnto Ioseph to shewe to hym his comyng. And he cam to Ioseph in Iessen, and anon Ioseph ascended his chare, wente for to mete his fader, and whan he sawe hym, he enbraced hym mekely and wepte. And his fader receyuyd hym ioyously and enbraced also hym. Thenne said the fader to Ioseph: 'Now shal I dye ioyously, bycause I haue seen thy vysage.' Thenne said Ioseph to his brethern and to alle the hows of his fader: 'I shal goo and ascende to Pharao, and shal saye to hym that my brethern

525 in] in \ in   533 f. 53] folio lvi

and the hows of my fader that were in the londe of Canaan be come to me, and ben men kepyng sheep and can the maner wel for to kepe the flockes of sheep, and that they haue brought with them their beestis and alle that euer they had. Whan he shal calle you and axe you of what occupacion ye be, ye shal saye: "We ben shepeherdes, thy seruauntes, from our chyldhode vnto now, and our faders also." This shal ye saye that ye may dwelle in the lond of Iessen, for th'Egipciens haue spyte vnto herdmen of sheep.'

Thenne Ioseph entred tofore Pharao and said to hym: 'My fader, my brethern, their sheep and beestis ben comen fro the londe of Canaan, and be in the londe of Iessen.' And he brouht fyue of his brethern tofore the kynge, whom he demanded of what occupacion
f. [53]rb they were of. They answerd: 'We ben kepers of | sheep, thy seruantes, we and our faders. We be come to duelle in thy lande, for ther is no grasse for the flockes of sheep of vs thy seruantis; the famyne is so grete in the londe of Canaan. We beseche the that thou comande vs thy seruantes to dwelle in the lande of Iessen.' Thenne said the kyng to Ioseph: 'Thy fader and thy brethern ben comen to the. The lande of Egipt is at thy commandement. Make thou them to duelle in the beste place and delyuer to them the londe of Iessen. And yf thou knowe them for connyng, ordeyne them to be maistres of my beestis.' After this Ioseph brought his fader in and made hym stande tofore the kynge, whiche blessid hym, and was demanded of the kynge how old he was. He answerd: 'The dayes of the pylgremage of my lif ben an C xxx yere, smale and euyll, and yet I am not comen vnto the dayes of my faders that they haue lyuyd.' And he blessyd the kynge and wente out. Thenne Ioseph gaf to his fader and brethern possession in Egipte in the best soyle of Ramesses, lyke as Pharao had commanded, and there fedde them, gyuyng to eche of them vytaylle.

In all the world was scarcete of brede, and hungre and famyne oppressyd specyally and most the land of Egypte and the londe of Canaan. Of whiche londes Ioseph gate all the money for sellyng of whete and brought it into the kynges tresorye. Whan alle peple lacked money, all Egypte cam to Ioseph, sayeng: 'Gyue vs brede. Why deye we to the, lackyng money?' To whom he answerd: 'Brynge to me your beestis and I shal gyue you for them vitailles, yf ye haue no money.' Whiche whan they brought, he gaf to them vitailles and food for horses, sheep, oxen and asses, and susteyned them one yere for chaungyng of theyr beestis.

Thenne cam they agayn the second yere and sayd: 'We hyde not fro the, our lorde, that our money is faylled, and also our beestis ben goon. And ther is nothyng lefte but our bodyes and our londe. Why thenne shal we deye in thy syght? And we ourself and also our lande shal be thyne. Bye vs into bondship and seruytude of the kynge, and gyue | vs seed to sowe leste the erthe torne into wildernes.' Thenne f. [53]va Ioseph bought all the lond of Egypte, euery man sellyng his possessions for the vehement hungre that they hadde. He subdued all vnto Pharao, and all his peple fro the laste termes of Egipte vnto the vtterist endes of the same, exepte the lande langyng to the preestes, which was gyuen to them by the kynge; to whom were gyuen vitaillis openly out of alle the barnes and garners, and therfore they were not compellid to selle their possessions. Thenne said Ioseph to all the peples: 'Lo, now ye se and know that Pharao oweth and is in possession of you and of your lande. Take to you seed and sowe ye the feldes, that ye may haue fruyte. The fyfte part therof ye shal gyue to the kynge, and four partes I promyse to you to sowe and for mete to your seruauntes and to your chyldren.' Whiche answerd: 'Our helth is in thyn honde. Late our lord only beholde vs, and we shal gladly serue þe kynge.' Fro that tyme vnto this present day, in alle the lande of Egipte, the fifte part is paid to the kynge, and it is holden for a lawe, exept the londe longyng to the prestes, whiche is fre fro this condicion.

Thenne Israhel dwellid in Egipte, in the londe of Iessen, and was in possession therof. He encreced and multiplied gretly and lyuyd therin xvij yere, and alle the yeres of his lyf were an honderd and seuen and fourty yere. Whan he vnderstode that the day of his deth approched, he callid to hym his sone Ioseph and said to hym: 'Yf I may fynde so moche grace in thy sight, do to me so moche mercy as thou promyse and swere that thou berye me not in Egipte, but that I may reste with my faders, and take and carye me fro this lande and leye me in the sepulchre of my fornfaders.' To whom Ioseph answerd: 'I shal doo that thou hast commanded.' Thenne said he: 'Swere that to me.' And so he swore. And thenne Israhel adoured and worshipped Our Lord and torned hym toward his beddes heed.

Thenne this don, anon after it was told to Ioseph that his fader was seke and feble; who anon toke his sones Manasses and Effraim and | cam to his fader. Anon it was told to the fader: 'Lo, thy sone Ioseph f. [53]vb cometh to the.' Whiche thenne was conforted; satte vp in his bedde. And Ioseph entrid in, and Iacob saide: 'Almyghty God apperid {t}o me in Luza, whiche is in the lond of Canaan, and he blessid me and saide: "I shal encrece the and multeplye into tourbes of peples. I shal gyue to the this londe and to thy seed after the in sempyternal possession." Therfore thy two sones that ben born to the in this londe of Egypte tofore I cam hether to the shal ben my sones; Effraim and Manasses, they shal be reputed to me as Symeon and Ruben. The other that thou shalt gete after them shal be thyn, and shal be called in the name of theyr brethern in theyr possessions.'

Thenne he, seyng Iosephs sones, said to hym: 'Who ben thyse chyldren?' Ioseph answerd: 'They be my sones, whiche God haue gyuen to me in this place.' 'Brynge them hether', said he, 'to me, that I may blesse them.' Israels eyen were dymmed and myght not see clerly for grete age. He toke them to hym and kyssed them, and said to Ioseph: 'I am not defrauded fro the sight of the, and furthermor God hath shewd to me thy seed.' Thenne, whan Ioseph toke them fro his faders lappe, he worshippid hym, knelyng lowe to th'erthe, and sette Effraym on his right side and on the lyft syde of Israhel, and Manasses on the right side of his fader Israhel. Whiche toke his right hande and leyde it on the heed of Effraim the yonger brother, and his lyft hande on the heed of Manasses, which was first born. Thenne Iacob blessyd the sones of Ioseph and said: 'God, in whos sight walked my faders Abraham and Ysaac, God, that had fedde me fro my yongthe vnto this present day, the angele that hath kepte me from alle euyllis, blesse thyse chyldren, and my name be called on them and the names of my fadres Abraham and Ysaac, and growe they into multytude vpon th'erthe.' Thenne Ioseph, seeyng that his fader sette his right hand vpon the heed of Effraim the yonger brother, toke it heuyly, and toke f. [54][ra] / sig. [g6] his faders hande and wold haue leyd it on the heed of | Manasses, and said to his fader: 'Nay fader, it is not conuenyent that ye doo. This is the first begoten sone; sette thy right honde on his heed.' Whiche renyed that and wold not doo so, but said: 'I wote, my sone, I wote what I doo; and this sone shal encrece into peples and multeplye, but his yonger brother shal be gretter than he, and his seed shal growe into gentyles.' And blessyd them, sayeng that same tyme: 'In the shal be blessyd Israhel, and shal be said: "Make God the like to Effraim and Manasses."' And said to Ioseph his sone: 'Lo, now I dye, and God shal be with yow and shal reduce and brynge you agayn vnto the londe of your faders. And I gyue to the one parte aboue thy brethern, whiche I gate and wan fro the hande of Amorrey with my swerd and my bowe.'

658 f. 54] folio lv

Thenne Iacob called his sones tofore hym and said to hem: ‘Gadre ye all togydre tofor me, that I may shewe to yow thynges that ben to come. And here your fader Israhel.’ And there he told to eche of them his condi[ci]on singulerly. And whan he had blessid his xij sones, he comanded them to berye hym with his faders in a double spelunke, whiche is in the felde of Ephron Ethey, ayenst Mambre in the londe of Canaan, whiche Abraham bought. And this saide, he gadred to hym hys feet and deyde.

Whiche anon as Ioseph sawe, fylle on his visage and kissed hym. He comanded to his maistres of phisik and medicines, whiche were his seruauntes, that they shold enbame the body of his fader with swete spices aromatykes. Whiche was alle don, and thenne wente they sorowyng hym xl dayes. The Egypcyens waylled hym lxx dayes, and whan the wayllyng was passyd, Ioseph dyde saye to Pharao how he had sworn and promysid to berye hym in the londe of Canaan. To whom Pharao saide: ‘Goo and berye thy fader lyke as thou hast sworn.’ Whiche thenne toke his faders body and wente, and with hym were accompanyed all the aged men of Pharaos hous and the noblest men of burthe of all the londe of Egypte, the hows of Ioseph with his brethern, without the yong children, flockes and beestis, whiche | they lefte in the londe of Iessen. He had in his felawship chares, cartes f. [54]rb and horsmen, and was a grete tourbe and companye, and cam ouer Iordan, whereas they halowed th’exequyes by grete wayllyng vij days long. And whan they of the contre sawe this plancte and sorowyng, they saide: ‘This is a grete sorow to th’Egypcyens.’ And that same place is named yet ‘the bewayllyng of Egypte’.

The children of Israhel dyde as they were commanded and bare hym into the londe of Ca[na]an, and buryed hym in the double spelunke whiche Abraham had bought. Thenne, whan Iacob their fader was buryed, Ioseph with alle his felowship retorned into Egypte.

Thenne his brethern, after the deth of their fader, spaken togydre pryuely, and dredyng that Ioseph wold auenge the wronge and euyll that they had don to hym, camen to hym and saide: ‘Thy fader comanded vs er he deyde that we shold saye thus to the: “We praye the that thou wilt forgete and not remembre the synne and trespaas of thy brethern, ne the malyce tha{t} they executed in the.” We beseche the that thou wilt forgyue to thy fader, seruaunt of God, this wickednes.’ Whiche whan Ioseph herde, wepte bitterly. And his

673 condicion] condi– \ on 697 Canaan] Caanan 706 of] of \ of

brethern cam to hym, knelyng lowe to the grounde and worshippid hym and sayd: 'We ben thy seruauntes.' To whom he answerd: 'Be ye nothyng aferd, ne drede you not. Wene ye that we may resiste Goddes wyll? Ye thought to haue don to me euyl, but God hath torned it into good, and hath exalted me as ye see and knowe, that he shold saue moche peple. Be ye nothyng aferde. I shal fede you and your children.' And conforted them with fair wordes and spack frendely and ioyously to them. And he abode and duellyd stylle in Egypte with alle the hous of his fader, and lyuyd an hondred and ten yere, and sawe the sones of Effraym into the thirde generation.

After thyse thynges, he said to his brethern: 'After my deth, God shal vysyte you and shal doo you departe fro this londe, vnto the londe that he promysed to Abraham, Ysaac and Iacob. Whan that tyme shal
f. [54]va come, take my bones and | lede them with you fro this place.' And thenne deyde. Whos body was enbamed with swete spyces and aromatikes, and leyde in a chest in Egypte.

Thus endeth th'ystorye of Ioseph and his brethern.

[6. MOSES]

Hyer next foloweth th'ystorye of Moyses, whiche is redde in the chirche on Mydlente Sonday.

Thyse ben the names of the children of Israhel that entryd into Egipt with Iacob, and eche entrid with their houshold and meyne: Ruben, Symeon, Leuy, Iudas, Ysachar, Zabulon, Beniamyn, Dan, Neptalyn, Gad and Aser. They were alle in nombre that entred lxx. Ioseph was tofore in Egypte. And whan he was deed, and all his brethern and kynred, the chyldren of Israhel grewe and multeplyed gretly and fylled the erthe.

Thenne was ther a newe kynge vpon Egypte whiche knewe nothyng
f. [54]vb Ioseph and | said to his peple: 'Loo and see, the peple of the children of Israhel is grete and strenger than we be. Come and late vs wysely oppresse them leste they multeplye and gyue vs bataylle and fyght with vs and dryue vs out of our londe.' Thenne he ordeyned prouostes and maystres ouer them to sette them awerke and put them to affliction of burthens. They bylded to Pharao two to[u]nes, Phiton and Ramesses. How moche more they oppressid them, so moche more

3 Thyse] T *five-line capital supplied by hand in red*   16 tounes] to– \ nes

they encreced and multeplyed. The Egypcyens hated the chyldren of Israhel and put them to affliction, scornyng and hauyng enuye at them, and oppressyd bytterly theyr lyf wyth hard and sore labours of tyle and claye, and greuyd alle them in suche werkis.

The kynge of Egypte said to the mydwyues of the Hebrews, of whom that one was callyd Sephora and that other Phua, and comanded: 'Whan-so is that the tyme of burth is and that ye shal doo your offyce in helpyng in the burthe of chyldren, yf it be a man chyld, slee hym; yf it be a maid childe, kepe it and late it lyue.' The mydwyues dredde God and dyde not as the kyng comanded them, but reseruyd and kepte the men chyldren. For whom the kynge sente and said: 'What is the cause that ye reserue and kepte the men chyldren?' They answerd: 'Ther ben of th'Ebrewys wymen that can the crafte of mydwyuys as wel as we, and er we come, the chyldren be born.' God dyde wel herfore vnto the mydwyues. And the peple grewe and were gretly comforted. And bycause the mydwyues dredde God, they edefyed to them howses.

Thenne Pharao commanded to his peple, sayeng: 'Whatsomeuer is born of males, caste ye into the ryuer, and what of wymen, kepe ye them and late ye them lyue.' After this, was a man of the hows of Leui wente out and toke a wyf of hys kynrede, whiche conceyuyd and brought forth a sone. And he sawe hym elegaunt and fayr; hydde hym thre monethes. And whan he myght no lenger hyde hym, toke a lytyl krybbe of rysshes and wykers, and pitchid it with glewe and pitche, and put therin the chylde and sette it on the ryuer | and lete it dryue doun in the streme; and the suster of the chyld, stondyng aferre, consyderyng what shold falle therof. f. 55[ra] / sig. [g7]

And it happed that same tyme the doughter of Kynge Pharao descended doun to the ryuer for to wasshe her in the water, and her maydens wente by the brynke. Whiche thenne, whan she sawe the lytyl crybbe or fiscelle, she sente one of her maydens to fetche and take it vp, whyche so fette and brought to her. She sawe therin lyeng a fayr chyld and she, hauyng pyte on it, said: 'This is one of the chyldren of the Ebrewis.' To whom anon spack the suster of the chyld: 'Wilt thou', said she, 'that I goo and calle the a woman of th'Ebrews, that shal and may norysshe this childe?' She answerd: 'Go thy waye.' The mayde wente and called his moder, to whom Pharaos doughter saide: 'Take this chylde and norysshe hym to me, and I shal gyue to the thy mede and rewarde.' The moder toke her chyld and norysshid it. And whan it was wened and coude goo, she delyured it to the doughter of

Kyng Pharao, whom s[h]e receyuyd and adopted in stede of a sone and named hym Moyses, sayeng that 'I toke hym out of the water'. And he ther grewe and wexe a praty chyld. And as Iosephus *Antyquitatum* saith, this dou[gh]ter of Pharao, whiche was named Termuthe, louyd wel Moyses and reputed hym as her sone by adopcion, and on a day brought hym to her fader, who for his beaute toke hym in hys armes and made moche of hym, and sette his dyademe on his heed wherin was his ydole. And Moyses anon toke it and caste it vnder his feet and trade on it; wherfore the kyng was wroth and demanded of the grete doctours and magyciens what shold falle of this child. And they kalked on his natyuyte and said: 'This is he that shal destroye thy regne and put it vnder foote, and shal rewle and gouerne th'Ebrews.' Wherfore the kynge anon decreed that he shold be put to deth. But other said that Moyses dyde it of chyldhood and ought not to dye therfor, and conceyled to make therof a preef. And so they dyde: they sette tofore hym a plater ful of coles brennyng f. 55rb and a | plater ful of cheryes, and bad hym ete. And he toke and put the hoote coles in his mouth and brenned his tongue, whiche letted his speche euer after. And thus he escaped the deth. Iosephus said that whan Pharao wold haue slayn hym, Thermuthe his doughter plucked hym away and sauyd hym.

Thenne on a tyme as Moyses was ful growen, he wente to his brethern and sawe the affliction of them and a man of Egypte smytyng one of the Hebrews his brethern. And he loked hether and theder and sawe no ma[n]; he smote th'Egypcien and slewe hym and hyd hym in the sonde. And another day he wente out and fonde two of the Hebrews braulyng and fyghtyng togydre. Thenne he said to hym that dyde wronge: 'Why smytest thou thy neyhbour?' Whiche answerd: 'Who hath ordeyned the prince and iuge vpon vs? Wilt thou slee me as thou slewest that other day an Egypcyen?' Moyses was aferde and said to hymself: 'How is this dede knowen and made open?' Pharao herd herof and sought Moyses for to slee hym, whiche thenne fledde fro his syght and dwellyd in the londe of Madyan and satte there by a pyt syde.

The preste of Madyan had vij doughters, whiche cam theder for to drawe water and to fylle the vessels, for to gyue drynke to the flockes of the sheep of their fader. Thenne cam on them the herdmen and putte them from it. Thenne roose Moyses and defended the maydens

58 she] se   61 doughter] douhgter   82 man] mam

and lete them watre their sheep. Whiche thenne retorned to their fader Ietro, and he said to them: ‘Why come ye now erlyer than ye were wont to doo?’ They sayde that ‘A man of Egypte hath delyueryd vs fro the hande of the herdmen, and also he drewe water for vs and gaf to the sheep drynke.’ ‘Where is he?’ saide he; ‘Why lefte ye the man after you? Goo calle hym that he may ete somme brede with vs.’ Thenne Moyses sware that he wold dwelle with hym. And he toke Sephora, one of his doughters, and wedded her to his wyf, whiche conceyuyd and bare hym a sone, whom he callyd Gersam, sayeng: ‘I was a straunger in a straunge londe.’ She brought to hym forth another sone, whom he named Eleazar, sayeng: | [f. 55va] ‘The God of my fader is my helper, and hath kept me fro the hande of Pharao.’

Longe tyme after this deyed the kyng of Egypte. And the chyldren of Israhel, wayllyng, made grete sorowe for th’oppressyon of theyr labour, and cryde vnto God for helpe. Their crye cam vnto God of theyr werkis, and God herde theyr wayllyng and remembryd the promyse that he made with Abraham, Ysaac and Iacob. And Our Lord beheld the chyldren of Israhel and knewe them.

Moyses fedde the sheep of Ietro, his wyues fader. Whan he had brought the sheep into the innerest part of deserte, he cam vnto the mount of God, Oreb. Our [L]ord apperid to hym in flamme of fyre in the myddys of a busshe; and sawe the fyre in the busshe, and the busshe brenned not. Thenne said Moyses: ‘I shal goo and see this grete vysyon, why the busshe brenneth not.’ Our Lord thenne, beholdyng that he wente for to see it, callyd hym, beyng in the busshe, and said: ‘Moyses, Moyses!’ Whiche answerd: ‘I am here.’ Thenne said Our Lord: ‘Approche no ner hytherward. Take of thy shone fro thy feet. The place that thou stondest on is holy ground’; and said also: ‘I am God of thy fader, God of Abraham and God of Ysaac and God of Iacob.’ Moyses thenne hydde his face and durst not loke toward God.

To whom God saide: ‘I haue seen th’affliction of my peple in Egypte, and I haue herde theyr crye of the hardnes þat they suffre in their werkis. And I, knowyng the sorow of them, am descended to delyuer them fro the hand of th’Egypcyens, and shal lede them fro this londe into a good londe and spacyous, into a land that floweth mylke and hony, vnto the places of Cananeis, Ethei, Amorrey, Pheresey, Euey and Iebusey. The crye of the chyldren of Israhel is

116 Lord] bord

comen to me. I haue seen theyr affliction, how they ben oppressyd of th'Egypcyens. But come to me and I shal sende the vnto Pharao, that thou shalt lede the chyldren of Israhel out of Egypte.'

Thenne Moyses said to hym: 'Who am I that shal goo to Pharao and lede the chyldren out of Egypte?' To whom God said: 'I shal be with f. 55vb the. And this shal be the signe | that I sende the: whan thou shalt haue [l]edde out my peple of Egypte, thou shalt offre to God vpon this hylle.' Moyses said vnto God: 'Loo, yf I goo to the chyldren of Israhel and saye to them, "God of your faders hath sente me to you", yf they saye, "What is his name?", what shal I saye?' Our Lord said to Moyses: *Ego sum qui sum*, 'I am that I am.' He said: 'Thus shal thou saye to the children of Israhel: "He that is sente me to you." And yet shalt thou saye to them: "The Lord God of your fadres, God of Abraham, God of Ysaac and God of Iacob, hath apperid to me, sayeng: Thys is my name for euermore, and this is my memoryall fro generacion to generacion."

'Go and gadre togydre the senyors and aged men of Israhel and saye to them: "The Lord God of your faders hath apperyd to me, God of Abraham and God of Ysaac and God of Iacob, sayeng: "Vysytyng I haue vysited you, and haue seen all that is fallen in Egypte, and I shal lede you out of th'affliction of Egypte into the londe of Canane, Ethei *etc.*, vnto the londe flowyng mylk and hony." And they shal here thy voys. Thou shalt goo and take with the senyors of Israhel to the kynge of Egypte and shalt saye to hym: "The Lord God of th'Ebrewes hath called vs. We shal goo the io[rn]ey of iij dayes in wyldernes, that we may offre to Our Lord God." But I knowe wel that the kynge of Egypte shal not suffre you to goo but by stronge hande. I shal stratche out my hand and shal smyte Egypte in all my meruaylles that I shal doo amyd-emong them. After that he shal lete you goo. I shal thenne gyue my grace to this peple tofore th'Egypciens. And whan ye shal goon out, ye shal not departe voyde ne wyth nought, but euery woman shal borowe of her neyh[b]our and of her hostesse vessel of syluer and of gold and clothes, and them shal ye leye on your sones and on your doughtres, and ye shal robbe Egypte.'

Thenne Moyses answerd and saide: 'They shal not byleue me ne here my voys, but shal saye: "God hath not apperyd to the."' God f. 56ra / sig. [g8] saith thenne to hym: 'What is that thou holdest in thyn honde?' He | answerd: 'A rodde.' Our Lord said: 'Caste it on the ground.' He

140 ledde] bedde 158 iorney] Ionrey 165 neyhbour] neyħlour

threwe it doun, and it torned vnto a serpent, wherof Moyses was aferde and wold haue fledde. Our Lord said to hym: ‘Put forth thy hande and holde hym by the taylle.’ He stratched forth hys honde and helde hym, and it torned agayn into a rodde. ‘To this that they byleue the that I haue apperid to the.’

And yet Our Lord said to hym: ‘Put thy honde into thy bosom.’ Whiche whan he hath put in and drawen out agayn, it was lyke a lepres hand. Our Lord bad hym to withdrawe it into hys bosom agayn; and drewe it out, and it was thenne lyke that other flesshe. ‘Yf they here not the and byleue by the fyrst signe and tokene, they shal byleue the by the seconde. Yf they byleue none of the two ne here thy voys, thenne take water of the ryuer and poure it on the drye ground, and whatsomeuer thou takest and drawest shal torne into blood.’

Thenne Moyses said: ‘I pray the Lord sende som other, for I am not eloquente but haue a lettyng in my speche.’ Our Lord said to hym: ‘Who made the mouth of a man, or who hath made a man dombe or deef, seeyng or blynde? Not I? Go therfor; I shal be in thy mouth and shal teche the what thou shalt saye.’ Thenne said Moyses: ‘I beseche the Lord,’ said he, ‘sende somme other whom thou wilt.’ Our Lord was wroth on Moyses and said: ‘Aaron thy brother deken, I knowe that he is eloquent. Lo, he shal come and mete with the, and seeyng the, he shal be glad in hys herte. Speke thou to hym and put my wordes in his mouth, and I shal be in thy mouth and in his mouth, and I shal shewe to you what ye ought to doo. And he shal speke for the to the peple and shal be thy mouth, and thou shal be in suche thynges as parteyne to God. Take with the this rodde in thyn hande, by whiche thou shallt doo signes and meruaylles.’

Thenne Moyses wente to Ietro, his wyuys fader, and said to hym: ‘I shal goo and retorne to my brethern into Egypte, and see yf they yet lyue.’ To whom Ietro said: ‘Goo in Goddes name and pees.’

Thenne said Our Lord to Moyses: ‘Goo and retorne | into Egypte. f. 56rb
Alle they ben now deed that sought for to slee the.’ Thenne Moyses toke his wyf and hys sones and sette them vpon an asse and retorned into Egypte, beryng the rodde of God in hys honde.

Thenne Our Lord said to Aaron: ‘Goo ayenst Moyses and mete with hym in deserte.’ Whiche wente for to mete with hym vnto the mount of God, and there kyssed hym. And Moyses told vnto Aaron alle that Our Lord had said to hym for whiche he sente hym, and alle the tokenes and signes that he bad hym doo. They cam bothe togydre and gadred and assamblyd alle the senyors and aged men of the chyldren of Israhel. And Aaron told to them alle that God had said to Moyses, and made the sygnes and tokenes tofore the peple, and the peple byleuyd it. They herd wel that Our Lord had vysyted the chyldren of Israhel and that he had beholden th'affliction of them, wherfore they fyll doun lowe to the ground and worshipped Our Lord.

Aft{e}r this Moyses and Aaron wente vnto Pharao and said: 'This said the Lord God of Israhel: "Suffre my peple to departe that they may sacrefyse to me in deserte."' Thenne said Pharao: 'Who is that lord þat I may here his voys and leue Israhel? I knowe not that lorde ne I wylle not leue Israhel.' They said to hym: 'God of the Hebrewis hath callid vs that we goo the iourney of thre dayes in the wyldernes and sacrefyse vnto Our Lord God, leste parauenture pestelence or warre falle to vs.' The Kynge of Egypte said to them: 'Why sollycyte ye, Moyses and Aaron, the peple fro theyr werkis and labour? Goo ye vnto your werke.'

Pharao also said: 'The peple is moche. See how they growe and multeplye, and yet moche more shold doo yf they rested fro theyr labour.' Therfore he comanded the same day to the prefectes and maistres of theyr werkis, sayeng: 'In no wyse gyue no more chaf to the peple for to make lome and claye, but late them goo and gadre stopple, and make them to doo as moche labour as they dyde tofore, and lasse it nothyng. They doo now but crye: "Late vs goo and make sacrefyse
f. 56va to our God." Late them be | oppressid by labour and excercisid, that they attende not to lesynges.' Thenne the prefectes and maistres of theyr werke said to them that Pharao had comanded to gyue them no chaf, but they shold goo and gadre suche as they myght fynde, and that theyr werke shold not therfor be mynusshed. Thenne the chyldren were dysperplyd for to gadre chaf. And their maistres awayted on them and bad them: 'Make an ende of your werke as ye were wonte to doo whan that chaf was delyured to yow.' And thus they were put to more affliction, and wold make them to make as many tyles as they dyde tofore.

Thenne the vpperist of the chyldren of Israhel cam to Pharao and complayned, sayeng: 'Why puttest thou thy seruants to suche affliction?' He said to them: 'Ye be so ydle that ye saye ye will goo and sacrefyse to your God. Ye shal haue no chaf gyuen to you, yet ye shal werke your custumable werke and gadre your chaf also.' Thenne the eldest and vpperist emonge th'Ebrews wente to Moyses and Aaron and said: 'What haue ye don? Ye haue so don that ye haue made our odour to stynke in þe sight of Pharao and haue encoraged hym to sle vs. God see and iuge this bytwene you and vs.'

Thenne Moyses counseylled with Our Lord how he shold doo and said: 'Lord, why hast thou sente me hether? For sith I haue spoken to Pharao in thy name, he hath put thy peple to more affliction than they had tofore and thou hast not deliueryd them.' Our Lord said to Moyses: 'Now thou shal see what I shal doo to Pharao. By strong hande he shal late you goo, and in a boystous he shal caste you fro his land.' Yet said Our Lord to Moyses: 'I am the Lord God that apperid to Abraham, Ysaac and Iacob in my myght, and my name is Adonay; I shewd to them not that. I promysed and made couenaunt with them that I shold gyue to them the lond of Canaan, in which they duellyd. I now haue herd the wayllyng, and the tribulacions that th'Egypciens oppresse them with, for whiche I shal delyure and brynge them from the seruytude of th'Egypciens.' Moyses told all thyse thynges | to the f. 56vb chyldren of Israhel. And they byleuyd hym not, for the anguyssh of their spiretes that they were inne and hard labour.

Thenne said Our Lord to Moyses: 'Goo and entre in to Pharao, and bydde hym delyure my peple of Israhel out of his land.' Moyses answerd: 'How shold Pharao here me whan the children of Israhel byleue me not?' Thenne Our Lord said to Moyses and Aaron that they bothe shold goo to Pharao and gyue hym in comandement to late the chyldren of Israhel to departe. And he said to Moyses: 'Lo, I h[a]ue ordeyned the to be God of Pharao, and Aaron thy brother shal be thy prophete. Thou shalt saye to hym all that I saye to the, and he shal saye to Pharao that he suffre the chyldren of Israhel to departe fro hys land; but I shal enharde his herte and shal multeplye my signes and tokenes in the land of Egypt. And he shal not here ne byleue you. And I shal lede the chyldren of Israhel my peple, and shal shewe myn hande and suche wonders on Egypte that Egypciens shal knowe that I am the Lord.' Moyses and Aaron dyde as Our Lord commanded them. Moyses was lxxx yer old whan he cam and stode tofore Pharao, and A[aro]n lxxxiij yere whan they spack to Pharao.

Thenne, whan they were tofore Pharao, Aaron caste the rodde doun tofore Pharao and anon the rodde torned into a serpent. Thenne Pharao callid his magyciens and iogelers and badde them do the same. And they made theyr witchecraft and inuocacions and caste doun their roddes, whiche torned in lyke wyse into serpentes. But the rodde

275 haue] heue   284 Aaron] Aroan

of Aaron deuoured their roddes. Yet was the herte of Pharao hard and so endurat that he wold not doo as God bad.

Thenne said Our Lord to Moyses: 'The herte of Pharao is greuyd and wil not delyuer my peple. Goo to hym tomorn in the mornyng. And he shal come out, and thou shal stande whan he cometh on the banke of the ryuer and take in thy hande the rodde that was torned into the serpent and saye to hym: "The Lord God of th'Ebrews sendeth me to the, sayeng: Delyure my peple that they may offre and f. 57ra / sig. h1 make sacrefise to | me in deserte. Yet thou hast no wille to here me." Therfor Our Lord said: "In this shalt thou knowe that I am the Lord. Loo, I shal smyte with the rodde that is in my hand the water of the flood, and it shal torne into blood. The fysshes that ben in the water shal deye and th'Egipciens shall be put to affliction, drynkyng of it."'

Thenne said Our Lord to Moyses: 'Saye thou to Aaron: "Take this rodde and stratche thyn hand vpon all the waters of Egypt, vpon the floodes, ryuers, pondes and vpon all the lakes where ony water is in, that they torne into blood, that it may be a vengeaunce in all the land of Egypte, as well in treen vessels as in vessels of erth and stone."' Moyses and Aaron dyde as God had comanded them and smote the flood with the rodde tofore Pharao and his seruaunts, which torned into blood. And the fisshes that were in the ryuer deyde, and the water was corrupt and th'Egypciens myght not drynke the water. And all the water of Egipte was torned into blood. And in lyke wyse dyde th'enchantours with theyr witchecraft. And the herte of Pharao was so indurat that he wold not lete the peple departe, as Our Lord had comanded, but he retorned home for this tyme. Th'Egypciens wente and doluen pittes for water all aboute by the ryuer, and they fonde no water to drynke, but alle was blood. And this plaghe endured vij dayes, and whatsomeuer water the chyldren of Israhel toke in this whyle was fair and good water. This was the first plaghe and vengeance.

The seconde was that God sente frosshes, so many that all the londe was ful, the ryuers, the howses, chambres, beddes, that they were woo-begoon. And thyse frosshes entrid into their mete, so many that they couerd all the londe of Egypte. Thenne Pharao prayd Moyses and Aaron that God wold take awaye these frosshes and that he wold goo suffre the peple to doo sacrefise. And thenne Moyses axid whan he wold delyure them yf þe frosshes were voided. And Pharao said: 'On the morn.' And thenne Moyses prayde, and they uoyded alle. And whan Pharao sawe that he was quyt of them, he kepte not his promyse, and wold not lete them departe.

The thirde vengeange that God sente to them | was a grete f. 57rb multitude of hongry horseflyes, as many as th[e d]uste of th'erthe, which were on men and bote them and beestis. And th'enchantours said thenne to Pharao: 'This is the fyngre of God.' Yet wold not Pharao lete them departe.

The fourth vengeance was that God sente alle maner kynde of flyes and lyse, in suche wyse the vnyuersal londe of Egypte was ful of all maner flyes and lyse; but in the lande of Iessen were none. Yet was he so indurate that he wold not lete them goo, but wold that they shold make their sacrefyse to God in that londe. But Moyses wold not so, but goo iij dayes iourney in deserte and sacrefyse to God there. Pharao said: 'I wil wel that ye goo into deserte, but goo not fer and come sone agayn, and praye ye for me.' And Moyses prayd for hym to Our Lord. And the flyes voyded, that ther was not one lefte, and whan they were goon, Pharao wold not kepe his promyse.

Thenne the fyfthe plaghe was that God shewd his honde vpon the feldes and vpon the horses, asses, camels, sheep and oxen, and was a grete pestelence on alle the beestis. And God shewd a wonder myracle bytwene the possessyons of the Egypcyens and the possessions of his peple of Israhel, for of the beestis of the chyldren of Israhel ther was not one that perisshid. Yet was Pharao so hardherted that he wold not suffre the peple to departe.

The sixt plaghe was that Moyses toke asshes out of the chymney and casted on the londe. And anon alle the peple of Egypte, as wel men as beestis, were ful of botchis, beelis and blaynes and woundes and swellyng in their bladders, in suche wise that th'enchantours coude ne myght not stonde for payne tofor Pharao. Yet wold not Pharao here them ne doo as God had comanded.

The seuenth plaghe was an haylle so grete that ther was neuer none like tofore, and thondre and fire, that it destroied all the gras and herbes of Egipte and smote doun alle that was in the feld, men and beestis, but in the londe of Iessen was none herd ne harm doon. Yet wold not Pharao delyure them.

The eygth, Our Lord sente to them locustes, whiche is a maner grete flye, callyd in somme place an adder-bolte, whiche bote | them f. 57[va] and ete vp all the corn and herbes that was left, in suche wyse that the peple cam to Pharao and desyred hym to delyure, sayeng that the lond perysshyd. Thenne Pharao gaf to the men lycence to goo and make

331 the duste] thuste

their sacrefyse and leue theyr wyues and chyldren there stylle tyl they come agayn. But Moyses and Aaron said that they must goo all, wherfor he wold not lete them departe.

The ix plage and vengeance was that God sente so gret derknes vpon all the londe of Egypte, that the derknesse was so grete and horryble that they were palpable, and it endured iij dayes and iij nyghtes. Whersomeuer the chyldren of Israhel wente it was lyght. Thenne Pharao callid Moyses and Aaron and said to them: 'Goo ye and make your sacrefyse vnto your Lord God, and late your sheep and beestis only abyde.' To whom Moyses saide: 'We shal take with vs suche hostyes and sacrefyses as we shal offre to Our Lord God. All our flockes and beestis shal goo with vs; ther shal not remayne as moche as an naylle that shal be necessarye in the honour of Our Lord God. For we knowe not what we shal offre tyl we come to the place.' Pharao was so indurate and hardherted that he wold not lete them goo, and bad Moyses that he shold no more come in his sight: 'For whan thou comest, thou shalt deye.' Moyses answerd: 'Be it as thou hast said. I shal no more come to thy presence.'

And thenne Our Lord said to Moyses: 'There resteth now but one plage and vengeange, and after that he shal lete you goo. But first saye to all the peple that euery man borowe of his frende and woman of her neyghbour vessell of gold, of syluer and clothes. Our Lord shal gyue to his peple grace and fauour to borowe of th'Egypciens.' And thenne gaf to them a comandement how they shold departe. And Our Lord said to Moyses: 'At mydnyght I shal entre into Egypte, and the first begoten chyld and heyr of alle Egypte shal deye, fro the first begoten sone of Pharao that sytteth in his trone vnto the first begoten sone of the handmayd that sytteth atte mylle, and all the first begoten of the beestis. Ther shal be a grete crye and clamour in alle the londe of f. 57vb Egypte, in suche wyse that ther was | neuer none lyke ne neuer shal be after, and emong all the chyldren ther shal not an hound be hurt, ne no man ne beest; wherby ye shal knowe by what myracle God deuydeth th'Egypcyens and Israhel.' Moyses and Aaron shewd alle thyse sygnes and plaghes tofore Pharao, and his herte was so indurate that he wold not late them departe.

Thenne whan Moyses had said to the chyldren how they shold doo er they departed and ete theyr pask lambe and all other cerymonyes as ben expressyd in the Byble (for a lawe t'endure euer emong them, whiche the chyldren of Israhel obeyed and accomplysshyd), it was so that at mydnyght Our Lord smote and slew euery fyrst begoten sone thurghout all the londe of Egypte, begynnyng at the first sone and heyr of Pharao vnto the sone of the caytyf that laye in pryson, and also the first begoten of the beestis. Pharao ar[ose] in the nyght and all his seruauntes and all Egypte, and ther was a grete clamour and sorouful noyse and crye. For ther was not an hows in all Egypte but ther laye therin one that was deed. Thenne Pharao dyde do calle Moyses and Aaron in the nyght and said: 'Aryse ye and goo your waye fro my peple, ye and the chyldren of Israhel, as ye saye ye wyll. Take your sheep and beestis with you lyke as ye desyred, and at your departyng blesse ye me.' Th'Egypcyens constrayned the chyldren to departe and goo theyr waye hastely, sayeng: 'We all shalle deye.' The chyldren of Israhel toke thenne mele and put it on their sholdres as they were comanded, and borowed vessels of syluer and of gold and moche clothyng. Our Lord gaf to them suche fauour tofore th'Egypcyens that th'Egipcyens lente to them all þat they desyred, and spoylled and robbed Egypte.

A[n]d so the children of Israhel departed, nyhe the nombre of vj honderd thousand footmen besyde wymen and chyldren, whiche were innumerable, and an huge grete multytude of beestis of dyuerse kynde. The tyme that the chyldren of Israhel had dwellyd in Egypte was four honderd yere.

And so they departed out of Egypte and wente not the ryght way by the Philisteis, but Our Lord lad them by the way of deserte, whiche is by the Reed See. | And the chyldren descended out of Egipt armed. f. 58[ra] /
Moyses toke with hym the bones of Ioseph, for he charged them so to sig. [h]2
doo whan he deyde. They wente in th'extreme endes of the wyldernes, and Our Lord went[e] tofore them, by daye in a columpne of a clowde and by nyght in a columpne of fyre, and was theyr leder and duc. The pyler of the clowde faylled neuer by daye, ne the pyler of fyre by nyght tofore the peple.

Our Lord said to Moyses: 'I shal make his herte so hard that he shal folowe and pursyewe you, and I shal be gloryfyed in Pharao and in all his hoost. Th'Egipciens shal knowe that I am Lord.'

And anon it was told to Pharao that the chyldren of Israhel fledde, and anon his herte was chaunged and also the hertes of his seruauntes, and said: 'What shal we doo? Shal wc suffre the chyldren to deparrte and no more to serue vs?' Forthwith he toke his chare and alle his peple with hym. He toke with hym vjC chosen chares and all the

410 arose] areos 424 And] Aed 431 sig. h2] g ii 434 wente] wento

chares and waynes of Egipte and the dukes of all his hoostes, and he poursyewyd the chyldren of Israhel and folowed them in grete pryde. And whan he approched, that the chyldren of Israhel sawe hym come, they were sore aferd and cryed to Our Lord God, and said to Moyses: 'Was ther not sepulture ynough for vs in Egypt but that we must now deye in wyldernesse? Said not we to the: "Goo fro vs and late vs serue th'Egypcyens"? It had ben moche better for vs to haue seruyd th'Egypciens than to dye here in wyldernes.' And Moyses said to the peple: 'Be ye not aferd. Stande and see ye the grete wondres that Our Lord shal doo for you this daye. Th'Egypciens that ye now see, ye shal neuer see them after this daye. God shal fyght for you, and be ye stylle.' Our Lord said thenne to Moyses: 'What cryest thou to me? Saye to þe chyldren of Israhel that they goo forth. Take thou and reyse the rodde and stratche thy hande vpon the see and departe it, that the chyldren of Israhel may goo drye thurgh the myddle of it. I shal so indurate the herte of Pharao that he shal folowe you and alle th'Egypciens, and I shal be gloryfyed in Pharao and in alle his hoost, his cartes and horsmen. And th'Egypciens shal knowe that I am Lord whan I shal so be gloryfyed.'

f. 58rb The angel of God wente tofore the castellis of Israhel, and another cam after in the clowde, whiche stode bytwene them of Egypte and the chyldren of Israhel. And the clowde was derke, that þe hoost of Pharao myght not come to them of all the nyght.

Thenne Moyses stratched his hond vpon the see and ther cam a wynde blowyng in suche wyse that it waxe drye. And the chyldren of Israhel wente in thurgh the myddes of the Reed See alle drye-foot. For the waters stode vp as a walle on the ryght syde and on the lyft syde. Th'Egypciens thenne, poursyewyng them, folowed and entryd after them, and alle the cartes, chares and horsmen thurgh the myddle of the see. And thenne Our Lord behelde that the chyldren of Israhel were passyd ouer and were on the land on that other syde. Anon torned the water on them, and the wheles on theyr cartes torned vp-so-doun; and drouned all the hoost of Pharao, and sancke doun into the depe of the see. Thenne said th'Egypciens: 'Late vs flee Israhel; the Lord fightith for them ayenst vs.'

And Our Lord said to Moyses: 'Stratche out thyn hand vpon the see and lete the water retorne vpon th'Egypcyens, vpon theyr carres and horsmen.' And so Moyses stratched out his hand and the see retorned into his first place. And thenne th'Egypcyens wold haue fledde, but the water cam and ouerflowed them in the myddys of the flood. And it couerid the chares and horsmen and all th'oost of Pharao, and ther was not one sauyd of them. And the chyldren of Israhel had passyd thurgh the myddel of the drye see and cam alonde. Thus delyueryd Our Lord the chyldren of Israhel fro the hond of th'Egypcyens, and they sawe th'Egypcyens lyeng deed vpon the brynkes of the see. Alle the peple thenne dred Our Lord and byleuyd in hym, and to Moyses his seruaunt.

Thenne Moyses and þe children of Israhel songe this songe to Our Lord: *Cantemus domino*: *magnificatus est*: 'Late vs synge to Our Lord. He is magnefied; he hath ouerthrowen the horsmen and carre-men in the see.' And Marie the suster of Aaron, a prophetesse, toke a tympane in her hande, | and alle the wymen folowed her with tympanes and (f. 58va) cordes; and she wente tofore syngyng *Cantemus Domino*.

Thenne Moyses brought the chyldren of Israhel fro the see into the Deserte of Sur, and walked with them iij dayes and iij nyghtes and fonde no water, and cam into Marath, and the waters there were so bytter that they myght not drynke therof. Thenne the peple grutched ayenst Moyses, sayeng: 'What shal we drynke?' And he cryde vnto Our Lord, whiche shewd to hym a tre, whiche he toke and put into the water, and anon they were torned into swetnes. There Our Lord ordeyned comandementis and iugements. And ther he tempted hym, sayeng: 'Yf thou herest the voys of thy Lord God, and that thou doo that is rightful tofore hym and obeyest his comandements and kepe his preceptis, I shal not brynge none of the langours no sorowes vpon the that I dyde in Egypte. I am Lord thy sauyour.'

Thenne the chyldren of Israhel cam in to Helym, whereas were xij fontaynes of waters and lxx palme trees, and they abode by tho watres.

Thenne fro thens wente alle the multytude of the chyldren of Israhel into the Deserte of Syn, whiche is bytwene Helym and Synay, and grutched ayenst Moyses and Aaron in that wildernes and said: 'Wold God we had duellyd stylle in Egypte, whereas we satte and hath plente of brede and flesshe. Why haue ye brought vs into the deserte for to slee alle this multytude by hungre?' Our Lord said thenne to Moyses: 'I shal rayne brede to you fro heuen. Late the peple goo out and gadre euery day, that I may proue them whether they walke in my lawe or none. The sixte day late them gadre doble as moche as they gadred in one day of the other.' Thenne said Moyses and Aaron to all the chyldren of Israhel: 'At euyn ye shal knowe that

497 hande] hande | de

God hath brought you fro the londe of Egypte, and tomorn ye shal see þe glorye of Our Lord. I haue wel herd your murmour ayenst Our Lord. What haue ye mused ayenst vs? What be we?' And yet said Moyses: 'Our Lord shal gyue you at euen flesshe for to ete, and f. 58vb tomorn brede vnto your fylle, for as moche as ye | haue murmured ayenst hym: "What be we?" Your murmour is not ayenst vs but ayenst Our Lord.'

As Aaron spack to all the companye of the chyldren of Israhel, they beheld toward the wyldernes, and Our Lord spack to Moyses in a clowde, and said: 'I haue herd the grutchynges of the chyldren of Israhel. Saye to them: "At euen ye shal ete flessh and tomorn ye shal be fyllyd wyth brede, and ye shal knowe that I am your Lord God."' And whan the euen was come, ther cam so many curlews that it couerid all their lodgyngis. And on the morn ther laye lyke dewe all aboute in their circuyte, which whan they sawe and cam for to gadre it, was smal and white lyke to colyandre. And they wondred on it and said *Manhu*, that is as moche to saye: 'What is this?' To whom Moyses sayd: 'This is the brede that God hath sente you to ete, and God comandeth that euery man shold gadre as moche for euery heed as is the mesur of gomor. And late not[h]yng be left tyl on the morn. And the syxthe day gadre ye doble so moche, that is two mesures of gomor. And kepe that one mesure for the Sabate, whiche God hath sanctefyed and comandeth you to halowe it.' Yet somme of them brake Goddes comandement and gadred more than they ete and kept it tyl on the morn. And thenne it began to putrefye and be ful of wormes; and that they kept for the Sabate day was good and putrefyed not. And thus Our Lord fedde the chyldren of Israhel xl yere in deserte. And it was called manna. Moyses toke one gomor therof and put it in the tabernacle for to be kept for a perpetuel memorye and remembraunce.

Thenne wente they forth, alle the multytude of the chyldren of Israhel, in the deserte of Syn in her mansyons and cam in to Raphydym, whereas they had no water. Thenne, alle grutchyng, they said to Moyses: 'Gyue vs water for to drynke.' To whom Moyses answerd: 'What grutche ye ayenst me? Why tempte ye Our Lord?' The peple thirsted sore for lacke and penurye of water, sayeng: 'Why hast thou brought vs out of Egipte for to sle vs and our chyldren and f. 59[ra] / sig. h3 beestis?' Thenne Moyses cryde vnto Our Lord, sayeng: | 'What shal I doo to this peple? I trowe within a whyle they shal stone me to deth.'

543 nothyng] notyng

Thenne Our Lord said to Moyses: ‘Goo tofore the peple and take with the the oldremen and senyors of Israhel, and take the rodde that thou smotest with the flood in thy hand, and I shal stonde tofore vpon the stone of Oreb. And smyte thou the stone with the rodde, and the waters shal come out therof, that the peple may drynke.’ Moyses dyde so tofore the senyors of Israhel, and callyd that place Temptacion, bycause of the grutche of the chyldren of Israhel, and said: ‘Is God with vs or not?’

Thenne cam Amalech and fought ayenst the chyldren of Israhel in Raphidim. Moyses said thenne to Iosue: ‘Chese to the men and goo out and fyght ayenst Amalech tomorow. I shal stande on the toppe of the hylle, hauyng the rodde of God in my hand.’ Iosue dyde as Moyses comanded hym, and faught ayenst Amalech. Moyses, Aaron and Hur ascended into the hylle. Whan Moyses helde vp his handes, Israhel wan and ouercam their enemyes, and whan he leyd them doun, thenne Amalech had the better. The handes of Moyses were heuy; Aaron and Hur toke thenne a stone and put it vnder hem, and they susteyned his handes on eyther syde, and so his handes were not wery vnto the goyng doun of the sonne. And so Iosue made Amalech to flee, and his peple, by strength of his swerd.

Our Lord said to Moyses: ‘Wryte this for a remembraunce in a book, and delyure it to the eeris of Iosue: “I shal destroye and put awaye the memorye of Amalech vnder heuen.”’ Moyses thenne edefied an aulter vnto Our Lord, and callyd there on the name of Our Lord: ‘The Lord is myn exultacion’, sayeng: ‘For this is the hand only of God, and the batayll of God shal be ayenst Amalech fro generacion to generacion.’

Whan Ietro the prest of Madyan, whiche was cosyn of Moyses, herd saye what Our Lord had don to Moyses and to the chyldren of Israhel his peple, toke Sephora the wyf of Moyses and his ij sones Gersam and Elyazar, and cam with them to hym into deserte; whom Moyses receyuyd wyth worship and kyssyd hym. And whan they were togydre, Moyses told hym all what Our Lord had don to Pharao and to | th’Egypcyens for Israhel, and all the labour that they endured and f. 59rb how Our Lord had delyuered them. Ietro was glad for alle thise thynges that God had so sauyd them fro the handes of th’Egypciens, and said: ‘Blessid by the Lord that hath delyuerid you fro the hand of th’Egypcyens and of Pharao, and hath sauyd his peple. Now I know that he is a grete lord aboue all goddes, bycause they dyde so proudly ayenst them.’ And Ietro offred sacrefyces and offryngis to Our Lord.

Aaron and alle the senyors of Israhel cam and ete with hym [t]ofore Our Lord.

The next day Moyses satte and iuged and demed the peple fro mornyng vnto euenyng, whiche whan his cosyn sawe, he said to hym: 'What doost thou? Why sittest thou allone, and all the peple tarye fro the morn til euen?' To whom Moyses answerd: 'The peple come to me demaundyng sentence and the dome of God. Whan ther is ony debate or dyfference emonge them, they come to me to iuge them and to shewe to them the preceptes and lawes of God.' Thenne said Ietro: 'Thou dost not wel ne wysely, for by folye thou consumest thyself and the peple with the. Þou doost aboue thy myght. Thou maist not allone susteyne it. But here me and doo therafter, and Our Lord shal be with the. Be thou vnto the peple in tho thynges that apparteyne to God, þat thou telle to them what they shold do and the cerymonyes and ryte to worship God and the way by whiche they shold goo and what werk they shal doo. Poruyde of all the peple wyse men and dredyng God, in whom is trouth, and them that hate auaryce and couetyse, and ordeyne of them trybunes and centuriones and denes, that may in all tymes iuge the peple. And yf ther be of a grete charge and weight, late it be referrid to the; and late them iuge the smale thinges. It shal be the esyer to the to bere the charge whan it is so parted. Yf thou doo soo, thou shalt fulfylle the comandement of God and susteyne his preceptis, and the peple shall goo hom to theyr places in pees.' Which thynges whan Moyses had herde and vnderstonden, he dyde all that he had counceyllyd hym, and chase out þe strengest and wysest peple of all Israhel and ordeyned them prynces of the peple, tribunes, f. 59va centuriones, quinquagenaries | and denes, whiche at alle tymes sh[o]ld iuge and deme the peple. And alle the grete and weyghty maters they referryd to hym, demyng and iugyng the smale causes. And thenne his cosyn departed and wente into his contre.

The thirde moneth after the children departed out of Egypte, that same day they cam into the wyldernesse of Synay, and ther aboute the regyon of the mounte they fyxed theyr tentes. Moyses ascended into the hylle vnto God. God callid hym on the hylle and said: 'This shalt thou saye to the hows of Iacob and to the chyldren of Israhel: "Ye yourself haue seen what I haue don to the Egypciens, and how I haue born you on the whynges of egles and haue taken you to me. Yf ye therfor here my voys and kepe my couenaunt, ye shal be to me in the

602 tofore] so fore 629 shold] sheld

regne of preesthod and holy peple." Thyse ben the wordes that thou shalt saye to the chyldren of Israhel.'

Moyses cam doun and gadred all the most of byrthe, and expowned in them alle the wordes that Our Lord had comaunded hym. Alle the peple answerd: 'Alle that euer Our Lord hath said we shal doo.'

Whan Moyses had shewd to the peple the wordes of Our Lord, Our Lord said to hym: 'Now I shal come to the in a clowde, that the peple may here me spekyng to the, that they byleue the euer after.' Moyses wente and told this to the peple, and Our Lord bade them to sanctefye the peple this day and tomorow, 'and late them wesshe their clothes and be redy the thirde day. The thirde day Our Lord shal descende tofore all the peple on the Mount of Synay and ordeyne to the peple the markes and termes in the circuyte'; and said to them: 'Beware that ye ascende not on the hylle ne towche the endes of it. Whosomeuer towcheth the hylle shal dye by deth. Ther shal no hande towche hym, but with stones he shal be oppressid, and with castyng of them on hym he shal be to[sl]en; whether it be man or beest, he shal not lyue. Whan thou herest the trompe blowen, thenne ascende to the hylle.' Moyses wente doun to the peple and sanctefyed and halowed them, and whan they had wasshen herr clo|this, he said to them: 'Be ye redy f. 59vb
at the thirde daye, and approche not your wyues.'

Whan the thirde daye cam and the mornyng wexed clere, they herde thondre and lyghtnyng and saw a grete clowde coure the mounte. And the crye of the trompe was so shrylle that the peple was sore aferd. Whan Moyses had brouht them forth vnto the rote of the hylle, they stode there. All the mounte of Synay smoked, forsomoche as Our Lord descended on it in fyre. And the smoke ascended fro the hylle as it had be fro a fornays. The mount was terryble and dredeful, and the soun of the trompe grewe a lytyl more and contynued lenger. Moyses spack and Our Lord answerd hym. Our Lord descended vpon the toppe of the mounte of Synay, euen on the toppe of hit, and called Moyses to hym. Whiche whan he come, said to hym: 'Goo doun and charge the peple þat they come not to the termes of the hylle for to see the Lord, for yf they doo, moche multitude shal perisshe of them. The preestis that shal come, late them be sanctefyed, lest they be smeton doun. And thou and Aaron shal ascende the hylle; alle the peple and preestes, late them not passe

656 toslen] tolben

theyr boundes, leste God smyte them.' Thenne Moyses descended and told to the peple alle that Our Lord hath said.

After this Our Lord callyd Moyses and said: 'I am the Lord God that brought you out of Egypte and of thraldom', and gaf hym the comandementis, first by spekyng and many cerymonyes, as ben rehersed in the Byble, whiche is not requysyte to be wreton here, but the Ten Comandementes euery man is bounden to knowe. And er Moyses receyued them wreton, he wente vp into the mount of Synay and fasted there xl dayes and xl nyghtes er he receyuyd them. In whiche tyme he comanded hym to make many thynges and to ordeyne the lawes and cerymonyes, which now ben not had in the Newe Lawe. And also, as doctours saye, Moyses lerned that tyme all th'ystoryes tofore wreton of the makyng of heuen and erthe, of Adam, Noe, Abraham, Ysaac, Iacob and of Ioseph with his brethern. And atte laste
f. 60ra / sig. h4 delyueryd to hym | two tables of stone, bothe wreton with the honde of God, whiche folowen.

[7. TEN COMMANDMENTS]

Here folowen the Ten Comandemens of our lawe.

The first comandement that God comanded is this: thou shal not worshipe no straunge ne dyuerse goddes, that is to seye, thou shalt worshipe no god but me, and thou shalt not reteyne thyn hope but in me; for who that setteth pryncypally his hope on ony creature, or faith or byleue in onythyng more than in me, synneth dedly. And suche ben they that worshippe ydoles and make their god of a creature. Whosomeuer so doth synneth ayenst this comandement. And so doo they þat ouermoche loue their tresours, gold or syluer or ony other erthely thynge that ben passyng and transytorye, or sette their herte or hope on onythynge by whiche they forgete and leue God their creatour and maker, whiche hath lente to them alle that they lyue by. And therfor ought they to serue hym with al their goodes, and aboue alle thynge to loue hym and worshipe hym wyth all theyr herte, with alle their soule and with all their strengthe, lyke as the first comandement enseigneth and techeth vs.

The seconde comandement is this: that thou shalt not take the name of God in vayn; that is to saye, thou shalt not swere by hym for nothyng. In this comandement Our Lord comandeth in the Gospel

2 The] T *four-line capital supplied by hand in red*

that thou shalt not swere by the heuen, ne by erthe, ne by other cr[e]ature. But for good cause and rightful a man may swere without synne, as in iugement or in requyryng of trouthe or without iugement in good and nedful causes; and in none other maner without reson by the name of Our Lord and for nought. Yf he swere false wetyngly, he is forsworn, and that is ayenst the comandement and synneth dedely, for he swerith ayenst his conscience, and that is whan he swerith by auys and by delyberacion. But a man shold swere truly, and yet not for nought or for ony | vayn or ylle thynge ne malycyously. But to swere f. 60rb lyghtly, without hurte or blame, is venyal synne. But the custome therof is perylous and may wel torne to dedly synne, but yf he take hede. But he thenne that swereth horri[b]ly by Our Lord or by ony of his membris or by his sayntes in despyte, and blasphemeth in thynges that ben not trewe, or other wyse, he synneth dedely; he may haue no reson wherby he may excuse hym. And they that most accustome them in this synne, they synne most *etc.*

The thirde comandement is that thou shalt haue mynde and remembre that thou halowe and kepe holy thy Sabate day or Sonday. That is to saye, that thou shalt doo no werke ne operacion on the Sonday or holy daye, but þou shalt reste fro alle worldly labour and entende to prayer and to serue God thy maker, whiche restid the vij day of the werkes that he made in the vj dayes tofore, in whiche he made and ordeyned the world. This comandement accomplyssheth he þat kepeth to his power þe pees of his conscience, for to serue God more holyly. Thenne this day, that the Iewes called Sabate, is as moche to saye as 'reste'. This comandement may no man kepe spirituelly that is accombred in his conscience with dedely synne. Suche a conscience can not be in reste ne in pees as longe as he is in suche astate. In the stede of the Sabate day, which was straitly kept in the Olde Lawe, Holy Chirche hath stablysshid the Sonday in the Newe Lawe. For Our Lord aroos fro deth to lyf on þe Sonday, and therfore we ought to kepe it holyly and be in reste fro the werkes of þe weke tofore and to cesse of the werke of synne and t'entende to doo ghoostly werkes and to folowe Our Lord, besechyng hym of mercy and to thancke hym for his benefaites. For they that breke the Sonday and the other solempne festes that ben stablysshed to be halowed in Holy Chir[c]he, they synne dedly, for they do dyrectly ayenst the comandement of God aforsaid and Holy Chyrche, but yf it be for

21 creature] crature 26 and] & \ & 31 horribly] horri \ ly 56 Chirche] chirhe

somme necessite that Holy Chirche amytteth and graunteth. But they synne moche more thenne þat employe the Sondayes and the festes | f. 60va in synnes, in lecherye, in goyng to tauernes in the seruyse tyme, in gloutonye and drynkyng dronke and in other synnes, oultrages ayenst God. For alas for sorowe, I trowe ther is more synne commysed on the Sonday and holy dayes and festes than in the other werke-dayes. For thenne ben they dronke, fyghte and slee, and ben not ocupyed vertuously in Goddes seruyce as they ought to doo; and as God comandeth vs to remembre and haue in mynde to kepe and halowe the holy day, they that so doo synne dedely and obserue and kepe not this third comandement. Thyse thre comandementes ben wreton in the first table and apparteynen only to God.

The fourth comandement is that thou shalt honoure and worshippe thy fader and moder, for thou shalt lyue the lenger on th'erthe. This comandement admonesteth vs that we be wel ware to angre fader and moder in ony wyse; or who that curseth them or sette hande on them in euyl wylle synneth dedely. In this comandement is vnderstanden th'onour that we shold doo to our goostly and spirytuel faders, that is to them that haue the cure of vs to teche and chastyse vs, as ben the prelates of the chirche and they that haue the charge and cure of our sowles and to kepe our bodyes. And he that wil not obeye to hym that hath the cure ouer hym whan he enseigneth and techeth hym good that he is bound to doo, he synneth greuously and is inobedyent, whiche is dedely synne.

The fyfthe comandement is that thou shal slee no man. This comandement wil that no man shal slee other for v[e]ngeance, ne for his goodes or for ony other euyl cause; it is dedely synne. But for to slee malefactours in executyng of iustice for other good cause, yf it be lawful, it may wel be doon. In this comandement is defended the synne of wrath and hate, of rauncour and of yre. For, as the Scripture saith, who hateth his brother is an homycide whan it is by his wylle, and he sinneth dedely, and he that bereth angre in his herte longe; for f. 60vb suche ire longe holden in the herte is rauncour and hate, which | is dedly synne and is ayenst this comandement. And yet synneth he more that doth or pourchaceth shame, vylonye or hurte to another wrongfully, or counseylleth or helpeth to greue another for t'auenge hym. But wrath or angre lyghtly passed without wyll to noye or greue ony other is not dedly synne.

83 vengeance] vngeance

The sixthe comandement is thou shalt not doo aduoultrye, that is to saye thou shall not haue flesshly companye with another mannes wyf. In this comandement it is forboden and defended all maner synne of the flesshe, which is called generally lecherye, whiche is a right fowle synne and vylaynous, howbeit that ther is somme braunche of it that is not dedly synne, as ofte meuynges of the flesshe that may not be eschewed, whiche men oughte to restrayne and refrayne as moche as they maye. And this cometh oftetymes by outrageous drynkyng and etynge, or by euyl thought or foule touchyng. For in suche thynges may be grete peryll. And in this comandement is defended alle synne ayenst nature, in what maner it be don, in his persone or other.

The seuenth comandement is that thou shal do no thefte. This comandement forbedeth to take away other mennes thynges, whatsomeuer they bee, without reson ayenst the wyll of them that owe or make them. In this comandement is defended rauayne, vsure, robberye and deceyte, and begylyng other for to haue theyr hauoyr or good. And he that doth ayenst this comandement is bounden to make restitucion and yeld agayn that he hath so goten or taken, yf he knowe to whom he ought to rendre it. And yf he knowe not, he is bounden to gyue it for Goddes sake or doo by the counseyl of Holy Chirch. For who reteyneth wrongfully and without reson other mennes good agayn theyr wyll synneth dedely, yf he paye not whereas he oweth, yf he knowe where and be in his power and hath wherof. And yf he knowe not, late hym doo by the counseyl of Holy Chirche. And whoso doth not so synneth ayenst this comandement dedely.

The viij comandement is that thou | shalt not bere false witnesse f. 61ra / sig. [h5] ayenst thy neyghbour. In this comandement is forboden that no man shall lye wetyngly, for whoso lyeth doth ayenst this comandement. And also that he forswere not hym in iugement ne make no lesynges to noye ne greue another; ner he ought not to myssaye ne speke euyl of other in entencion t'enpayre his good name and fame, for it is dedly synne. Ayenst this comandement do they that saye euyl of good men behynde them and bacbyte them, and do this wetyngly by malyce, whiche is called detraction. And also they that accuse somme of theyr folye, or herkene, by maner of adulacion or flateryng, whan they that men speke of be not present; they that doo thus and saye suche wordes doo ayenst this comandement, for they be all false witnessis.

The nyne comandement is that thou shalt not desyre the wyf of thy

98 comandement] comādemnēt

neyghbour, ne shalt not coueyte her in thyn herte; that is to saye, thou shalt not consente to synne with her with thy body. This comandement defendeth to desyre to haue companye with all maner wymen out of maryage. And the euyl sygnes that ben without-forth make men for to drawe them to synne, as the euyl wordes of suche matere or the foule and euyl attouchyng, kyssyng, handlynge and suche other. And the dyfference bytwene this comandement and the syxthe aforsaid is that the syxthe comandement forbedeth the dede wythout-forth; and this forbedeth the consentyng within-forth. For the consentyng within-forth to haue companye with a woman that is not his by maryage is dedely synne, after the sentence of the Gospel that saith: 'Who that seeth a woman and coueyteth her in his herte, he hath now synne[d] in his herte and dedly.' This is to vnderstonde of the consentyng e[x]presse in his thought.

The tenth comandement is that thou shalt not coueyte nothyng that is or longeth to thy neyghbour. This comandement defendeth wylle to haue thynges that longe to other men by euyll rayson or wrongfully.
f. 61rb In this comandement is defended enuye of other mennes | wele, of other mennes grace or welfare. For suche enuye cometh of euyl couetyse to haue suche good or suche grace or fortune as he seeth in other. And this couetyse is whan the consentyng and thoughte be certaynly one; thenne is it dedly synne. And yf ther be ony ylle mouynges without wyll and consentyng of damage or hurte of other, this is not dedly synne. Yf he synne herin, it is but venyel synne.

Thyse ben þe Ten Com[an]dement[s] of Our Lord, of whiche the iij first belonge to God, and the vij other ben ordeyned for our neyghbours. Euery persone that hath witte and vnderstandyng in hymself and age is bounde to knowe them and t'obeye and kepe thise ten comandemens aforsaid, or ellis he synneth dedly.

Thus Moyses abode in the hill xl dayes and xl nyghtes, and receyued of Almyghty God the tables with the comandements wreton with the hond of God, and also receyued and lerned many cerymonyes and statutes that God ordeyned, by whiche the children of Israhel shold be reuled and iuged by. And whiles that Moyses was thus with Our Lord on the mounte, the children of Israhel sawe that he taried and descended not, and somme of them said that he was dede or goon away and wold not retorne agayn. And somme said nay, but in conclusion they gadred them togydre ayenst Aaron and said to

146 synned] synneth   147 expresse] eypresse   151 comandement] comande \ demēt   153 couetyse] couety \ tyse   158 Comandements] co \ mdement

hym: 'Make to vs somme goddes that may goo tofore vs. We knowe not what is befallen to Moyses.' Thenne Aaron saide: 'Take the gold that hangeth in the eeris of your wyues and your chyldren and brynge it to me.' The peple dyde as he bad and brought the gold to Aaron, whiche he toke and molte it, and made therof a calf. Thenne they sayd: 'Thyse ben thy goddes, Israhel, that brought the out of the londe of E[g]ypte.' And the peple made an aulter tofore it, and made grete ioye and myrthe, and ete and dronke and daunced and pleyed tofore the calf, and offrid and made sacrefises therto.

Our Lord spack to Moyses, sayeng: 'Goo hens and descend doun. Thy peple haue synned, whom thou hast brought fro the lond of Egypte. They haue sone | forsake and lefte the waye which thou hast f. 61va shewd to them. They haue made to them a calf blowen and haue worshyped it and offred sacrefyses therto, sayeng: 'Thise be thy goddes, Israhel, that haue brought the out of the londe of Egypte.' Yet sayd Our Lord to Moyses: 'I see wel that this peple is of euyl disposicion. Suffre me that I may wreke my wrath on them, and I shal destroye them. I shal make the gouernour of grete peple.' Moyses thenne prayd Our Lord God, sayeng: 'Why art thou wroth, Lord, ayenst thy peple that thou hast brought out of the londe of Egypte in a grete strengthe and a boystous hande? I beseche the, Lord, late not th'Egypcyens saye that their god hath locked them out for to slee them in the montayns. I praye the, Lord, that thy wrath may aswage, and be thou pleysid and benygne vpon the wickednes of thy peple. Remembre Abraham, Ysaac and Iacob thy seruauntes, to whom thou promysyst and swarest by thyself, sayeng: "I shal multeplye your seed as the sterres of heuen, and the vnyuersal londe of whiche I haue spoken I shal gyue to your seed, and ye shal possede and haue it euer."' And with thise wordes Our Lord was pleased, that he wold do no h{a}rme, as he had said, vnto his peple.

And Moyses retorned fro the mount beryng two tables of stone, wreton both with the hande of God. And the scripture that was in the tables were the Ten Comandementis as fore be wreton.

Iosue, heering the grete noyse of the chyldren of Israhel, said to Moyses: 'I trowe they fyght benethe.' Whiche answerd and said: 'It is no crye of exortyng men to fyght, ne noyse to compelle men to flee, but I here the voys of syngyng.' Whan he approc{he}d to them, he sawe the calf and the instrumentis of myrthe. And he was so wroth

178 Egypte] Eypte

that he threwe doun the tables and brake them atte fote of the hylle, and ran and raught doun the calf that they had made and brente and smote it al to pouldre, whiche he caste into water and gaf it to drynke to the chyldren of Israhel. Thenne said Moyses to Aaron: 'What hath this peple don to þe that thou hast made to synne greuously?' To f. 61vb whom | he answerd: 'Late not my lord take none indignacion at me. Thou knowest wel that this peple is prone and redy to synne. They said to me: "Make to vs goddes that may goo tofore vs. We knowe not what is fallen to this Moyses that lad vs out of Egypte." To whom I said: "Who of you that hath gold geue it me." They toke and gaf it to me, and I caste it into the fire, and therof cam out this calf.'

And thenne said Moises: 'Alle they that ben of Goddis parte and haue not synned in this calf, late hem ioyne to me', and the chyldren of Leui ioyned to hym; and bade eche man take a swerd on his side and take vengeance and slee euerych his brother, his frende and neygbour that haue trespaced. And so the chyldren of Leui wente and slewe xxxiijM of the children of Israhel. And thenne said Moyses: 'Ye haue halowed this day your handes vnto Our Lord, and ye shal be therfore blessyd.'

The second day, Moyses spack to the peple and said: 'Ye haue commysed and don the grettest synne that may be. I shal ascende vnto Our Lord agayn and shal praye hym for your synne.' Thenne Moyses ascended agayn and receyuyd afterward two tables agayn, whiche Our Lord bad hym make. And therin Our Lord wrote the comandements. And after, Our Lord comanded hym to make an arke and a tabernacle, in whiche arke was kepte thre thinges: first the rodde, with whiche he dide meruaillis, a potte ful of manna and the ij tables with the comandementis. And thenne after, Moyses taught hem the lawe, how eche man shold behaue hym ayenst other and what he shold doo and what he shold not doo, and departed them in xij tribus, and comanded that euery man shold brynge a rodde into the tabernacle. And Moyses wrote eche name on the rodde; and Moyses shytte fast the tabernacle. And on the morn ther was founde one of the roddes that burgeyned, bare leuys and fruyt, and was of [a]n almonde tree. That rodde fyl to Aaron.

And after thys longe tyme the chyldren desireden to ete flesshe and f. 62ra / sig. [h6] remembrid of the flesshe | that they ete in Egypte, and grudchyd agayn Moyses, and wold haue ordeyned to them a duc for to haue

243 an] on

retorned into Egypte. Wherfore Moyses was so woo that he desired of Our Lord to delyure hym fro this lyf, bycause he sawe them so vnkynde ayenst God. Thenne God sente to them so grete plente of curlews that two dayes and one nyght they flewe so thycke by the ground that they toke g[r]ete nombre, for they flewhe but the hey[gh]t of two cubytes; and they had so many that they dreyde hem, hangyng on their tabernacles and tentes. Yet were they not content, but euer grutchyng. Wherfore God smote them and toke vengeaunce on hem by a grete plaghe, and many deyde and were buryed there. And thenne fro thens they wente into Aseroth and dwellyd.

After this Maria and Aaron, brother and suster of Moyses, began to speke agayn Moyses bycause of his wif, whiche was of Ethyope, and said: 'God hath not spoken only by Moyses: hath he not also spoken to vs?' Wherfore Our Lord was wroth. Moyses was the humblest and mekest man that was in all the world.

Anone thenne Our Lord said to hym and to Aaron and to Marye: 'Goo ye thre only vnto the tabernacle.' And there Our Lord said that ther was none lyke to Moyses, to whom he had spoken mouth to mouth, and repreuyd Aaron and Maria bycause they spack so to Moyses, and beyng wroth departed fro them. And anone Maria was smeton and made lepre and whyte lyke snowe. And whan Aaron behelde her and sawe her smeton with lepre, he said to Moyses: 'I beseche the, lord, that thou sette not this synne on vs whiche we haue commysed folyly, and late not this our suster be as a deed woman or as born out of tyme and caste away from her moder. Beholde and see, half her flesshe is deuoured of the lepre.' Thenne Moyses cryed vnto Our Lord, sayeng: 'I beseche the Lord that thou hele her.' To whom Our Lord said: 'Yf her fader had spytte in her face, shold she not be put to shame and rebuke vij dayes? Late her departe out of þe castellis vij dayes, and after she shal be callyd | in agayn.' So Maria was shytte f. 62rb
out of the castellis vij dayes, and the peple remeuyd not fro the place tyl she was callyd agayn.

After this Our Lord commanded Moyses to sende men into the londe of Canaan, that he shold gyue them charge for [to] see and considere the goodnes therof, and that of euery trybe he shold sende somme. Moyses dyde soo as Our Lord had comaunded. Whiche wente in and brought of the fruytes wyth hem, and they brought a braunche with one clustre of grapes as moche as two men myght bere

252 grete] gete heyght] heyhgt 281 to] *om.*

bytwene them vpon a colestaf. Whan they had seen the contre and consydered by the space of xl dayes, thei retorned and tolde the commodytees of the londe. But somme said that the peple were stronge, and many kynges and gyauntes, in suche wyse that they said it was inprenable, and that the peple were moche strenger than they were. Wherfore the peple anon were aferde and murmured agayn Moyses and wold retorne agayn into Egypte.

Thenne Iosue and Chaleph, whiche were two of them that had consydered the londe, said to the peple: 'Why grutche ye? And wherof be ye aferd? We haue wel seen the contrey, and it is good to wynne. The contrey floweth ful of mylke and hony. Be not rebelle ayenst God; he shal gyue it vs. Be ye not aferd.' Thenne alle the peple cryed ayenst hem. And whan they wold haue taken stones and stoned hem, Our Lord in his glorye apperyd in a clowde vpon the coueryng of the tabernacle and said to Moyses: 'Thys peple byleueth not the sygnes and wondres that I haue shewd and don to hem. I shal destroye them alle by pestylence. And I shal make the a prynce vpon peple gretter and strenger than this is.' Thenne prayd Moyses to Our Lord for the peple, that he wold haue pyte on them and not destroye them, but to haue mercy on them after the magnytude of his mercy. And Our Lord at his request forgaf them. Neuertheles Our Lord said that all tho men that had seen his mageste and the sygnes and meruaylles that he dyde in Egypte and in deserte, and haue tempted hym ten tymes and not obeyed vnto his voys, 'shal not see | [f. 62va] ne come into the contrey and londe that I haue promysed to theyr faders. But Iosue and Caleph, my seruantes, shal entre into the londe, and theyr seed shal possesse it.' Moyses told all this vnto the chyldren, and they waylled and sorowed gretly therfor.

After this the peple remeuyd fro thens and cam into the Deserte of Syn. And there Maria, suster of Moyses and Aaron, deyde and was buryed in the same place.

Thenne the peple lacked water and cam and grutched ayenst Moyses and yet wesshed they had abyden in Egypte. Thenne Moyses and Aaron entryd into the tabernacle and fylle doun to the ground lowe and prayd vnto Our Lord, seyeng: 'Lord God, here the clamour of thy peple, and opene to them thy tresour, a fontayn of lyuyng water, that they may drynke and the murmuracion of them may cesse.'

Our Lord said to hym thenne: 'Take the rodde in thy hande, and thou and Aaron thy brother assemble and gadre the peple, and speke ye to the stone and it shal gyue out water. And whan the water cometh, late alle the multytude drynke, and theyr beestis.’ Moyses thenne toke the rodde as Our Lord badde, and gadred all the peple tofore the stone and said to them: ‘Here ye rebelles and out of byleue. Trow ye not that we may gyue you watre out of this stone?’ And he lefte vp his hand and smote twyes the stone, and water cam and flowed out in the most largest wyse, in suche wyse that the peple and beestis dronke theyr fylle.

Thenne said God to Moyses and Aaron: ‘Bycause ye haue not byleuyd me and sanctefyed my name tofore the chyldren of Israhel and gyuen to me the laude, but haue don this in your name, ye shal not brynge this peple into the londe that I shal gyue to them.’ And therfor this water was callyd the water of contradiction, where the chyldren grutched agayn God.

Anon after this, by Goddes comandement Moyses toke Aaron vpon the hylle and despoylled of his vesture, and clothid therwith his sone Eleazar and made hym vpperist bysshop for his fader Aaron. And there Aaron deyde in the | toppe of the hylle. And Moyses descended f. 62vb
with Eleazar. And whan alle the multytude of peple sawe that Aaron was deed, they wepte and waylled on hym xxx dayes in euery trybe and famylye.

After this the peple wente aboute the londe of Edom, and began to wexe wery and grutchyd ay{e}nst Our Lord and Moyses, and sayd yet: ‘Why hast thou ledde vs out of the lond of Egypte for to slee vs in this deserte and wildernes? Breed failleth vs, ther is no water, and our sowles abhorre and lothe this light mete.’ For whiche cause God sente emonge them fyry serpentes, whiche bote and wounded many of them and slewe also. Thenne they that were hurte cam to Moyses and said: ‘We haue synned, for we haue spoken ayenst Our Lord and the. Praye for vs vnto God that he delyuer fro vs thise serpentes.’ Thenne Moyses prayd Our Lord for the peple, and Our Lord said to hym: ‘Make a serpente of brasse and sette it vp for a signe. And whosomeuer be hurte, and loketh theron and beholdeth it, shal lyue and be hole.’ Thenne Moyses made a serpente of brasse and sette it vp for a sygne. And whan they that were hurte beheld it, were made hole.

After this, whan Moyses had shewid to them all the lawes of Our Lord and cerymonyes, and had gouerned them xl yere and that he was an C xx yere old, he ascended fro the feldes of Moab vpon the montayn of Nebo into the toppe of Phasga ayenst Ierico, and there Our Lord shewd to hym alle the londe of Galaad vnto Dan, and all the londe of promyssyon fro that one ende to that other. And thenne Our Lord sayd to hym: 'This is the land that I promysed to Abraham, Ysaac and Iacob, sayeng: "I shal gyue it to thy seed." Now thou hast seen it with thyn eyen, and shalt not entre ne come therin.'

And there in that place deyede Moyses, seruaunt of Our Lord, as God comanded, and was buryed in the vale of the londe of Moab ayenst Phogor. And yet neuer man knewe his sepulcre vnto this day. Moyses was an honderd and twenty yere old whan he deyde; his eyen neuer dimmed ne his teeth were neuer meuyd. | [f. 63ra / sig. [h7]] The chyldren of Irahel wepte and morned for hym xxx dayes in the feldes of Moab. Iosue, the sone of Num, was replenessyd with the spyrite of wisdom, for Moyses sette on hym his handes. And the chyldren obeyed hym, as Our Lord had comanded to Moyses. And ther was neuer after a prophete in Israhel lyke vnto Moyses, whiche knewe and spack to God face to face, in alle signes and tokenes that God dyde and shewd by hym in the londe of Egypte to Pharao and alle hys seruauntes.

Here endeth the lyf and th'ystorye of Moyses.

[8. JOSHUA]

After Moyses, Iosue was duc and ledar of the chyldren of Israhel and brought them into the londe of beheste, and dyde many grete batayllis; for whom God shewd many grete meruayllys, and in especyal one that was that the sonne stode stylle at his request tyl he had ouercome his enemyes by the space of a day. And Our Lord, whan he faught, sent doun suche haylstones, that slewe moo of his enemyes wyth tho stones than wyth mannes hond.

Iosue was a noble man and gouerned wel Israhel, and deuyded the londe vnto the xij trybus by lotte. And whan he was C x yere old he deyde. And dyuerse dukes after hym iuged and demed Israhel, of whom ben noble hystoryes, as of Iepte, Gedeon and Sampson, whiche I passe ouer vnto th'ystoryes of the kynges, whiche is redde in Holy Chyrche fro the fyrst Sonday after Trynyte Sonday vnto the first Sonday of August. And in the moneth of August is redde the Book of Sapience. And in the moneth of Septembre ben redde th'ystoryes of Iob, of Thobye and of Iudi[t]h; and in Octobre the hystorye of the Machabeis, and in Nouembre the book of Ezechiel and his visions,

374 f. 63] *a stray type* i *a little apart after* folio lxiij C+, *no stray type* CcHM$_1$
1 After] A *four-line capital supplied by hand in red* 16 Iudith] Iudich

and in Decembre the hystorye of Aduent and the book of Ysaye vnto Crystemasse; and after the fest of Epyphanye | f. 63rb vnto Septuagesme ben red th'Epistles of Paule. And this is the rewle of the Temporal thurgh the yere *etc*.

[9. SAUL]

The first Sonday after Trynyte Sonday vnto the first Sonday of the moneth of August [i]s redde the Book of Kynges.

This hystorye maketh mencion that ther was a man named Helcana, whiche had two wyues. That one was named Anna, and the name of the seconde Fenenna. Fenenne had chyldren; and Anna had none, but was bareyn.

The good man, at suche dayes as he was bounden, wente to his cyte for to make hys sacrefyse and worshipe God. In this tyme Ophny and Phynees, sones of Hely the grete preest, were preestes of Our Lord. This Helcana gaf to Fenenna, at suche tyme as he offred, to her sones and doughters certayn partes, and vnto Anna he gaf but one parte. Fenenne dyde moche sorow and repreef to Anna bycause she | f. 63va had no chyldren, and thus dyde euery yere and prouoked her to wrath; but she wepte for sorow and ete no mete. To whom Helcana her husbond said: 'Anna, why wepest thou and wherfor etest thou not? Why is thyn herte put to afflyction? Am I not better to the than ten sones?'

Thenne Anna aroose after she had eten and dronken in Sylo and wente to praye vnto Our Lord. Hely that tyme satte tofore the postes of the hows of Our Lord. And Anna besought and prayd Our Lord, makyng to hym a vowe, yf that she myght haue a sone, she shold offre hym to Our Lord.

And it was so that she prayd so hertely in her thought and mynde that her lyppes meuyd not. Wherfor Hely bare her an hand that she was dronke. And she said: 'Nay, my lord, I am a synful woman. I haue dronken no wyn ne drynke that may cause me to be dronken, but I haue made my prayers and cast my sowle in the sight of Almyghty God. Repute me not as one of the doughters of Belial, for the prayer that I haue made and spoken yet is of the multytude of the heuynes and sorow of my herte.' Thenne Hely the preest said to her: 'Goo in pees. The God of Israhel gyue to the the peticion of thy herte, for that thou hast prayd hym.' And she said: 'Wold God that thy hand-

2 is] CcHM$_1$, s C+ 3 This] T *six-line capital supplied by hand in red*

seruaunt myght fynde that grace in thy syght.' And so she departed. And on the morn they wente home agayn into Ramatha.

After this Our Lord remembryd her, and H[e]lcana knewe her and she conceyuyd, and at tyme acustomed brought forth and bare a fair sone and named hym Samuel, for so moche as she axed hym of Our Lord. Wherfor Helcana her husbond wente and offred a solompne sacrefyce and his vowe acomplysshyd, but Anna ascended not with hym. She said to her husbond that she wold not goo tyl her chyld were wened and taken fro the pappe.

And after, whan Samuel was wened and was an infaunt, the moder toke hym and iij caluys and iij mesures of mele and a botel of wyn and brought hym vnto the hows of Our Lord in Sylo, and sacrefyed that f. 63[vb] calf and offred the chylde to Hely, and told to Hely| that she was the woman that prayd Our Lord for that chyld. And there Anna worshyppid Our Lord and thankyd hym; and ther made this psalme, which is one of the canticles, *Exultauit cor meum in Domino et exaltatum est cornu meum in Deo meo* and so forth, all the remenaunt of that psalme. And thenne Helcana with his wif retorned home to his hows. After this Our Lord vysyted Anna and she conceyuyd iij sones and two doughters, whiche she brought forth. And Samuel abode in the hows of Our Lord and was mynyster in the syght of Hely.

But the two sones of Hely, Ophny and Phynees, were chyldren of Belyal, not knowyng Our Lord, but dyde grete synnes ayenst the comandementis of God. And Our Lord sente a prophete to Hely because he corrected not his sones, and said he wold take th'office from hym and from his hows, and that ther shold not be an old man in his hows and kynrede but shold dye er they cam to mannes estate, and that God shold reyse a preest that shold be faithful and after his herte.

Samuel seruyd and mynystred Our Lord in a surplys tofore Hely. And on a tyme as Hely laye in his bedde, his eyen were so dymmed that he myght not see the lanterne of God til it was quenchyd and put out; Samuel slepte in the temple of Our Lord, whereas þe arke of God was. And Our Lord callyd Samuel, whiche answerd: 'I am redy', and ran to Hely and said: 'I am here redy; thou caldest me.' Whiche said: 'I callyd the not my sone; retorne and slepe.' And he retorned and slept.

And Our Lord callid hym the second tyme, and he aroos and wente to Hely and said: 'Lo, I am here; thou calledest me.' Whiche answerd:

34 Helcana] CcChHLM_1, Hlcana C+

'I callid the not; go thy waye and slepe.' Samuel knewe not the callyng of Our Lord yet, ne ther was neuer reuelacion shewd to hym tofore.

And Our Lord callid Samuel the thirde tyme, whiche aroos and cam to Hely and said: 'I am here; for thou calledest me.' Thenne Hely vnderstode that Our Lord had callyd hym, and said to Samuel: 'Goo and slepe. And yf thou be callid agayn, thou shalt saye: "Speke Lord, for thy seruaunt hereth the."' | Samuel retorned and slepte in his place. f. 64ra / sig. [h8]

And Our Lord cam and callid hym: 'Samuel, Samuel!' And Samuel said: 'Saye Lord what it pleseth, for thy seruaunt hereth.' And thenne Our Lord said to Samuel: 'Loo, I make my word to be knowen in Israhel, that whoso hereth, his eeris shal rynge and sowne therof. In that day I shal reyse agayn Hely. All that I haue said opon his hows, I shal begynne and accomplyssh hit. I haue gyue hym in knowleche that I shal iuge his hous for wyckednes, for as moche as he knoweth his sones to doo wickedly and hath not corrected them. Therfor I haue sworn to the hows of Hely that the wickednes of his hows shal not be made clene with sacrefyses ne yeftes neuer.'

Samuel slepte tyl on the morn. And thenne he roos and opend the dores of the hous of Our Lord in his surplis. And Samuel was aferd to shewe this vysyon vnto Hely. Hely callyd hym and axid what Our Lord hath said to hym and chargyd hym to telle hym alle. And Samuel told to hym all that Our Lord hath said, and hyd nothyng from hym. And he said: 'He is Our Lord; what it plesith hym late hym doo.'

Samuel grewe, and Our Lord was with hym in all his werkis. And it was knowen to all Israhel fro Dan to Bersabee that Samuel was the trewe prophete of Our Lord.

After this it was so that the Philisteis warryd ayenst the chyldren of Israhel, agayn whom ther was a batayll, and the chyldren of Israhel ouerthrowen and put to flyght. Wherfor they assemblyd agayn and toke with them the arke of God, whiche Ophny and Phynees, sones of Hely, bare. And whan they cam with a grete multytude wyth the arke, the Philisteis were aferd. Notwythstondyng, they faught ayenst them manly and slew xxxM fotemen of the chyldren of Israhel and token the arke of God, and the two sones of Hely were slayn, Ophny and Phynees.

And a man of the tribe of Beniamyn ran for to telle this vnto Hely, whyche satte abydyng somme tydynges of the batayll. This man, as sone as he entrid into the toun, told how the feld was lost, the peple

f. 64rb slayn and how the arke was taken. And ther was | a grete sorow and crye.

And whan Hely herd thys crye and wayllyng, he demanded what this noyse was and mened, and wherfor they so sorowed. Thenne the man hyed and cam and told to Hely. Hely was at that tyde lxxxxviij yere old and his eyen were woxen blynde and myght not see. And he said: 'I am he that cam fro the batayll and fledde this daye fro th'oost.' To whom Hely said: 'What is ther don, my sone?' He answerd: 'The hoost of Irahel is ouerthrowen and fledde tofore the Phylisteis, and a grete ruyne is made emong the peple. Thy two sones ben slayn and the arke of God is taken.' And whan Hely herd hym name the arke of God, he fylle doun backward by the dore and brake his necke and there deyde. He was an old man and had iuged Israhel xl yere.

Thenne the Philisteis toke þe arke of God and sette it in their temple of Dagon, by theyr god Dagon in Azote. On the morn the next day erly whan they of Azote cam into their temple, they sawe theyr god Dagon laye on the ground tofore the arke of God vpon his face. And the heed and the two handes of Dagon were cutte of, and there abode no more but the tronke only in the place.

And God shewed many vengeances to them of the contre as longe as the arke was with hem. For God smote them with sekenesses in their secrete partyes, and wellis boylled in townes and feldes of that regyon, and ther grewe emong them so many myes that they suffred grete persecucion and confusyon in that cyte. The peple, seeyng this vengeance and plaghe, sayde: 'Late not the arke of the God of Israhel abyde lenger with vs, for his hond is hard on vs and on Dagon our god'; and sente for the grete maistres and gouernours of the Philisteis. And whan they were gadred, they said: 'What shal we doo with the arke of the God of Israhel?' And they answerd: 'Late it be ladde alle aboute the cytees.' And so it was, and a grete vengeance and deth was had vpon all the cytees and smote euery man with plaghe fro the most to the leste, in suche wyse that the nether partes of them putrefyed
f. 64va and roted of them, and that they | made to them setes of furres and skynnes to sytte softe.

And thenne they sente the arke of God into Acharon. And whan they of Acharon sawe the arke, they cryed, sayeng: 'They haue brought the arke of the God of Israhel to vs for to slee vs and our peple.' They cryed that the arke shold be sente home agayn; for moche peple were deed by the vengeaunce that was taken on them in their secrete partyes, and a grete howlyng and wayllyng was emong them.

The arke was in the regyon of the Phylysteis seuen monethes. After this they counceyllid with their preestis what they shold doo with the arke, and it was concluded it shold be sente home agayn, but the prestes said: 'Yf ye sende it home, sende it not uoyde, but what ye owe paye for your trespaas and synne, and thenne ye shal be heled and cured of your seknessis.' And so they ordeyned, after the nombre of the fyue prouyncis of the Philisteis, fyue pieces of gold and fyue myes of gold, and lad to a wayne and 'putte in it two wylde kyen which neuer bere yoke, and leue their calues at home, and take the arke and sette it on the wayn and also the vessels and peces of gold that ye haue payd for your trespaas, sette them at the syde of the arke and late them goo wher they will'. And thus they sente the arke of God vnto the chyldren of Israhel.

Samuel thenne gouernyd Israhel longe, and whan he was old, he sette his sones Iuges on Israhel, whos names were Iohel and Abya. And thyse two his sones walked not in hys wayes, but declyned after couetyse and toke yeftes and peruerted iustyse and dome. Thenne assemblyd and gadred togydre all the grettest of byrthe of the chyldren of Israhel and cam to Samuel and said: 'Loo, thou art old and thy sones walke not in thy weyes. Wherfor ordeyne to vs a kynge that may iuge and reule vs, lyke as all other nacions haue.' This displesid moche to Samuel whan they said: 'Ordeyne on vs a kynge.' Thenne Samuel counseylled on this mater with Our Lord. To whom God saide: 'Here the voys of the peple that speke to the. They haue not caste only the away but me, that I shold not regne on them. For they doo | now lyke as they euer haue don sith I brought them out of [f. 64vb] Egypte vnto this day; that is that they haue seruyd false goddes and straunge, and so doo they to the. Notwithstondyng, here them and telle to them tofore the right of the kynge and how he shal oppresse them.'

Samuel told all this to the peple that demaunded to haue a kyng, and said: 'This shal be the right of a kyng that shal regne on you. He shal take your sones and make them his men of warre and sette them in his carris, and shal make them his carters and ryders of his hors in his chares and cartes, and shal ordeyne of them trybunes and centuryons, erers and tylyers of his feldes and mowars and repers of his corn, and he shal make them smythes and armorers of harnoys and carres. And he shal also take your doughters and make them his vnguentaryes and redy at his will and playsir. He shal also take fro you your feldes and vyneyerdes and the beste olyues and gyue them to his seruauntes. And he shal taske and dyme your corn and sheues, and the rentes of your vynyerdes he shal value for to gyue to his offycers and seruauntis, and shal take fro you your seruauntes, bothe men and wymen, and sette them to his werkis. And your asses and beestis he also shal take to his labour; your flockes of sheep he shal taske and take the tenthe or what shal plese hym. And ye shal be to hym thral and seruauntis, and ye shal crye thenne, wesshyng to flee fro the face of your kynge. And Our Lord shal not here you ne delyure you, bycause ye haue askyd for you a kyng.'

Yet for all this, the peple wold not here Samuel but said: 'Gyue to vs a kynge. For a kynge shal regne on vs and we shal be as all other peple been. And our kynge shal iuge vs and goo byfore vs, and he shal fyght our batailles for vs.' And Samuel herde all this and counseillid with Our Lord. To whom God comanded to ordeyne to them a kyng, and so he dyde.

For he toke a man of the trybe of Beniamyn whos name was Saul, a good man and chosen, and ther was not a better emong alle the children of Israhel, and he was heyer of stature fro the sholdre vpward than | ony other of all the peple. And Samuel enoynted hym kynge (f. 65ra / sig. i1) upon Israhel and said to hym: 'Our Lord God hath enoynted the vpon his heritage and ordeyned þe a prynce, and thou shal delyuer his peple fro the handes of hys enemyes that ben in the circuyte and contrees aboute'; and so departed from hym.

And Samuel after this gadred the peple togydre and said: 'Our Lord saith that he hath brought you fro the lond of Egipte and sauyd you fro the handes of all the kynges that were your enemyes and pursyewed you, and ye haue forsaken Our Lord God that hath only delyuryd you from all your euyll and trybulacions, and haue said: "Ordeyne vpon vs a kynge." Wherfor now stande euerich in his tribe and we shal lote who shal be our kyng.'

And the lotte fylle on the tribe of Beniamyn, and in that trybe the lotte fylle vpon Saul the sone of Cys. And they souht hym and coude not fynde hym, and it was told hem that he was hyd in his hous at home, and the peple ran thyder and fette hym and sette hym amyddes all the peple. And he was heyer than ony of alle the peple fro the sholdre vpward. Thenne Samuel saide to the peple: 'Nowe ye see and beholde whom Our Lord hath chosen. For ther is none lyke hym of all the peple.' And thenne all the peple cryed *viuat rex*, 'Lyue the kynge!'

Samuel wrote the lawe of the royame to the peple in a book and put it tofore Our Lord.

Thus was Saul made the first kynge in Israhel; and anon had moche warre. For an all sides men warrid on the chyldren of Israhel and he defended them. And Saul had dyuerse bataylles and had victorye.

Samuel cam on a tyme to Saul and said God comanded hym to fight agaynst Amalech and that he shold slee and destroye man, woman and chyld, oxe, cowe, camel and asse and sheep, and spare nothyng. Thenne Saul assemblyd hys peple and had ijC M footmen and xxM men of the tribe of Iuda and wente forth and fought ayenst Amalech and slewe them, sauf he sauyd Agag the kynge of Amalech alyue, and alle other he slewe; but he spared the best flockes of sheep and of other beestis and also good clothis and wethers, and all þat was good he spared, and whatsomeuer was fowle he destroyed.

And this was shewd | f. 65rb to Samuel by Our Lord, sayeng: 'Me forthynketh that I haue ordeyned Saul kynge vpon Israhel; for he hath forsaken me and not fulfylled my comandements.' Samuel was sory herefore and waylled all the nyght. On the morn he roos and cam to Saul, and Saul offrid sacrefise vnto Our Lord of the pyllage that he had taken. And Samuel demaunded of Saul what noyse that was that he herde of sheep and beestis. And he saide that they were of the beestis that the peple had brouht fro Amalech to offre vnto Our Lord; and the residue were slayn. 'They haue spared the best and fattest for to doo sacrefyse with vnto thy Lord God.'

Thenne said Samuel to Saul: 'Remembrest thou not that where thou were leste emong the trybus of Israhel, thow were made vpperist? And Our Lord enoynted the and made the kynge. And he said to the: "Goo and slee the synners of Amalech and leue none alyue, man ne beest." Why hast thou not obeyed the comandement of Our Lord, and hast ronne to roberye and don euyl in the sight of God?' And thenne said Saul to Samuel: 'I haue taken Agag kynge of Amalech and brought hym wyth me, but I haue slayn Amalech. The peple haue taken of the sheep and beestis of the beste for to offre vnto Our Lord God.' And thenne said Samuel: 'Trowest thou that Our Lord wold rather haue sacrefise and offrynges then not t'obeye his comandements? Better is obedyence than sacrefise, and better it is to take hede to doo after thy lord than to offre the fatte kedeneys of the weders. For it is a synne to withstande and to repugne ayenst his lord, lyke the synne of ydolatrye. And bycause thou hast not obeyed Our

Lord and caste awaye his worde, Our Lord hath caste the away, that thou shalt not be kynge.'

Thenne said Saul to Samuel: 'I haue synned, for I haue not obeyed the word of God and thy wordes, but haue dredde the peple and obeyed to their request. But I pray the to bere my synne and trespaas and retorne with me, þat I may worshipe Our Lord.' And Samuel answerd: 'I shal not retorne with the.' And so Sammuel departed; and yet er he departed, | f. 65va he dyde do sle Agag the kyng. And Samuel sawe neuer Saul after, vnto his deth.

Thenne Our Lord bad Samuel to goo and enoynte one of þe sones of Ysay, otherwise called Iesse, to be kynge of Israhel. And so he cam into Bethleem vnto Iesse and bad hym brynge his sones tofore hym. This Iesse had viij sones; he brought tofore Samuel vij of them. And Samuel said ther was not he that he wold haue. Thenne he said that ther was no moo, sauf one whiche was yongest and yet a chyld and kept sheep in the felde. And Samuel said: 'Sende for hym, for I shal ete no brede tyl he come.' And so he was sente for and brought; he was rough and fayr of vysage and wel fauoured. And Samuel aroos and toke an horne with oyle and enoynted hym in the myddle of his brethern. And forthwyth the spyryte of Our Lord cam directly in hym, that same day and euer after. Thenne Samuel departed and cam into Ramatha.

And the spyryte of Our Lord wente away fro Saul and an euyl spirite ofte vexid hym. Thenne his seruants said to hym: 'Thou a[r]t o[f]te vexid with an euyl spirite. It were good to haue one that coude harpe, to be with the; whan the spirite vexeth the, thou shalt bere it the lyghter.' And he said to his seruauntes: 'Prouyde ye to me suche one.' And thenne one said: 'I saw one of Ysayes sones pleye on a harpe, a fayr chyld and strong, wyse in hys talkyng, and Our Lord is with hym.' Thenne Saul sente messagers to Ysaye for Dauid, and Ysaye sente Dauid his sone with a presente of brede, wyn and a kydde to Saul. And alway whan the euyl spyryte vexid Saul, Dauid harped tofore hym, and anon he was easyd and the euyl spyryte wente his waye.

After this, the Philisteis gadred them into grete hoostes to make warre agaynst Saul and the chyldren of Israhel. And Saul gadred the children of Israhel togidre and cam agayn them in the Vale of Therebinthi. The Philisteis stode vpon the hille on þat one parte

293-4 art ofte] aft orte

and Israhel stode vpon the hille on þat other parte, and the valeye was bytwene them. And ther cam out of the hoost of the Philisteis a grete geaunt named Golye of Geth. He was vj cubytes hye and a palme, | and a helme of brasse on his heed, and was cladde in a habergeon. The f. 65vb weight of his habergeon was of vM sicles of weight of metal. He had botes of brasse in his cartes and his sholdre[s] were couerid with plates of brasse. His glayue was as a grete colestaf and ther was theron vj sicles of yron. And his squyer wente tofor hym and cryde ayenst them of Israhel, and said that they shold chese a man to fight a synguler batail ayenst Golyas; and yf he were ouercomen, the Philisteis shold be seruauntes to Israhel, and yf he preuaile and ouercome his enemye, they of Israhel shold serue the Phylisteis. And thus he dyde crye xl dayes long. Saul and the children of Israhel were sore aferd.

Dauid was at this tyme in Bethleem with his fader and kept sheep, and iij of his brethern were in the hoost with Saul. To whom Ysay said: 'Dauid, take this potage, x loues of breed and x cheses, and goo renne vnto the hoost to thy brethern and see how they doo and lerne how they ben arayed.' Dauid delyueryd his sheep to one to kepe them, and bare thise thynges vnto the hoost. And whan he cam thether, he herde a grete crye, and he demaunded after his brethern. And that same tyme cam forth that geaunt Golyas and said as he had doon tofore, and Dauid herde hym speke. Alle they of Israhel fledde for fere of hym.

And Dauid demaunded what he was, and it was told hym that he was comen to destroye Israhel, and also that what man that myght slee hym, the kyng shold enriche hym with grete rychessis and shal gyue to hym his doughter and shal make the hous of hys fader withoute trybute. And Dauid said: 'What is this incircumcised that hath despysed the hoost of the God of Israhel? And what reward shal he haue that shal slee hym?' And the peple said as afore is said. And whan his oldest brother herde hym speke to the peple, he was wroth with hym and said: 'Wherfor art thou comen hether and hast lefte the fewe sheep in deserte? I knowe wel thy pryde; thou art comen for to see the bataille.' And Dauid said: 'What haue I doo? Is it not as þe peple haue said? I dar fight wel with this geaunt'; and declyned fro hys brother to other of the peple.

And all this was shewd to Saul. And Dauid was brouht to hym and f. 66ra /
said to Saul: 'I thy seruaunt shal fight ayenst this geaunt, yf thou sig. {i2}

312 of^{1}] of \ of 313 sholdres] sholdre

wylt.' And Saul said to hym: 'Thou maist not withstonde this Phyliste ne fight ayenst hym, for thou art but a chyld. This geaunt hath ben a fightar fro his chyldehod.' Dauid said to Saul: 'I thy seruaunt kept my faders sheep, and ther cam a lyon and a bere and token away a weder fro the myddle of my flocke, and I pursiewed after and toke it agayn fro their mouthes. And they aroose and wold haue deuouryd me, and I caught them by the iawes and slewe them. I thy seruaunt slewe the lyon and the bere. Therfor this Phyliste incircumcised shal be as one of them. I shal now goo and delyure Israhel fro this oprobrye and shame. How is this Phyliste incircumcised so hardy to curse the hoost of the lyuyng God?' And yet said Dauid: 'The Lord that kept me fro the myght of the lyon and fro the strengthe of the bere, he shal wel delyure me fro the power of this P[h]ilistee.' Saul said thenne to Dauid: 'Goo, and Our Lord be with the.' Saul dyde do arme hym with his armour and gyrd his swerd about hym. And whan he was armed, Dauid said: 'I may not ne can not fight thus, for I am not acustomed ne vsid', and vnarmed hym, and toke his staff that he had in his hond and chase to hym v good round stones fro the brook and put them in his bagge and toke a slyng in his honde, and wente forth ayenst the geaunt.

And whan Golye sawe hym come, he despised hym and said: 'Wenest þou th[a]t I am a hounde, that comest with thy staf to me?' And he cursid Dauid by his goddes and said to Dauid: 'Come hether, and I shal gyue thy flessh to the fowles of heuen and to the beestis of th'erthe.' Dauid said vnto Golye: 'Thou comest to me with thy swerd and glayue, and I come to the in the name of þe Lord God of th'oost of Israhel, which thou hast this day despised. And that Lord shal gyue the in my hande, and I shal slee the and smyte of thy heed. And I shal gyue this daye the bodyes of the men of warre of the Philisteis to the fowles of heuen and to the beestis of th'erthe.'

Thenne Golye roos and hyed toward Dauid, and Dauid on that |
f. 66rb o{t}her syde hyed and toke a stone and leyde it in his slynge and threwe it at the geaunt, and smote hym in the forhede in suche wyse that the stone was fyxed therin, that he fyl doun on his vysage. Thus preuaylled Dauid ayenst the Phylistee with his slynge and stone, and smote hym and slewe hym. And he had no swerd, but he wente and toke Golyes owen swerd and therwith smote of his heed. And thenne þe Phylisteis, seeyng this geaunt thus slayn, fledde. And th'Ysrahe-

358 Philistee] pilistee 367 that] thut

lytes after folowed and slewe many of them, and retorned agayn and cam into the tentes, pauillons and lodgynges of the Phylistees, and toke all the pyllage. Dauid toke the heed of Golye and brought it into Iherusalem, and his armes he brought into his tabernacle.

And Abner brought Dauid, hauyng the heed of Golye in hys hand, tofore Saul. And Saul demanded of hym of what kynred that he was, and he said that he was sone of Ysay of Bethleem.

And forthwith that same tyme Ionathas the sone of Saul louyd Dauid as his owen sowle. Saul thenne wold not gyue hym licence to retorne to his fader. And Ionathas and he were confederid and swore eche of them to be true to other. For Ionathas gaf hys cote that he was cladd withall and alle his other garmentis, vnto his swerd and spere, vnto Dauid. And Dauid dyde alle that euer Saul bad hym doo, wysely and prudently.

And whan he retorned fro the bataylle and Golye was slayn, the wymen camen out fro euery toun, syngyng wyth choris and tympanes ayenst the comyng of Saul with grete ioye and gladnesse, sayeng: 'Saul hath slayn a thousand, and Dauid hath slayn ten thousand.' And this sayeng dysplesyd moche to Saul, whiche said: 'They haue gyuen to Dauid ten thousand and to me one thousand. What may he more haue sauf the royame and to be kynge?' For this cause Saul neuer louyd Dauid after that day, ne neuer lokyd on hym frendly, but euer sought menes afterward to destroye Dauid, for he dredde that Dauid shold be lord with hym, and put hym from hym. And Dauid was wise and kepte hym wel from hym.

And after this he wedded Mychol, | doughter of Saul, and Ionathas f. 66va
made {of}tymes peas bytwene Saul and Dauid, yet Saul kepte no promyse but euer laye in awayte to slee Dauid. And Ionathas warned Dauid therof, and Dauid gate hym a companye of men of warre to the nombre of iiijC and kept hym in the montaynes.

And on a tyme Dauid was at home with his wif Mychol, and Saul sente theder men of warre to slee hym in his hous in the mornyng. And whan Mychol herd herof, she said to Dauid: 'But yf thou saue thyself this nyght, tomorne thou shalt dye.' And she lete hym out by a wyndowe, by which he escaped and saued hymself. Mychol toke an ymage and leyd in his bedde, and a rowhe skynne of a ghoot on the heed of the ymage, and couerd it with clothis. And on the morn Saul sente spyes for Dauid. And it was answerd to them that he laye seke in his bedde. Thenne after this sente Saul messagers for to see Dauid, and said to them: 'Brynge hym to me in his bedde, that he may be slayn.' And whan the messagers cam, they fonde a symylacre or an ymage in his bedde and ghotes skynnes on the heed.

Thenne said Saul to Mychol his doughter: 'Why hast thou mocked me so and hast suffrid myn enemy to flee?' And Mychol answerd to Saul and said: 'He said to me: "Late me goo or I shal slee the."' Dauid wente to Samuel in Ramatha and told hym all that Saul had don to hym.

And it was told to Saul that Dauid was with Samuel, and he sente theder messagers to take hym. And whan they cam, they fonde hem with the companye of prophetes, and they satte and prophecied with them. And he sente moo, and they dyde also so. And the thyrde tyme he sente mo messagers and they also prophecyed. And thenne Saul, beyng wroth, askyd where Samuel and Dauid were, and wente to them and he prophecyed whan he cam also, and toke of his clothis and was naked alle that day and nyght byfore Samuel.

Dauid thenne fledde from thens and cam to Ionathas and complayned to hym, sayeng: 'What haue I offended that thy fader secheth to slee me?' Ionathas was sory therfore, for he louyd wel Dauid.

f. 66vb After | this, Saul euer sought for to slee Dauid. And on a tyme Saul wente into a caue for to ease hym. And Dauid was within the caue, to whom his squyer said: 'Now hath God brought thyn enemye into thyn hand; now go and slee hym.' And Dauid said: 'God forbede that I shold leye ony honde on hym. He is enoynted; I shal neuer hurte ne greue hym. Late God doo his playsyr.' And he wente to Saul and cutte of a gobet of his mantel and kepte it.

And whan Saul was goon out, sone after yssued Dauid out and cryed to Saul, sayeng: 'Loo Saul, God hath brought the in my handes. I myght haue slayn the yf I had wolde, but God forbede that I shold leye honde on the my lord, enoynted of God. And what haue I offended that thou sechest to slee me?'

'Who art thou?', said Saul. 'Arte not thou Dauid, my sone?' 'Yes,' said Dauid, 'I am thy seruaunt', and kneled doun and worshiped hym. Thenne said Saul: 'I haue synned', and wepte and also saide: 'Thou arte rightfuller than I am. Thou hast don to me good, and I haue don to the euylle. And thou hast wel shewde me this day that God had brought me into thyn hande; and hast not slayn me. God rewarde the for this that thou hast don to me. Nowe I knowe wel that thou shalt regne in Israhel. I praye the to be frendly to my seed and destroye not my hows, and swere and promyse me that thou take not away my name fro the hows of my fader.' And Dauid sware and promysed to Saul. And thenne Saul departed and wente home; and Dauid and his peple wente into surer places.

Anon after this, Samuel deyde and was buryed in hys hows in Ramatha, and alle Israhel bewaylled hym gretly.

Thenne ther was a riche man in the Mounte of Carmel, that on a tyme he share and clypped his sheep. To whom Dauid sente certayn men and bad them saye that Dauid grette hym wel, and whereas afortymes his shepherdes kepte his sheep in deserte he neuer was greuous to them, ne they lost not as moch as a sheep as longe as they were wyth vs, and | that he myght aske his seruantes for they coude telle, and that I wold [that he] now in their nede sende them what it pleased hym. f. 67ra / sig. i3

Nabal answerd to the children of Dauid: 'Who is that Dauid? Trowe ye that I shal sende the mete that I haue made redy for them that shere my sheep, and sende it to men that I knowe not?'

The men retorned and told to Dauid alle that he had sayd. Thenne said Dauid to his men: 'Late euery man take his swerd, and gyrde hym wythalle.' And Dauid toke his swerd and gyrde hym. And Dauid wente and iiijC men folowed hym, and he lefte ijC behynde hym.

One of the seruauntes of Nabal told to Abygayl, Nabals wyf, how that Dauid had sente messagers fro the deserte vnto his lord, and how wroth and weyward he was, and also he said that tho men were good ynough to hem whan they were in deserte, 'ne neuer perisshed beest of our as longe as they were there. They were a wal and a shelde for vs, both day and nyht all the tyme that we kepte our flockes there. Wherfor consydere what is to be don; they purpose to do harme to hym and to his hous. For he is the sone of Belial, in suche wise that no man may speke with hym.'

Thenne Abygail hyed her and toke ijC loues of breed, ij botelles of wyn, v weders sothen and v mesures of potage and C bondes of grapes dreyde and ijC masses of cariacares, and leyde all this vpon asses, and said to her seruauntes: 'Goo ye tofore and I shal folowe after.' She told herof nothyng to her husbond Nabal. Thenne she toke an asse and rode after, and whan she cam to the foot of þe hille, Dauid and his men descended, to whom she ran. And Dauid said: 'I haue for nought sauyd alle the beestis of this Nabal in deserte, and ther perisshed nothyng of his that perteyned to hym; and hath yelded euyl for good.

475 that he] *om.*

By the lyuyng God I shal not leue as moche of his alyue as shal pisse ayenst a walle.'

As sone as Abigail sawe Dauid, she descended fro her asse and fill doun tofore Dauid vpon her visage and worshipped hym on th'erthe, and fylle doun to his feet and said: 'In me,' said she, 'my lord, be this wickednes. I beseche that I thyn handmayde may speke to thyn eeris
f. 67rb and that thou wilt here the wordes of | me thy seruaunte. I praye and requyre the, my lord, late not thy herte be sette ayenst this wicked man Nabal, for acordyng to his name he is a fool, and folye is with hym. I thyn handmayde sawe not thy chyldren that thou sendest. Now therfor my lord, for the loue of God and of thy soule, suffre not thy hond to shede no blood; and I beseche God that thyn enemyes may be lyke Nabal and they that wold the harme, and I beseche the to resseyue this blessyng and presente, whiche I thyn handmayde haue brought to the, my lord, and gyue it to thy men that folowe the, my lord. Take away the wyckednes fro me thy seruaunt. And I beseche God to make to the, my lord, a hous of trouthe. For thou, my lord, shal fight the bataillis of Our Lord God. And late no malyce be founde in the, neuer in alle the dayes of thy lyf. Yf euer ony man aryse ayenst the or wold pursiewe or wold hurte the, I beseche God to kepe þe. And whan Our Lord God hath accomplisshid to the, my lord, all that he hath spoken good of the, and hath constytued the duke vpon Israhel, late this not be in thy thought ne scropule in thy herte þat thou sholdest shede blood not gylty, ne be thou not now auengid. And whan Our Lord God hath don wel to the, my lord, haue thou ramembraunce on me thy handmayde and doo wel to me.'

And Dauid said to Abygayl: 'Blessid be God of Israhel that sente the this day to mete me, and blessyd be thy speche. And blessid be thou that hast withdrawen me fro bloodshedyng, and that I auengyd me not on myn enemye with my hande. Elles by the lyuyng Lord God of Israhel, yf thou haddest not comen vnto me, ther shold not haue blyuen vnto Nabal, tomorn in the mornyng, one pyssyng ayenst a walle.' Thenne Dauid receyuyd alle that she brouht and said to her: 'Goo pesibly into thy hous. Loo, I haue herde thy voys and I haue honoured thy visage.'

And so Abygail cam vnto Nabal, and Dauid retorned into the place he cam fro. Nabal made a grete feste in his hows, lyke the feste of a kynge. And the herte of Nabal was iocunde; he was dronken. And Abygail his wyf told to hym no worde tyl on the morn, lytyl ne moche.
f. 67va On the morn, whan | Nabal had dygestid the wyn, his wyf told hym

alle thyse wordes. And his herte was mortefyed wythin hym and he was deed lyke a stone.

For the tenthe day after Our Lord smote hym, and he deyde. And whan Dauid herde that he was deed, he said: 'Blessyd be the good Lord that hath iuged the cause of myn obprobrye fro the hand of Nabal and hath kepte me his seruaunt from harme. And Our Lord hath yolden the malyce of Nabal on his owen heed.' Thenne Dauid sente to Abygayl for to haue her to his wyf. And she humbled herself and said she his handmayde was redy to wasshe the feet of his seruauntes. And she aroos and toke with her fyue maydens, whiche wente afoote by her, and she rood vpon an asse and folowed the messagers, and was made wyf to Dauid.

And Dauid also toke another wyf called Achynoem of Iesrahel, and bothe two were hys wyues.

After this, Saul alway sought Dauid, for to slee hym. And the peple called Zyphei told to Saul that Dauid was hyd in the hille of Achylle, whiche was on the after part of the wyldernes. And Saul toke with hym thre thousand chosen men, and folowed and sought Dauid.

Dauid, whan he herde of the comyng of Saul, wente into the place whereas Saul was. And whan he was aslepe, he toke one with hym and wente into the tente where Saul slepte, and Abner with hym and alle his peple. Thenne said Abysay to Dauid: 'God hath put thyn enemye this day in thy handes. Now I shal goo and smyte hym thurgh with my spere, and thenne after that we shal haue no nede to drede hym.' And Dauid said to Abysay: 'Slee hym not. Who may extende his hande into the enoynted kyng of God, and be innocent?' And Dauid said yet more: 'By þe lyuyng God, but yf God smyte hym or the dayes come that he shal deye or perisshe in batayl, God be mercyful to me as I shal not leye my hond on hym that is enoynted of Our Lord. Now take the spere that stondeth at his heed and the cuppe of watir, and late vs |
goo.' Dauid toke the spere and the cuppe and departed thens, and ther f. 67vb
was not one that sawe them ne awaked, for they slepte all.

Thenne, whan Dauid was on the hylle fer from hem, Dauid cryed to the peple and to Abner, saieng: 'Abner, shal not thou answere?' And Abner answerd: 'Who art thou that cryest and wakest the kynge?' And Dauid said to Abner: 'Art not thou a man? And ther is none lyke the in Israhel. Why hast not thou therfor kepte thy lord the kynge? Ther is one of the peple goon in to slee the kynge thy lord. By the lyuyng Lord, it is not good that ye doo, but ye be worthy to dye bycause ye haue not kepte your lord, enoynted of Our Lord. Now loke and see where the kynges spere is and the cuppe of water that stode at his heed.'

Saul knewe the voys of Dauid and said: 'Is not this thy voys, my sone Dauid?' And Dauid said: 'It is my voys, my lord kynge. For what cause doost thou my lord pursyewe me, thy seruaunt? What thyng haue I don? And what euyl haue I commysed with my hand? Thou seest wel I myght haue slayn the yf I wold. God iuge bytwene the and me.'

And Saul saide: 'I haue synned. Retorne, my sone. I shalle neuer herafter doo the harme ne euyl, for thy soule is precious in my sight this day. Hit apperith now that I haue don folily and am ignouraunt in many thynges.' Thenne said Dauid: 'Lo, here is the spere of the kynge. Late a chyld come fetche it. Our Lord shal reward to euery man after his iustice and faith. Our Lord hath this day brought the into my handes, and yet I wold not leye myn honde on hym that is enoynted of Our Lord. And lyke as thy sowle is magnyfyed this day in my syght, so be my sowle magnefyed in the sight of God and delyuer me from all anguysse.' Saul said thenne to Dauid: 'Blessyd be thou, my sone Dauid.' And Dauid wente thenne his waye, and Saul retorned home agayn.

And Dauid said in his herte: 'Somtyme it myght happe me to falle and come into the handes of Saul. It is better I flee fro hym and saue me in the londe of the Phylysteis'; | [f. 68ra / sig. i4] and wente thens with vjC men and cam to Achis kynge of Geth, and dwellyd there. And whan Saul vnderstode that he was with Achis, he cessed to seche hym. And Achis delyueryd to Dauid a toun to dwelle in named Sychelech.

After this, the Philisteis gadred and assembled moche peple ayenst Israhel. And Saul assemblid alle Israhel and cam vnto Gelboe. And whan Saul sawe alle th'oost of the Phylysteis, his herte dredde and faynted sore. He cryed for to haue counseylle of Our Lord, and Our Lord answerd hym not, ne by sweuenes, ne by preestis, ne by prophetes. Thenne said Saul to his seruantes: 'Fetche to me a woman hauyng a phiton, otherwyse callyd a phytonesse or witche.' And they said that ther was suche a woman in Endor. Saul thenne changed his habyte and clothyng, and dyde on other clothyng and wente, and two men with hem, and cam to the woman by nyght, and made her by her crafte to reyse Samuel. And Samuel said to Saul: 'Why hast thou put me fro my reste for to aryse?' And Saul said: 'I am coarted therto, for the Phylysteis fighte ayenst me, and God is goon fro me and wyl not here me, neyther by prophetes ne by sweuenes.'

And Samuel said: 'What axest thou of me whan God is gon fro the and goon vnto Dauid? God shal doo to the as he hath said to the by me, and shal cutte thy regne fro thyn hande and shal gyue it to thy neyghbour Dauid. For thou hast not obeyed his voys, ne hast not don his comandement in Amalech; therfor thou shalt lose the batayll and Israhel shal be ouerthrowen. Tomorow thou and thy chyldren shal be with me. And Our Lord shal suffre the chyldren of Israhel falle in the handes of the Phylysteis.'

Anon thenne Saul fylle doun to the erthe. The wordes of Samuel made hym aferde, and ther was no streng[th] in hym, for he had eten no brede of all that day; he was gretly trobled. Thenne the phytonesse desired hym to ete, and she slewe a paske lambe that she had, and dighted and sette it tofore hym, and breed, and whan he had eten, he walked with his | seruauntes alle that nyght. f. 68rb

And on the morn the Philisteis assailled Saul and them of Israhel and fought a grete bataylle, and the men of Israhel fledde fro the face of the Philisteis. And many of them were slayn in the Mounte of Gelboe. The Philysteis smote in agaynst Saul and his sones, and slewe Ionathas and Amynadab and Melechesue sones of Saul. And alle the burthen of the bataylle was torned on Saul. And the archers folowed hym and wounded hym sore. Thenne said Saul to his squyer: 'Plucke out thy swerd and slee me, that thyse men incircumcised come not and, scornyng, slee me.' And his squyer wold not, for he was gretly aferd. Thenne Saul toke his swerd and slewe hymself; whiche thyng whan his squyer sawe, that is, that Saul was deed, he toke his swerd and fylle on hit and was deed with hym. Thus was Saul deed, and his thre sones and his squyer and all his men that day togydre. Thenne the chyldren of Israhel that were theraboutes and on that other syde of Iordan, seeyng that the men of Israhel fledde and that Saul and his thre sones were deed, lefte theyr cytees and fledde. The Philisteis cam and duellyd there.

And the next daye, the Philisteis wente for to ryfle and pylle them that were deed, and they fonde Saul and his thre sones lyeng in the hylle of Gelboe. And they cut of the heed of Saul, and robbed hym of hys armours, and sente it into the londe of Phylistym all aboute, that it myght be shewd in the temple of their ydollis and vnto the peple; and sette vp his armes in the temple of Astaroth, and henge his body on the walle of Bethsan.

628 chyldren] chyldreen 631 strength] strenght

And whan the men that dwellyd in Iabes sawe what the Phylisteis had doon vnto Saul, alle the strongest men of them aroos and wente alle that nyght and toke doun thc bodyes of Saul and of his sones fro the walle of Bethsan, and brente them and toke the bones and buryed them in the wood of Iabes, and fasted seuen dayes.

f. 68va Thus endeth the lyf of Saul, whiche was first kynge vpon Israhel, and for disobedyence of Godes comandement was slayn, and his heyres neuer regned long after.

[10. DAVID]

Here foloweth how Dauid regned after Saul and gouerned Israhel, shortly taken out of the Bible the most historyal maters and but litil towched.

After the deth of Saul, Dauid retorned fro the iorney that he had ayenst Amalech. For whiles Dauid had ben out with Achis the kyng, they of Amalech had ben in Sychelech and taken all that was therin prysoners, and robbed and caryed away with hem the two wyues of f. 68vb Dauid, and had sette fyre and brente | the toun. And whan Dauid cam agayn home and sawe the toun brente, he pursyewed after. And by the conueyeng of one of them of Amalech, that was lefte by the waye seke, for to haue hys lyf he brought Dauid vpon the hoost of Amalech whereas they satte and ete and dronke. And Dauid smote on them with his meyne and slewe doun alle that he fonde, and rescowed his wyues and all the good that they had taken and toke moche more of them.

And whan he was come to Secelech, þe thirde day after ther cam one from the hoost of Saul, and told to Dauid how that Israhel had loste the batayll and how they were fledde and how Saul the kyng and Ionathas his sone were slayn. Dauid said to the yong man that brought thyse tidynges: 'How knowest thou that Saul and Ionathas ben deed?' And he answerd: 'It was so by aduenture that I cam vpon the Mounte of Gelboe, and Saul rested vpon his spere. And the horsmen and chares of the Phylisteis approched to hym ward. And he looked byhynde hym and sawe me, and callyd me and said to me: "Who art thou?" And I said: "I am Amalechytes." And than he said: "Stonde vpon me and slee me, for I am ful of anguysshes and yet my sowle is in me." And I thenne, stondyng on hym, slewe hym, knowyng wel that

4 After] A *six-line capital supplied by hand in red*

he myght not lyue after the ruyne. And I toke the dyademe from his heed and the armylle fro hys arme, whiche I haue brought hether to the, my lord.'

Dauid toke and rente his vestement, and alle the men that were with hym, and waylled and sorowed moche the deth of Saul and Ionathas and of all the men of Israhel, and fasted that day tyl euen. And Dauid said to the yong man: 'Of whens art thou?' And he said: 'I am the sone of Amalechites.' And Dauid said to hym: 'Why dreddest not thou to put thy hand forth to slee hym that is enoynted of God?' Dauid called one of his men and bad hym to sle hym. And he smote hym and slewe hym. And Dauid saide: 'Thy blood be on thy heed. Thyn owen mouth hath spoken ayenst the, sayeng: "I haue slayn Saul, which was kyng enoynted of Our Lord."' Dauid | sorowed and f. 69ra / sig. [i5] bewaylled moche the deth of Saul and of Ionathas.

After this, Dauid counceylled with Our Lord and demaunded yf he shold goo into one of the cytees of Iuda. And Our Lord bad hym goo, and he asked whyder. And Our Lord said: 'Into Ebron.' Thenne Dauid toke his two wyues and all the men that were with hym, euerich with his houshold, and dwellyd in the townes of Hebron. And theder cam the men of Iuda, and enoynted Dauid kynge to regne vpon the trybe of Iuda.

And Abner, prynce of th'oost of Saul, and other seruantes of Saul toke Hisboseth, the sone of Saul, and ladde hym aboute, and made hym kynge ouer Israhel exept the tribe of Iuda. Hisboseth was xl yere whan he began to regne, and he regned two yere. The hows of Iuda only folowed Dauid.

After this it happed that Abner, prynce of þe hoost of Hisboseth, with certayn men went out of the castellis. And Ioab, with certayn men of Dauid, wente also out and ran by the piscene of Gabaon. One partye was on that one side, and that other on that other. And Abner said to Ioab: 'Late our yong men pleye and scarmusshe togydre', and Ioab agreed. And ther roose xij of Beniamyn of the party of Hysboseth and xij of the chyldren of Dauid. And whan they mette togydre, eche toke other by the heed and roof their swerdes into eche other sydes, and were alle ther slayn. And ther aroose a grete batayll, and Abner and his felawship were put to flight by the men of Dauid. And emonge all other ther was Asahel, one of the brothern of Ioab, and was the swiftest rennar that myght be, and pursiewed Abner. And Abner loked behynde hym, and bad hym: 'Declyne on the right side or on the lyft side, and take one of the yong men and his harnoys, and come not at me.' Asahel wold not leue hym. Yet Abner said to hym: 'Goo fro me and folowe not me, lest I be compellyd to slee the, and thenne I may not make my pees with Ioab thy brother.' Whiche wold not here Abner, but despysed hym. And Abner thenne torned and slewe hym in the same place. And anon the sonne wente doun and they | f. 69rb withdrewe. Ther were slayn of the chyldren of Dauid xix men, and of them of Beniamyn iijC lx were slayn.

And thus ther was longe stryf and contencion bytwene the hows of Dauid and the hous of Isboseth. After this, Abner toke a concubyne of Saul and helde her, wherfor Hisboseth repreuyd hym of it. And Abner was wroth gretly therof, and cam to Dauid and made frendship with hym. Ioab was not there whan Abner made his pees with Dauid, but whan he knewe it, he cam to Abner with a fayr semblaunt and spack fayr to hym by dissimylacion and slew hym, for to auenge the deth of Asa[h]el his brother. And whan Dauid herde how Ioab had slayn Abner, he cursed hym and bewaylled gretly the deth of Abner and dyde do burye hym honourably, and Dauid folowid the bere hymself.

And whan Hisboseth, the sone of Saul, herde that Abner was deed, he was alle abasshed and alle Israhel sore trobled. Ther were two prynces of theues with Hisboseth, named Banaa and Rechab, whiche cam on a day into Hisboseth where he laye and slepte, and ther they slewe hym and toke pryuely his heed and brought it to Dauid into Hebron, and said: 'Lo, here is the heed of thyn enemye Isboseth, that sought to sle the. This day God hath gyuen to the, my lord, vengeaunce of Saul and of his seed.' Dauid answerd to them: 'By the lyuyng God that hath delyuerd me fro all anguysshe, hym that told me that he had slayn Saul and had thought to haue had a reward of me I dyde doo slee. How moche more ye, that be so wicked to slee hym that is not gylty in his hows and vpon his bedde? Shal I not aske his blood of your hondes and throwe you out of this world? Yes, certaynly.' And Dauid comaunded to his seruantes to slee them, and so they were slayn and cutte of their handes and feet, and henge them on the pyscene in Ebron and toke the heed of Hysboseth and buryed it in the sepulcre of Abner.

And thenne cam all the tribus of Israhel to Dauid in Ebron, sayeng: 'We ben thy mouth and thy flesshe. Whan Saul lyued and was kynge f. 69va on vs and regned, thou were comyng and goynge, and bycause | God

82 Asahel] asabel

hath said: "Thou shalt regne vpon my peple and be theyr gouernour", therfore we shal obeye the.' And alle the senyors of Israhel cam and dyde homage to Dauid in Hebron, and enoy[nte]d hym kynge ouer them.

Dauid was xxx yere old whan he began to regne. And he regned xl yere. He regned in Hebron vpon Iuda vij yer and vj monethis, and in Iherusalem he regned xxxiij yere vpon all Israhel and Iuda.

Dauid thenne made hym a dwellyng place in the hylle of Syon in Iherusalem. And after this, the Philisteis made warre agayn hym, but he ofte ouerthrewe hem and slewe many of them and made them trybutarye to hym; and after brought the arke of God in Iherusalem and sette it in his hows. After this yet, the Phylisteis made warre agayn vnto hym, and other kynges were aydyng and helpyng them ayenst Dauid, whom Dauid ouercome and slewe and put vnder.

And on a tyme whan Ioab was out with his men of warre, lyeng at a syege tofore a cyte, Dauid was at home and walkid in his chambre. And as he looked out at a wyndow, he sawe a fair woman wasshe her and bayne her in her chambre, whiche stode ayenst his hows, and demanded of his seruantes who she was. And they said she was Vries wyf. He sente for her and laye by her and gate her with chylde.

And whan Dauid vnderstode that she was with chyld, he sente lettres to Ioab and bad hym to sende home to hym Vrye. And Ioab sente Vrye to Dauid, and Dauid demaunded how the hoost was rewlid, and after bad hym goo home to his hows and wasshe his feet. And Vrye wente thens and the kynge sente to hym his disshe with mete. Vrye wold not goo home, but laye tofore the yate of the kynges hous with other seruauntes of the kynges. And hit was told to the kynge that Vryas wente not home. And thenne Dauid said to Vrye: 'Thou comest fro a farre waye; why goste not home?' And Vrye said to Dauid: 'The arke of God and Israhel and Iuda ben in the pauylions and my lord Ioab and the seruauntes of the, my lord, lye on the ground, and wold ye that I shold goo to my hous and ete | and drynke (f. 69vb) and slepe with my wyf? By thy helthe and by the helthe of my sowle, I shal not doo soo.' Thenne Dauid said to Vrye: 'Abyde here thenne this nyght, and tomorow I shal delyure the.' Vrye abode there that day and the next, and Dauid made hym ete tofore hym and made hym dronke. Yet for alle that, he wold not goo home, but laye wyth the seruauntes of Dauid.

108 enoynted] enoytend

Thenne on the morn, Dauid wrote a lettre to Ioab, that he shold sette Vrye in the weykest place of the batayl and where most ieopardye was, and that he shold be lefte there, that he myght be slayn. And Vrye bare this lettre to Ioab, and it was so don as Dauid had wreton. And Vrye was so slayn in the batayll. And Ioab sente worde to Dauid how they had foughten and how Vrye was slayn and deed.

Whan Vryes wyf herd that her husbond was deed, she morned and waylled hym, and after the mornyng Dauid sente for her and wedded her, and she bare hym a sone. And this that Dauid had commysed in Vrye displeysyd gretly Our Lord.

Thenne Our Lord sente Nathan the prophete vnto Dauid, whiche whan he cam said to hym: 'Ther were two men dwellyng in a cyte, that one ryche and þat other poure. The ryche man hadde sheep and oxen right many, and þe poure man hadde but one lytyl sheep, whiche he bought and nourisshid and grewe with his chyldren, etyng of hys brede and drynkyng of his cuppe and slepte in his bosom; she was to hym as a doughter. And on a tyme whan a certayn pylgryme cam to the riche man, he, sparyng his owen sheep and oxen to make a feste to the pylgrym that was comen to hym, toke the only sheep of the poure man and made mete therof to his gheest.'

Dauid was wroth and said to Nathan: 'By the lyuyng God, the man that hath so doo is þe childe of deth. The man that hath so doo shal yelde therfore iiij double.' Thenne said Nathan to Dauid: 'Thou art the same man that hath don this thynge. This said the Lord God of Israhel: "I haue enoynted the kynge vpon Israhel and I haue kept the fro the hande of Saul, and I haue gyuen to the an hows to kepe in thy houshold and wyues in thy bosom. I haue gyuen to the the hous of Israhel | (f. 70ra / sig. [i6]) and the hous of Iuda. And yf thyse be smale thynges, I shal adde and gyue to the moche more and gretter. Why hast thou therfor despysed the word of God and hast don euyl in the sight of Our Lord? Thou hast slayn Vrye with a swerd, and his wyf hast thou taken vnto thy wif, and thou hast slayn hym with the swerd of the sones of Ammon. Therfor the swerd shal not goo fro thy hows, world withoute ende, for as moche as thou hast despysed and hast taken Vryes wyf vnto thy wyf." This said Our Lord: "I shal reyse euyl ayenst the, and shal take thy wyues in thy sight and gyue them to thy neyghbour; and shal lye wyth thy wyuys tofore thyn eyen. Thou hast don it pryuely, but I shal make this to be don and open in the sight of alle Israhel."'

And thenne said Dauid to Nathan: *Peccaui*, 'I haue synned ayenst Our Lord.' Nathan said: 'Our Lord hath taken away thy synne; thou shalt not dye. But for as moche as thou hast made the enemyes to blaspheme the name of God, therfor the sone that is born to the shal dye by deth.’ And Nathan retorned home to his hous.

And for this synne Dauid made this psalme *Miserere mei, Deus*, whiche is a psalme of mercy. For Dauid dide grete penaunce for thyse synnes of aduoultrye and also of homycyde. For as I ones was byyonde the see, rydyng in the companye of a noble knyght named Syr Iohan Capons, and was also doctour in bothe lawes and was born in Malyorke and had ben viceroye and gouernour of Aragon and Catelone, and that tyme counceyllour vnto the Duc of Bourgonye, Charloys, it happend we comened of the hystorye of Dauid. And this said noble man told me that he had redde that Dauid dyde this penaunce folowyng for thyse said synnes: that he dalf hym in the ground, standyng nakyd, vnto the heed so longe that the wormes began to crepe in his flesshe, and made a verse of this psalme *Miserere* and thenne cam out. And whan he was hole therof, he wente in agayn and stode so agayn as longe as afore is said and made the second verse, and so as many tymes he was doluen in the erth as | ben verse in the f. 70rb said psalme of *Miserere mei Deus*, and euery tyme was abydyng therin tyl he felte the wormes crepe in his flesshe. This was a grete penaunce and a token of grete repentaunce. For ther ben in the psalme xx verses, and xx tymes he was doluen. Thus thys noble man told me rydyng bytwene the toun of Gaunt in Flaundres and the toun of Bruxellis in Braband.

Therfor God toke away this synne and forgaue it hym, but the sone that she brought forth deyed. And after this Bersabee, that had ben Vryes wyf, conceyuyd and brought forth another sone named Salomon, whiche was wel-byloued of God; and after Dauid Salomon was kynge.

After this, Dauid had moche warre and trouble and angre, in so moche that on a tyme Ammon, oldest sone of Dauid, louyd Thamar his suster. This Thamar was Absalons suster by the moder syde. And Ammon forced and laye by her, and whan he had don his pleasir he hated her and threwe her out of his chambre, and she complayned her vnto Absalon. Dauid knewe herof and was right sory for it, but he wold not rebuke his sone Ammon for it, for he louyd hym bycause he was his first-begoten sone. Absalon hated Ammon euer after.

And whan Absalon on a tyme dyde do shere his sheep, he prayd alle his brethern to come ete with hym, and made hem a feste lyke a kynges feste, at whiche feste he dyde do slee his brother Ammon. And anon it was told to the kynge Dauid that Absalon had slayn all the kynges sones, wherfor the kynge was in grete heuynes and sorowe. But anon after, it was told hym that ther was no mo slayn but Ammon. And the other sones cam home, and Absalon fledd into Gessur and was there thre yere and durst not come home.

And after, by the moyen of Ioab, he was sente for and cam into Iherusalem, but yet he myght not come in his fader the kynges presence, and dwellyd there two yere and myght not see the kynge his fader. This Absalon was the fayrest man that euer was, for fro the sole f. 70va of his foot vnto his heed ther was not a spotte. He | had so moche heere on his heed that it greuyd hym to bere, wherfore hit was shorn of ones a yere. It weyed two hondred cycles of good weight.

Thenne whan he abode so longe that he myght not come to his faders presence, he sente for Ioab to come speke with hym, and he wold not come. He sente agayn for hym and he cam not. Thenne Absalon said to his seruauntes: 'Knowe ye Ioabs felde, that lyeth by my felde?' They said: 'Ye.' 'Goo ye', sayde he, 'and sette fyre in the barle[y] that is therin and brenne it.' And Ioabs seruauntes cam and told to Ioab that Absalon had sette fyre on his corn. Thenne Ioab cam to Absalon and said: 'Why hast thou sette fyre on my corn?' And he said: 'I haue sente tweys to the, prayeng the to come to me, that I myght sen[d]e the to the kyng and that thou sholdest saye to hym: "Why I cam fro Gessur? It had be better to me for to haue abyden there." I praye the that I may come to his presence and see hys vysage. And yf he remembre my wickednes, late hym slee me.' Ioab wente into the kynge and told to hym all thyse wordes. Thenne was Absalon callyd and entred into the kynge, and he fylle doun and worshipped the kynge, and the kyng kyssyd hym.

Aftir this, Absalon dyde doo make for hymself chares and horsmen and fyfty men to goo byfore hym, and walked emong the tribus of Israhel and grette and salued them, takyng them by the hond and kyssed hem, by whiche he gate to hym the hertes of the peple, and said to hys fader that he had auowed to make sacrefise to God in Hebron. And hys fader gaf hym leue. And whan he was there, he gadred peple to hym and made hymself kynge, and dyde doo crye that all men shold obeye and wayte on hym as kynge of Israhel. Whan Dauid herd this, he was sore abasshed and was fayn to flee out of Iherusalem. And Absalon cam wyth hys peple and entrid into

241 barley] barle   245 sende] sente

Iherusalem into his faders hows and laye by his fadres concubynes, and after pursyewid his fader to depose hym.

And Dauid ordeyned his peple and batayll ayenst hym, and sente Ioab prynce of his hoost | ayenst Absalon, and deuyded hys hoost into f. 70vb thre partyes and wold haue goon with them. But Ioab counceyllid that he shold not goo to the batayll, whatsomeuer happid. And thenne Dauid badde them to saue his sone Absalon.

And they wente forth and fought. And Absalon with his hoost was ouerthrowen and put to flyght. And as Absalon fledde vpon his mule, he cam vnder an ooke and his heere flewe aboute a bowhe of the tre, and helde so fast that Absalon henge by his heer, and the mule ran forth. Ther cam one to Ioab and told hym how that Absalon henge by his heer on a bowhe of an oke. And Ioab said: 'Why hast thou not slayn hym?' The man said: 'God forbede that I shold sette honde on the kynges sone. I herde the kynge saye: "Kepe my sone Absalon alyue and slee hym not."' Thenne Ioab wente and toke thre speres, and fyxed them in the herte of Absalon as he henge on the tree by his heer. And yet after this x yong men, squy[r]es of Ioab, ranne and slewe hym. Thenne Ioab tromped and blewe the retrayt, and reteyned the peple that they shold not pursyewe the peple fleyng. And they toke the body of Absalon and caste it in a grete pytte and leyde on hym a grete stone.

And whan Dauid knewe that his sone was slayn, he made grete sorow and said: 'O my sone Absalon, my sone Absalon, who shal graunte to me that I may dye for the, my sone Absalon, Absalon my sone?'

It was told to Ioab that the kynge wepte and sorowed the deth of his sone Absalon, and all their vyctorye was torned into sorowe and wayllyng, in so moche that the peple eschewed to entre into the cyte. Thenne Ioab entrid to the kynge and said: 'Thou hast this day discoraged the chere of alle thy seruauntes, bycause they haue sauyd thy lyf and the lyues of thy sones and doughtres, of thy wyues and of thy c[o]ncubynes. Thou louest them that hate the and hatest them that loue the, and shewyst wel thys day that thou settyst lityl by thy dukes and seruauntes. And truly I knowe now wel that yf Absalon had lyuyd and alle we thy seruauntes had ben slayn, thou haddest ben plesyd. Therfor | aryse now and come forth and satisfye the peple, or f. 71ra / ellis I swere to the by the good Lord that ther shal not one of thy sig. [i7]

279 squyres] squy \ es 294 concubynes] cancubynes

seruauntes abyde with the tyl tomorow. And that shal be worse to the than all the harmes and euylles that euer yet fylle to the.'

Thenne Dauid the kyngc aroos and satte in the yate. And anon it was shewd to all the peple that the kyng satte in the yate; and thenne all the peple cam in tofore the kyng. And they of Israhel that had ben with Absalon fledde into their tabernacles, and after cam agayn vnto Dauid whan they knewe that Absalon was deed.

And after, one Siba, a cursid man, rebellyd and gadred peple ayenst Dauid. Ayenst whom Ioab with the hoost of Dauid pursyewed, and drof hym vnto a cyte whiche he byseged. And by the meane of a woman of the same cyte, Sibas heed was smeton of and delyuerd to Ioab ouer the walle. And so the cyte was saued and Ioab plesid.

After this Dauid callid Ioab and bad hym nombre the peple of Israhel. And so Ioab walked thurgh alle the tribus of Israhel, fro Dan to Bersabee, and ouer Iordan and all the contre. And ther were founden in Israhel viijCM strong men that were able to fight and to drawe swerd, and of the tribe of Iuda fyfty thousand fyghtyng men.

And after that the peple was nombred, the herte of Dauid was smeton by Our Lord and was heuy, and said: 'I haue synned gretly in this dede, but I praye the Lord to take away the wickednes of thy seruaunt, for I haue don folyly.' Dauid roos on the morn erly, and the word of Our Lord cam to Gad the prophete, sayeng that he shold goo to Dauid and bidde hym c{h}ese one of thre thyngis that he shold saye to hym. Whan Gad cam to Dauid he said that he shold chese whether he wold haue vij yere hungre in his londe, or thre monthes he shold flee his aduersaryes and enemyes, or to haue thre dayes pestylence. 'Of this thre God biddeth the chese whiche t{h}ou wylt. Now auyse the and conclude what I shal answere to Our Lord.' Dauid said to Gad: 'I am constrayned {t}o a grete thyng, f. 71rb but it is better for me to put me in þe handes | of Our Lord, for his mercy is moche more than in men.' And so he chees pestylence.

Thenne Our Lord sente pestylence the tyme constytute. And ther deyed of the peple fro Dan to Bersabee lxxM men. And whan the angele extended his hond vpon Iherusalem for to destroye it, Our Lord was mercyful vpon th'affliction and said to the angele so smytyng: 'It suffiseth. Nowe withdrawe thyn hand.' Dauid said to Our Lord whan he sawe th'angele smytyng the peple: 'I am he that haue synned and don wickedly. What haue thyse sheep don? I beseche the that thy hand torne vpon me and vpon the hows of my fader.'

Thenne cam G[a]d to Dauid and bad hym make an awter in the same place where he sawe th'aungel; and bought the place and made the aulter and offred sacrefises vnto Our Lord. And Our Lord was mercyful, and the plaghe cessed in Israhel.

Dauid was old and feble and sawe that his deth approched, and ordeyned that his sone Salomon shold regne and be kynge after hym, howbeit that Adonyas hys sone toke on hym to be kynge duryng Dauids lyf. For whiche cause Bersabee and Nathan cam to Dauid, and tofore them he said that Salomon shold be kynge and ordeyned that he shold be sette on his mule by hys prophetes Nathan, Sadoch the preest and Banayas, and brought into Syon. And ther Sadoch the preest and Nathan the prophete enoynted hym in kynge vpon Israhel, and blewe in a trompe and saide: 'Lyue the kynge Salomon!' And fro thens they brought hym into Iherusalem and sette hym vpon his faders sete, in his fadres trone. And Dauid worshipped hym in his bedde and said: 'Blessid be the Lord God of Israhel, that hath suffred me to see my sone in my trone and sete!' And thenne Adonyas and all they that were with hym were aferd and, dredyng Salomon, ran away, and so cessed Adonyas.

The dayes of Dauid approched faste that he shold deye, and dyde do calle Salomon tofore hym. And ther he comanded hym to kepe the comandementis of Our Lord and walke in his wayes and to obserue his cerymonyes, | his preceptes and his iugementis, as it is wreton in f. 71va
the lawe of Moyses, and said: 'Our Lord conferme the in thy regne and sende to the wysedom to rewle it wel.' And whan Dauid had thus counceyllyd and comanded hym to do iustise and kepe Goddes lawe, he blessid hym and deyde, and was buryed with his fadres.

This Dauid was an holy man and made the holy Psawter, whiche is an holy booke, and is conteyned therin the Olde Lawe and Newe Lawe. He was a grete prophete, for he prophecyed the comyng of Cryst, his natyuyte, his passyon and resurrection and also his ascencion, and was grete with God. Yet God wold not suffre hym to bylde a temple for hym, for he had shedde mans blood. But God said to hym his sone, that shold regne after hym, shold be a man pesyble and he shold bylde the temple to God. And whan Dauid had regned xl yere, kynge of Iherusalem oucr Iuda and Israhel, he deyed in good mynde and was buryed with his faders in the cyte of Dauid.

Thus endeth the lyf of Dauid, seconde kynge of Israhel.

340 Gad] god

[11. SOLOMON]

After Dauid regned Salomon his sone, whiche was in the begynnyng a f. 71vb good man and walked in | the wayes and lawes of God, and all þe kynges aboute hym made pees with hym; and was kynge confermed, obeyed and pesible in his possession; and acordyng to hys faders comandement dyde iustice, first on Ioab, that had ben prynce of his faders hoost, bycause he slewe two good men by trayson and gyle, that was Abner the sone of Ner and Amasa the sone of Gether. And Ioab was aferd and dredde Salomon, and fledde into the tabernacle of Our Lord and helde the ende of the aulter. And Salomon sente Banayas and slewe hym there, and after buryed hym in his hows in deserte.

And after this on a nyght, as he laye in his bedde after that he had sacrefyed to Our Lord in Gabaon, Our Lord apperid to hym in his sleepe, sayeng to hym: 'Aske and demaunde what thou wilt, that I may gyue to the.' And Salomon saide: 'Lord, thou hast don to my fader grete mercy bycause he walked in thy wayes, in trouthe, iustyce and in a rightful herte. Thou hast alwaye kepte for hym thy grete mercy, and hast gyuen to hym a sone, syttyng vpon his trone, as it is this daye. And now, Lord, thou hast made me thy seruaunt to regne for my fader Dauid. I am a lytyl chyilde and knowe not my goyng out and entryng in. And I thy seruaunt am sette in the myddle of the peple that thou hast chosen, whiche ben infynyte and may not be nombred for multytude. Therfor, Lord, gyue to me thy seruaunt a herte docyle and taught in wysdom, that may iuge thy peple and dyscerne bytwene good and euyl. Who may iuge this peple, thy peple that ben here so many?'

Thys requ{e}st and demande plesyd moche vnto God, that Salomon had asked suche a thynge. And God said to Salomon: 'Bycause thou hast requyred and axed this, and hast not axed longe lyf ne rychesses ne the sowles of thy enemyes, but hast askyd sapyence and wysedom to discerne dome and iugement, I haue gyuen to the after thy desyre and request. And I haue gyuen to the a wyse herte and vnderstandyng in so moche that ther was neuer none such{e} tofore | f. 72[ra] / sig. [i8] ne neuer after shal be. And also tho thynges that thou hast not asked I haue gyuen also to the, that is to saye rychesse and glorye, that no man shal be lyke to the emong alle the kynges that shal be after thy dayes. Yf thou walke in my wayes and kepe my preceptes and obserue my comandements as thy fader walked, I shal make thy dayes longe.'

1 After] A *four-line capital supplied by hand in red*

After this Salomon awoke, and cam to Iherusalem and stode tofore the arke of Our Lord and offred sacryfises and victymes vnto Our Lord, and made a grete feste vnto alle his seruantes and houshold.

Thenne cam tofore hym two comyn wymen, of whiche that one said: ‘I beseche the, my lord, here me. This woman and I dwellyd togydre in one hows, and I was delyueryd of a chyld in my cubycle. And the thyrde day after, she bare a chyld and was also delyueryd. And we were togydre and none other in the hows but we tweyne. It was so that this womans sone was deed in the nyght, for she, slepyng, ouerlaye and oppressid hym. And she aroos in the derkest of the nyght pryuyly, and toke my sone f[ro] the syde of me thy seruant and layd hym by her. And her sone that was deed she leyde by me. Whan I aroos in the mornyng for to gyue mylke to my sone, it apperid deed; whom I toke, beholdyng hym dylygently in the clere lyght, vnderstode wel anon that it was not my sone that I had born.’ The other woman answerd and said: ‘It was not so as thou saist, but my sone lyueth and thyn is deed.’ And contrarye that other said: ‘Thou lyest. My sone lyueth and thyn is deed.’ Thus in this wyse they stroof tofore the kynge.

Thenne the kynge said: ‘This woman saith: “My sone lyueth and thyn is deed.” And this answerth: “Nay, but thy sone is deed and myn lyueth.”’ Thenne the kynge said: ‘Brynge to me here a swerd.’ Whan they had brouht forth a swerd, the kynge said: ‘Dyuyde ye’, said he, ‘the lyuyng chyld in two partyes and gyue that one half to that one and that other half to that other.’

Thenne said the woman that was moder of the lyuyng child to the kynge, for all her membris and bowellis were | meuyd vpon her sone: f. 72rb
‘I beseche and praye the, my lord kynge, gyue to her the chyld alyue and slee hym not.’ And contrarye said that other woman: ‘Late it not be gyuen to me ne to the, but late it be deuided.’ The kynge thenne answerd and said: ‘Gyue the lyuyng chylde to this woman and late it not be slayn. This is veryly the moder.’ Alle Israhel herd how wysely þe kynge had gyuen this sentence and dredde hym, seeyng that the wysedom of God was in hym, in demyng of rightful domes.

After this, Salomon sente his messagers to dyuerse kynges for cedre trees and for werkmen, for to make and bylde a temple vnto Our Lord. Salamon was ryche and gloryous, and all the royames, fro the ryuer of the endes of the Phylisteis vnto th’ende of Egypte, were

47 fro] for

acorded with hym and offryd to hym yeftes, and to serue hym all the dayes of his lyf. Salomon had dayly for the mete of hys housho[l]d xxx mesures, named chores, of corn and lx of mele, x fatte oxen and xx oxen of pasture, and hondred wethers, without veneson, that was taken as hertes, ghotes, bubals and other fleyng fowles and byrdes. He obteyned all the regyon that was fro Tapsa vnto Gazam, and had pees with alle the kynges of alle the royames that were in euery parte rounde aboute hym. In that tyme Israhel and Iuda dwellyd wythout fere and drede, euerich vnder his vyne and fygge-tre, fro Dan vnto Bersabee.

And Salamon had xlM rackes for the horses of his cartes, chares and curres, and xijM for horse to ryde on, by whyche prefectes brought necessarye thyngis for the table of Kynge Salomon with grete dylygence in their tyme.

God gaf to Salamo[n] moche wysedom and prudence in hys herte, lyke to the grauel that is in the seesyde. And the sapyence and wysedom of Salamon passed and wente tofore the sapyence of alle them of th'oryent and of Egypte. And he was wysest of all men and so he was named. He spack thre thousand parablis and fyue th[ou]sand songes, and dysputed vpon alle maner trees and vertue of them, fro the cedre that is in Libano vnto the ysope that groweth on the walle, |
f. 72va and discerned the propretees of beestis, fowles, reptyles and fysshes. And ther cam peple from all regyons of the world for to heere the wysedom of Salamon.

And Salamon sente lettres to Hyram, Kynge of Tyre, for to haue his men to cutte cedre trees with his seruauntis, and he wold yelde to them theyr hyre and mede, and lete hym wete how that he wold bylde and edefye a temple to Our Lord. And Hyram sente to hym that he shold haue all that he desyred, and sente to hym cedre trees and other woode; and Salamon sente to hym corne in grete nombre. And Salomon and Hyram confederyd them togydre in loue and frendship.

Salamon chaas out werkmen of alle Israhel, the nombre of xxxM men, of whom he sente to Libane xM euery moneth. And whan xM wente, the other cam home and so two monethis were they at home. And Adonyras was ouerseer and comandour on them. Salamon had lxxM men that dyde nothyng but bare stone and morter and other thynges to the edefyeng of the temple, and were berars of burthens only. And he had lxxxM of hewers of stone and masons in the

76 houshold] houshod 89 Salamon] Salamom 93 thousand] thuosand

montayn, wythout the prefectes and maisters, whiche were iijM and iijC, that dyde nothyng but comande and ouersee them that wrought. Salamon comanded the werkmen to make square stones grete and precyouse, for to laye in the foundement whiche the masons of Israhel and masons of Hyram hewed, and the carpenters made redy the tymbre.

Thenne began Salomon the temple to Our Lord. In the fourthe yere of his regne hee began to bylde the temple. The hous that he bylded had lx cubytes in lengthe and xx cubytes in brede and xxx in heyght. And the porche tofore the temple was xx cubytes longe, after the mesure of the brede of the temple, and had x cubytes of brede tofore the face of the temple. And for to wryte the curiosyte and werke of the temple and the necessaryes, the tables and cost that was don in gold, syluer and laton, it passeth my connynge to expresse and Englysshe them. Ye that ben clerkys may see it in the S[e]cond Bo{ok} | of Kynges and the Seconde Book of Paralipomenon. It is f. 72vb wondre to here the costes and expencis that was made in that temple, but I passe ouer. It was on makyng vij yere, and his palays was xiij yere er it was fynysshed. He made in the temple an aulter of pure gold and a table to sette on the loues of proposicion of gold, fyue candelstiks of gold on the right syde and fyue on the lyft syde, and many other thynges; and toke all the vessels of gold and syluer that hys fader Dauid had sanctefyed and halowed, and brought hem in the tresory of the hows of Our Lord.

After thys he assemblyd alle the noblest and grettest of burthe of them of Israhel, with the prynces of the trybus and dukes of the famylyes, for to brynge the arke of God fro the cyte of Dauid, Syon, into the temple. And the prestes and Leuytes toke the arke and bare it and alle the vessels of the sanctuarye that were in the tabernacle. Kynge Salamon, with alle the multytude of þe chyldren that were there, wente tofore the arke and offred sheep and oxen without extimacion and nombre. And the preestes sette the arke in the hows of Our Lord, in the oracle of the temple, in *sancta sanctorum*, vnder the wynges of cherubyn. In the arke was nothyng but the two tablys of Moyses of stone, which Moyses had put in.

And thenne Salamon blessyd Our Lord tofore all the peple and thanked hym that he had suffred hym to make an hous vnto hys name, and besought Our Lord that whosomeuer prayd Our Lord for ony

127 Second] sccond

petycion in that temple, that he of his mercy wold here hym and be mercyful to hym. And Our Lord appered to hym whan the edefyce was accomplysshed perfightly and said to Salamon: 'I haue herde thy prayer and thyn oracion that thou hast prayd tofore me. I haue sanctefyed and halowed this hows that thou hast edefyed for to put my name therin for euermore. And myn eyen and herte shal be theron allewaye. And yf thou walke byfor me lyke as thy fader walked in the f. 73ra / sig. k1 symplycyte of herte and in equyte | and wylt doo alle that I haue commanded the and kepe my iugements and lawes, I shal sette the trone of thy regne vpon Israhel euermore, lyke as I haue said to thy fader Dauid, sayeng: "Ther shal not by taken away a man of thy generacion fro the regne and sete of Israhel." Yf ye auerte and torne fro me, ye and your sones, not folowyng ne kepyng my comandements and cerymonyes that I haue shewd tofore you, but goo and worshyp straunge goddes and honoure them, I shal cast away Israhel fro the face of the erthe that I haue gyuen to them. And the temple that I haue halowed to my name, I shal cast it away fro my syght. And it shal be a fable and prouerbe, and thys hows an example shal be to alle peple. Euery man that shal goo therby shal be abasshyd and astonyed and shal saye: "Why hath God don thus to this londe and to thys hows?" And they shal answere: "For they haue forsaken theyr Lord God that brought their fadres fro the londe of Egypte, and haue folowed straunge goddes and them adoured and worshipped. And therfor God hath brought on them all thys euyll."' Here may euery man take ensample how peryllous and dredeful it is to breke the comandements of God.

XX yere after that Salamon had edefyed the temple of God and hys hows and fynysshyd it perfyghtly, Hyram the Kynge of Tyre wente for to see townes that Salamon had gyue to hym, and they plesyd hym not. Hyram had sente to Kynge Salamon an hondred and twenty besaunts of gold, whyche he had spente on the temple and hys hows, and on the walle of Iherusalem and other townes and places that he had made.

Salamon was ryche and gloryous, that the fame ranne of hys sapyence and wysedom and of hys byldyng and dyspense in hys hows thurgh the world, in so moche that the Quene of Saba cam fro fer contreys to see hym and to tempte hym in demaundes and questyons. And she cam into Iherusalem with moche peple and richessis, with camelles charged with aromatykes and gold infynyte. f. 73rb And she cam and spack to Kynge Salamon alle that euer she | had in her herte. And Salamon taught her in all that euer she purposed tofore hym. She coude saye nothyng but that the kyng answerd to her; ther was nothyng hyd fro hym.

The Quene of Saba thenne, seeyng alle the wysedom of Salamon, the hows that he had bylded, and the mete and seruyse of hys table, the habytacles of hys seruauntes, the ordre of the mynystres, theyr clothyng and araye, hys botellers and offycers, and the sacrefyses that he offred in the hows of Our Lord, whan she sawe alle thyse thynges, she had no spyrite to answere. But she said to Kynge Salamon: 'The word is trew that I herde in my lande of thy wordes and thy wysedom. And I beleuyd not them that told it to me, vnto the tyme that I myself come and haue seen it with myn eyen. And I haue now wel seen and prouyd that the half was not told to me. Thy sapyence is more, and thy werkis also, than the tydynges that I herde. Blessyd be thy seruantes, and blessyd ben thyse that stande alwaye tofore the and here thy sapyence and wysedom. And thy Lord God be blessyd, whom thou hast plesid, and hath sette the vpon the trone of Israhel, for so moche as God of Israhel loueth the and hath ordeyned the a kynge for to do rightwysnes and iustyse.' She gaf thenne to the kynge an C and xx besauntes of gold, many aromatykes and gemmes precious. There were neuer seen tofore so many aromatykis ne so swete odours smellyng as the Quene of Saba gaf to Kyng Salamon. Kynge Salamon gaf to the Quene of Saba alle that euer she desyred and demaunded of hym; and after r[e]torned into her contre and londe.

The weight of pure gold that was offred euery yere to Salamon was vj honderd lxvj talentes of gold, exept that that the marchantes offred, and alle they that solde and alle the kynges of Arabye and dukes of that londe.

Salamon made two C sheldes of the purest gold and sette them in þe hows of Lybane. He made hym also a trone of yuorye, which was grete and was clad with gold, whiche had vj grees or stappes, whiche was rychely wrought with two lyons | of gold holdyng the sete aboue f. 73va
and xij smale lyons standyng vpon þe stappes, on euerich tweyne, here and there. Ther was neuer suche a werke in no royame.

And all the vessellis that Kynge Salomon dronke of were of gold. And the seelyng of the hows of Lybane, in which his sheldes of gold were in, was of the most pure gold. Syluer was of no prys in the dayes of Kyng Salamon; for the nauye of the kynge wyth the nauye of

214 retorned] rotorned

Hyram wente, in thre yere ones, into Tharse and brouht thens gold and siluer, teeth of olyphauntes and grete rychesses.

The kynge Salamon was magnefyed aboue all the kynges of the world in rychessis and wysedom. And all the world desyred to see the chyere and vysage of Salamon, and to here hys wysedom that God had gyuen to hym. Euery man brought to hym yeftes, vessellis of gold and syluer, clothes and armours for warre, aromatikes, horse and mules euery yere. Salamon gadred togydre charis and horsmen. He had a thousand a{n}d foure hondred charis and carris and xij thousand horsmen; and were lodged in smale cytees, and townes abowte Iherusalem by the kyng. Ther was as grete habundance and plente of gold and syluer in tho dayes in Iherusalem as stones or sichomours that growe in the felde. And horses were brought to hym fro Egypte and Chao. What shal I al-daye wryte of the rychesses, glorye and magnyfycence of Kynge Salamon? It was so grete that it can not be expressyd, for ther was neuer none lyke tofore hym, ne neuer shal none come after hym lyke vnt{o} hym. He made the Book of the Parables conteynyng xxxj chapytres, the Booke of the Canticles, the Book of Ecclesiastes conteynyng xij chapytres and the Booke of Sapience conteynyng xix chapytres.

Thys Kynge Salamon louyd ouermoche wymen and specially straunge wymen of other sectes, as Kyng Pharaos doughter and many other of the gentyles, of whom God had comanded to the chyldren of Israhel that they shold not haue to doo wyth them ne they
f. 73vb with theyr doughtres. For God said certaynly they shold | torne your hertes to serue theyr goddes. To suche wymen Salamon was coupled with most brennyng loue. He had vijC wyues whyche were as quenes and iijC concubynes, and thyse wymen torned hys herte. For whan he was olde, he so doobted and loued hem that they made hym honoure their straunge goddes, and worshyppid Astaroth, Chamos and Moloch, ydollys of Sydone, of Moabytes and Amonytes, and made to them tabernacles for to plese hys wyues and concubynes.

Wherfor God was wroth with hym, and said to hym: 'Bycause thou hast not obserued my preceptes and my comandementis that I comanded the, I shal cutte thy kyngdom and deuyde it, and gyue it to thy seruaunt. But not in thy dayes I shal not do it, for loue that I had to Dauid thy fader. But fro the hand of thy sone I shal cutte it, but not alle: I shal reserue to hym one trybe for Dauids loue and Iherusalem that I haue chosen.' And after thys, dyuerse kynges becam aduersaryes to Salamon, and was neuer in pees after.

It is said, but I fynde it not in the Byble, that Salamon repentyd hym moche of thys synne of ydolatrye and dyde moche penaunce therfor, for he lete hym be drawe thurgh Iherusalem and bete hymself wyth roddes and scorgys, that the blood flowed in the syght of alle the peple. He regned vpon alle Israhel in Iherusalem xl yere and deyde, and was buryed with hys fadres in the cyte of Dauid. And Roboas hys sone regned after hym.

Thus endeth the lyf of Salamon.

[12. REHOBOAM]

After Salomon, regned hys sone Roboas. He cam to Sychem, and f. 74ra / theder cam alle the peple for to ordeyne hym kynge. Iheroboas and all sig. k2 the multytude of Israhel spack to Roboas, and said: 'Thy fader sette on vs an harde yoke and grete imposicions. Now thou hast not so moche nede. Wherfor lasse it and mynuysshe it, and ease vs of the grete and hard burthen, and we shal serue the.' Roboas answerd, and said: 'Goo ye and come agayn the thyrde day, and ye shal haue an answere.' Whan the peple was departed, Roboas made a counseyl of the senyors and old men that had assysted hys fader Salomon whylis he lyuyd, and said to them: 'What saye ye and counseylle me, that I may answere to the peple?' Whyche said to Roboas: 'Yf thou wylt obeye and agree to this peple, and agree to theyr petycion and speke fayr and frendly to them, they shal serue the alleway.' But Roboas forsoke the counseyl of the olde men, and called the yong men that were of hys age and axid of them counseyll. And the yong men that had ben norisshyd with hym bad hym saye to the peple in thys wyse: 'Is not my fyngre | gretter than the backe of my fader? Yf my fader f. 74rb hath leyed on you an heuy burthen, I shal adde and put more to your burthen. My fader bete you with scorgis, and I shal bete you with scorpions.'

The thyrde day after, Iheroboam and alle the peple cam to Roboas to haue theyr answere. And Roboas lefte the counseyl of the olde men, and saide to them lyke as the yong men had counseylled hym. And anon the peple of Israhel forsoke Roboas. And of xij trybus ther abode with hym no moo but the trybe of Iuda and of Beniamyn; and the other ten trybus departed and made Iheroboam theyr kynge, and neuer retorned vnto the hows of Dauid after, vnto thys day.

272 flowed] folowed
1 After] A *six-line capital supplied by hand in red*

And thus for synne of Salomon, and bycause Roboas wold not doo after the counseyl of the old men but was counseylled by yong men, the ten tribus of Israhel forsoke hym and departed fro Iherusalem, and seruyd Iheroboam and ordeyned hym kynge vpon Israhel. Anon after thys, Iheroboas fylle to ydolatrye, and grete deuysyon was euer after bytwene the kynges of Iuda and the kynges of Israhel. And so regned dyuerse kynges eche after other in Iherusalem after Roboas, and in Israhel after Iheroboam.

And here I leue alle th'ystorye and make an ende of Booke of Kynges for thys tyme *etc.* For ye that lyste to knowe how euery kyng regned after other, ye may fynde it in the fyrst chapytre of Saynt Mathew, whyche is redde on Crystemas Day in the mornyng tofore *Te Deum*, whyche is the genelagye of Our Lady.

[13. JOB]

f. 74va Here foloweth th'ystorye of Iob, red on the first Sonday of Septembre.

Ther was a man in the londe of Hus named Iob. And this man was symple, rightful and dredyng God and goyng from all euyll. He had vij sones and thre doughtres. And his possessyon was vijM sheep, iijM camellis, vC yok of oxen, vC asses, and hys famylye and houshold, passyng moche and grete. He was a grete man and riche emong all the men of the oryent.

And his sones wente dayly eche to other hows, makyng grete festes, euerich as his day cam, and they sente for their thre susters for to ete and drynke with hem. Whan they had thus fested eche other ofte, Iob sente to them and blessyd and sanctefyed them, and rysynge euery day erly, he offred sacrefyses for them all, sayeng: 'Leste my chyldren synne and blesse not God in theyr hertes.' And thus dyde Iob euery daye.

On a daye whan the sones of God were tofore Our Lord, Sathan cam and was emonge them. To whom Our Lord saide: 'Whens comest thou?' Whiche answerd: 'I haue goon round aboute the erthe f. 74vb and thurgh|walked it.' Our Lord saide to hym: 'Hast thou not consyderyd my seruaunt Iob, that ther is none lyke vnto hym in the erthe, a man symple, rightful, dredyng God and gooyng from euyl?' To whom Sathan answerd: 'Doth not Iob drede God ydelly? Yf so

3 Ther] T *six-line capital supplied by hand in red*

were that thou ouerthrewest hym, hys hows and alle hys substaunce rounde aboute, he shold sone forsake the. Thou hast blessyd the werkes of hys handes and hys possessyon is encrecyd moche in th'erthe. But stratche out thy hond a lytyl and towche all that he hath in possessyon, and he shal soone grutche and not blesse the.' Thenne sayd Our Lord to Sathan: 'Loo, all that whiche he oweth and hath in possession, I wyl it be in thy hand and power, but on hys persone ne body sette not thy hand.' Sathan departed and wente fro the face of Our Lord.

On a day as hys sones and doughtres ete and dronke wyn in the hows of the oldest brother, ther cam a messager to Iob, whiche said: 'The oxen erid in the ploughe and the asse pastured in the pasture by them, and the men of Sabey ran on them and smeten thy seruauntes and slewe them with swerd, and I only escaped for to come and to shewe it to the.' And whyles he spack, ther cam another and saide: 'The fyre of God fylle doun from heuen and hath brente thy sheep and seruauntes and consumed them, and I only escaped for to come and shewe it to the.' And yet whylys he spack, cam another and sayd: 'The Chaldeys made thre hoostes and haue enuayhed thy camels, and taken them and hath slayn thy seruantes with swerd, and I only escaped for to brynge the word.' And yet he spekyng, another entryd in and said: 'Thy sones and doughtres drynkyng wyn in the hows of thy first begoten sone, sodenly cam a vehemente wynde fro the regyon of deserte and smote the iiij corners of the hows, whiche fallyng, oppressyd thy chyldren, and ben all deed, and I only fledde for to telle to the.'

Thenne Iob aroos and cutte his kote and dyde do shaue his heed and, fallyng doun to the ground, worshipped and adowred God, sayeng: 'I am comen out naked fro the wombe of my moder, | [f. 75ra / sig. k3] and naked shal retorne agayn therto. Our Lord hath gyuen, and Our Lord hath taken away. As it hath plesid Our Lord, so is it don. The name of Our Lord be blessyd.' In all thyse thynges Iob synned not with hys lippes ne spack nothyng folyly ayenst Our Lord, but toke it all pacyently.

After thys, it was soo that on a certayn day whan the children of God stood tofore Our Lord, Sathan cam and stode emong them, and God said to hym: 'Whens comest thou?' To whom Sathan answerd: 'I haue gon rounde the erthe and walked thurgh it.' And God said to Sathan: 'Hast thou not consydered my seruaunt Iob, that ther is no man lyke hym in th'erthe, a man symple, ryghtful, dredyng God and goyng fro euyl, and yet reteynyng hys innocencye? Thou hast meuyd me ayenst hym, that I shold put hym to afflyction without cause.' To whom Sathan said: 'Skynne for skynne, and all that euer a man hath he shal gyue for hys sowle. Neuertheles, stratche thyn hande and towche his mouth and hys flesshe, and thou shalt see þat he shal not blesse the.' Thenne said God to Sathan: 'I wyl well that hys body be in thyn hande, but saue hys sowle and hys lyf.'

Thenne Sathan departed fro the face of Our Lord, and smote Iob with the worst botchys and blaynes, fro þe plante of hys foot vnto the toppe of hys heed, whiche was made lyke a lazar, and was caste out and satte on the dongehyll. Thenne cam hys wif to hym and said: 'Yet thou abydest in thy symplenes. Forsake thy God and blesse hym no more, and goo deye.' Thenne Iob said to her: 'Thou hast spoken lyke a folissh woman. Yf we haue receyuyd and taken good thyngis of the hande of Our Lord, why shal we not susteyne and suffre euyll thynges?' In all thyse thynges Iob synned not with his lippes.

Thenne thre men that were frendes of Iob, heeryng what harme was happed and comen to Iob, camen euerich fro hys place to hym. That one was named Eliphas Themanytes, another Baldad Scintes, and the thyrde Sophar Naamathites. And whan they sawe hym fro fer,
f. 75rb they knewe hym not, and cryeng they wepte. | They cam for to conforte hym, and whan they considered hys myserye, they tare theyr clothis and caste duste on theyr heedys, and satte by hym seuen dayes and seuen nyghtes, and no man spake to hym a word, seeyng hys sorow.

Thenne after that, Iob and they talked and spoken togydre of hys sorowe and myserye, of whyche Seynt Gregory hath made a grete book callyd the *Morallys* of Seynt Gregory, whiche is a noble book and a grete werk. But I passe ouer all tho maters and retorne vnto the ende, how God restored Iob agayn to prosperyte.

It was so that, whan thyse thre frendes of Iob had ben longe wyth Iob and had sayd many thynges, eche of them to Iob and Iob agayn to hem, Our Lord was wroth with thyse thre men and said to them: 'Ye haue not spoken ryghtfully as my seruaunt Iob hath spoken. Take ye therfore seuen bulles and seuen weders and goo to my seruaunt Iob, and offre ye sacrefise for you; Iob my seruaunt shal praye for you. I shal receyue hys prayer and shal take hys vysage.' They wente forth and dyde as Our Lord comanded them.

And Our Lord beheld the vysage of Iob and sawe hys penaunce whan he prayd for hys frendes, and Our Lord added to Iob double of all that Iob had possessyd. Alle hys brethern came to hym, and alle hys susters, and all they that tofore had knowen hym, and ete with hym in hys hows, and meuyd theyr heedys vpon hym, and conforted hym vpon all the euyl that God had sente to hym. And eche of them gaf hym a sheep and a golde ryng for hys eere.

Our Lord blessyd more Iob in hys last dayes than he dyde in the begynnyng, and he had thenne after xiiij thousand sheep, vj thousand camellys, a thousand yok of oxen, a thousand asses, and he had vij sones and thre doughtres. And the first doughters name was Diem, the seconde Cassiam, and the thyrde Cornustib[ii]. Ther were nowher founden in the world so fair wymen as were the doughters of Iob. Theyr fader Iob gaf to them herytage emong their brethern.

And thus Iob by his pacience gate so moche loue of God that he | was restored double of all his lossis. And Iob lyuyd after one hondred f. 75va and xl yere, and sawe hys sones and the sones of hys sones vnto the fourth generacion, and deyed an old man and ful of dayes.

Thus endeth the storye of Iob.

[14. TOBIT]

Here foloweth th'ystorye of Tobye, whyche is red the Thyrde Sondaye of Septembre.

Thobye, of the tribe and of þe cyte of Neptalym, whiche is in the ouerpartyes of Galylee vpon Nason, after the waye þ{at} ledeth men westward hauyng on his lyfte syde the cyte of Sepheth, was taken in the dayes of Salmanasar kynge of th'Assyryens and put in captyuyte. Yet he forsoke not the waye of trouthe, but alle that he had or coude gete he departed dayly with his brethern of hys kynred, which were prysoners wyth hym.

And howbeit that he was yongest in alle the trybe of Neptalym, yet dyde he nothyng chyldesly. Also, whan alle other wente vnto the golden calues that Iheroboas | kynge of Israhel had made, this Thobye f. 75vb only fledde the felowships of them alle and wente to Iherusalem into the temple of Our Lord. And there he adowred and worshypped the Lord God of Israhel, offryng truly hys fyrst fruytes and tythes, in so moche that in the thyrde yere he mynystred vnto proselytys and straungers alle the tythe. Suche thynges and other lyke to thyse he obseruyd whylis he was a chylde. And whan he cam to age and was a

112 Cornustibii] Cornustibu
3 Thobye] T *six-line capital supplied by hand in red*

man, he toke a wyf named Anne of hys trybe, and gate on her a sone, namyng after hys owne name Thobye, whom fro hys chyldehode he taught to drede God and absteyne hym fro alle synne.

Thenne after, whan he was brouht by captyuyte wyth hys wyf and his sone into the cyte of Nynyue with alle hys trybe, and whan alle ete of the metes of the gentyles and paynems, thys Thobye kepte hys sowle clene and was neuer defowled in the metes of them. And bycause he remembryd Our Lord in all hys herte, God gaf hym grace to be in the fauour of Salmanasar the kynge, whiche yaf to hym power to goo where he wold, hauyng lyberte to doo what he wolde. He wente thenne to alle them in captyuyte and gaf to them warnynges of helthe. Whan he cam on a tyme in Rages, cyte of the Iewes, he had suche yeftys as he had be honoured wyth of the kynge, ten besauntes of syluer. And whan he sawe one Gabele beyeng nedy, whych was of hys trybe, he lente hym the sayd weight of syluer vpon hys oblygacion.

Longe tyme after thys, whan Salmanasar the kynge was deed, Sennacheryb hys sone regned for hym, and hated and loued not the chyldren of Israhel. And Thobye wente vnto alle hys kynred and conforted them, and deuyded to euerich of them as he myght of hys facultees and goodes. He fedde the hungry and gaf to the naked clothes, and dylygently he buryed the dede men and them that were slayn. After this, whan Sennacheryb retorned, fleyng the plaghe fro the Iewery that God hath sente hym for hys blasphemye, and he, beyng wroth, slewe many of the chyldren of Israhel, | [f. 76ra / sig. k4] and Thobye alwaye beryed the bodyes of them. Whiche was told to the kynge, whyche comanded to slee hym and toke awaye all hys substaunce.

Thobye thenne with hys wyf and hys sone hyd hym and fledde away all naked, for many louyd hym wel. After thys xlv dayes, the sones of the kynge slewe the kynge. And thenne retorned Thobye vnto hys hous, and all hys facultees and goodes were restored to hym agayn.

After this, on an hye festful day of Our Lord whan that Thobye had a good dyne{r} in hys hows, he said to hys sone: 'Goo and fetche to vs somme of our trybe dredyng God, that they may come and ete with vs.' And he wente forth and anon he retorned, tellyng to hys fader that one of the chyldren of Israhel was slayn and laye deed in the strete. And anon he lepe out of his hows, leuyng hys mete and fastyng, cam to the body, toke it and bare it into hys hows pryuely, that he myht secretly berye it whan the sonne wente doun. And whan he had hyd the corps, he ete his mete with waillyng and drede, remembryng that worde that Our Lord said by Amos the prophet: 'The daye of youre feste shal be torned into lamentacion and wayllyng.' And whan the sonne was gon doun, he wente and buryed hym. Alle hys neyghbours repreuyd and chydde hym, sayeng: 'For thys cause thou were comanded to be slayn and vnneth thou escapedest the comandement of deth, and yet thou beryest dede men.' But Thobye, more dredyng God than the kynge, toke vp the bodyes of dede men and hyd them in hys hows, and at mydnyht he buryed them.

Hit happed on a day after thys that he was wery of beryeng dede men, cam home and leyde hym doun by a walle and slepte. And fro a swalows neste aboue ther fylle doun hote donge of them on hys eyen, and he was therof blynde. Thys temptacion suffred God to falle to hym, that it shold be example to them that shal come after hym of hys pacience, lyke as it was of holy Iob. For fro hys infancye he dredde euer God and kepte hys preceptis and | [f. 76rb] was not grutchyng ayenst God for hys blyndnes, but he abode vnmeuable in the drede of God, gyuyng and rendryng thankyngis to God alle the dayes of hys lyf. For lyke as Iob was assaylled, so was Thobye assaylled of hys kynnesmen, sko{r}nyng hym and sayeng to hym: 'Wher is now thy hope and reward, for whiche thou gauest thy almesses and madest sepultures?' Thobye blamed them for suche wordes, sayeng to them: 'In no wyse saye ye not soo. For we be the sones of holy men and we abyde that lyf that God shal gyue to them that neuer shal chaunge theyr faith fro hym.'

Anna hys wyf wente dayly to the werke of weuyng, and gate by the labour of her handes theyr lyuelode as moche as she myght. Wherof on a day she gate a kydde and brought it home. Whan Thobye herde the voys of the kyd bletyng, he saide: 'See that it be not stolen; yelde it agayn to the ownar, for it is not leeful to vs to ete ne touche onythyng that is stolen.' To that hys wyf, all angry, answerd: 'Now manyfestely and openly is thyn hope made vayne, and thy almesses lost.' And thus wyth suche and lyke wordes she chydde hym.

Thenne Thobye began to syghe and began to praye Our Lord with t[e]eris, sayeng: 'O Lord thou art rightful, and alle thy domes ben trewe and alle thy wayes ben mercy, trouthe and ryghtwisnes. And now, Lord, remembre me and take thou no vengeance of my synnes, ne remembre not my trespaces ne the synnes of my fadres. For we haue not obeyed thy comandementis; therfore we ben betaken into

92 teeris] theris

dyrepcyon, captyuyte, deth, fables, and into repreef and shame to alle nacions in whiche thou hast dysperclyd vs. And now, Lord, grete be thy iugements; for we haue not don accordyng to thy preceptes, ne haue not walkyd wel tofore the. And nowe, Lord, doo to me after thy wylle, and comande my speryte to be receyuyd in pees. It is more expedyent to me to dye than to lyue.'

The same day, it happed that Sara doughter of Raguel in the cyte of f. 76va Medes, þat she was rebuked and herde rep[r]eef | of one of the handmaidens of her fader, for she had be yeuen to vij men, and a deuyl named Asmodeus slewe them as sone as they wold haue gon to her. Therfor the mayde repreuyd her, sayeng: 'We shal neuer see sone ne doughter of the on the erthe, thou slear of thy husbondes. Wilt thou slee me as thou hast slayn vij men?' Wyth thys voys and rebuke, she wente vp in the vpperist cubicle of the hows; and thre dayes and thre nyghtes she ete not ne dranke not, but was contynuelly in prayers, besechyng God for to delyuer her fro this repreef and shame.

And on the thirde day, whan she had accomplysshed her prayer, blessyng Our Lord, she said: 'Blessyd be thy name, God of our fadres, for whan thou art wroth thou shal doo mercy. And in a tyme of trybulacion thou forgyuest synnes to them that calle to the. Vnto the Lord I conuerte my vysage, and vnto the I addresse myn eyen. I aske and requyre the that thou assoylle me fro the bonde of the repreef and shame, or certaynly vpon the erthe kepe me. Thou knowest wel, Lord, that I neuer desired man, but I haue kepte clene my sowle from all co[n]cupyscence. I neuer medlyd me with players, ne neuer had parte of them that walke in lightnes. I consented for to take an husbond wyth thy drede, but I neuer gaf consente to take one with my luste. Or I was vnworthy to them, or happely they were vnworthy to me, or happely thou hast conseruyd and kepte me for som other man. Thy counseyl is not in mannes power; this knoweth euery man that worshippeth the. For the lyf of hym, yf it be in probacion, shal be crowned, and yf it be in trybulacion, it shal be delyuerd, and yf it be in correction, it shal be leefull to come to mercy. Thou hast none delectacion in oure perdicion, for after tempeste thou makest tranquyllyte, and after wepynge and shedyng of teeris thou bryngest in exultacion and ioye. Thy name, God of Israhel, be blessyd, world without ende.'

In that same tyme were the prayers of them bothe herde, in the

104 repreef] repeef   121 concupyscence] comcupyscence

sight of the glorye of the hye God; and the holy angele of God, Raphael, was sente to hele them bothe, | of whom in one tyme were f. 76vb the prayers recyted in the syght of Our Lord God.

Thenne, whan Tobie supposed his prayer to be herd that he myght deye, he called to hym his sone Thobye and said to hym: ‘Here, my sone, the wordes of my mouth and sette them in thy herte as a fundamente. Whan God shal take away my sowle, burye my body and thou shalt worshippe thy moder alle the dayes of her lyf. Thou owest to remembre what and how many peryllis she hath suffred for the in her wombe. Whan she shal haue accomplisshid the tyme of her lyf, burye her by me. Alle the dayes of thy lyf haue God in thy mynde, and beware that thou neuer consente to synne, ne to disobeye ne breke the comandements of God. Of thy substance doo almesse, and torne neuer thy face fro ony poure man; so doo that God torne not hys face fro the. As moche as thou mayst be mercyful. Yf thou haue moche good, gyue habundantly. Yf thou haue but lytyl, yet studye to gyue and to departe therof gladly. Thou makeste to the therof good tresour and mede in the daye of necessyte; for almesse delyuerith a man fro alle synne and fro deth, and suffreth not hys sowle to goo into derknesse. Almesse is a grete sykernesse tofore the hye God vnto all them that doo it. Beware, my sone, kepe the fro alle fornycacion, and suffre not thyself sauf with thy wyf to knowe that synne. And suffre neuer pryde to haue domynacion in thy wytte ne in thy worde; that synne was the begynnyg of alle perdicion. Whosomeuer werke to the onythynge, anon yelde to hym hys mede and hyre. Late neuer the hyre of thy seruaunt ne mede of thy mercenarye remayne in no wyse wyth the. That þou hatest to be don to the of other, see that thou neuer doo to another. Ete thy brede wyth the hungry and nedy, and couer the naked wyth thy clothis. Ordeyne thy brede and wyn vpon the sepulture of a rightwys man, but ete it not ne drynke it not wyth synners. Aske and demaunde counseyl of a wyse man. Alleway and in euery tyme blesse God, and desyre of hym that he adresse thy wayes and late all thy counseilles abyde in hym.

‘I | telle to the, my sone, that whan thou were a lytyl chylde I lente f. 77ra / to Gabele x besauntes of syluer, duellyng in Rages, the cyte of Medes, sig. [k5] vpon an oblygacion whiche I haue by me. And therfore spyre and aske how thow maist goo to hym, and thou shalt receyue of hym the said weight of syluer and restore to hym his oblygacion. Drede thou not, my sone. Though we lede a poure lyf, we shal haue moche good yf we drede God and goo fro synne and doo well.’

Thenne yonge Thobye answerd to his fader: 'Alle that thou hast comanded to me I shal do, fader, but how I shal gete this moneye, I wote neuer. He knoweth not me, ne I knowe not hym. What token shal I gyue hym? And also I knowe not the waye thether.' Thenne his fader answerd to hym and said: 'I haue his oblygacion by me, whiche whan thou shewest hym, anon he shal paye the. But goo now first and seche for the somme trewe man, that for hys hyre shal goo with the whilis I lyue, that thou mayst receyue it.'

Thenne Thobye wente forth, and fonde a fair yong man gyrt vp and redy for to walke, and not knowyng that it was the aungele of God, salewed hym and said: 'Fro whens haue we the, good yong man?' And he answerd: 'Of the chyldren of Israhel'. And Thobyas sayd to hym: 'Knowest thou the waye that ledeth one into the regyon of Medes?' To whom he answerd: 'I knowe it wel, and alle the iorneyes I haue ofte walked and haue dwellyd with Gabele our brother, whiche dwellyth in Rages the cyte of Medes, whyche stondeth in the hylle of Egbathanis.' To whom Thobye said: 'I pray the tarye here a whyle, tyl I haue told this to my fader.' Thenne Thobye wente in to his fader and told to hym alle thyse thynges, wheron his fader meruaylled and prayde hym that he shold brynge hym in. Thenne the angel cam in and salewed the old Thobye and said: 'Ioye be to the alewaye.' And Thobye said: 'What ioye shal be to me that sytte in derknesses and see not the light of heuen?' To whom the yonglyng said: 'Be of stronge byleue; it shal not be longe but of
f. 77rb God thou shalt | be cured and heled.' Thenne said Thobye to hym: 'Mayste thou lede my sone vnto Gabele in Rages, cyte of Medes? And whan thou comest agayn, I shal restore to the thy mede.' And the angele saide: 'I shal lede hym thether and brynge hym agayn to the.' To whom Tobye said: 'I pray the to telle me of what hows or of what kynred art thou?' To whom Raphael the aungele said: 'Thou nedest not to aske the kynred of hym that shal goo with thy sone, but lest happely I shold not delyure hym to the agayn, I am Azarias, sone of grete Ananye.' Thobye answerd: 'Thou art of a grete kynred; but I pray the be not wroth thaugh I wold knowe thy kynrede.' The aung{e}le said to hym: 'I shal sauely lede thy sone theder, and saufly brynge hym and rendre hym to the agayn.' Thobye thenne answeryng said: 'Wel mote ye walke, and Our Lord be in your iourneye, and hys aungele felawshype wyth you.'

Thenne whan all was redy þat they shold haue wyth hem by the waye, yong Thobye toke leue of his fader and moder and bad them farewel. Whan they shold departe, the moder b[e]gan to wepe and saye: ‘Thou haste taken away and sente fro vs the staf of our old age. Wold God that thilke money had neuer ben, for whiche thou hast sente hym. Our pouerte suffyseth ynough to vs that we myght haue seen our sone.’ Thobye said to her: ‘Wepe not; our sone shal come saufly agayn, and thyn eyen shal see hym. I byleue that the good aungele of God felawshipeth with hym and shal dyspose all thynge that shal be nedeful to hym, and that he shal retorne agayn to vs with ioye.’ With this the moder cessed of her wepyng and was stylle.

Thenne yong Thobye wente forth, and an hounde folowed hym. And the fyrst mansion that they made was by the Ryuer of Tygre. And Thobye wente out for to wasshe hys feet, and ther cam a grete fissh for to deuoure hym, whom Thobye, feryng, cryde out with a grete voys: ‘Lord, he cometh on me!’ And the aungele said to hym: ‘Take hym by the vynne and drawe hym to the.’ And so he dyde, and drewe hym out of the water to the drye londe. Thenne said | the f. 77va
angele to hym: ‘Open the fysshe and take to the the herte, the galle and the mylte, and kepe them by the. They be prouffitable and necessarye for medycynes.’ And whan he had don so, he rosted of the fysshe and toke it with hem for to ete by the waye, and the remenaunt they salted, that it myght suffyse them tyl they cam into the cyte of Rages. Thenne Thobye demanded of the angele and said: ‘I pray the, Azaria brother, to telle me wherto thyse be good that thou hast boden me kepe.’ And the aungele answerd and said: ‘Yf thou take a lytyl of hys herte and put it on the coles, the smoke and fume therof dryueth away all maner kynde of deuylles, be it fro man or fro woman, in suche wyse that he shal no more come to them.’

And Thobye said: ‘Where wilt thou that we shal abyde?’ And he answerd and said: ‘Herby is a man named Raguel, a man nyghe to thy kynrede and trybe, and he hath a doughter named Sara, and he hath neyther sone ne doughter more than her. Thou shalt owe all his substaunce, for the behoueth to take her to thy wyf. Therfor aske thou her of her fader, and he shal gyue her to the for to be thy wyf.’

Thenne Thobye answerd and said: ‘I haue herde saye that she hath be gyuen to vij men and they ben deed; and I haue herd that a deuyl sleeth them. I drede therfor that it myght happe so to me; and I, that am an only sone to my fader and moder, I shold depose theyr olde age with heuynes and sorow to helle.’ Thenne Raphael th’aungele said to

215 began] bagan 231 and] & \ and 244 a] a \ a

hym: 'Here me, and I shal shewe to the wherwith thou mayst preuayle ayenst that deuyll. Thyse that toke their wedlok in suche wyse that they exclude God fro them and their mynde and wayte but to their luste, as an hors and mule in whom is none vnderstondyng, the deuyl hath power vpon them. Thou, therfor, whan thou shalt take a wyf and entrest into her cubycle, be thou contynent by the space of thre dayes fro her, and thou shal do nothyng but bee in prayers with her. And that same nyght put the herte of the fysshe on the fyre, and that shal f. 77vb put away the deuyl. The | seconde nyght thou shal be admytted in copulacion of holy patryarkes. The iij nyght ye shal folowe the blessyng, that sones may be begoten of you bothe. And after the thyrde nyght, thou shalt take the vyrgyne wyth drede of God more for loue of procreacion of chyldren than for luste of thy body, that thou mayst folowe the blessyng of Abraham in hys seed.'

Thenne they wente and entryd into Raguels hows, and Raguel receyuyd them ioyously. And Raguel, beholdyng wel Thobye, sayd to Anna hys wyf: 'How lyke is thys yong man vnto my cosyn!' And whan he had so said, he asked them: 'Whens be ye, yong men, my brethern?' And they said: 'Of the trybe of Neptalym, of the captyuyte of Nynyue'. Raguel saide to them: 'Knowe ye Thobye my brother?' Whiche said: 'We know hym wel.' Whan Raguel had spoken moche good of hym, th'aungele said to Raguel: 'Thobye, of whom thou demaundest, is fader of this yonge man.' And thenne wente Raguel and with wepyng eyen kyssed hym and wepyng vpon hys necke saide: 'The blessyng of God be to the my sone, for thou art sone of a blessyd and good man.' And Anna hys wyf and Sara hys doughter wepte also.

After they had spoken, Raguel comanded to slee a weder and make redy a feste. Whan he thenne shold bydde them sytte doun to dyner, Thobye said: 'I shal not ete here thys day ne drynke but yf thou fyrst graunte to me my petycion and promyse to me to gyue me Sara thy doughter.'

Whyche whan Raguel herde, he was astonyed and abasshid, knowyng what had fallen to vij men that tofore had wedded her, and dredde leste it myght happen to this yong man in lyke wyse. And whan he helde his pees and wold gyue hym none answere, the angele said to hym: 'Be not aferde to gyue thy doughter to thys man dredyng God, for to hym thy doughter is ordeyned to be hys wyf. Therfor none other may haue her.' Thenne said Raguel: 'I doubte not God hath admytted my prayers and teres in hys syghte. And I byleue that therfor he hath made you to come to me, that thyse | may be ioyned in [f. 78ra / sig. [k6]] one kynrede after the lawe of Moyses. And now haue no doubte but I shal gyue her to the.'

And he, takyng the right honde of his doughter, delyueryd it to Thobye, seyeng: 'God of Abraham, God of Ysaac and God of Iacob be wyth you, and he conioyne you togydre and fulfyl hys blessyng in yow'; and toke a chartre and wrote the conscrypcion of the wedlok. And after thys they ete, blessyng Our Lord God. Ragu{e}l callyd to hym Anne hys wyf and bad her to make redy another cubycle. And she brought Sara her doughter therin, and she wepte. To whom her moder said: 'Be thou stronge of herte, my doughter. Our Lord of heuen gyue to the ioye for the heuynes that thou hast suffred.'

After they had souped, they lad the yong man to her. Thobye remembryd the wordes of th'aungele and toke out of hys bagge parte of the herte of the fysshe, and leyde [it] on brennyng coles. Thenne Raphael th'angel toke the deuyll and bonde hym in the vpperyst deserte of Egypte. Thenne Thobye exhorted the vyrgyne and sayd to her: 'Aryse, Sara, and late vs praye to God thys day and tomorow and afte[r] tomorow. For thyse thre nyghtis we be ioyned to God, and after the thyrde nyght we shal be in our wedlok. We ben sothly the chyldren of saynctes and we may not so ioyne togydre as peple doo that knowe not God.' Thenne they bothe arysynge prayde togydre instantly that helth myght be gyuen to them. Thobye said: 'Lord God of our fadres, heuen and erthe, see, welles and floodes, and all creatures that ben in them, blesse the. Thou madest Adam of the slyme of th'erthe, and gauyst to hym for an helpe Eue. And now, Lord, thou knowest that for the cause of lecherye I take not my suster to wyf, but only for the loue of posteryte and procreacion of chyldren, in whyche thy name be blessyd world without ende.' Thenne said Sara: 'Haue mercy on vs Lord, haue mercy, and late vs wexe olde bothe togydre in helthe.'

And after this the cokkes began to crowe, at whiche tyme Raguel comanded hys seruauntes to come to hym. And they togydre | wente [f. 78rb] for to make and delue a sepulcre. He said: 'Lest happely it happen to hym a[s] it hath happed to the vij men that wedded her.' Whan they had made redy the fosse and pytte, Raguel retorned to hys wyf and said to her: 'Sende one of thyn handmaydens and late her see yf he {be} deed, that he may be beryed er it be lyght day.' And she sente

307 it] *om.* 311 after] aftee 327 as] at

forth one of her seruauntes, whiche entryd into the cubycle and fonde them bothe sauf and hole and slepyng togydre. And she retorned and brought good tydynges. And Raguel and Anna blessyd Our Lord God and said: 'We blesse the Lord God of Israhel that it hath not happed to vs as we supposid. Thou hast don to vs thy mercy, and thou hast excluded fro vs our enemye poursyewyng vs. Thou hast don mercy on two only chyldren. Make them, Lord, to blesse the to fulle and to offre [t]o the sacrefyse of praysyng and of theyr helth, that the vnyuersyte of peples may knowe that thou art God only in the vnyuersal erthe.'

Anone thenne Raguel comanded his seruauntes to fylle agayn the pytte that they had made er it wexid lyght, and bad hys wyf to ordeyne a feste and make all redy that were necessarye to mete. He dyde doo slee ij fatte kyen and foure weders and to ordeyne mete for all hys neyghbours and frendys. And Raguel desired and adiured Thobie that he shold abyde with hym two wekys. Of all that euer Raguel had in possessyon of goodys, he gaf half parte to Thobye, and made to hym a writyng that þat {ot}her half parte he shold haue after the deth of hym and hys wyf.

Thenne Thobye called th'angele to hym, whiche he trowed had ben a man, and said to hym: 'Azaria brother, I praye the to take heed to my wordes. Yf I make myself seruaunt to the, I shal not be worthy to satysfye thy prouydence. Neuertheles, I pray the to take to the the bestes and seruauntes, and goo to Gabele in Rages, the cyte of Medes, and rendre to hym hys oblygacion and receyue of them the money, and praye hym to come to my weddynge. Thou knowest thyself that my fader nombreth the dayes of my beyng oute, and yf I tarye more,
f. 78va hys sowle shal | be heuy. And certaynly thou seest how Raguel hath adiured me, whos desire I may not despyse.'

Thenne Raphael, takyng foure of the seruauntis of Raguel and two camels, and wente to Rages, the cyte of Medes, and there fyndyng Gabele, gaf to hym hys oblygacion and receyuyd alle the money, and tolde to hym of Thobye, sone of Thobye, alle that was don, and made hym come wyth hym to the weddyng. Whan thenne he entred the hows of Raguel, he fonde Thobye syttyng at mete, and cam to hym and kyssed hym. And Gabele wepte and blessyd God, sayeng: 'God of Israhel blesse the, for thou art sone of the best man and iuste, dredyng God and doyng almesse; and the blessyng be said vpon thy wyf and your parentis, and that ye may see the sones of your sones vnto the

338 to] do

thyrde and fourth generacion. And your seed be blessyd of God of Israhel, whyche regneth *in secula seculorum*.' And whan alle had said amen, they wente to the feste, and with the drede of God they excersised the feste of theyr weddynges.

Whyles that Thobye taryed bycause of hys maryage, hys fader Thobye began to be heuy, sayeng: 'Trowest [thou], wherfor my sone tarieth and why he is holden there? Trowest thou that Gabele be deed and no man is there that shal gyue hym his money?' He began to be sory and heuy gretly, bothe he and Anna hys wyf wyth hym, and began bothe to wepe bycause at the day sette he cam not home. His moder therfor wepte with vnmesurable teeris and said: 'Alas my sone, wherfore sente we the to goo this pylgremage, the lyght of our eyen, the staf of our age, the solace of our lyf, the hope of our posteryte; all thyse only hauyng in the, we ought not to haue laten the goo fro vs.' To whom Thobye said: 'Be stylle and troble the not. Our sone is sauf ynough; the man is trewe and faithful ynough with whom we sente hym.' She myght in no wyse be conforted, but euery day she wente and loked and espyed the waye that he shold come yf she myght see hym come fro ferre.

Thenne Raguel said to Thobye his sone-in-lawe: 'Abyde here with me, and I shal sende messagers of thy helthe and | welfare to Thobye f. 78[vb] thy fader.' To whom Thobias saide: 'I knowe wel that my fader and my moder acompte the dayes, and the spyrite is in grete payne within them.' Raguel prayd hym with many wordes, but Thobye wold in no wyse graunte hym. Thenne he delyueryd to hym Sara hys doughter, and half parte of all hys substaunce in seruauntis, men and wymen, in beestis, camellis, in kyen and moche money. And sauf and ioyeful he lete hym departe fro hym, sayeng: 'Th'angel of God, that is holy, be in your iourney and brynge you home hool and sound, and that ye may fynde alle thynge weel and ryghtful aboute your fader and moder, and þat myn eyen may see your sones er I deye.' And the fader and moder, takyng their doughter, kyssyd her and lete her departe, warnyng her to worshipe her husbondes fader and moder, loue her husbond, to rewle wel the meyne, to gouerne the hows and to kepe herself irreprehensyble, that is to saye wythout repreef.

Whan they thus retorned and departed, they came to Charram, which is the half waye to Nynyue, the thertenst day. Thenne said the angele to Thobye: 'Thobye brother, thou knowest how thow hast lefte

374 thou] *om.*

thy fader. Yf it plese the, we wyl go tofore, and late thy famylye come softly after with thy wif and with thy bestes.' Thys plesed wel to Thobye. And thenne said Raphael to Thobye: 'Take with the of þe galle of the fysshe; it shal be necessarye.' Thobye toke of the galle and wente forth tofore.

Anna hys moder satte euery daye by the waye in the toppe of the hylle, fro whens she myght see hym come fro ferre. And whylis she satte there and loked after hys comyng, she sawe aferre and knewe her sone comyng. And rennyng home, she tolde to her husbonde, sayeng: 'Loo, thy sone cometh.' Raphael thenne said to yong Thobye: 'Anon as thou entrest into the hows, adowre thy Lord God and, gyuyng to hym thankyngis, goo to thy fader and kysse hym. And anone thenne enoynte hys eyen with the galle of the fysshe that þou berest with the. Thou shalt wel knowe that hys eyen shal be opened and thy fader shal see the lyght of heuen and shal ioye in thy syght.' Thenne ranne | f. 79ra / sig. [k7] the dogge that folowed hym and had ben with hym in the waye, and cam home as a messager, fawnyng and makyng ioye with hys tayll. And the blynde fader aroos and began, offendyng hys feet, to renne to mete hys sone, gyuyng to hym hys honde; and so takyng, kyssed hym with hys wyf and began to wepe for ioye. Whan than they had worshyped God and thanked hym, they satte doun togydre.

Thenne Thobye, takyng the galle of þe fysshe, enoynted hys faders eyen and abode as it had be half an houre. And the slyme of hys eyen began to falle away, lyke as it had be the whyte of an egge, whiche Thobye toke and drewe fro hys fadres eyen, and anone he receyuyd sight. And they gloryfyed God, that is to wete he and hys wyf and all they that knewe hym. Thenne said Thobye the fader: 'I blesse the, Lord God of Israhel, for thou hast chastysed me and thou hast saued me. And loo, I see Thobye my sone.'

After thys vij dayes, Sara the wyf of hys sone cam and entryd in with alle the famylye and the beestis hole and sound, camellys and moche money of hys wyuys, and also the money that he had receyuyd of Gabele. And he told to hys fader and moder alle the benefetes of God that was don to hym by the man that ladde hym. Thenne cam Achior and Nabath, cosyns of Thobye, ioyeng and thankyng God of all the goodes that God had shewde to hym. And vij dayes they ete togydre makyng feste, and were glad wyth grete ioye.

Thenne olde Thobye callyd hys sone Thobye to hym and sayde: 'What may we gyue to thys holy man that cometh with the?' Thenne Thobye, answeryng, said to hys fader: 'Fader, what mede may we gyue to hym or what may be worthy to hym for hys benefetes? He ladde me out and hath brouht me hole agayn; he receyuyd the money of Gabele; he dyde me haue my wyf and he put away the deuyl fro her; he hath made ioye to my parentis and saued myself fro deuoryng of the fysshe, and hath made the see the lyght of heuen; and by hym we be replenesshyd with all goodes. What may we thenne worthyly gyue to hym? Wherfor I praye | the, fader, that thou praye hym yf he f. 79rb v[ou]chesauf to take the half of all that I haue.' Thenne the fader and the sone, callyng hym, toke hym aparte and begonne to pray hym that he wold vouchesauf to take half the parte of all the goodes that they had brought.

Thenne said he to them pryuely: 'Blesse ye God of heuen, and byfore alle lyuyng peple knowleche ye hym, for he hath don to you hys mercy. Forsothe, to hyde the sacramente of the kynge it is good, but for to shewe the werkys of God and to knowleche them it is worshypful. Oracion and prayer is good with fastyng and almesse, and more than to sette vp tresours of gold. For almesse delyueryth fro deth, and it is she that purgeth synnes and maketh a man to fynde euerlastyng lyf. Who that doo synne and wyckednes, they ben enemyes of hys sowle. I shew to you therfor the trouthe, and I shal not hyde fro you the secrete worde. Whan thou praidest with teres and dydest berye the dede men and leftest thy dyner and hyddest dede men by daye in thy hows and in the nyght thou beryedest them, I offred thy prayer vnto God. And for as moche as thou were accepted tofore God, it was necessarye, thou beyng tempted, that he shold proue the. And now hath Our Lord sente me for to cure the; and Sara, the wyf of thy sone, I haue delyuerd fro the deuyl. I am sothly Raphael the angele, one of the seuen whyche stande tofore Our Lord God.'

Whan they herd thys, they were trobled, and tremblyng fyl doun groflyng on theyr faces vpon the ground. The aungele said to them: 'Pees be to you; drede you not. Forsothe, whan I was with you by the wylle of God—hym alleway blesse ye and synge ye to hym—I was seen to you to ete and drynke, but I vse mete and drynke inuysyble, whyche of men may not be seen. It is now therfor tyme that I retorne to hym whiche hath sent me. Ye alway blesse God and telle ye alle hys meruaylles.' And whan he had said this, he was taken away fro the sight of them, and after that they myght no more see hym. Thenne

454 vouchesauf] vuochesauf

f. 79va they fyl doun flatte on theyr faces by the space of iij | houres, and blessyd God. And arisyng vp, they told all the meruaylles of hym.

Thenne th'older Thobye, openyng hys mouthe, blessyd Our Lord and sayde: 'Grete art thou, Lord, euermore, and thy regne is into alle worldes; for þou scorgest and sauyst, thou ledyst to helle and bryngest agayn, and ther is none that may flee thy hand. Knowleche and confesse you to the Lord, ye children of Israhel, and in the syght of gentylis preyse ye hym. Therfor he hath desperpled you emong gentyles that knowe hym not, that ye telle hys meruaylles and make them to be knowen, for ther is none other God Almyghty but he. He hath chastysed vs for our wyckednesses and he shal saue vs for hys mercy. Take heed and see, therfor, what he hath don to vs, and with fere and drede knowleche ye to hym and exalte hym kynge of alle worldys in your werkys. I, sothly, in the londe of my captyuyte, shal knowleche to hym, for he hath shewd hys mageste into the synful peple. Confesse you therfor synners, and do ye iustyce tofor Our Lord, byleuyng that he shal doo to you hys mercy. I, sothly, and my sowle shal be glad in hym. Alle ye chosen of God, blesse ye hym, and make ye dayes of gladnes, and knowleche ye to hym. Iherusalem, cyte of God, Our Lord hath chastysed the in the werkys of hys hondys. Confesse thou to Our Lord in hys good thyngys, and blesse thou God of worldes, that he may re-edyfye in the hys tabernacle and that he may calle agayn to the alle prysoners and them that ben in captyuyte, and that thou ioye *in omnia secula seculorum*. Thou shalt shyne with a bright lyght, and all the endes of the erthe shal worshipe the. Nacions shal come to the fro ferre, and bryngyng yeftes shal worshype in the Our Lord and shal haue thy londe into sanctificacion. They shal calle in the a grete name. They shal be cursed that shal despyse the. And they all shal be condempned that blaspheme the. Blessyd be they that edefye the. Thou shalt be ioyeful in thy sones, for all shal be blessyd and shal be gadred togydre vnto Our Lord. Blessed be they that loue
f. 79vb the and that | ioye vpon thy pees. My sowle, blesse thou Our Lord, for he hath delyueryd Iherusalem hys cyte. I shal be blessyd yf ther be lefte of my seed for to see the clerenesse of Iherusalem. The yates of Iherusalem shal be edefyed of saphir and emerawde, and all the circuyte of hys walles, of precious stone. Alle the stretes therof shal be paued with whyte stone and clene, and alleluya shal be song by the wayes therof. Blessyd be the Lord, that hath exalted it, that it may be hys kyngdome *in secula seculorum*. Amen.'

And thus Thobye fynysshed thyse wordes. And Thobye lyuyd after he had receyuyd his sight xlij [y]ere and sawe the sones of hys neuewis, that is the sones of the sones of hys sone, yonge Thobye. And whan he had lyuyd C ij yere, he deyde and was honorably buryed in the cyte of Nynyue. He was lvj yere old whan he lost hys syght; and whan he was lx yere old, he receyuyd hys syght agayn. The resydue of hys lyf was in ioye, and with good profyght of the drede of God, he departed in pees.

In the houre of hys deth he called to hym Thobye hys sone, and vij of hys yonge sones, hys neuewes, and sayd to hem: 'The destruction of Nynyue is nygh; the worde of God shal not passe; and our brethern that ben desperpled fro the londe of Israhel shal retorne theder agayn. All the londe therof shal be fulfyllid with deserte, and the hows that is brente therin shal be re-edefyed, and theder shal retorne all peple dredyng God. And gentylis shal leue theyr ydolles, and shal come in Iherusalem and shal dwelle therin. And alle the kynges of the erthe shal ioye in her, worshypyng the kynge of Israhel. Here ye therfor, my sones, me your fader: serue ye God in trouthe, and seche ye that ye doo that may be plesyng to hym; and comande ye to your sones that they doo rightwisnessis and almesses, that they may remembre God and blesse hym in all tyme in trouthe and in alle theyr vertue. Now therfor, my sones, here me, and dwelle ye no lengre here but whansomeuer your moder shal deye, berye her by me, and fro than forth on dresse | ye your stappes that ye goo hens; I see wel that f. 80ra1 / wyckednesse shal make an ende of it.' sig. [k8]

Hyt was soo thenne, after the deth of hys moder, Thobye wente fro Nynyue with hys wyf and hys sones and the sones of hys sones, and retorned vnto hys wyues fader and moder, whom they fonde in good helthe and good age; and toke the cure and charge of them, and were with them vnto their deth and closyd theyr eyen. And Thobye receyuyd alle th'erytage of the hows of Raguel and sawe the sones of hys sones vnto the fyfthe generacion. And whan he had complesshyd lxxxxix yere, he deyde in the drede of God, and with ioye they beryed hym. | Alle hys cognacion and alle hys generacion f. 80rb1 abode in good lyf and in holy conuersacion, in suche wyse as they were acceptable as wel to God as to men and to alle dwellyng on the erthe.

Thus endeth the hystorye of Thobye th'older and of hys sone Thobye the yonger.

524 yere] xere

[15. JUDITH]

Here begynneth th'ystorye of Iudith, whiche is redde the last Sonday of Octobre.

f. 80ra2 Arphaxat, Kynge of the Medes, subdued vnto his empire many peoples and edefyed a myghty cite, whych he named Egbathanis, and made hyt with stones squared, and polysshed them. The walles therof were of heyght lxx cubitis and of brede xxx cubitis, and the towres therof were an honderd cubytis hye. And gloryfyed hymself as f. 80rb2 he that was myghty in puyssance | and in the glorye of hys hoost and of hys chares. Nabugodonosor thenne, in the xij yere of hys regne, whyche was kynge of th'Assyryens and regned in the cite of Nynyue, fought agayn Arphaxat and toke hym in the felde. Wherof Nabugodonosor was exalted and enhaunsed hymself, and sente vnto all regyons aboute and vnto Iherusalem tyl the mountes of Ethyope for t'obeye and holde of hym. Whyche all gaynsaid hym with one wille, f. 80va and without | worshype sente home hys messagers voyd and setted nought by hym.

Thenne Nabugodonosor, hauyng herat grete indygnacion, swore by hys regne and by hys trone that he wold auenge hym on them all, and therupon callyd all hys dukes, prynces and men of warre and helde a counseyl, in which was decreed that he shold subdue alle the world vnto hys empyre. And therupon he ordeyned Olyfernes prynce of hys knyghthode and bad hym goo forth and in especial agayn them that had despysed hys empyre, and bad hym spare no royame ne towne but subdue all to hym. Thenne Olifernes assemblyd dukes and maistres of the strength of Nabugodonosor and nombred CxxM fotemen and horsmen shoters xijM. And tofore them he comanded to goo a multitude of innumerable camellis, laden with suche thyngis as were nedeful to the hoost, as vytayll, gold and syluer moche that was taken out of the tresorye of the kynges; and so wente to many royames which he subdued and ocupyed a grete parte of th'oryent, tyl he cam approchyng the londe of Israhel.

And whan the chyldren of Israhel herde herof, they drede sore leste he shold come emong them into Iherusalem and destroye the temple, for Nabugodonosor had comanded that he shold extyncte alle the goddes of the erthe, and that no god shold be named ne worshiped but he hymself of all the nacions that Olifernes shold subdue. Eliachym

3 Arphaxat] A *six-line capital supplied by hand in red*

thenne, preest in Irahel, wrote vnto all them in the montayns that they shold kepe the strayte wayes of the montayns. And so the chyldren of Israhel dyde as the preest had ordeyned. Thenne Eliachym the preest wente aboute alle Israhel and said to them: ‘Knowe ye that God hath herde your prayers, yf ye abyde and contynue in your prayers and fastyngis in the sight of God. Remembre ye of Moyses, the seruaunt of God, whyche ouerthrewe Amalech, trustyng in hys strengthe and in hys power, in hys hoost, in hys helmes, in hys chares and in hys horsmen, not fyghtyng wyth yron but with prayeng of holy prayers. In lyke wyse shal be all the enemy|es of Israhel yf ye perseuere in this f. 80vb werke that ye haue begonne.’ With this exortacion they contynued prayeng God. They perseuered in the sight of God, and also they þat offred to Our Lord were clad with sackcloth and had asshes on theyr heedes, and with all their herte they prayd God to visite hys peple Israhel.

It was told to Holofernes, prynce of the knyghthode of th’Assyryens, that the chyldren of Israhel made them redy to resyste hym and had closed þe wayes of the montayns. And he was brenned in ouermoche furour, in grete ire. He callid all the prynces of Moab and dukes of Amon and said to them: ‘Saye ye to me what peple is this that bisege the montaynes, or what or how many cytes haue they? Also what is theyr vertue and what multytude is of them, or who is kyng of their knyghthode?’ Thenne Achior, duke of all them of Amon, ansueryng said: ‘Yf thou daignest to here me, I shal telle the trouthe of this peple that dwelleth in þe montayns, and ther shal not yssue out of my mouth one false worde. This peple dwelled fyrst in Mesopotamye and was of the progenye of the Caldees, but wold not dwelle there, for they wold not folowe the goddes of their faders that were in the londe of Caldees, and goyng and leuyng the cerymonyes of their fadres whiche was in the multitude of many goddes, they honoured one God of heuen, which comanded them to goo thens and that they shold dwelle in Carran. Thenne after was there moche hongre, that they descended into Egypte and there abode iiijC yere and multeplied, that they myht not be nombred. Whan the Kynge of Egipt greuyd them in his bildyngis, beryng claye tyles, and subdued them, they cryed to Our Lord and he smote the londe of Egypte with dyuerse plaghes. Whan they of Egipt had caste them out fro them, the plaghe cessed fro them. And thenne they wold haue taken hem agayn and wold haue called them to their seruyse. And they fleyng, their God opend the see to them that they wente thurgh drye-foot, in whiche the innumerable hoost of th'Egipciens poursyewyng them were drowned, that ther was not one of them sauyd for to telle to them that cam after [f. 81ra / sig. l1] them. They passed thus the Reed See and | them with manna xl yere and made bytter waters swete and gaf them water out of a stone. And wheresommeuer this peple entred without bowe or arowe, sheld or swerd, theyr God fought for them. And ther is no man may preuayle ayenst this peple but whan they departe fro the culture and honour of theyr God. And as ofte as they haue departed fro theyr God and worshypped other strange goddes, so ofte haue they ben ouercomen with their enemyes. And whan they repente and come to the knowlege of their synne and crye their God mercy, they ben restored agayn and theyr God gyueth to them vertue to resiste their enemyes. They haue ouert[h]rowen Cananeum the kyng, Iebusee, Pheresee, Eueum, Etheum and Amorreum and all the myghty men in Esebon, and haue taken their londe and cytees and possesse them, and shal as longe as they plese their God. Their God hated wickednesse, for tofore thys tyme whan they wente fro the lawes that theyr God gaf to them, he suffred them to be taken of many nacions into captiuyte, and were disperplid. And nowe late they be comen agayn and possede Iherusalem, wherein is *sancta sanctorum*, and ben comen ouer thise montaynes whereas somme of hem dwelle. Now therfor, my lord, see and serche yf ther be ony wickednesse of them in the sight of their God, and thenne late vs goo to them, for their God shal gyue them into thy hondes and they shal be subdued vnder þe yock of thy power.'

And whan Achior had said thus, all the grete men aboute Holyferne were angry and had thought for to haue slayn hym, sayeng eche to other: 'Who is this that may make the chyldren of Israhel resiste the kynge Nabugodonosor and hys armee and hoost? Men cowardis and without myght and without ony wysedom of warre. Therfor, that Achior may knowe that he saith not trewe, late vs ascende the montayns. And whan the myghty men of them be taken, late hym be slayn wyth theym, that all men may knowe that Nabugodonosor is god of the erthe and that ther is none other but he.' Thenne whan they cessed to speke, Holofernes, hauyng indignacion, said to Achior: [f. 81rb] 'Bycause thou hast prophecied to vs of the chyldren | of Israhel, sayeng that their God defended them, I shal shewe to the that ther is no god but Nabugodonosor. For whan we haue ouercomen them all

89 ouerthrowen] ouertrowen

and slayn them as one man, thenne shalt thou dye with them by the swerd of Assyryens, and all Israhel shal be put into ruyne and perdicion, and thenne shal be knowen that Nabugodonosor is lord of all the erthe. And the swerd of my knyghthode shall passe thurgh thy sydes. And thou shalt departe hens and goo to them, and shal not dye vnto the tyme that I haue them and the. And whan I haue slayn them with my swerd, thou shalt in lyke wyse be slayn with lyke vengeaunce.' After this, Holofernes comanded hys seruauntis to take Achior and lede hym to Bethulye and to put hym in the handes of them of Israhel.

And so they toke Achior and ascended the montayns; ayen whom cam out men of warre. Thenne the seruantes of Holofernes torned aside and bonde Achior to a tree, hondes and feet, with cordes and lefte hym, and so retorned to their lord. Thenne the sones of Israhel, comyng doun fro Bethulye, loosed and vnbonde hym and brought hym to Betulye. And he, beyng sette amydde the peple, was demaunded what he was and why he was so sore there bounden. And he told to them alle the mater lyke as it is aforsaid and how Holofernes had comanded hym to be delyuerd vnto them of Israhel. Thenne all the peple fylle doun into their faces worshypyng God, and with grete lamentacion and wepyng wyth one wylle made their prayers vnto Our Lord God of heuen, and that he wold behold the pryde of them and to the mekenes of them of Israhel, and take hede to the faces o{f} hys halowes and shewe to them his grace and not forsake them; and praid God to haue mercy on them and defende them fro their enemyes.

And on that other side, Holofernes comanded his hoostis to goo vp and assaille Bethulye, and so wente vp of footmen an C and xxM, and xij thousand horsmen and byseged the toun and toke their water fro them, in so moche that they þat were in þe toun were in grete penurye
of water, | for in all the toun was not water ynowgh for one daye, and f. 81va
suche as they had was gyuen to the peple by mesure. Thenne all the peple, yong and old, cam to Osias, whiche was their prynce with Carmy and Gothoniel, all with one voys cryeng: 'God the Lord deme bytwene vs and the. For thou hast don to vs euyl what þou spakest not pesybly wyth th'Assyryens, for now we shal be delyueryd into the hondes of them. It is better for vs to lyue in captyuyte vnder Holofernes and lyue than to dye here for thurst and see our wyues

134 faces] facess

and chyldren dye byfore our eyen.' And whan they had made thys pyetous cryeng and yollyng, they wente all to theyr chyrche and ther a longe whyle prayden and cryeden vnto God, knowlechyng theyr synnes and wyckednes, mekely besechyng to shewe hys grace and pyte on them. Thenne at laste Ozias aroos vp and said to the peple: 'Late vs abyde yet fyue dayes, and yf God sende vs no rescowe ne helpe vs not in that tyme that we may gyue glorye to hys name, ellis we shal doo as ye haue said.'

And whan that Iudith herde herof, whiche was a wydowe and a blessyd woman and was left wydowe iij yere and vj monethis after that Manasses her husbond deyde, anon she wente into ouerest parte of her hows, in which she made a pryue bedde which she and her seruauntes closed, and hauyng on her body an heyr had fasted all the dayes of her lyf, sauf Sabottis and newe mones and the festis of the hows of Israhel. She was a fayr woman, and her husbond had left her moche riches wyth plentyfull meyne and possessyons of droues of oxen and flockes of sheep, and she was a famous woman and dredde God gretly. And whan she had herde that Ozias had said that the fyfthe day the cyte shold be gyuen ouer yf God helped hem not, she sente for the prestis of Cambre and of Carmy and said to hem: 'What is this worde in whiche Ozias hath consented that the cyte shold be delyuerd to th'Assyryens yf within fyue dayes ther come no helpe to vs? And who be ye that tempte the Lord God? Thys worde is not [t]o styre God to mercy, but rather to areyse wrath and wodenes: ye haue f. 81vb sette a tyme of mercy-doyng by God. And | in your dome ye haue ordeyned a daye to hym. O God Lord, how pacyent is he! Late vs aske hym foryefnes with wepyng teeris. He shal not threten as a man ne enflawme in wrath as a sone of a man. Therfore meke we our sowles to hym, and in a contryte spyryte and mekyd serue we to hym, and saye we wepyng to God that after hys wylle he shewe to vs hys mercy. And as our herte is troubled in the pryde of them, so also of our humblenes and meknes late vs be ioyful. For we haue not folowed the synne of our fadres that forsoken theyr God and worshiped straunge goddes, wherfor they were gyuen and bytaken into hydous and grete vengeance, into swerde, ravayne and into confusyon to theyr enemyes. We forsothe knowen none other god but hym. Abyde we mekely the comforte of hym; and shal kepe vs fro our enemyes, and he shal meke all gentiles that arise ayenst hym, and shal make them without

175 to] so 179 teeris] teeeris

worship the Lord Our God. And now ye brethern, ye that ben prestes, on whom hongeth the lyf of the peple of God, praye ye vnto Allmyghty that he make me stedfaste in the purpose that I haue purposed. Ye shal stande atte gate and I shal goo out with my handmayde. And praye ye the Lord that he stedfast make my sowle. And do ye nothyng tyl I come agayn.'

And thenne Iudith wente into her oratorye and arayed her with her precious clothyng and aournements, and toke vnto her handmayde certayn vytayllys suche as she myg[h]t lawfully ete. And whan she had made her prayers vnto God, she departed in her most noble araye toward the gate, whereas Osias and the prestes abode her. And whan they sawe her, they meruaylled of her beaute. Notwithstandyng, they lete her goo, seyeng: 'God of our fadres yeue the grace and strengthe, all the counseyl of thyn herte with hys vertue and glorye to Iherusalem, and be thy name in the nombre of seyntis and of ryghtwys men.' And they, all they that were there, said Amen and *fiat, fiat*. Thenne she, praysyng God, passed thurgh the yate and her handmayde wyth her.

And whan | she cam doun the hylle aboute the spryngyng of the (f. 82ra / sig. l2) day, anon the espyes of th'Assiryens toke her, sayeng: 'Whens comest þou or whyther goost þou?' The whiche answerd: 'I am a doughter of th'Ebrews and flee fro them, knowyng that they shal be taken by you, and come to Holofernes for to telle hym theyr pryuetees. And I shal shewe hym by what entre he may wynne them, in suche wyse as one man of his hoost shal not perisshe.' And the men that herd their wordes beheld her vysage and wondred of her beaute, sayeng to her: 'Thou hast sauyd thy lyf bycause thou hast founden suche counseyl. Come therfor to our lord, for whan thou shal stonde in his sight, he shal accepte þe.' And they ladde her to the tabernacle of Holofernes.

And whan she cam byfor hym, anon Holofernes was caught by hys eyen. And his tiraunt knyghtis said to hym: 'Who despised þe peple of Iewes that haue so fayr wymen, that not for hem of right we ought to fight ayenst hem?' And so Iudith, seeyng Holofernes syttyng in hys canape that was of purpure, of gold, smaragdes and precious stones within wouen, and whan she had seen hys face she honowrid hym, fallyng doun herself vnto th'erthe. And the seruantes of Holofernes toke her vp, he so comandyng. Thenne Holofernes said to her: 'Be thou not aferd ne drede the not. I neuer greuyd ne noyed man that

199 myght] myggt

wold serue Nabugodonosor. Thy peple, sothly, yf they had not despised me, I had not reysed my peple ne strengthe ayenst them. Now telle to me the cause why thou wentist fro them, and that it hath plesi[d] the to come to vs.' And Iudith said: 'Take the wordes of thy handmayde, and yf thou folowe them, a perfight thyng God shal doo with the. Forsothe, Nabugodo[no]sor is the lyuyng kynge of th'erthe and thou hast hys power for to chastyse alle peple. For men only serue not hym, but also the beestis of the felde obeyen to hym. Hys myght is knowen ouerall and the chyldryn of Israhel shal be yolden to the, for their God is angry with them for their wickednes. They ben enfamyned and lacke brede and watre. They ben constrayned to ete their horse and beestis and to take suche holy thynges as ben forboden by theyr lawe, as whete, wyn and oyle. All thyse thynges God hath shewd to me. And they purpose to wast suche thyngis as they ought
f. 82rb not | touche. And herfor and for their synnes, they shal be put in the handes of their enemyes. And Our Lord hath shewde me thyse thynges to telle the. And I, thyn handmayde, shal worshipe God and shal goon out and praye hym, and come in and telle the what he shal seye to me, in suche wyse that I shal brynge the thurgh the myddle of Iherusalem, and thou shalt haue all the peple of Israhel vnder the as the sheep ben vnder the shepherde, in so moche þat ther shal not an hound barke ayenst the. And bycause thyse thynges ben said to me by the prouydence of God and that God is wroth with them, I am sente to telle the thyse thynges.'

Forsothe, all thyse wordes plesed moche to Holofernes and to hys peple. And they meruaylleden of þe wysedom of her, and one said to another: 'Ther is not suche a woman vpon erthe in sight, in fairnesse and in witte of wordes.' And Holofernes said to her: 'God hath doo wel that he hath sente þe hether for to lete me haue knowleche, and yf thy God do to me thise thynges, he shal be my God and thou and thy name shal be grete in the hows of Nabugodonosor.' Thenne comanded Holofernes her to goo in wher hys tresor laye and to abyde there, and to gyue to her mete fro his feste. To whom she said that she myht not ete of hys mete, but that she hath brouht mete with her for to ete. Thenne Holofernes saide: 'Whann that mete faylleth, what shal we gyue to the to ete?' And Iudith said that she shold not spende alle 'tyl God shal do in my hondes tho thynges þat I haue thought'. And the seruantes lad her into hys tabernacle.

232 plesid] plesith 234 Nabugodonosor] Nabugodo \ sor

And she desyred that she myght goo oute in the nyght and byfore daye to praye and come in agayn. And the lord comanded hys cubyculyers that she shold goo and come at her playsyr, thre dayes duryng. And she wente out into the valeye of Bethulye and baptysed her in the water of the welle. And she stratched her hondes vp to the God of Israhel, prayeng the good Lord that he shold gouerne her waye for to delyuer hys peple. And thus she dyde vnto the fourth day.

Thenne Holofernes made a grete feste, and sente a man of hys whyche was ghelded, named Vago, for to entrete Iudith for to lye with his lord and to come, ete and drynke wyn wyth hym. And Iudyth sayd: 'What am | I, that shold gaynsaye my lordes desire? I am at hys f. 82va
comandement. Whatsommeuer he wil that I doo, I shal doo and plese hym all the dayes of my lyf.' And she roos and aourned herself with her riche and precious clothes, and wente in and stode byfore Holofernes. And Holofernes herte was percyd with her beaute and brenned in the lust and desyre of her, and said to her: 'Sitte doun and drynk in ioye, for thou hast founden grace byfore me.' Iudith said: 'I shal drynk, my lord, for my lyf is magnefyeed this day bifore all the dayes of my lyf.' And she ete and dronke suche as her handmayde had ordeyned for her. And Holofernes was mery, and dranke so moche wyn þat he neuer dranke so moche in one day in all his lyf, and was dronken. And at euen, whan it was nyght, Olofernes wente vnto his bedde and Vago brought Iudith into his chambre and closid the dore.

And whan Iudith was allone in the chambre and Holofernes laye and slepte in ouermoche dronkenesse, Iudith said to her handmayde that she shold stonde without-forth byfore the dore of the preuy chambre and wayte aboute. And Iudith stode bifore the bedde, prayeng with teeris and with meuyng of her lippes, secretly sayeng: 'O Lord God of Israhel, conferme me in this houre to the werkes of my hondes, that thou reyse vp the cyte of Iherusalem as thou hast promysed, and that I may performe this that I haue thought to doo.' And whan she had thus said, she wente to the pyler that was at his beddes heed, and toke hys swerd and losed it. And whan she had drawen it out, she toke hys heer in her hand and said: 'Conferme me, God of Israhel, in this hour', and smote twyes in the necke and cutte of his heed, and lefte the body lye stylle and toke the heed and wrapped it in the canape, and delyueryd it to her mayde and bad her to put it in her scryppe. And they two wente oute, after their vsage, to pray.

And they passed the tentes and, goyng aboute the valeye, camen to the yate of the cytee. And Iudyth said to the kepers of the walles:

'Opene the yates, for God is with vs that hath don grete vertue in Israhel.' And anon, whan they herd her calle, they called the preestis of the cyte. And they comen rennyng, for they had supposed no more to haue seen her. And lyghtyng lightes, all wente aboute her. She f. 82vb thenne entrid in, stode vp in | an hye place and comanded scylence, and said: 'Prayse ye the Lord God that forsaketh not men hopyng in hym, and in me, hys handwoman, hath fulfyllyd hys mercy that he promysed to the hous of Israhel, and hath slayn in my hand th'enemye of hys peple this nyght.' And thenne she brought forth the heed of Holofernes and shewde it to them, sayeng: 'Loo, here the heed of Holofernes, prynce of the chyualrye of Assyriens. And lo the canope of hym, in whyche he laye in hys dronkenhed, where Our Lord hath smeton hym by the honde of a woman. Forsoth God lyueth, for hys aungel kepte me, hens goyng, ther abidyng and fro thens hyther retornyng. And the Lord hath not suffre[d] me his handwoman to ben defowled, but without pollucion of synne hath callyd me agayn to you, ioyeng in hys vyctorye, in my escapyng and in your delyueraunce. Knoweleche ye hym all for good, for hys mercy is euerlastyng, world withouten ende.' And all they, honouryng Our Lord, sayden to her: 'The Lord blesse the in hys virtue, for by the he hath brought our enemyes to nought.' Thenne Ozias, the prynce of the peple, said to h{e}r: 'Blessyd be thou of the hye God byfore alle wymen vpon erthe. And blessyd be the Lord that made heuen and erthe, that hath addressid the in the woundes of the heed of the prynce of our enemyes.'

After this Iudith bad that the heed shold be hanged vp on the walles. 'And at the sonne risyng, euery man in hys armes yssue out vpon your enemyes, and whan their espies shal see yow, they shal renne vnto the tente of their prynce to reyse hym and to make hym redy to fight. And whan his lordes shal see hym deed, they shal be smeton with so grete drede and feer that they shal flee, whom ye thenne shal pursyewe. And God shal brynge them and trede them vnder your feet.' Thenne Achior, seeyng the vertue of þe God of Israhel, lefte his olde hethens custom and byleuyd in God and was circumsised in his preuy membre, and put hymself to the peple of Israhel and all the successyon of hys kynred vnto thys day. Thenne, at the spryngyng of the daye, they henge the heed of Holofernes on the walles. And euery man toke hys armes and wente out with grete

321 suffred] suffre

noyse. Whyche thyng seeyng, th'espyes ronnen togydre to the tabernacle of Holofernes, | f. 83ra / sig. l3 and cam makyng noyse for to make hym t'aryse and that he shold awake, but no man was so hardy to knocke or entre into his preuy chambre.

But whan the dukes and leders of thousandes camen and other, they said to the preuy chamberlayns: 'Goo and awake your lord, for myes ben gon out of their caues and ben hardy to calle vs to bataylle.' Thenne Vago, his bawde, wente into his preuy chambre and stode byfore the curtyne and clapped hys handes togydre, wenyng he had slepte with Iudith. And whan he perceuyd noo meuyng of hym, he drewe the curteyn and, seeyng the dede body of Holofernes without heed lyeng in his blood, cryed with a grete voys, wepyng and rendyng hys clothes, and wente into the tabernacle of Iudith and fonde her not, and sterte out to the peple and said: 'A woman of th'Ebrewes hath made confusion in the hous of Nabugodonosor. She hath slayn Holofernes, and is deed, and she hath his heed with her.'

And whan þe prynces and capytayns of th'Assyryens herde this, anone they rente their clothes and intollerable drede fylle on them, and were sore troblyd in their wittes and made an horrible crye in their tentis. And whan all th'oost had herde how Olofernes was byheded, counseyl and mynde flewh fro them, and with grete tremblyng for socoure bygonne to flee, in suche wise that none wold speke with other, but with their heedes bowed doun fledde for t'escape fro th'Ebrews, whom they sawe armed, comyng vpon them; and departed, fleyng by feldes and weyes of hilles and valeyes. And the sones of Israhel, seeyng them fleyng, folowed them, cryeng wyth trumpes and showtyng after them, and slewe and smote doun al them þat they ouertoke. And Osias sent forthwith vnto all the cytees and regyons of Israhel. And they sente after alle the yong men and valiaunt to pursiewe them by swerd, and so they dyde vnto the vttermest coostis of Israhel. The other men, sothly, þat weren in Bethulye wente into the tentis of th'Assyrens and toke all the praye that th'Assyryens had lefte. And whan the men þat had pursiewed them were retorned, they toke all their beestis and all the meuable goodes and thynges þat they had lefte, so moche that euery man, fro þe moste to the leste, were made riche by the | f. 83rb praye that they toke.

Thenne Ioachim, the highe bisshop of Iherusalem, cam vnto Bethulye with all the preestis for to see Iudith. And whan she cam tofore them, all they blessid her with one vois, sayeng: 'Thou glorye of Iherusalem, thou gladnes of Israhel, thou the worship-doyng of our peple, þou dyde manly and thyn herte is comforted, bycause þou louedyst chastyte and knewest no man after the deth of thy husbond. And therfor the honde of God hath comforted the. And therfor þou shalt be blessyd, world without ende.' And all the peple said *Fiat, fiat*, 'Be it don, be it don.' Certaynly the spoylles of th'Assyriens were vnnethe gadred and assembled togydre in xxx dayes of the peple of Israhel. But all the propre rychesses þat were apperteynyng to Holofernes and coude be founden þat had ben hys, they were gyuen to Iudith as wel, gold, syluer, gemmes, clothis, as all other appertenancis to houshold. And all was delyuerd to her of the peple. And the folkes, with wimen and maydens, ioyeden in organs and harpes.

Thenne Iudith songe this song vnto God, saieng: 'Begynne ye in tymbres, synge ye to the Lord in cymbalis, manerly synge to hym a newe psalme. Fully ioye ye and inwardly calle ye hys name', and so forth. And for this grete myracle and victorye, all the peple cam to Iherusalem for to gyue laude, honour and worship vnto Our Lord God. And after they were purified, they offred sacrefices, vowes and behestis vnto God, and the ioye of this victorye was solempnysed duryng iij monethis. And after þat, eche wente home agayn into his owen cyte and hous.

And Iudith retorned into Bethulye and was made more grete and cleer to alle men of the londe of Israheel. She was ioyned to the vertue of chastyte, so that she knewe no man alle the dayes of her lyf after þe deth of Manasses her husbond, and duellyd in the hous of her husbond an hondred and fyue yere. And she lefte her damoyselle free. And after this she deyde, and is buryed in Bethulye. And all the peple bewayled her seuen dayes. Duryng her lyf, after this iourney, was no troble emong the Iewes, and the daye of this victorye of þe Hebrews was accepted for a festful day and halowed of the Iewes and nombred emong their feestis vnto this day.

NOTES ON THE TEXT

As discussed in the Introduction (vol. i, pp. xxxi–xxxiii; see also Taguchi, 'The Use of Sources'), nearly everything in the Old Testament section is ultimately derived from the Bible, with varying use of intermediate sources. While much of it is translated from the Vulgate, in other places the immediate source is Petrus Comestor's *Historia scholastica* (particularly in the earlier legends), *Bible historiale*, or *Cursor mundi*. In the later legends, direct use of the Vulgate comes to predominate, with some signs of influence from the existing Wycliffite translation. A few passages suggest the use of Flavius Josephus' *Jewish Antiquities*. As these are largely parallel accounts of the same biblical material, there is sometimes uncertainty about the proximate source, even leaving aside the verbatim quotations from the Vulgate within *Hs*.

The translation is characteristically free: the notes do not normally record the persistent abridgement and recasting of source material, and where sources have been combined, it is not always possible to say which one a particular phrase or sentence is derived from. The comparisons between *GoL* and the earlier texts are not exhaustive, but are intended to illustrate the various ways in which sources are treated.

Hs is cited by the chapter numbers of the 1543 Lyon edition (wikisource version). For Genesis, *Bh* is cited from Taguchi, *The Historye of the Patriarks*, by page/line, or simply by page when the text is relegated to the Commentary; the remainder by folio and column is from British Library MS Royal 19. D. iii (see Pl. 1). *HP* is also cited from Taguchi by page/line. WB is cited from *The Holy Bible*, ed. Forshall and Madden, and *Cm* from *Cursor Mundi*, ed. Morris; the Göttingen version is used, except where Cotton, Fairfax, or Trinity is specified. Unless otherwise stated, *JA* is cited by book, chapter, and section from the edition by Pollard, Timmermann, di Gregorio, and Laprade. *LgD* is cited from the British Library copy of the (c) version (IC.50152), using its handwritten foliation.

1. ADAM

Much of the material is drawn from *Hs* (Gen.), chs. 1–29, particularly from the beginnings and ends of chapters, but some is taken directly from Gen. 1–5, and there are passages that could be from either source, particularly where *Hs* quotes Gen., as often at the beginning of chapters.

The running head is *The lyf of Adam/adam*.

1 This line is preceded by a double-columned space for a woodcut that was never inserted.

3–7 **In . . . derknes nyght:** Gen. 1: 1–5.

7–8 **And thus . . . fyrst:** *Hs*, 3, *Primo enim cum coelo et terra lux est creata.*

8–17 **and euen and mornyng . . . and said:** Summarizes Gen. 1: 5–26. For *The second day, the thyrde day*, etc., compare the *Hs* chapter openings *Secunda die, Tercia die*, etc.

13–14 **God made the sonne and mone and sterres** *etc.*: Cf. *Hs* (Gen.), 6, *Fecit enim eadem die luminaria, solem, et lunam et stellas.*

14 **fisshes:** *Hs* (Gen.), 7, *Pisces vocauit Moyses reptilia*; Gen. identifies the sea-creatures only as *reptile* and *cete grandia.*

17–20 ***Faciamus*** **. . . nombre:** *Hs* (Gen.), 9, *Faciamus hominem etc. (Gen. I). Et loquitur Pater ad Filium, et Spiritum sanctum. Vel est quasi communis vox trium personarum, Faciamus et nostram.*

20–4 **Man was . . . beestis:** *Hs* (Gen.), 9.

24–7 **Whan God . . . allone:** *Hs* (Gen.), 10. Horrall, 'William Caxton's Biblical Translation', 92, attributes the retention of the Latin words to forgetfulness, but perhaps a direct quotation from the Vulgate (cf. Gen. 1: 10) has been inattentively extended to the following clause.

26 **for yet he was not parfyght til the woman was made:** *Hs* (Gen.), 10, *vel quia nondum homo perfectus erat.*

27–9 **Thus . . . rested:** Gen. 2: 1–2.

29–30 **not for that . . . operacion:** *Hs* (Gen.), 11, *Non enim quasi fessus dicitur quievisse, sed quia cessavit.*

30–1 **and shewd . . . blessyd:** Gen. 2: 3. This seems to be duplicated in the next sentence but one (*and the seuenth day he sanctefyed and made holy*); the translator may have separately rendered both the biblical passage and its paraphrase in *Hs* (Gen.), 11.

31–2 **Thus . . . vj dayes:** *Hs* (Gen.), 11.1. For *determynat*, cf. *Hs*, *determinant.*

34–5 **God . . . delyces:** Gen. 2: 8, but for the final word cf. the explanation in *Hs* (Gen.), 13, of *Eden* as *deliciae.*

35 **man was . . . Damaske:** *Hs* (Gen.), 13.

35–6 **He was made . . . erthe:** Gen. 2: 7; *Hs* (Gen.), 13.

36–9 **Paradyse . . . euyll:** Gen. 2: 9; *Hs* (Gen.), 13.

40–8 *Hs* (Gen.), 14; *moder* (41) translates *matrix.*

49–60 *Hs* (Gen.), 15.

61–78 *Hs* (Gen.), 16, which glosses Gen. 2: 18–21.

73 extasi: *Hs* (Gen.), 16, *exstasim*; *MED* has only 2 citations.

79–82 Whiles . . . my flessh: Gen. 2: 21–3.

82–4 And Adam . . . taken of a man: *Hs* (Gen.), 18.

84–5 And anon . . . the syde of a man: *Hs* (Gen.), 19.

85–7 therfor . . . flesshe: Gen. 2: 24.

87–90 And thaugh . . . owne flesshe: *Hs* (Gen.), 19.

90–2 They were . . . innocensye: *Hs* (Gen.), 20.

93–112 *Hs* (Gen.), 21.

93 hotter: Contrast Gen. 3: 1, *callidior* (quoted in *Hs*); *callidus* 'clever' has been confused with *calidus* 'hot'. Horrall, 'William Caxton's Biblical Translation', 95–7, suggests influence from *Cm*, 901–2, which mentions 'heat' as the serpent's natural state: *þou þu wild euer hat stede, / In cald sal euer be þi bede.*

111 willyng be lyke to God: Perhaps *to* should be added, but for *willing* with bare infinitive, cf. the quotation from *Gesta Romanorum* [a1500 (?1450)] in *MED willen* v.1, 1f: *þe sonne willing obey to the fadir, he come to him.*

113–27 The woman . . . asshamed: *Hs* (Gen.), 22.

128–33 And thus . . . thou: Gen. 3: 7–9.

132–57 Our Lord called . . . heede *etc.*: *Hs* (Gen.), 23. But the words *and thy seed and her seed* (156), absent in *Hs*, are from Gen. 3: 15.

158–81 In two thyngis . . . his wyf Eue: *Hs* (Gen.), 23.

174 shalst: Should perhaps be emended, but *MED*, *shulen* v.(1) 15a, has one example, c1450(c1415), Berkshire.

182 whiche is to saye, 'moder of all lyuyng folke': *Hs* (Gen.), 18, *Eva, scilicet post peccatum, quod sonat vita, eo quod futura esset mater omnium viventium.*

183–5 Thenne God made . . . mortalite: *Hs* (Gen.), 24.

185–7 and sayde . . . lyue euer: Gen. 3: 22.

187–8 Beware . . . of lyf: *Hs* (Gen.), 24.

188–92 And so . . . of lyf: Combines material from Gen. 3: 23–4 and *Hs* (Gen.), 24.

193–200 *Hs* (Gen.), 25.

201–12 *Hs* (Gen.), 26. For *he offryd wethes and thornes*, cf. *Bh*, 36/45–6, *les pires espiz offrit*. The final clause, *for the sacrefyse wold not belight ne brenne clere in the light of God* (of Cain), may have been generated by analogy from the statement in *Hs* about Abel: *Ignis enim de coelo oblationem ejus incendit.* Perhaps derived from *Hs*, the idea seems to have been widespread that God showed the acceptance of a sacrifice by allowing it to burn. Cf. Taguchi, 'The

Legend of the Cross', 28, *Chaym saw þat þe offrynge of his broþer Abel pleside more God þan his, fore þe smyche of Abellis offrynge wente vpward bute his dide nat so.*

213 Wherof Cayn . . . Abel: *Hs* (Gen.), 27.

213–21 wiche roose . . . th'erthe: Gen. 4: 8–12.

221–38 This Cayn . . . no penaunce: *Hs* (Gen.), 27, which includes part of Gen. 4: 13–15.

232 personaly: Contrast *Hs*, *additur impersonaliter* ['without naming the person'], *septuplum punietur.*

236 departed not truly: *Hs* (Gen.), 27, *Non recte divisit.* Cf. *MED departen* 4a, 'divide . . . (possessions . . .) among . . . recipients'. The corresponding passage in *Bh*, 315, has *Il ne disma mye a droit*, with the more specific sense 'tithe', not attested for *departen.*

239–290 *Hs* (Gen.), 28.

256–7 and vnderstode the fedyng . . . yere: *Hs* (Gen.), 28, *et commissuras certis temporibus faciendas intellexit.* While *fedyng* gives acceptable sense, emendation to *sedyng* in the sense of 'coupling' (*MED seden* 3a, 'to beget children, procreate', with one citation) would produce closer correspondence to *commissuras.*

261 suche as shepherdes . . . sportes: Cf. *Hs* (Gen.), 28, *ut labor pastoralis quasi in delicias verteretur.*

264–5 pilers or colompnes: *Hs* (Gen.), 28, *columnis.* Cf. Caxton, *Mirror of the World* (translated from French sources), *colompnes or pylers* (*OED column* n. 1a).

273 texture: *Hs* (Gen.), 28, *texturae. MED* has only one citation of the sense 'the art of weaving'.

277–8 Cayn was alway aferde: Not here in *Hs* (Gen.), but cf. 27, *Timens ergo Cain.*

288 he fered hym by payne: Mistranslates *Hs* (Gen.), 29, *tamen terrebat eas* [Cain's wives], *subdendo poenam.*

291–5 After that . . . chyldren: *Hs* (Gen.), 29.

295–6 And so . . . ymage of God: *Hs* (Gen.), 29.1.

296–7 This Seth was a good man: Not in Gen. or *Hs*; cf. *JA*, 1 II.iii, *fuisset uir egregius.*

297–303 he gate Enos . . . into the sones: *Hs* (Gen.), 29.1.

304–5 And Adam . . . doughtres: Gen. 5: 4; but compare also *Bh*, 44/38–9, *Et vesquit Adam puis qu'il ot engendre Seth viii*[c] *ans et engendra filz et filles.*

305–7 xxx sones . . . in the Bible: While *Hs*, ed. Sylwan, 29, *Additio* 1, mentions thirty sons and the same number of daughters, none of the sources consulted gives the number fifty.

307–8 alle . . . yere: Gen. 5: 5.

308–19 And in th'ende . . . heuen: This is an abridged account of the common legendary narrative about Seth's mission to the paradise for the oil of mercy and the early history of the cross tree. This story occurs integrated in various biblical narratives both in prose and verse, including the Middle English *Liber Aureus and Gospel of Nicodemus* (see Marx, *The Middle English Liber Aureus*, 27–8 and 86–7). For the legend, see Taguchi, 'The Legend of the Cross'; and in a broader context, Murdoch, *The Apocryphal Adam and Eve*. Cf. *Cm*, 1237–1412.

2. NOAH

Combines material from Gen. 5: 32–10: 32, *Hs*, chs. 29–36, and *Cm*, 1627–2138.

The running head is *The lyf of Noe*.

1–2 This heading is followed by a woodcut depicting Noah receiving animals into the ark (Hodnett 247; see frontispiece).

3 After that Adam . . . buryed by hym: *Hs* (Gen.), 24, mentions that Adam and Eve were buried in a double sepulchre.

3–9 At the begynnyng . . . ijM ***etc.***: Selectively summarizes material from *Hs* (Gen.), 29.1.

9 Methodius: Methodius of Olympus (died *c.*311), author of a lost commentary on Genesis; but the source here is Pseudo-Methodius, *Reuelationes in nouissimis temporibus*.

10–11 Noe thenne . . . comandement: Gen. 6: 9.

11–23 whan he was . . . C xx yere: Selectively summarizes material from *Hs* (Gen.), 30.

12–13 the chyldren of God, that is to saye of Seth, as religious: *Hs* (Gen.), 30, *filii Dei, id est Seth, religiosi*; the sense is clearer in *Bh*, 48/39–41, *les filz de Dieu (ce furent les filz qui de Seth estoient issuz, religieux et bons)*.

24–38 Thenne Noe . . . crystall: *Hs* (Gen.), 31, integrated with material from Gen. 6: 5–15. For *warderops* (28), cf. *Cm*, 1686, *wardrop*.

38–9 This arcke . . . C xx yere: *Hs* (Gen.), 30, discusses the length of time taken to build the ark.

39–44 In whiche tyme . . . wickednes: Up to this point, the selection of material has been similar to that in *Cm*, and for this passage *Cm*, 1729–44 is the closest source, with possible verbal parallels in *And hu god had him teld in* *speche; / He teld þat resun to mani a man, / Quarfor he suilk a schip bigan* (1732–4), in accordance with which *told* is supplied in 40.

45–9 Thenne whan . . . commanded hym: Gen. 6: 19–22, with some material from *Hs*, 32.

48 comestible: This word does not derive from any of the identified sources. *MED* has only two citations, both a1484, and this is the earliest in *OED*.

50–66 Thenne said . . . xl nyghtes: Gen. 7: 1–11, with some material from *Hs* (Gen.), 33.

66–73 And the arke . . . of th'erthe: Gen. 7: 17–22 is integrated with *Hs* (Gen.), 33, which may be the reason for the duplication (*GoL*, 68 and 72) of the detail, not in *Cm*, that the waters reached fifteen cubits above the mountains.

73–4 And whan Noe . . . glewe: Cf. *Hs* (Gen.), 33, *Et cum intrasset Noe clausit ostium Deus, et bituminavit exterius*, in which it is God that shut the door, etc.

74–96 And so . . . Our Lord: Gen. 7: 24–8: 14, integrated with material from *Hs* (Gen.), 33; in particular, *Yet thenne were not the toppes of the hillis bare?* (89–90) translates *Sed nonne cacumina montium jam erant nudata?*; and *but he durst not goo out but abode the commandement of Our Lord* (95–6) resembles *sed egrediendi exspectabat Domini praeceptum*. Some material not in either source suggests influence from *Cm*: *desired sore to haue tydynges of cessyng of the flood* (83–4) is similar in substance to *Cm*, 1874–6, *"Childer," he said, "quat rede ȝe, / Hou sal we of þis water witt, / Queþer þai be aught fallen ȝeitt?"*; and *for parauenture she fonde . . . was lefte there* (85–7) to *Cm*, 1885–8, *Apon þe water sone he fand, / A drinkled best þar fletand, / Of þat fless was he so fain, / To schip cam he neuer egain.*

97–105 Gen. 8: 14–19, integrated with material from *Hs* (Gen.), 34; for example, *He commanded . . . disiunctly entred* (99–100) is based on *Hs*, the following sentence on Gen.

106–21 Noe thenne . . . of heuen: Gen. 8: 20–9: 17. But *for he is prone and redy to fall* (109–10) abridges 8: 21 in a way that resembles *Hs* (Gen.), 34, *quia proni sunt ad malum*; and *And in token therof . . . in the clowdes of heuen* (120–1) abridges 9: 13–17 in a way that resembles *Hs* (Gen.), 34, *et in signum foederis hujus, posuit arcum suum in nubibus.*

121–2 For who . . . on hym: *Cm*, 1979–80, *If man misdo in oþer wise, / On þaim i sal take mi iustise.*

123 Noe lyuyd after the flood iijC l yere: The equivalent in Genesis (9: 28) occurs at a later point, after the drunkenness of Noah. In *JA* also, this information (1 III.ix) immediately follows the episode of the rainbow.

123–8 Fro the tyme . . . eten: *Cm*, 1988–98, with verbal resemblances in

1988–9, *þat bituix adam and noe / þe time was euer elike grene*. However, *Hs* (Gen.), 31, also includes an account of the effect of the deluge on the fecundity of the earth, which leads people to start eating meat.

128–49 And thenne . . . sones of Noe: Abridges *Cm*, 2007–58, 2081–138, with a number of verbal resemblances: e.g. *liuelad* (2009), *tilth* (2013), *breris* (2014), *Drunken on slepe lai bi him ane* (2021), *His middelest sun* (2025), *To skorning he his fader logh* (2028), *foli* (2035), *wok* (2049; T, *awoke*), *scornyng* (2050), *couering* (2057), *bituix þaim delt* (2088), *best* (2101), *blomen* (2118), *where maste to day / Reinys of þe cristen lay* (2123–4). However, *Cm* does not mention Noah's curse on Canaan (*Hs* (Gen.), 35), or the position of Asia in the east and that of Europe in the north; that of Asia may arise from a misreading of *Cm*, 2101, [*Asia*] *es þe best, for þar in es*.

3. ABRAHAM

Based on Gen. 11–25, with extensive use of *Cm* in the earlier part and some similarities to *Hs* and *Bh* in the later part.

The running head is *The lyf of Abraham*.

1 This line is followed by a woodcut depicting the imminent sacrifice of Isaac (Hodnett 248).

3–4 This Thare . . . of Sem: Ultimately derived from Gen. 11: 10–26.

4–13 Iaphet . . . yet doth: Follows with abridgements *Cm*, 2151, 2191–287. *Cm*, 2199–200, *þis nembrot wid his mekil pride / He wend to wirke wondris wide*, has verbal resemblances to *GoL*, 6–7; *Cm*, 2260, *þat naman oþer vndirstode*, (Cotton, similarly Fairfax) to *GoL*, 9; and *Cm*, 2283–4, 2287, *þis nembrot was þe first king / þat in maumet fand mistrouing, / . . . þat he bigan lastes ȝeit*, to *GoL*, 12–13. *Cm*, 2272, *Fyf thousand steppis*, is one of only two citations of *step* as a unit of distance in *MED* (cf. *GoL*, 12, *steppes*) and there are similarities in the numbers given for languages (though *Cm* makes this sixty-two) and breadth in miles.

14–17 Thare . . . and Sara: *Cm*, 2305–12.

17–18 Now I shal speke of Abram: *Cm*, 2315.

18 of whom Our Blessid Lady come: *Cm* (Trinity), 2323.

18–19 He weddyd Sara . . . Aram: *Cm*, 2333–4.

19 Abram was euer faithful and trewe: *Cm*, 2329–30.

20–1 He was . . . comforted hym: *Cm*, 2355–8.

21–7 whiche said . . . erthe: Gen. 12: 1–3.

28–36 Gen. 12: 4–8, though Gen. 12: 4 gives Abraham's age as seventy-five. The *ylle peple* (*GoL*, 31) echoes *Cm*, 2381, *feloun folk*; and the last two sentences are closer to *Cm*, 2389–94 than to Gen.

37–53 *Cm*, 2395–436; cf. Gen. 12: 10–20. Verbal parallels are evident in *Cm* (Fairfax), 2395–6, *bot sone quen he had seised þe lande / þer-in fel an hungre strange* (*GoL*, 37–8); *Cm* (Cotton), 2405–6, *"Lemman," he said, "sare .i me dred; / þar we weind to þis laules lede* (*GoL*, 40–1); *Cm*, 2409–10, *Say þu þar-for till an and oþer, / þat þu ert my sister and i þi broþer* (*GoL*, 42–3); *Cm*, 2414, *wid þis þai com in þat contre* (*GoL*, 43–4); and *Cm* 2421–2, *þat miht na man wid lichurye / Hir bodi nehy wid vilanye* (*GoL*, 47–8).

54–73 Gen. 13: 1–13, integrated with *Cm*, 2437–81. The duplication of *Lo, this contre* (*GoL*, 61–2) and *Lo, beholde all the contrey* (*GoL*, 64–5) arises from successively giving two versions of the same material, from *Cm*, 2459–60 and Gen. 13: 9. The mention of Mambre (cf. *GoL*, 71 and 81) comes at the end of this section in *Cm*, but at a later point (13: 18) in Gen.

74–82 Gen. 13: 14–18. For *GoL*, 82, *tabernacle*, cf. the same word in *Cm*, 2489; Gen. 13: 18 has *altare*.

83–94 Gen. 14: 8–16, integrated with *Cm*, 2493–532. There are verbal resemblances in *Cm*, 2493, *Four kinges werrid apon fijf* (*GoL*, 83–4); *Cm*, 2510–11, *A man unethes miht passe away, / To cum til abram for to tell* (*GoL*, 87–8); *Cm*, 2515–16, *He did to gadir samen his men, / Thre hunderd eyt sergauntis and ten* (*GoL*, 89–90); *Cm*, 2521–2, *And þar he delt his folk in tua / þat þai suld noght schape þaim fra* (*GoL*, 90–1); and *Cm* (Cotton, similarly Fairfax), 2526, *þat haiþen lede he smat a-mang* (*GoL*, 91–2).

95–101 Gen. 14: 17–21, 23, integrated with *Cm*, 2535–48. There are verbal resemblances in *Cm*, 2537–8, *Of ierusalem and all þat land, / was king and preist* (*GoL*, 97); and *Cm*, 2545–6, *Mekil it was þat loueword þan / þat abram gat o mani a man* (*GoL*, 100–1); whereas, for example, *þe lachet of a shoo* (100), is derived from the Vulgate rather than *Cm*.

102–19 Gen. 15: 1–2, 4–8, 13–16; with influence from *Cm*, 2549–90: for *GoL*, 104–5, cf. *Cm*, 2557–9, *Lauerd . . . / Quat es þi will to giue to me? / þu wat wele child nou haue i nan*; for *GoL*, 115–16, cf. *Cm*, 2582, *In egipte suld his sede exile*.

110 ofspryngyng: Cited only from here in *MED*; not in *OED*.

111–12 and it was reputed to hym to iustice: Gen. 15: 6, *et reputatum est ei ad iustitiam*. The only other record of *reputen* in *MED* with *to* of the thing as well as the person is from a translation of the same Latin words: a1425(a1400) Northern Pauline Epistle, *Abraham trowyde to god; and it is repute to hym to riȝtwisnesse*. (This translates Rom. 4: 3, which quotes Gen. 15: 6 verbatim.)

120–42 Gen. 16: 1–13, 15–16, integrated with *Cm*, 2591–640. There are verbal resemblances in *Cm*, 2593–4, *Scho had wid hir an hand womman, / þat agar hite, egipcian* (*GoL*, 120–1); *Cm* (Trinity), 2596, *þou seest no childer bere may I* (*GoL*, 121–2); *Cm*, 2602, *I now it held it als for mine* (*GoL*, 123–4); *Cm*,

2617, *In wilderness right bi a welle* (*GoL*, 132); and *Cm*, 2633, *Egain him all, egain all he* (*GoL*, 139–40).

143–85 Gen. 17: 1–27, integrated with *Cm*, 2643–702. There are verbal resemblances in *Cm*, 2647, *Multipli þi sede i sall* (*GoL*, 146); *Cm*, 2656, *Of þe sal cum bath prince and king* (*GoL*, 151); and *Cm*, 2677, *þu and þi childer it sal biginne* (*GoL*, 162).

181 99: Printed in arabic numerals.

183–4 they were receyuyd this newe lawe: While there are possible instances of the indirect passive in the 15th century (see Fischer, 'Syntax', 384–5, and the references there), in view of the sense, it is likely that *in* or a similar preposition has dropped out after *receyuyd*. Cf. *Cm*, 2700, *þai vndertok þis neu lay*.

186–207 Gen. 18: 1–15, integrated with *Cm*, 2703–32. There are verbal resemblances in *Cm*, 2703–4, *apon a tide, / Abraham satt his huus bisyde* (*GoL*, 186); and *Cm*, 2709, 2711, *Bot an alone he onered of þa / . . . / þe trinite sau he bi þat sith* (*GoL*, 189–90).

206 smylid ne lawhed not: Contextually the sense is 'neither smiled nor laughed'. *OED*, *ne* conj. 1b, 'With omission of preceding negative', gives other late ME instances. Cf. Gen. 18: 15, *non risi*, and *Cm*, 2731, *for-soth ne smile i noght*; also 492 below, *reteyne ne lette me not*, and in vol. i, *Pentecost*, 309, *attrybue ne take*.

208–21 *Cm*, 2733–64, though with details that come from the longer account in Gen. 18: 16–33, such as *Yf there be xl, I shal spare them* (*GoL*, 218; Gen. 18: 32).

218–19 And so . . . Our Lord said: The abridgement of the original repetitive passage (Gen. 18: 30–32) is quite different in *Cm* (2758–9); here *GoL* is closer to *Hs* (Gen.), 51, *Item, si quadraginta. Quid, si triginta? Quid, si viginti? Quid si decem?*

222–48 Gen. 19: 1–14, but the opening clause is closer to *Cm*, 2765–6, *At an euyntide into sodom, / To lothes hous tua angeles com*. There are several deviations from Gen. unsupported by *Cm*: *shette the dore and stode byhynde* (*GoL*, 231; cf. Gen. 19: 6, *post tergum adcludens ostium*); *Loth withstode them myghtily* (*GoL*, 238–9; cf. Gen. 19: 9, *vimque faciebant Loth vehementissime*, in which *Lot* is the object); *they had raued or iaped* (*GoL*, 248; cf. Gen. 19: 14, *et visus est eis quasi ludens loqui*, in which it is Lot who is thought to be joking).

249–63 Gen. 19: 15–23. In 252, *God shold spare hem*, for Gen. 19: 16, *eo quod parceret Dominus illi*, the plural *hem* is derived from the context.

264–87 Gen. 19: 24–38. The additional information that the statue of Lot's wife can still be seen (268) occurs in *Cm*, 2853–4, but the wording is closer to *Hs* (Gen.), 52, *quam Josephus dicit se vidisse, et hactenus manere*.

278 may doo haue adoo: The appearance of auxiliary DO between a modal and an infinitive is unexpected. Possibly *doo* is an anticipation of *adoo*, or *haue adoo* is a euphemistic substitute for an original noun object.

288–320 Gen. 20: 1–18.

318 and conceyuyd: The expected subject, denoting Abimelech's wife and handmaids, is missing. Cf. Gen. 20: 17, *sanavit Deus Abimelech et uxorem ancillasque eius et pepererunt.*

321–29 Gen. 21: 1–8. For *was wened fro the pappe* (328–9), cf. *Cm* (Trinity), 3018, *was wened fro þe pappe.*

330–53 Gen. 21: 9–21. Close lexical resemblances include *GoL*, 340, *erryd*, Gen. 21: 14, *errabat*; *GoL*, 341, *consumed*, Gen. 21: 15, *consumpta*; and *GoL*, 349, *pytte*, Gen. 21: 19, *puteum.*

350 And God abode with hym: In Gen. 21: 20, *Et fuit cum eo*, the omitted subject is God. Its absence in *GoL* may be attributable either to the translator or a compositor.

354–64 Gen. 21: 22–6, with the final sentence summarizing 21: 27–34.

365–99 Gen. 22: 1–19; in 374, *children* translates Gen. 22: 5, *pueros*; contrast *Bh*, 114/13, *ses seruiteurs.*

381 hym: Reflexive, referring to God. Cf. Gen. 22: 8, *Deus providebit sibi victimam.*

400–3 Gen. 23: 1–2 and 19; with Gen. 23: 3–18 summarized in *and bought of the children of Heth a felde.*

404–18 Gen. 24: 1–9, omitting the details of the Hebrew manner of taking an oath.

419–54 Gen. 24: 10–27; *sette doun her potte* (428) is an addition.

455–75 The mayde . . . my sone: Gen. 24: 28–38. For 458, *poynettis or armylles*, cf. Gen. 24: 30, *armillas* (*Bh*, 126/20, has *les ioyaux* collectively for the earrings and bracelets); 462, *strowed* is erroneous for Gen. 24: 32, *destravit* ('unharnessed'); 465–6, *and said*: '*wherfor I am comen*' is a *GoL* addition, but cf. *Hs* (Gen.), 59, *donec loqueretur sermones pro quibus venerat* (not in *Bh*).

475–9 Wherfore . . . lordes sone: Summarizes Gen. 21: 39–49.

480–501 Gen. 24: 50–61. For 493, *wherfor late me goo to my lord*, cf. *Bh*, 130/11–12, *si m'en laissiez aler a mon seigneur* (contrast Gen. 24: 56, *dimittite me ut pergam ad dominum meum*); for 496, *Thenne . . . wyth her*, cf. *Bh*, 130/20–1, *Lors l'en laissierent ilz aler, et sa nourrice auec elle* (contrast Gen. 24: 59, *dimiserunt ergo eam et nutricem illius*).

502–11 Gen. 24: 62–7, though the first two clauses in *GoL* are heavily abridged and recast.

512–18 Summarizes Gen. 25: 1–10.

4. ISAAC

For the most part a free translation of Gen. 25: 20–35: 27, with frequent omissions, expansions and paraphrasing; some influence from *Bh*, and in the earlier parts from *Cm* and *Hs*, in addition to two parallels to *HP*.

The running head is *The lyf of ysaac*.

1 This line is preceded by a woodcut depicting Esau and Isaac (Hodnett 249).

3–33 **Ysaac was . . . patremony:** Gen. 25: 20–34.

4–5 **that she myght . . . fruyt:** Not in Gen. *Hs* and *Bh* have parallel expansions, entirely different in their wording.

6–7 **of hym . . . were born:** Not in Gen.

7–8 **For whiche . . . whiche apperid:** Not in Gen., but cf. *Cm*, 3449–51, *To pray to godd ay was scho prest, / To consail hir quat were best, / Quat hir war best he suld hir rede*; and *Bh*, 134/44–5, *Adonc s'en ala Rebeque pour conseillier a Nostre Seigneur.*

27 **Lo, I dye for hungre:** Gen. 25: 32, *en morior*; *Cm* (Cotton), 3547, *for hunger loo i dei right now.*

28–9 **yf I dye . . . this potage:** Not in Gen. Cf. *Hs* (Gen.), 67, *Esau . . . se moriturum, nisi comederet in instanti, putans, dedit ei primogenita pro edulio lentis.*

30–1 **that thou shalt . . . enioye it:** Not in Gen. Cf. *Cm*, 3543–4, *þat þu sal neuer fra þis night / In þi for-birth clayme na right.*

33–5 **This aforsaid . . . in the chirche:** Not in sources examined. Gen. 26 is omitted, as also in *Cm*.

36–133 Gen. 27: 1–46.

45 **Whiche all thise wordis Rebecca herde:** Gen. 27: 5, *quod cum audisset Rebecca*. See *OED*, *which* 14a, for this pleonastic linking use, and cf. note to 232 below.

52–3 **whiche whan . . . and hath eten:** For the missing subject of the second verb, cf. Gen. 27: 10, *quas cum intuleris et comederit*. See vol. i, Introduction, p. xxxvii, and notes to 246 and 253–4 below.

88 **and oyle:** The Stuttgart edn. records the addition of *et olei* as a variant in Gen. 27: 28; similarly *Bh* and *Hs*.

99–102 **And thenne . . . haue the blessyng:** Cf. *Hs* (Gen.), 71, *et in hac extasi vidit in spiritu a Domino factum esse hoc, et significationem piae fraudis intellexit.*

111 **secondly:** *MED* records the sense 'for the second time' only twice, from WB.

vndernome: This is the sole citation under *OED undernim* 4b, 'To take away by stealth' (sense not in *MED*), which comments 'Also OE'.

114 stablysshed: Gen. 27: 37, *stabilivi* 'I have sustained', but neither *MED* nor *OED* records such a sense. Cf. WB (LV), *stablischid* (EV *stablid*).

115 and oyle: Not in Gen. (27: 37), nor in *Hs* or *Bh*; cf. note to line 88 above.

117 with a grete syghyng and wepyng: The equivalent words in Gen. 27: 38 refer to Esau; similarly in *Bh*.

134–79 Gen. 28: 1–22.

139 tourbes: Gen. 28: 3, *turbas*. This is the only citation in *MED* for sense c 'a multitude'.

168 dredyngly: This is the only example in *MED*; earliest *OED* citation of *dreadingly* 1589.

180–242 Gen. 29: 1–35.

204 mouth: Gen. 29: 14, *os*; normally interpreted as *os* 'bone'. See notes to *David* 104 and *Job* 67.

221–2 brought Lya to me: Gen. 29: 25, *imposuisti mihi*; similarly *Bh*.

224 coplement: Gen. 29: 27, *copulae*. Not in *MED*; the earliest *OED* citation for *couplement* is from 1548.

228–30 Neuertheles . . . were but shorte: Contrast Gen. 29: 30, *tandemque potitus optatis nuptiis amorem sequentis priori praetulit serviens apud eum septem annis aliis*; similarly *Bh*.

232 Whiche thenne Lya: *Whiche* qualifies *Lya*, but *thenne*, which has no equivalent in the Latin, obscures the construction.

236 sawe: Cf. *Bh* 158/28, *veoit*. Contrast Gen. 29: 33, *audivit*.

241 I shal knowleche me to Our Lord: Gen. 29: 35, *confitebor Domino*. Forms of the verb *knowleche* occur twice in OT in the widely attested sense 'acknowledge': *Joseph* 163 (translating *confiteor*) and *Judith* 155 (in free paraphrase). The other eight occurrences, like that in *Joseph*, correspond to forms of *knoulechen* in WB (both EV and LV), and are instances of *OED knowledge* v. 6, 'give thanks or praise to', translating Vulgate *confiteri* (*MED knoulechen* 5a ~ *to*, 'praise or honor'). The only non-WB citations in either dictionary are from Coverdale, possibly derived from WB, and Trevisa's *Gospel of Nicodemus*. All the WB occurrences except Tobit 12: 7 (= *GoL*, *Tobit* 459) have a personal object, preceded by *to*, whereas in OT the verb is also used transitively in this sense (see glossary). The reflexive use here is unparalleled in WB or elsewhere; but see further the note on the syntactically ambiguous *Tobit* 489–90.

243–309 Gen. 30: 1–43.

246 and hath pryued fro the the fruyt of thy bely: Gen. 30: 2, *qui privavit te fructu ventris tui.* The semantic subject of *hath* is 'God', and *he* should perhaps be supplied. The use of this verb with accusative for the thing and *from* for the person is not recorded in *MED* or *OED*.

253–4 I haue avayled: Possibly an example of the translator's notably free ellipsis of pronoun subjects rather than a printing error.

258 generations: Gen. 30: 13, *mulieres*; similarly *Hs* and *Bh*. Influenced by the development of this verse in Luke 1: 48, *beatam me dicent omnes generationes.*

279 obprobrye: *MED* has only 4 quotations, all from Higden. *OED* adds quotations from the Caxton/de Worde *Vitas Patrum* and later writers.

285 I haue founden grace: Similarly *Bh*, 162/32–3, *I'ai trouue grace.* Contrast Gen. 30: 27, *inveniam gratiam.*

286 I haue ordeyned: Contrast Gen. 30: 28, *constitue*; similarly *Bh*.

293 and departe: Gen. 30: 32, *gyra omnes greges tuos et separa.*

296 And Laban graunted therto: After this, Gen. 30: 35–6, relating Laban's removal of variegated animals and black lambs, is omitted.

297–307 Thenne Iacob toke . . . of one colour: This corresponds only very loosely to Gen. 30: 37–42; Laban's changing of the agreement and Jacob's response are not found there (though subsequently implied in Gen. 31: 8), but the motif occurs in the equivalent passage of *HP*, 167/23–9, with substantial differences in detail.

310–25 After that Iacob . . . gyuen it to me: Gen. 31: 1–9.

322 party colour: *MED* records *parti(e* with reference to colours, but not this collocation. The first citation of *particoloured* in *OED* is from 1530.

325–7 And now God . . . departe hens: Heavily abridges Gen. 31: 10–13, omitting mention of Jacob's dream.

328–83 Thenne answerd . . . confedersy togydre: Gen. 31: 14–44.

353–4 I departed, the not knowyng; I dredde: Gen. 31: 31, *quod inscio te profectus sum / timui.*

361 lytter: Gen. 31: 34, *stramen* 'straw, litter'; the variant *stramenta* can also mean 'bedding'.

372 I shal make alle good: Cf. Gen. 31: 39, *ego damnum omne reddebam.*

372–3 I prayd therfore . . . and in colde: Gen. 31: 39–40, *a me exigebas / die noctuque aestu urebar et gelu.* While *die noctuque* modify the second verb (similarly *Bh*), it is difficult to construe *day and nyght* in this way.

382 leghe: *MED* has only two earlier examples of *liege*, 'a pact between two governments, an agreement'.

383–5 Thenne Iacob . . . euer after: A selective summary of Gen. 31: 45–54.

385–413 And after this Laban . . . beestis: Gen. 31: 55–32: 16.

398 turmes: Gen. 32: 7, *turmas*. MED has only three earlier citations.

402 I am the leste in all thy mercyes: Gen. 32: 10, *minor sum cunctis miserationibus* (with variant + *tuis*).

413–15 and bad . . . with yeftes: A selective summary of Gen. 32: 16–23.

416 The nyght folowyng, hym thought: Jacob's wrestling is introduced differently in Gen. 32: 24: *remansit solus / et ecce*.

416–67 a man wrastlyd . . . of Israhel: Gen. 32: 24–33: 20.

426 whiche is meruayllous: Not in Gen. 32: 29 (nor *Hs* nor *Bh*), but cf. *HP*, 181/4–5, *the which is mirable and mervelus to thy andrestoundynge*.

445–7 Whos ben . . . vnto th'ende: Gen. 33: 8, *quaenam sunt istae turmae quas obviam habui / respondit ut . . .*

452 Vnneth, by compellyng, he takyng it: Abbreviates Gen. 33: 11.

455 ouerlaboured: This is the only example in *MED*. The first in *OED* is from 1530.

462–4 And fro thens . . . londe of Canaan: Various details from Gen. 33: 17–19 have been omitted.

468–515 Gen. 34: 1–31.

491 incircumsiced: Gen. 34: 14, *incircumciso*. Not in *MED*. *OED* has only two quotations: one from elsewhere in *GoL*, the other dated 1554.

496–7 and ther was no yong man . . . the damoyselle: Contrast Gen. 34: 19, *nec distulit* ['did not delay'] *adulescens quin statim quod petebatur expleret / amabat enim puellam valde / et ipse erat inclitus in omni domo patris sui*.

507–8 and slewe all that they fond: Contrast Gen. 34: 27, *et depopulati sunt* ['pillaged'] *urbem*.

516–52 Gen. 35: 1–20.

538 Folkes and peples of nacions: Gen. 35: 11, *gentes et populi nationum*.

544 in veer tyme: Gen. 35: 16, *verno tempore*.

553–7 Gen. 35: 27–9.

5. JOSEPH

A translation of Gen. 37: 2–50: 26, sometimes abridged, expanded, or paraphrased, with a few parallels to *Bh*, *Cm*, *Hs*, and *JA*.

The running head is *Thystorye of Ioseph*.

2 This line is followed by a woodcut depicting the selling of Joseph (Hodnett 250).

3–71 Gen. 37: 2–36.

18 fume: Contrast Gen. 37: 8, *fomitem* ('kindling-wood'). *MED fume* n. 3, 'Any "exhalation" said to be generated in the body; such an "exhalation" as producing emotions, dreams, dullness, etc.', records similar uses.

48 spyces and reysyns: Gen. 37: 25, *aromata et resinam et stacten* ('spices and resin and myrrh'). *MED* records one instance (a1398) of 'resin' spelt *reysyn*, with etymological warrant in OF *reisine* and AL *reisina*, but the plural is suspicious and erroneous translation as 'raisins' is likely. Cf. note on 339–40 below.

54 xxx pecis of syluer: Contrast Gen. 37: 28, *viginti argenteis.*

55–6 At this tyme . . . with his beestis: Cf. *Hs* (Gen.), 86, *et recessit Ruben, meliora quaerens pascua.*

59–60 He had supposed . . . they had don: Not in Gen. Cf. *Hs* (Gen.), 86, *credens eum interemptum.*

72–114 Gen. 39: 1–23.

79 of Egypte: Gen. 39: 5, *Aegyptii* ('of the Egyptian').

84–6 and wold not . . . a werke: Not in Gen. Cf. *Bh*, 210/21–2, *qui a nulle mauvaise oeuure ne se vouloit accorder.*

113 And what he dyde was doon: Cf. Gen. 39: 22, *et quicquid fiebat sub ipso erat.*

115–49 Gen. 40: 1–23.

133–4 when thou art at thyn aboue: Gen. 40: 14, *cum tibi bene fuerit.*

145 emong the meles: Gen. 40: 20, *inter epulas.*

150–238 Gen. 41: 1–57.

160 coniectours: Gen. 41: 8, *coniectores*; *MED* has only two other citations of this word.

166 prodyges: *MED* has only one other citation of this word, a1500(a1470), which is the earliest in *OED.*

171 bayned: No equivalent in Gen., nor in *Bh.* This is the earliest *MED* citation for the sense 'bathe' (both earlier examples meaning 'moisten or drench'), but it comments that it 'may be read as belonging to *bainen* v.(2), i.e. "to ready (sb.), prepare", though the concrete specificity of the other verbs ("shave", "dress"), as well as the occurrence of the verb elsewhere in Caxton (see OED s.v. *bain* v.) argue for its placement here'.

175–7 Thenne Pharao told . . . of the eeris: Summarizes Gen. 41: 17–24, which essentially repeats Gen. 41: 1–8, corresponding to 150–9 above.

178 The kyngis dreme . . . shewde to Pharao: Contrast Gen. 41: 25, *somnium regis unum est / quae facturus est Deus ostendit Pharaoni*; the point that the two dreams have the same meaning is made in *Hs* and more explicitly in *Bh*, as well as in Gen. 41: 26, *eandemque vim somnii conprehendunt*, which is omitted in *GoL*.

180 comodyous: The sense 'fertile' is recorded in *MED* but not *OED*.

184 sterilite bareyne and scarcete: Gen. 41: 30, *sterilitatis*; *bareyne* appears to be a postnominal adjective. *MED* records no nominal use of the word, and *OED* records no abstract sense for the noun.

195 enfamyned: *OED* has no citations later than Caxton.

208 the second trompet cryeng: Contrast Gen. 41: 43, *fecitque ascendere super currum suum secundum clamante praecone*.

226 and the hous of my fader hath forgoten me: Contrast Gen. 41: 51, *oblivisci me fecit Deus . . . domus patris mei*.

239–316 Gen. 42: 1–38.

244–5 bycause whatsomeuer . . . her iourney: Cf. Gen. 42: 4, *Iacob qui dixerat fratribus eius / ne forte in itinere quicquam patiatur mali*. There seems to be an omission in *GoL*.

272 doo as Y haue said: Gen. 42: 18, *facite quod dixi*.

287–8 aboue that . . . in their way: Cf. Gen. 42: 25, *datis supra cibariis in via*.

292 My money is gyuen to me agayn: Cf. Gen. 42: 28, *reddita est mihi pecunia*.

306 thenne forthon: Gen. 42: 34, *deinceps*. *MED forth-on* 1b, 'henceforth, ?forthwith' has only one citation, a1325(c1250). *OED* has three further citations of *forth on/forthon* 2a (of time), the earliest being from Caxton.

317–87 Gen. 43: 1–34.

331–2 Sende the child: In Gen. 43: 8, these words are preceded by *Iudas quoque dixit patri suo*.

339–40 a lytyl reysyns and hony, storax, stacten, therebinthe and dates: Gen. 43: 11, *modicum resinae* ['resin'] *et mellis et styracis et stactes et terebinthi et amigdalarum*. Cf. note on 48 above; here too *reysyns* is likely to be in error.

362–3 It is not . . . put it: Gen. 43: 22, *non est in nostra conscientia quis eam posuerit*.

383–5 he set his brothern . . . with th'Ebrewis: Condenses, rearranges, and changes the seating arrangements of Gen. 43: 32–3, *seorsum Ioseph et seorsum fratribus / Aegyptiis quoque qui vescebantur simul seorsum / inlicitum est enim Aegyptiis comedere cum Hebraeis / et profanum putant huiuscemodi* *convivium / sederant coram eo / primogenitus iuxta primogenita sua / et minimus iuxta aetatem suam.*

388–452 Thenne Ioseph . . . shall take: Gen. 44: 1–34.

400 doth to vs his seruaunts suche lettyng: Contrast Gen. 44: 7, *ut servi tui tantum flagitii commiserint*, normally interpreted as an exclamation, though WB (LV) has *Whi spekith oure lord so, that thi seruauntis han do so greet trespas?* (similarly EV). Neither *Hs* nor *Bh* has anything similar to *GoL* here, but cf. *Cm* (Cotton), 4914, *For drightin dos vs na letting.*

413–14 in the science of knowleche: Gen. 44: 15, *in augurandi scientia. MED* has *knoulech(e* 1c, 'also foreknowledge'; the only relevant citation is ?c1475, *Knawlege: . . . presciencia.* This sense is not in *OED.*

421–2 and spack with a hardy chere to hym: Not in Gen. *JA*, 2 VI.viii, says here of Judah, *erat uir efficax.*

452–8 Wherfore I beseche the . . . to th'Ismaelites: Not in Gen. Cf. *JA*, 2 VI.viii, for Judah's speech, and 2 VI.ix for Joseph's motive in hiding the cup.

459–513 Gen. 45: 1–28.

491 Lade ye your beestis: Gen. 45: 17 simply has *onerantes iumenta*, but for the emendation cf. *Bh*, 242/7–8, *Chargiez vos asnes.*

514–28 Thenne Israhel . . . into Egypt: Gen. 46: 1–8.

526 and children ***etc.*****:** Cf. Gen. 46: 7, *et nepotes filiae et cuncta simul progenies.*

528–39 The first begoten . . . in nombre vij: Condenses Gen. 46: 9–25 by omitting names and some other details.

539–625 Alle the sowles . . . beddes heed: Gen. 46: 26–47: 31.

547–8 And his fader . . . enbraced also hym: Not in Gen.

586 to the: Gen. 47: 15, *coram te* ('in your presence'); cf. *MED to* prep. 4b, 'in company with, together with'.

595 bondship: *MED* has only three citations; *OED* adds quotations from Caxton and Udall (1542).

619–20 do to me . . . and swere: Contrast Gen. 47: 29, *pone manum sub femore meo / et facies mihi misericordiam et veritatem. Bh*, 252/16–17, includes a similar paraphrase: *met ta main sur ma cuisse et me fai ceste misericorde & ceste verite que tu me iures.*

626–38 Thenne this don . . . possessions: Gen. 48: 1–6.

639–72 Thenne he . . . fader Israhel: Gen. 48: 8–49: 2.

664 gentyles: Gen. 48: 19, *gentes. MED* has *gentil* n. 3c, '?a nation or people [translating L *gentes* as if *gentiles*]', citing only this passage. *OED* has no appropriate sense.

672–3 And there he told . . . his xij sones: Briefly summarizes Gen. 49: 3–28. Compare *Cm*, 5455–6 and 5459–60, *His sonis he bifore him cald, / And mani resunes he þaim tald, . . . Quan he endid of his saue, / His sonis blissed he on a rau.*

673–6 he comanded . . . whiche Abraham bought: Abbreviates Gen. 49: 29–32. *HP*, 271/17–19, abbreviates the passage similarly: *burie ye me with my forefaders Abraham and Isaac in the dowble cave in the lond of Ephron Ethei biside Mambre in the region of Canaan, the which Abraham bought.*

676–723 And this saide . . . in Egypte: Gen. 49: 33–50: 26.

681 spices aromatykes: The adjective is also postposed in two of the other *MED* citations, and *OED* 2nd edn. (1989) records *wynes aromatyques* from Caxton's *The Curial.*

681–2 thenne wente they sorowyng hym xl dayes: Contrast Gen. 50: 3, *transierunt quadraginta dies / iste quippe mos erat cadaverum conditorum.*

683–4 how he had sworn . . . londe of Canaan: Summarizes Gen. 50: 4–5.

692 exequyes: In *MED*, the singular of this word always has final *-s(e*, but *OED* records the modern singular form from Caxton.

697–8 and buryed hym . . . had bought: Condenses Gen. 50: 13. The version in *Bh*, 274/18–19, begins similarly: *et l'enseuelirent en la double fosse que Abraham auoit achetee.* Cf. also 673–6 above, and note.

706 forgyue to thy fader, seruaunt of God: As in *Hs* (Gen.), 105, it is the father that is to be forgiven: *ut patri tuo dimittas iniquitatem hanc.* Contrast Gen. 50: 17, *servis Dei patris* ['the servants of the God of your father'] *tui dimittas iniquitatem hanc.*

6. MOSES

Largely follows Exod. 1: 1–20: 2, with abridgements, paraphrases, and omissions, particularly of repetitive passages and ritual details, of which only exceptional instances are noted below. There is additional information from *Hs*, sometimes further supplemented from or conflated with *JA* (one of its sources), as well as from *Bh*.

The running head is *Thystorie/The lyf of Moyses.*

2 This line is followed by a woodcut depicting Moses receiving the tables of the Law (Hodnett 251).

3–34 Exod. 1: 1–21.

33–4 And bycause . . . howses: Contrast Exod. 1: 21, *et quia timuerant obstetrices Deum aedificavit illis domos* (*Hs* (Exod.), 2, explains the last clause with *id est locupletavit eas*). The word *they* is erroneous.

35–59 Exod.1: 22–2: 10.

39 elegaunt: Exod. 2: 2, *elegantem*. Not in *MED*. Cf. *OED*, *elegant* adj. 3a, 'Of a person . . . : graceful; free from awkwardness or clumsiness', first cited from elsewhere in *GoL*.

48 fiscelle: Exod. 2: 5, *fiscellam*. There are only two other quotations under *MED*, *fishelle*; *OED* adds the present example and one from *Vitas Patrum*.

60–3 And he ther grewe . . . by adopcion: *JA*, 2 IX.vi–vii. *Hs* (Exod.), 4, has only *Suscepit ergo Terimith alendum puerum*.

63–76 on a day . . . the deth: *Hs* (Exod.), 4, partly closely translated and partly abridged and paraphrased, but with details from *JA*, 2 IX.vii: *took him in his arms* = *sumens eum et ad pectus applicans*; *dyademe* = *diadema* (rather than the *coronam* of *Hs*); *trade on it* = *calcauitque suis pedibus*; in addition, *they kalked on his natyuyte* has possibly been influenced by *qui eius natiuitatem praedixerat ita futurum ad humiliationem principatus*. However, the episode of Pharaoh calling for his magicians (*Hs sacerdos*) to divine (67–8) has been altered, probably influenced by a previous prophecy that occasioned the killing of the children.

76–8 Iosephus said . . . sauyd hym: *JA*, 2 IX.vii; not in *Hs*.

79–113 Exod. 2: 11–25.

97 Ietro: Cf. Exod. 2: 18, *Raguhel* (but *Iethro* in 3: 1); *Hs* (Exod.), 6, *Raguel, agnominatus Jethro*.

105–7 She brought . . . the hande of Pharao: Not in Exod.; cf. *Bh*, 43vb, *Et puis elle lui en engendra vn autre quil nomma eleazar et dist. . . . Le dieu de mon pere est mon ayde. et ma oste de la main pharaon*. (Contrast the briefer equivalent in *Hs* (Exod.), 6, *peperitque alterum, quem dixit Eliezer, id est Dei mei adjutorium*.)

114–201 Exod. 3: 1–4: 18.

131–2 floweth mylke and hony: Exod. 3: 8, *fluit lacte et melle*. *OED*, *flow* v. 14 identifies the anomalous transitive use of the verb in the WB (EV) translation of the same verse and a similar passage in Mandeville as arising from the influence of the Vulgate. Similarly *flowyng* in 155 below.

155 *etc.*: Abbreviates Exod. 3: 17, *et Amorrei / Ferezei et Evei, et Iebusei*.

162 amyd-emong them: Exod. 3: 20, *in medio eorum*. *MED*, *amid-mong*, gives two quotations; *OED*, s.v. *amid*, has one example of *amidmong*, from 1548.

202–5 Ex. 4: 19–20.

206–47 Thenne Our Lord . . . affliction: Exod. 4: 27–5: 15.

243 and wold make them: In Exod. 5: 14, the subject is clearly the Hebrew foremen.

245 vpperist: *MED* records the sense 'highest in rank' only from the OT of *GoL*.

247–53 He said . . . and vs: Exod. 5: 17–21, heavily adapted and abridged.

249 and gadre your chaf also: Not here in Exod., but cf. 238 above.

254–74 Thenne Moyses . . . to departe: Exod. 5: 22–6: 6, 6: 9–13.

259 in a boystous: Exod. 6: 1, *in manu robusta*; *hande* is to be understood from the preceding *strong hande*, or has been omitted by the compositor.

261–2 my name . . . couenaunt with them: Cf. Exod. 6: 3–4, *nomen meum Adonai non indicavi eis / pepigique cum eis foedus*. Although the punctuation supplied is an attempt to give the English a similar sense, it is possible that *that* is actually intended to introduce a noun clause object of *shewd*.

274–84 And he said . . . Pharao: Exod. 7: 1–7.

285–317 Thenne, whan . . . was blood: Exod. 7: 10–24.

306–7 that it may . . . of Egypte: Contrast Exod. 7: 19, *et sit cruor in omni terra Aegypti*. For the use of the word 'vengeance' in *Cm*, see the notes on 319 and 320–85 below.

318–19 whatsomeuer . . . good water: *Hs* (Exod.), 13, *Josephus dicit quod Hebraeis fluvius potabilis erat, licet esset mutatus*, corresponding to *JA*, 2 XIV.i.

319 This was the first plaghe and vengeance: *Hs* (Exod.), 13, *Et haec est prima plaga*; *Cm*, 5915, *þe first vengans he on him send*.

320–85 The account of the second to ninth plagues extensively abridges Exod. 8: 1–10: 29, though some passages are closely translated. The numbering of the plagues is absent in the Vulgate, *JA*, and *Hs*, but found in the rubricated headings of *Bh*, 46r–48r (except for the last plague). Some of them are similarly introduced in *Cm*, 5927–6058: *þe toþer wengans*, *þe thrid vengans*, *þe sext*, *þe seuent vengans*, *þe tend wreche*. In addition, occasional verbal reminiscences and the overall structure suggest the influence of *Cm*.

354–5 botchis, beelis and blaynes and woundes and swellyng in their bladders: Cf. Exod. 9: 9–10, *vulnera* [v. l. *ulcera*] *et vesicae turgentes . . . vulnera* [v. l. *ulcera*] *vesicarum turgentium*. Compare WB (EV), *biles, and bleynes swellynge*, and LV, *botchis . . . and bolnynge bladdris*; and *Cm*, 6011, *Bile and blester, bolnand sare*, which also alliterates and is similar in rhythm. Both *vesica* and ME *bladdre* can mean 'blister' as well as 'bladder'.

356–7 Yet wold not . . . had comanded: Exod. 9: 12, *non audivit eos sicut locutus est Dominus ad Mosen*. The last clause in the Vulgate means that God had foretold Pharaoh's obduracy, a sense the English cannot bear.

364 adder-bolte: Not in *MED*; this is the first quotation in *OED*, the next being from 1665. Cf. Exod. 10: 4, *lucustam*.

365–70 in suche wyse . . . departe: Summarizes Exod. 10: 7–11: 20.

373 palpable: Exod. 10: 21, *ut palpari queant*; 10: 22 reads *tenebrae horribiles*, but *Hs* (Exod.), 20, quotes the verse with the variant *tenebrae palpabiles*.

378 hostyes: Exod. 10: 25, *hostias*. Not in *MED*; this is the earliest example in *OED*, s.v. *hostie* n.1.

386–402 Exod. 11: 1–7, 10.

388 borowe: *Bh*, 48[rb], *empruntent*. Cf. Exod. 11: 2, *postulet*; *MED* and *OED* lack clear examples of the sense 'take something without an intention to return'. See also note to 420 below.

389 clothes: Not in Exod. 11: 2, but taken from Exod. 12: 35.

398–9 emong all the chyldren ther shal not an hound be hurt, ne no man ne beest: Apparently derived from *Bh*, 48[rb], *entre les filz disrael ne criera mye vn chien. ne homme ne beste*, which recasts Exod. 11: 7, *apud omnes autem filios Israhel non muttiet canis / ab homine usque ad pecus* [i.e. there shall not even be a dog barking at the Israelites or their livestock]. The failure to specify that the children are those of Israel probably arises from an error on the part of the translator or compositor.

404–5 as ben expressyd in the Byble: i.e. Exod. 12: 1–28.

406–27 it was so . . . dyuerse kynde: Exod. 12: 29–38.

420 borowed: Exod. 12: 35 *petierunt*. See note on 388 above; possibly influenced by *commodarent* ('give, lend') and *spoliaverunt* in the following verse.

427–8 The tyme . . . yere: Exod. 12: 40.

429–37 Exod. 13: 17–22.

438–40 Exod. 14: 4.

441–92 Exod. 14: 5–31.

450 sepulture: Neither *MED* nor *OED* records such a generalized use of the singular.

465–6 another cam after: In Exod. 14: 19 there is one angel, who moves from the front of the host to the rear.

475–6 And thenne . . . other syde: Contrast Exod. 14: 24, *et ecce respiciens Dominus super castra Aegyptiorum per columnam ignis et nubis*.

488 and cam alonde: Replaces Exod. 14: 29, *et aquae eis erant quasi pro muro a dextris et a sinistris*.

493–6 Thenne Moyses . . . the see: Exod. 15: 1.

495 carre-men: See *MED carre* 1b.

496–543 And Marie . . . of gomor: Exod. 15: 20–16: 16.

498 cordes: While the context suggests a musical instrument, neither *MED* nor *OED* records such a sense, as opposed to 'string of a musical instrument'. Contrast Exod. 15: 20, *choris* 'dancing': perhaps a mistranslation.

526 **What haue ye mused . . . be we:** Exod. 16: 7, *nos vero quid sumus quia mussitatis contra nos*. Cf. WB (Bodley 959), *What forsoþ ben we þat ȝe moysen* [EV *grucchen*, LV *grutchen*] *aȝeyns vs?*

538 **in their circuyte:** Exod. 16: 13, *per circuitum castrorum*. This example is cited by *OED* under 2a, 'the space enclosed by a given circumference or boundary', but cf. *MED*, *circuit(e* 1c *in* (*the*) ~, 'all around'.

539 **lyke to colyandre:** While the rest of the sentence translates Exod. 16: 14, the comparison with the herb has been shifted from 16: 31 as in *Hs* (Exod.), 31, *granum minutum quasi semen coriandri*.

543 **And late nothyng . . . the morn:** Exod. 16: 19.

543–52 **And the syxthe . . . remembraunce:** Summarizes and rearranges material from Exod. 16: 20–35.

553–631 Exod. 17: 1–18: 27.

554 **in her mansyons:** Exod. 17: 1, *per mansiones suas*. All three quotations under *MED mansioun* n.1 1b, 'a stop in a stage of a journey', refer to the wanderings of the Israelites in the desert.

563 **oldremen:** *MED* and *OED* record no forms with initial *o*; this seems to be a crossing of the positive with *eldreman*, well attested in *MED* in biblical contexts.

587 **only:** Apparently a mistranslation of *solii* 'throne' (Exod. 17: 16).

617 **Poruyde:** There are no *por-* forms in *MED* or *OED*; but cf. *purvey*, of the same ultimate etymology.

619 **centuriones:** After this, a translation of *quinquagenarios* (Exod. 18: 21) is omitted, probably in error.

632–78 Exod. 19: 1–25.

639–40 **ye shal be to me in the regne of preesthod:** Translates literally Exod. 19: 6, *vos eritis mihi* [v. l. + *in*] *regnum sacerdotale*; cf. WB (LV), *ȝe shulen be to me in to a rewme of preesthod*. Before this, there is no equivalent of *eritis mihi in peculium de cunctis populis / mea est enim omnis terra* (Exod. 19: 5), perhaps through eyeskip.

642 **the most of byrthe:** Exod. 19: 7, *maioribus natu populi*. It is not clear from *MED* or *OED* that the English can give the expected sense of 'elders', as opposed to 'those highest in rank or lineage'; but cf. WB (EV), *the more men thurȝ birthe*.

645 **Whan Moyses had shewd to the peple the wordes of Our Lord:** Contrast Exod. 19: 8, *cumque rettulisset Moses verba populi ad Dominum*, with a similar change to the sense in the following sentence. Repeats, whether by

error or deliberate and contextually plausible rewriting, the basic sense found in lines 642–3 above, and in *JA*, 3 V.iii, *ut audirent quae illis dixisset deus.*

648–56 bade them . . . shal not lyue: The wavering between direct and indirect speech and the confusion over speakers and addressees are not found in the source, Exod. 19: 10–13.

655–6 with stones . . . he shal be toslen: Cf. Exod. 19: 13, *lapidibus opprimetur aut confodietur iaculis*; the arrows are omitted.

668 grewe a lytyl more: Cf. Exod. 19: 19, *crescebat in maius.*

679–80 After this . . . thraldom: Exod. 20: 1–2.

683 the Ten Comandementes . . . to knowe: Cf. Deut. 4: 13–14.

685 fasted there xl dayes and xl nyghtes: Exod. 34: 28.

689–90 Adam, Noe, Abraham, Ysaac, Iacob and of Ioseph: Although the content is different, cf. the enumeration at the same point in the narrative in *Hs* (Exod.), 36: *Adam de fructibus terrae comedit, Noe ex imbribus ereptus, vel exceptus est; Abraham Chananaeam obtinuit, Isaac natus est de senibus, Jacob prole ditatus, Joseph sublimatus.*

691–2 two tables . . . honde of God: Deut. 4: 13.

7. TEN COMMANDMENTS

Lines 1–162 are a close translation of *LgD*, 46vb–48rb (no equivalent in *LgA*, *D-L*, or *GiL*). Most of the remainder assembles material from the Vulgate, freely handled, with probable influence from *Cm*.

The running head *The lyf of Moyses* continues to the end of this section. (See Pl. 2 above.)

1 There is no space between this line and the last line of the preceding legend, though the table of contents lists *Commandments* separately from *Moses*. A single blank line follows.

5–6 or faith or byleue in onythyng: Not in *LgD*.

14–15 wyth all . . . strengthe: Cf. Deut. 6: 5, quoted in Matt. 22: 37 and Mark 12: 30. Not in *LgD*.

37–8 thy Sabate day or Sonday: *LgD*, 47ra, *le iour du sabat*; *thy* may well be an error for *the*.

60–1 in goyng to tauernes . . . drynkyng dronke: Not in *LgD*.

61 other synnes, oultrages: The last word may be a postposed adjective, but cf. *LgD*, 47rb, *aultres oultrages.*

62–8 For alas . . . this third comandement: Not in *LgD*.

62 commysed: *MED* has only two other examples of *commi(s)sen*, a1470 and a1475(1450).

109–10 that owe or make them: Cf. *LgD*, 47vb, *a qui elles font*.

118 and be in his power and hath wherof: *LgD*, 47vb, *et il le puist faire*.

139 attouchyng: *LgD*, 48ra, *atouchemens*. Not in *MED*; *OED* cites *attouch* only from Caxton.

139 kyssyng, handlynge and suche other: Not in *LgD*.

163–8 Thus Moyses . . . on the mounte: Cf. Exod. 24: 18 and 31: 18, with the intervening material briefly summarized.

168–9 the children . . . and descended not: Exod. 32: 1.

171–232 they gadred them . . . Moyses ascended agayn: Exod. 32: 1–31, with omissions.

232–7 and receyuyd afterward . . . with the comandementis: The corresponding scriptural material is widely scattered: the renewal of the tables, Exod. 34; the making of the ark and tabernacle, Exod. 35–7; the rods, Num. 17; the pot of manna, Exod. 16: 33–4; the tables to be placed in the ark, Deut. 10: 2 and Hebr. 9: 4. Cf. also *Cm*, 6647–66: *Apon þe morn quen it was day, / went moyses to fett þe lay, / He tok þe comandementis ten / For to lede wid all his men, / writen wid godes aun hand, / . . . / Of an ark to þaim he spac, / In goddes worschip for to mak, / A tabernacyl als for to dight, / þar-of he scheud þaim þe slight. / þan he tok vp þa wandis thrin, / And for to kepe did þaim þar-in, / For-to bere to ilka stede, / Queþer so he þee folk wild lede.*

237–44 Moyses taught hem . . . fyl to Aaron: The sequence of events and the wording of the last two sentences resemble that of *Cm*, 6881–96: *þis moyses þat i rede of here, / was tahut þe folk to lede and lere, / þat delt war in kinredis tuelue, / Moyses þaim bad him-selue / þat ilk kinred suld bere a wand. / . . . / And ilk-a wand þat þai þar bar, / He sperd þaim in þair seyntwar, / And wrat þe name and set þe sele, / . . . / Quen he þaim lokid on þe morn, / Fand an wid lef and flour born, / And for it was an almaunde wand, / þat ilk fruit þar-on þai fand, / Almaundes war growen þar-on, / þe wand þat fell to aron.* Cf. also Num. 17: 1–8.

245–6 And after thys . . . ete in Egypte: Cf. Num. 11: 4–5.

246–8 and grudchyd . . . into Egypte: Cf. Num. 14: 2 and 14: 4.

246 grudchyd: Should perhaps be emended to *grutchyd*, but may belong to the development of *grutch* into *grudge*, the latter being amply attested in *OED* from the later 15th century.

248–50 Wherfore Moyses . . . vnkynde ayenst God: Cf. Num. 11: 14–15.

250–83 Thenne God sente . . . had comaunded: Num. 11: 31–13: 3, with omissions.

281 for to see: The addition of *to* is perhaps not necessary; cf. vol. i, notes to *Pentecost* 480, and *Corpus Christi*, 21–2. But all three instances of *for* + inf. cited there are direct translations of *pour* + inf.

284–6 and brought of the . . . vpon a colestaf: Num. 13: 23.

286 colestaf: *MED*, s.v. *couel*, has one example, a1325(c1250), of *cuuel-staf*. *OED* adds the present instance and further examples from 1530 on.

286–8 Whan they had . . . of the londe: Cf. Num. 13: 25–6.

288–92 But somme said . . . agayn into Egypte: Cf. Num. 13: 32.

290 inprenable: *MED* has only two quotations s.v. *imprenable*, ?a1439 and 1440.

293–303 Thenne Iosue . . . than this is: Num. 14: 6–12.

303–10 Thenne prayd Moyses . . . to theyr faders: Num. 14: 19–23.

310–13 But Iosue and Caleph . . . sorowed gretly therfor: Num. 14: 38–9.

314–39 After this the peple . . . grutched agayn God: Num. 20: 1–13, with abridgements.

329 out of byleue: *OED*, *belief* 1b *out of belief*, 'outside the Christian faith, unbelieving'.

340–6 Anon after this . . . trybe and famylye: Num. 20: 27–9.

347–60 After this the peple . . . were made hole: Num. 21: 4–9.

363–81 he ascended fro the feldes . . . alle hys seruauntes: Deut. 34: 1–11.

374 ne his teeth were neuer meuyd: Deut. 34: 7, *nec dentes illius moti sunt* (Cf. WB (EV), *ne the teeth of hym ben meued*). *MED*, *meven* 1a includes the sense 'dislodge' but with no example similar to this; *OED* records no appropriate senses.

8. JOSHUA

This legend is set off by blank lines at the beginning and the end, and begins with a four-line decorative capital, but there is no woodcut, and the running head continues to be *The lyf of Moyses*. (See Pl. 2 above.)

1–10 After Moyses, Iosue . . . he deyde: Briefly summarizes information from Joshua, especially 10: 11–13. Cf. also *Cm*, 6927–8, 6951–6, 6966–7: *godd efter moysen, / Leder made him* [Iosue] *ouer his men / . . . / þis iosue was selcuth wight, / And maystri had in many a fiht, / He faght treuly for goddes lay, / For-þi god dublid him his day, / And did þe sonne stille for to stand, / Til Iosue wan þe ouer-hand. / . . . / þat delt bituix þaim ilk-a land. / þat ilk kinred of þa tuelue.*

10–20 And dyuerse dukes . . . th'Epistles of Paule: This passage is discussed in the Introduction, vol. i, p. xxviii–xxix.

20 Temporal: *MED* has just one example of the word in the present sense, c1384.

9. SAUL

This is a free translation of 1 Samuel, much paraphrased and abridged, with omissions of entire episodes and the supply of summarizing links. However, when it follows the Vulgate, the translation is often very close. There is some influence from *Hs*, and probably from *JA*.

The running head is *Thystorie of Saul.*

2 This line is followed by a woodcut depicting a crowned king with a scroll (see Pl. 2 above; Hodnett 252.) The same woodcut is also used for *Solomon* and *Rehoboam*.

3–46 ther was a man . . . and thankyd hym: 1 Sam. 1: 1–28.

24 synful: Contrast 1 Sam. 1: 15, *infelix*.

26 cast my sowle; 1 Sam. 1: 15, *effudi animam meam*. *MED* has no precisely similar use, but cf. *casten* v. 12a, 'To utter (a cry, complaint, threat, etc.); heave (a sigh)'; similarly *OED cast* v. 26.

31–2 hand-seruaunt: Not in *MED*; the first two citations in *OED* are from WB (EV), translating a different passage, and the present instance.

46–9 and ther made this psalme . . . the remenaunt of that psalme: Given in full in 1 Sam. 2: 1–10.

49–52 And thenne Helcana . . . of Hely: 1 Sam. 2: 11 and 2: 21.

53–5 the two sones of Hely . . . the comandementis of God: 1 Sam. 2: 12–17, with their names from 1 Sam. 2: 34.

55–9 And Our Lord . . . after his herte: Selectively summarizes 1 Sam. 2: 27–36.

56–7 he wold take . . . and from his hows: Interprets the metaphor of 1 Sam. 2: 31, *praecidam brachium tuum et brachium domus patris tui*, in similar terms to *Hs* (1 Kgs), 4, *auferam sacerdotium de domo tua*.

60 Samuel seruyd . . . tofore Hely: Blends 1 Sam. 2: 18 with 1 Sam. 3: 1.

61–123 And on a tyme . . . iuged Israhel xl yere: 1 Sam. 3: 2–4: 18.

62–3 see the lanterne of God til it was quenchyd and put out: Contrast 1 Sam. 3: 2–3, *nec poterat videre / lucerna Dei antequam extingueretur*; erroneously makes *lanterne* the object of *see* rather than the subject of *was quenchyd*.

124–9 1 Sam. 5: 1–4.

130–4 And God shewed . . . in that cyte: Closest to *Hs*, 7, *aggravata est manus Domini super Azotos, et percussit eos in secretiori parte natium . . . et mures ebullientes de agris corrodebant extales eorum*. The boiling wells, not mentioned in 1 Sam. or *JA*, may originate from *ebullientes*. The mice are in *JA*, 6 I.i, but cf. also 1 Sam. 6: 4. For *they suffered grete persecucion and confusyon*, cf. *JA*, 6 I.i (at a slightly earlier point), *in angustia et confusione grauissima constituti sunt*.

134–42 The peple . . . leste: 1 Sam. 5: 7–9.

142–44 in suche . . . softe: *Hs*, 7.

145–63 And thenne . . . they will: 1 Sam. 5: 10–6: 8.

163–4 And thus . . . the chyldren of Israhel: Summarizes 1 Sam. 6: 9–16.

165–205 Samuel thenne . . . ordeyne to them a kyng: 1 Sam. 7: 15, 8: 1–22.

187 erers: The latest *MED* citation is from 1440, but *OED* has a single later instance dated 1534.

190 vnguentaryes: 1 Sam. 8: 13, *unguentarias*. *MED* has a single citation, from WB (EV) Exod. 30: 25, glossed 'a maker of ointments, an apothecary'. *OED* adds the present instance, and two from the seventeenth century.

192 dyme: 1 Sam. 8: 15, *addecimabit*. Not in *MED*, and *OED* has only the present instance and one (in a different sense) from 1610; cf. French *di(s)mer*.

197 thral: The adjective is well attested, but emendation to *thrals* would give easier syntax.

206 and so he dyde: A linking addition.

207–10 For he toke . . . of all the peple: 1 Sam. 9: 1–2.

210–14 And Samuel enoynted . . . contrees aboute: 1 Sam. 10: 1.

214 and so departed from hym: Replaces 1 Sam. 10: 2–16.

215–31 1 Sam. 10: 17–25.

221 lote: *MED lotten* does not record this sense, and this is the only example before 1642 in *OED*.

232–5 Thus was Saul . . . and had victorye: Replaces 1 Sam. 10: 26–14: 51; cf. 14: 52.

236–76 Samuel cam on a tyme . . . retorne with the: 1 Sam. 15: 1–26.

276–8 And so Sammuel . . . vnto his deth: Summarizes 1 Sam. 15: 27–35.

279–81 Thenne Our Lord . . . tofore hym: Summarizes 1 Sam. 16: 1–5.

282–303 This Iesse had . . . wente his waye: 1 Sam. 16: 10–23.

287 rough: Contrast 1 Sam. 16: 12, *rufus* 'ruddy', and cf. the *pellem pilosam* of 19: 13, translated *rowhe skynne* in 419 below. But possibly a form of *rouge* 'red'; *MED* records the spellling *rouȝ*.

304–19 After this, the Philisteis . . . serue the Phylisteis: 1 Sam. 17: 1–9.

313 botes: *MED*, *bot(e* n.2 has 2b, '?a greave', the only citation being the WB (LV) translation of the same passage.

in his cartes: Contrast 1 Sam. 17: 6, *in cruribus* 'on his legs', evidently misread as *in curribus*.

sholdres: In view of the persistence into later ME of pl. forms descending from OE *sculdru/sculdra*, *sholdre* might be pl., but the dictionaries record no close parallels.

319–20 And thus he dyde crye xl dayes long: *Hs* (1 Kgs), 16, *Sic dicebat Goliath quadraginta diebus*. In 1 Sam., this information occurs at a later point (17: 16), and is differently expressed.

320 Saul and the children . . . sore aferd: 1 Sam. 17: 11.

321–2 Dauid was at this tyme . . . with Saul: Summarizes 1 Sam. 17: 12–15.

322–90 To whom Ysay said . . . Ysay of Bethleem: 1 Sam. 17: 17–58.

341–2 Is it not . . . this geaunt: Contrast 1 Sam. 17: 29, *numquid non verbum est*.

391–405 And forthwith . . . frendly: 1 Sam. 18: 1–9.

399 choris: *MED* has *chor(e* b. *pl.*, 'a troupe of dancers; ?dances', cited only from WB (EV) (Judg. 11: 34). Contextually, the second sense is likelier, and closer to *chorosque ducentes* (1 Sam. 18: 6).

405–6 but euer sought menes afterward to destroye Dauid: An addition. Cf. 556 below and note ad loc.

406–7 for he dredde . . . hym from hym: 1 Sam. 18:12–13.

407–8 And Dauid was wise and kepte hym wel from hym: An addition.

409–12 And after this . . . warned Dauid therof: Assembles material from 1 Sam. 18: 20 and 19: 1–4.

412–13 and Dauid gate hym . . . in the montaynes: Cf. *JA*, 6 XIII.i, *sumens quadringentos quicum eo erant de ciuitate, profectus est in desertum* (1 Sam. 23: 13–14 contains similar information, but is more diffusely expressed, and the number is given as six hundred).

414–38 1 Sam. 19: 11–24.

439–41 Dauid thenne fledde . . . to slee me: 1 Sam. 20: 1.

441–3 Ionathas was sory . . . to slee Dauid: Summarizes 1 Sam. 20: 2–24: 2, drawing particularly on 20: 17.

443–66 And on a tyme . . . into surer places: 1 Sam. 24: 3–23, with some rearrangement.

467–555 1 Sam. 25: 1–43.

474–6 that he myght . . . pleased hym: Cf. 1 Sam. 28: 8; this has been clumsily condensed in translation or mangled in the printing. The initial *that* may be a pronoun, referring to the treatment by David's men of Nabal's sheep, with *for* meaning 'because'. Instead of supplying *that he*, *I* could perhaps be emended to *he*.

495 masses of cariacares: 1 Sam. 25: 18, *massas caricarum*. The only *MED* citation s.v. *masse* for the sense 'cake (of dried figs)' is from WB (EV) (4 Kgs 20: 7). This is the only *OED* citation for *cariacare*; it is not in *MED*.

501 and hath yelded euyl for good: The omission of the subject is perhaps a compositor's error, but may be authorial, closely rendering 1 Sam. 25: 21, *et reddidit mihi malum pro bono*.

523 constytued: 1 Sam. 25: 30, *constituerit*. *MED* does not record *constitue(n*, and the earliest *OED* citation is from elsewhere in *GoL*. *MED* has only one citation for *constituten* in the sense 'appoint'.

524–5 þat thou sholdest . . . auengid: Contrast 1 Sam. 25: 31, *quod effuderis sanguinem innoxium aut ipse te ultus fueris*; the added negative preserves the sense, but the future-perfect time-reference is lost.

533 blyuen: According to *OED*, s.v. *belive*, this pa. p. (not recorded in *MED*) occurs only in Caxton, and is 'probably after Middle Dutch or Middle Low German'.

542 mortefyed: 1 Sam. 25: 37, *emortuum*. *MED* does not record this metaphorical use (but compare 2d, 'deaden (sensation), benumb').

556 After this, Saul alway sought Dauid, for to slee hym: An added linking passage, echoing 443.

556–601 And the peple called Zyphei . . . retorned home agayn: 1 Sam. 26: 1–25.

558 after part of the wyldernes: 1 Sam. 26: 1, *ex adverso* ('facing') *solitudinis*. Although *MED* lists no spatial senses, *after* probably has the sense 'rear', recorded by *OED* from OE and from 1652 onward.

602–7 1 Sam. 27: 1–4, 6.

608–9 After this, the Philisteis . . . ayenst Israhel: 1 Sam. 28: 1.

609–17 And Saul assemblid . . . to the woman by nyght: 1 Sam. 28: 4–8.

614 phiton: 1 Sam. 28: 7, *pythonem*. *MED* has only *phitoun* 'Python, the serpent slain by Phoebus', which itself has been 'reshaped by anal. with *phitonesse*'. The earliest *OED* citation for *python* n.1 is from 1548.

otherwyse callyd a phytonesse or witche: An addition. The word *pythonissam* occurs in *Hs* (1 Kgs), 25 and 27, in passages not present in 1 Sam. or *GoL*.

617–8 and made her by her crafte to reyse Samuel: Summarizes 1 Sam. 28: 8–14. Cf. *JA* in IC. 50150, Book 6, ch. 13, *iussit vt ei animam samuel euocaret* (similarly Frobenius 1524; the text of Pollard et al. 6 XIV.ii is deviant here: *eius sic ei animam samuhel euocaret*).

618–32 And Samuel said . . . all that day: 1 Sam. 28: 15–20.

632–3 he was gretly trobled . . . desired hym to ete: Summarizes 1 Sam. 28: 21–3. Cf. *Hs* (1 Kgs), 27, *coegit eum mulier, et servi ejus, ut comederet.*

633–5 and she slewe . . . alle that nyght: 1 Sam. 28: 24–5.

633 paske lambe: Contrast 1 Sam. 28: 24, *vitulum pascualem* ('fatted/ grazing calf'); the second word has been misinterpreted as referring to the Pasch, which in turn has prompted the substitution of *lambe*.

636–64 1 Sam. 31: 1–13.

10. DAVID

This combines close translation (with some recasting and abridgement) of sections of the Vulgate with summaries of some of the intervening material, brief narrative links, and two substantial additions (187–207 and 367–74). A few passages suggest the influence of *Bh* or *Hs*. The selection of material in *Cm* is generally different, but see the notes on 187–9 and 367–71.

The running head is *Thystorye of Dauid*.

2–3 but litil towched: Contextually, the sense appears to be 'reproduced with little intervention', which is true of the extensive sections of the Vulgate that are closely translated, but as this legend contains extensive Caxtonian additions, the words may have a pre-emptive intention. *MED* offers no appropriate sense for *towched*, but cf. *OED touch* v. 17d, 'to alter, make a change to', with the earliest citation from 1688.

3 This line is followed by a woodcut depicting a Hebrew king (Hodnett 253).

4–5 After the deth . . . ayenst Amalech: Cf. 2 Sam. 1: 1.

5–15 For whiles Dauid . . . more of them: Cf. 1 Sam. 30: 1–18.

16–17 whan he was come . . . the hoost of Saul: Cf. 2 Sam. 1: 1–2.

17–41 told to Dauid . . . Ionathas: 2 Sam. 1: 4–17.

21 by aduenture: *Bh*, 133va, *dauenture*. Cf. 2 Sam. 1: 6, *casu*.

29 armylle: The only *MED* citations are from a1475 and *Abraham* 446 above.

42–8 2 Sam. 2: 1–4.

49–53 Cf. 2 Sam. 2: 8–10.

54–72 After this it happed . . . in the same place: 2 Sam. 2: 12–23.

61 roof: See OED *rive* v.1 7b for this rare construction with the the weapon as object.

72–3 anon the sonne . . . they withdrewe: Cf. 2 Sam. 2: 24, 28.

73–4 Ther were slayn . . . were slayn: 2 Sam. 2: 30.

75–8 thus ther was . . . wroth gretly therof: Cf. 2 Sam. 3: 6–8. But for *Abner toke a concubyne of Saul . . . wherfor Hisboseth repreuyd hym of it*, compare *Hs* (2 Kgs), 5, *Abner intraret ad concubinam Saulis . . . Ob hoc objurgatus est adversus eum Isboseth*, with 2 Sam. 3: 7, *fuerat autem Sauli concubina . . . / dixitque Hisboseth ad Abner*.

78–9 cam to Dauid . . . frendship with hym: Cf. 2 Sam. 3: 20–1.

79–80 Ioab was not there . . . he knewe it: Cf. 2 Sam. 3: 23.

80–3 he cam to Abner . . . deth of Abner: Cf. 2 Sam. 3: 27–9.

84–5 dyde do burye . . . the bere hymself: Cf. 2 Sam. 3: 31–2.

86–8 whan Hisboseth . . . Banaa and Rechab: 2 Sam. 4: 1–2.

88–9 whiche cam on a day . . . laye and slepte: 2 Sam. 4: 5.

89–114 ther they slewe . . . Syon in Iherusalem: 2 Sam. 4: 7–5: 5.

104 mouth: 2 Sam. 5: 1, *os*, normally interpreted as 'bone'. See notes to *Isaac* 165 and *Job* 67.

114–17 after this . . . in his hows: Cf. 2 Sam. 5: 17–6: 17.

117–19 After this yet . . . put vnder: Cf. 2 Sam. 8: 1–14.

120–49 2 Sam. 11: 1–18, 21.

150–86 Whan Vryes wyf . . . home to his hous: 2 Sam. 11: 26–12: 15.

187–9 for this synne . . . of homycyde: Two lines after Nathan foretells the death of David's son, *Cm* (7963–70) also relates David's composition of this psalm, though without significant verbal similarities: *Quen dauid knew his cost of care, / Reued him thing neuer sua sare; / In takin þat he reud his sake / An orison sone gan he make, / þat high miserere mei deus, / Men au to say þat sinne es reus. / Of all þe psalmis of þe sautere, / þis salme of penance has na pere.*

189–207 For as I ones . . . Braband: Evidently an addition by Caxton himself. Depictions of David buried waist-deep in the ground in some books of hours suggest that the episode was popular. See Huttar, 'Frail Grass and Firm Tree', 48–9, and King'oo, *Miserere Mei*, 123–4.

190–1 Syr Iohan Capons: The Catalan Joan Copons was a frequent ambassador to the French court and a supporter of the engagement of Margaret of York to Peter of Coimbra, Constable of Portugal; Margaret eventually married Charles, Duke of Burgundy. Sutton ('Caxton was a Mercer', 119) dates the journey mentioned by Caxton to about 1467–9; see also Calmette, 'Dom Pedro', 13.

191 **bothe lawes:** Canon and civil law.

208–12 Cf. 2 Sam. 12: 15–24.

213–15 After this, Dauid . . . the moder syde: *Bh*, 138[va], *Apres ce auint que nostre seigneur suscita vn grant mal en la maison dauid. en ceste maniere. Amon lainsne filz dauid . . . aima sa suer thamar. qui nestoit sa suer que depar son pere. car elle estoit fille maacha sa mere.* Compare 2 Sam. 13: 1, *factum est autem post hae / ut Absalom filii David sororem speciosissimam vocabulo Thamar / adamaret Amnon filius David.*

216–17 Ammon forced . . . out of his chambre: Cf. 2 Sam. 13: 14–15. For *threwe her out of his chambre*, compare *Hs* (2 Kgs), 13, *ejecit eam a se*, with 2 Sam. 13: 15, *surge vade.*

217–20 she complayned her . . . first-begoten sone: Cf. 2 Sam. 13: 20–1.

220 Absalon hated Ammon euer after: Cf. 2 Sam. 13: 22.

221–3 whan Absalon . . . his brother Ammon: Cf. 2 Sam. 13: 23–9.

224–6 it was told . . . but Ammon: Cf. 2 Sam. 13: 30–3. For *ther was no mo slayn but Ammon*, compare *Bh*, 139[ra], *nul de tes filz nest occis fors amon*, with 2 Sam. 13: 33, *ne ponat . . . verbum istud dicens / omnes filii regis occisi sunt / quoniam Amnon solus mortuus est.*

227–8 the other sones . . . durst not come home: Cf. 2 Sam. 13: 36–8.

229–32 by the moyen . . . kynge his fader: Cf. 2 Sam. 14: 23–4, 28.

232–5 This Absalon . . . of good weight: 2 Sam. 14: 25–6.

236–54 Thenne whan he abode . . . salued them: 2 Sam. 14: 28–15: 2.

254–9 takyng them . . . kynge of Israhel: Cf. 2 Sam. 15: 5–10. For *all men shold obeye and wayte on hym as kynge of Israhel*, cf. both *Bh*, 139[vb], *et la vint a lui moult grant peuple. appareilliez a faire sa voulente*, and 2 Sam. 15: 10, *regnavit Absalom in Hebron.*

259–61 Whan Dauid herd . . . out of Iherusalem: Cf. 2 Sam. 15: 13–14.

261–2 Absalon cam . . . his fadres concubynes: Cf. 2 Sam. 16: 22.

264–8 Cf. 2 Sam. 18: 2–5.

269–70 And they wente forth . . . put to flyght: *Hs* (2 Kgs), 17, *Et factum est praelium in die illa juxta saltum Ephraim, et fugit exercitus Absalon.* Compare 2 Sam. 18: 6–7, *itaque egressus est populus in campum contra Israhel / et factum est proelium in saltu Ephraim / et caesus est ibi populus Israhel ab exercitu David / factaque est ibi plaga magna.*

270–83 as Absalon fledde . . . a grete stone: 2 Sam. 18: 9–17.

284 And whan Dauid knewe that his sone was slayn: Cf. 2 Sam. 18: 19–32.

284–90 he made gret sorow . . . into the cyte: 2 Sam. 18: 33–19: 3.

291–305 Thenne Ioab entrid . . . into their tabernacles: 2 Sam. 19: 5–8.

292 discoraged the chere: 2 Sam. 19: 5, *confudisti . . . vultus*.

305–6 and after cam . . . was deed: Cf. 2 Sam.. 19: 10–15.

307–11 after, one Siba . . . Ioab plesid: Cf. 2 Sam. 20: 1–22.

312–14 After this Dauid . . . all the contre: Cf. 2 Sam. 24: 1–2.

314–42 ther were founden . . . vnto Our Lord: 2 Sam. 24: 9–18.

329 I am constrayned to a grete thyng: 2 Sam. 24: 14, *artor nimis*. For the adverbial use, cf. *MED*, *thing* 13a(c), 'for an unspecified amount or measure', especially quotation c1440, *be a gret thynge*.

342–3 Our Lord was . . . cessed in Israhel: Cf. 2 Sam. 24: 25.

344–58 Cf. 3 Kgs 1: 1–53.

350 Syon: Contrast 3 Kgs 1: 38, *Gion*.

359–66 The dayes of Dauid . . . his fadres: Cf. 3 Kgs 2: 1–10.

367–71 This Dauid was an holy man . . . also his ascension: Immediately before relating David's death and burial, *Cm* (8521–9) also records his authorship and prophecies, though without significant verbal resemblances: *þis ilk it was, king dauy, / þat mekil spac of prophesy, / Of cristes birth ful lang biforn, / . . . / þis ilke dauid þe sauter made*.

374–6 whan Dauid had regned . . . cyte of Dauid: Cf. 3 Kgs 2: 10–11. For *ouer Iuda and Israhel*, compare *Bh*, 146rb, *sur iudee*, with 3 Kgs 2: 11, *super Israhel*; for *he deyed in good mynde* (no equivalent in the Vulgate), cf. *Bh*, 146rb, *mouru dauid en bonne vieillesse*.

11. SOLOMON

This combines close translation (with some recasting and abridgement) of sections of the Vulgate with summaries of some of the intervening material, brief narrative links, and several more subjectively expressed additions (124–30, 174–6, 242–8, and 269). A few passages suggest the influence of *Bh*, *Cm*, *Hs*, or *JA*.

The running head is *Thystorye of Salomon/Salamon*.

1 This line is preceded by the same woodcut as is used for *Saul* above (Hodnett 252).

1–4 After Dauid regned Salomon . . . in his possession: Cf. 3 Kgs 2: 12,

3–4. Compare also *Cm*, 8539–44, *Qven dauid was dede, sone salamon / was king sittand in his faderis tron, / He was a burli bacheler, / In all þis werld had he na pere. / Of witt and wisdam, as we rede, / was neuer nan wiser laue to lede.*

4–7 acordyng to hys faders . . . sone of Gether: Cf. 3 Kgs 2: 5–6.

8–10 and fledde . . . in deserte: *Hs* (3 Kgs), 4, *Joab fugit in tabernaculum Domini, et apprehendit cornu altaris. Et misit rex Banaiam . . . Et interfecit eum Banaias ad cornu altaris, et sepultus est in domo sua in deserto.* The same events are more diffusely related in 3 Kgs 2: 28–34.

11–70 3 Kgs 3: 4–28.

22 docyle: 3 Kgs 3: 9, *docile.* Not in *MED*; this is the earliest *OED* citation, the next being for 1584.

38 victymes: 3 Kgs 3: 15, *victimas.* Not in *MED*; the two earliest *OED* citations are for 1497 and 1582.

42 cubycle: 3 Kgs 3: 17, *cubiculo. MED* has only a single citation, c1450; this is the earliest citation in *OED*.

43 the thyrde day . . . delyueryd: Contrast 3 Kgs 3: 18, *tertia vero die postquam ego peperi / peperit et haec. GoL* is closer to *Bh*, 147[va], *Et au tiers iour apres enfanta aussi ceste un filz.*

73–88 all the royames . . . in their tyme: 3 Kgs 4: 21–7.

85–6 for the horses of his cartes, chares and curres: 3 Kgs 4: 26, *equorum currulium.* This is the only *OED* citation for *curre*; the only *MED* citation, s.v. *cure* n.2, is c1225(?c1200).

89–98 3 Kgs 4: 29–34.

99–102 Salamon sente lettres . . . to Our Lord: Cf. 3 Kgs 5: 2, 5–6.

102–5 Hyram sente . . . loue and frendship: Cf. 3 Kgs 5: 8, 10–12.

106–18 3 Kgs 5: 13–18. The redundancy in *dyde nothyng but bare . . . berars of burthens only* suggests the blending of two versions: for *berars of burthens*, compare 3 Kgs 5: 15, *eorum qui onera portabant*, and for *lxxM men that dyde nothyng but bare stone and morter and other thynges*, compare *JA*, 8 II.ix, *ad portandos lapides aliamque materiam septuaginta milia uiri.*

119–20 Thenne began Salomon the temple . . . began to bylde the temple: The words *in the fourthe yere of his regne* can be construed with either what precedes or what follows. The redundancy suggests the blending of 3 Kgs 6: 1 with another version, possibly *JA*, 8 III.i, *Coepit autem salomon aedificare templum anno quarto regni sui*; less probably, in view of the amount of material omitted, 2 Paral. 3: 1–2.

120–4 The hous that he bylded . . . face of the temple: 3 Kgs 6: 2–3.

124–30 And for to wryte . . . but I passe ouer: Not in identified sources.

125 necessaryes: Blake, *Caxton's Own Prose*, gives the glosses 'accoutrements' and 'indispensable parts'. Cf., in a related context, WB (EV), 3 Kgs 10: 21, *alle the vessels, of the whiche kyng Salamon drank, weren golden, and al the necessarie of the hows of the wijlde wode of Liban of moost pure gold.*

cost: The context suggests a concrete sense, and Blake, *Caxton's Own Prose*, gives the glosses 'adornments' and 'decoration'. Cf. *MED*, 'costly object', attested once, c1450(?a1400), and *OED*, *cost* n.3 4, 'a costly thing'.

127–8 the Second Book of Kynges: The reference is to 3 (also designated 1) Kgs *Hs* combines Kings and Paralipomenon, and several times cites the two in close proximity.

130–1 It was on makyng . . . it was fynysshed: Cf. 3 Kgs 6: 38–7: 1. But compare also *JA*, 8 V.i, *Post templi uero fabricam quam septem annis praediximus fuisse perfectam aedificium domum regalium construere coepit quod tredecim annis impleuit.*

131–6 He made in the temple . . . hows of Our Lord: Cf. 3 Kgs 7: 48–51.

137–47 3 Kgs 8: 1–6.

139 famylyes: 3 Kgs 8: 1, *familiarum. MED* has only the sense 'household', with a single citation 1607(?a1425); *OED family* 3a(a), 'those descended . . . from a common ancestor', is first cited from Caxton. Cf. note on *Job* 6.

143–4 without extimacion and nombre: 3 Kgs 8: 5, *absque aestimatione et numero. OED* lists *extymacion* as a ME spelling, and *MED* has one example of *exstymacion.*

148–52 And thenne Salamon . . . mercyful to hym: Cf. 3 Kgs 8: 14–15, 25–6.

152–74 Our Lord appered . . . all thys euyll: 3 Kgs 9: 1–9.

167–8 a fable and prouerbe: 3 Kgs 9: 7, *in proverbium et in fabulam.*

177–8 XX yere after that . . . fynysshyd it perfyghtly: Cf. 3 Kgs 9: 10.

178–80 Hyram the Kynge . . . plesyd hym not: 3 Kgs 9: 12.

180–1 Hyram had sente . . . besaunts of gold: 3 Kgs 9: 14.

181–3 whyche he had spente . . . he had made: Cf. 3 Kgs 9: 15.

186–212 the Quene of Saba . . . to Kyng Salamon: 3 Kgs 10: 1–10.

212–42 Kynge Salamon gaf . . . Egypte and Chao: 3 Kgs 10: 13–28.

214 retorned: The gapping of the pronoun subject is paralleled, but the 1498 [or 1499?] (STC 24876) de Worde print adds *she.*

238 smale cytees: Cf. 3 Kgs 10: 26, *civitates munitas* ('walled cities'); the second word may have been misread as *minutas.*

239–41 Ther was as grete . . . growe in the felde: 3 Kgs 10: 27 states that he made silver as abundant as stones, and cedar as sycamores.

242–8 What shal I . . . conteynyng xix chapytres: An addition.

245–8 He made the Book . . . conteynyng xix chapytres: Cf. 93–4 above, translating 3 Kgs 4: 32.

249–58 Thys Kynge Salamon . . . their straunge goddes: 3 Kgs 11: 1–4.

258–9 worshyppid Astaroth . . . Amonytes: *Hs* (3 Kgs), 16, *Et aedificavit in excelsis circa Jerusalem tria fana idolorum: unum Astarthae deae Sidoniorum, quae Juno dicitur; secundum, Chamos idolo Moabitarum; tertium, Moloch idolo Ammonitarum.* In 3 Kgs, this information is divided between 11: 5 and 11: 7.

261–7 Wherfor God . . . I haue chosen: 3 Kgs 11: 9, 11–13.

267–8 after thys . . . neuer in pees after: Cf. 3 Kgs 11: 14–40.

269–73 Salamon repentyd hym . . . alle the peple: Cf. *Cm*, 9041–4, 9087–8, 9100–4, *Qven salamon his wille had wroght, / wa was him þat euer he thoght / Godd to wreth, his saule to file, / And þan repentid him a quile. / . . . / And lais on me ful hard paynis, / For sore it es mi repentanis / . . . / And his bodi all to driue. / To skourge bar thoru þat thrang, / vte of his bac þe blode it sprang. / þat sor, þat schame, þat martyring, / was neuer sene on suilk a king.*

273–5 He regned . . . regned after hym: Cf. 3 Kgs 11: 42–3.

12. REHOBOAM

This combines close translation of a section of the Vulgate with summary and linking passages that could be based on the Vulgate, but at some points are closer to *Bh* or *Hs* (the repetition at the beginning of the third paragraph of information already given also suggesting the combination of sources), and a first-person conclusion.

The running head is *Thystorye of Roboas.*

1 This line is preceded by the same woodcut as is used for *Saul* above (Hodnett 252). On the text written in this scroll in C, see Introduction p. li.

1 After Salomon . . . Roboas: Cf. 3 Kgs 11: 43.

1–2 He cam to Sychem . . . ordeyne hym kynge: 3 Kgs 12: 1.

2–15 Iheroboas and all . . . of them counseyll: 3 Kgs 12: 3–8, but *Now thou hast not so moche nede* is an addition.

15–23 And the yong men . . . had counseylled hym: 3 Kgs 12: 10–14.

23–4 And anon the peple of Israhel forsoke Roboas: Cf. *Bh*, 155va, *Et lors se partirent ilz tous de roboam. et sen alerent en leurs lieux.* Contrast 3 Kgs 12: 16, *et abiit Israhel in tabernacula sua.*

24–6 And of xij trybus . . . Iheroboam theyr kynge: Cf. *Bh*, 155va, *et les .x. ligniees firent leur roy de iheroboam le filz nabath. Et la ligniee iudas et beniamin firent leur roy de roboam.*

26–7 and neuer retorned . . . vnto thys day: Cf. 3 Kgs 12: 19, *recessitque Israhel a domo David usque in praesentem diem.*

28–9 Roboas wold not doo . . . by yong men: Cf. 3 Kgs 12: 13–14.

30 the ten tribus . . . forsoke hym: Cf. *Hs* (3 Kgs), 17, *recesserunt decem tribus ab eo.*

31 ordeyned hym kynge vpon Israhel: Cf. 3 Kgs 12: 20.

32 Iheroboas fylle to ydolatrye: Cf. 3 Kgs 12: 28.

32–3 grete deuysyon . . . kynges of Israhel: Cf. *Hs* (3 Kgs), 17, *et tunc separata est monarchia regni Hebraeorum in duo regna, nec amplius ad unitatem rediit.*

13. JOB

Job 1, 2, and 42, with parallels to *Bh* and WB. In MS BL Royal 19. D. iii. of *Bh*, a shorter version of Job (243va–244va) is followed by a longer one (244va–256ra). (On the relationship between the two versions, found together in most copies of *Bh*, see Patterson, 'Interpreting Job's Silence'.) In several difficult passages, *GoL* agrees with the freer interpretations of LV and the longer version in *Bh*, as against the more literal renderings in EV and the shorter version in *Bh*.

The running head is *Thystorye of Iob*.

2 This line is followed by a woodcut depicting Job and Satan (Hodnett 254).

3–55 Ther was a man . . . ayenst Our Lord: Job 1: 1–22.

6 famylye: Job 1: 3, *familia*. See note on *Solomon* 139.

11 Whan they had thus fested eche other ofte: Cf. Job 1: 5, *cumque in orbem transissent dies convivii.*

12 blessyd and sanctefyed: Job 1: 5, *sanctificabat*. *MED* has s.v. *seintefien*, '? to dedicate (sb.) to God's service', citing a similar context (*Job his Children doth sanctifie*), while *OED* has 'to make (a person) holy', with citations from 1526 onward.

13–14 Leste my chyldren synne and blesse not God in theyr hertes: Cf. Job 1: 5 *ne forte peccaverint filii mei et benedixerint Deo in cordibus suis.* Both the context and the Latin preclude an affirmation that the children have in fact blessed God, but precise renderings vary, as illustrated by the shorter and longer versions in *Bh*: 243vb, *Sire ne soufrez que mes enfans ayent pechie. et donnez sire quilz vous ayent benoit en leurs cuers*; 245vb, *afin que par auenture ilz naient pechie. et pense mal contre nostre seigneur dieu en leurs cuers*. *GoL* is close to the longer version in *Bh* and to WB (LV): *Lest perauenture my sones do synne, and curse* [EV *blisse*] *God in her hertis*. Cf. notes on 27, 67–8, and 74–5 below.

19 thurghwalked: Job 1: 7, *perambulavi*. Neither *MED* nor *OED* records the word, though parallel formations such as *thurghfaren* and *thurghyede* are well attested. The word order is against taking *thurgh* as an adv.

22–4 Yf so were . . . forsake the: Contrast Job 1: 10, *nonne tu vallasti eum ac domum eius universamque substantiam per circuitum*; anticipates the sense of Job 1: 11, rendered by *But stratche . . . blesse the* in lines 26–7 below.

27 and he shal soone grutche and not blesse the: Job 1: 11, *nisi in facie tua benedixerit tibi*. *GoL* is closer to the longer version in *Bh*, 246[ra], *il te maudira appertement*, and WB (LV), *if he cursith not thee in the face, bileue not to me*, than to the shorter version in *Bh*, 243[vb], *il te beneyra*, and WB (EV), *but in the face he blesse to thee*.

34 asse: Job 1: 14, *asinae*. Perhaps an error for *asses*, but the sg. is semantically possible.

41 enuayhed: *Bh* (longer version), 246[ra], *enuahi*. Not in *MED*; *OED* has only two citations, the present passage and another from Caxton. (See also *MED*, *envoisen* v.1 and *OED*, *envahisshe*.) Cf. Job 1: 17, *invaserunt*.

55–6 but toke it all pacyently: Not in the Vulgate.

57–72 After thys . . . the toppe of hys heed: Job 2: 1–7.

67 mouth: Job 2: 5, *os*, normally interpreted as 'bone'. The same mistake is made in *Isaac* 204 and *David* 104.

67–8 þat he shal not blesse the: Job 2: 5, *quod in facie benedicat tibi*. *GoL* is closer to the longer version in *Bh*, 246rb, *quil te maudira plainement*, and WB (LV), *that he schal curse thee in the face*, than to the shorter version in *Bh*, 244ra, *comment il te beneyra*, and to WB (EV), *that in to the face he blisse to thee*.

72–3 whiche was . . . dongehyll: Cf. Job 2: 8, *qui testa saniem deradebat sedens in sterquilinio*.

73–4 Thenne cam . . . in thy symplenes: Job 2: 9.

74–5 Forsake thy God and blesse hym no more, and goo deye: Job 2: 9, *benedic Deo et morere*. *GoL* is closer to the longer version in *Bh*, 246[rb], *Maudi dieu. et muires*, and WB (LV), *Curse thou God, and die*, than to the shorter version in *Bh*, 244[ra], *or pues tu bien beneyr et mourir*, and WB (EV), *Blisse to God, and die*.

74 symplenes: Job 2: 9, *simplicitate*, intepreted (e.g. in the *Glossa ordinaria*) as 'integrity'. However, negative senses of *symplenes* are well attested in the 15th century (cf. *MED simplenes(se* 4), and WB (LV), records the gloss [*symplenesse*] *that is, fonnednesse*.

75–82 Thenne Iob said . . . Naamathites: Job 2: 10–11.

82–3 And whan they . . . cryeng they wepte: Job 2: 12, *cumque levassent procul oculos suos non cognoverunt eum et exclamantes ploraverunt*.

83–4 They cam . . . hys myserye: Cf. Job 2: 11, *condixerant enim ut pariter venientes visitarent eum et consolarentur.*

84–7 they tare . . . hys sorow: Job 2: 12–13.

88–95 Thenne after that . . . Iob agayn to hem: Not in the Vulgate. *Bh* (shorter version) also skips from Job 2 to Job 42, but the bridging passage is different and longer.

90 ***Morallys*** **of Seynt Gregory:** Gregory the Great, *Moralia in Job.*

95 Our Lord . . . to them: Cf. Job 42: 7, *postquam autem locutus est Dominus verba haec ad Iob / dixit ad Eliphaz Themaniten / iratus est furor meus in te et in duos amicos tuos.*

95–8 Ye haue not . . . praye for you: Job 42: 7–8.

98–9 I shal receyue hys prayer and shal take hys vysage: Job 42: 8, *faciem eius suscipiam.* Cf. WB (EV), *his face I shal take*, and LV, *Y schal resseyue his face*; *MED* and *OED* record no similar metaphorical uses of *face/ visage.* The shorter and longer versions in *Bh* give, respectively, an interpretation and a literal rendering of the metaphor: 244[rb], *ie receurai son sacrefice en gre*; 256[ra], *ie receurai sa face.* (The *Glossa ordinaria* gives successively the interpretations found in *Bh* (longer version) and *GoL*: *id est gratum habuit sacrificium per eum oblatum. Et eius orationem non solum pro ipso, sed etiam amicis suis. ideo subditur.*) Compare, in 101 below, *Our Lord beheld the vysage of Iob*, translating Job 42: 9, *suscepit Dominus faciem Iob.*

99–114 They wente forth . . . emong their brethern: Job 42: 9–15.

105 and meuyd theyr heedys vpon hym: Job 42: 11, *moverunt super eum caput.* Cf. WB (LV), *moueden the heed on hym* (similarly EV). In *Bh*, the shorter version omits the clause, while the longer translates it literally.

115–16 And thus Iob . . . all his lossis: Not in the Vulgate.

116–18 And Iob lyuyd . . . ful of dayes: Job 42: 16.

14. TOBIT

This is a translation of the entire Book of Tobit. There are several notable agreements with WB and one with *Hs.*

The running head is *Thystorye of T(h)obie.*

2 This line is followed by a woodcut depicting Tobit (Hodnett 255).

3–49 Tobit 1: 1–25.

4 ouerpartyes: Tobit 1: 1, *superioribus. MED* has a single citation of *over-parti(e*, suggesting that the first element may be construed as an adj.; WB (EV) has *ouere partis* here.

11 chyldesly: *MED*, *childishli* has only one citation (glossed ‘clumsily’); the first citation in *OED* of the sense 'in a manner not befitting maturity' is from 1533.

17–18 Suche thynges . . . whylis he was a chylde: Cf. Tobit 1: 8, *haec et his similia secundum legem Dei puerulus observabat.*

29 warnynges of helthe: Tobit 1: 15, *monita salutis.*

30 Iewes: Contrast Tobit 1: 16, *Medorum*; correctly rendered as *Medes* in the remainder of the legend.

50–90 Tobit 2: 1–23.

75–7 For lyke as Iob . . . skornyng hym: Cf. Tobit 2: 15, *sicut beato Iob insultabant reges ita isti parentes et cognati eius / et inridebant vitam eius.*

89 thy almesses lost: *Hs* (Tob.), 1, *eleemosynae tuae perierunt*. Cf. Tobit 2: 22, *eleemosynae tuae modo paruerunt*, paraphrased by Knox in *the Holy Bible* as 'what hast thou to shew, now, for all thy almsgiving?'

91–137 Tobit 3: 1–25.

97 dyrepcyon: Tobit 3: 4, *direptionem*. Not in *MED*; this is the earliest citation in *OED*.

107 the mayde repreuyd her: Contrast Tobit 3: 9, *cum pro culpa sua increparet puellam respondit ei.*

119 kepe: Contrast Tobit 3: 15, *eripias.*

138–74 Tobit 4: 1–23.

138 Thenne: This word is preceded by a printed paraph.

159–60 the hyre of thy seruaunt ne mede of thy mercenarye: Tobit 4: 15, *merces mercennarii apud te* [v.l. *tui*]. Earlier citations of *mercenary* all have a pejorative sense. The earliest *OED* citations in this neutral sense are from 1523 (n.) and 1569 (adj.).

163 Ordeyne: Tobit 4: 18, *constitue.*

175–223 Tobit 5: 1–28.

198 it shal not be longe but: *OED but* C 10f(b): 'After *not long* . . . etc.: *when, before*'.

201 I shal restore to the thy mede: Tobit 15: 14, *restituam tibi mercedem tuam*. This sense of *restore* is not in *OED*, but cf. *MED*, *restoren* 2c, 'give reward (to sb.)' (latest citation c1426).

204–5 Thou nedest not to aske the kyndred of hym: Contrast Tobit 5: 17, *genus quaeris mercennarii an ipsum mercennarium.*

205–6 but lest happely . . . to the agayn: Cf. Tobit 5: 18, *sed ne forte sollicitum te reddam.*

215 shold departe: Contrast Tobit 5: 23, *profecti essent.*

218 Our pouerte suffyseth ynough to vs: Following this, Tobit 5: 25, *ut divitias computaremus hoc*, is omitted.

224–66 Tobit 6: 1–22.

229 vynne: Tobit 6: 4, *brancia. MED, fin* n.1 1b: 'used, perhaps mistakenly, to translate ML brancia or OF branche'; cited from WB (EV) translation of the same verse (LV *gile*) and Chauliac. *OED* does not record this sense.

230 to the drye londe: Following this, Tobit 6: 4, *et palpitare* ['struggle'] *coepit ante pedes eius*, is omitted.

232 mylte: Tobit 6: 5, *iecur* ('liver'). The usual sense of the English word is 'spleen', but this passage provides the earliest citation for sense 2 'the semen or the testes of a male fish' in *OED*, which comments, 'The sense "soft roe of fish" . . . may have been adopted < Dutch'; this sense is not in *MED*. In 260 and 307 below, the same word is rendered by *herte*, in agreement with Tobit 6: 8, *cordis* (translated *herte* in 239); all three passages refer to the burning of an organ on coals to drive away devils, and the Vulgate is inconsistent about whether this is the liver or the heart. *Liver* and *milt* are contrasted in Caxton, *Sonnes of Aymon* i. 52, *His nayles stacke in to my lyuer and my mylte* (*MED*, s.v. *milt(e)*).

241 shal no more come to them: Following this, Tobit 6: 9, explaining that the gall is a healing ointment for the eyes, is omitted.

251 depose: Tobit 6: 15, *deponam.*

262 copulacion: Tobit 6: 20, *copulatione. MED* has three citations, glossed 'joining, uniting' and 'association, affiliation'; the sexual sense of the word is first recorded in *OED* from Caxton. The meaning of the entire verse in the Vulgate is uncertain.

262 folowe: Tobit 6: 21, *consequeris* 'attain'; but the nearest sense recorded in *MED* and *OED* is 'strive for/after'.

267–304 Tobit 7: 1–20.

299 conscrypcion: Tobit 7: 16, *conscriptionem.* The use by WB (EV) of the same word here provides the earliest *MED* citation, and the only one in this sense, for which *OED* has only one other citation, ?a1425.

305–48 Tobit 8: 1–24.

307 it: Later editions include this word.

320 and procreacion of chyldren: Not in Tobit.

337–8 to blesse the to fulle . . . of theyr helth: Tobit 8: 19, *plenius benedicere te / et sacrificium tibi laudis tuae et suae sanitatis offerre.*

349–72 Tobit 9: 1–12.

351 Yf: Tobit 9: 2, *si*; the sense is 'even if'.

364–5 syttyng at mete . . . kyssed hym: Contrast Tobit 9: 8, *discumbentem / et exiliens osculati sunt se alterutrum.*

373–403 Tobit 10: 1–13.

374 Trowest thou, wherfor: Tobit 10: 1, *putas quare*. Later editions have the pronoun. The interrogative seems to introduce a direct question; perhaps the verb is parenthetical in effect ('Why, do you think . . .?'). Cf. WB (EV), *Wenest thou, whi* (LV, *Gessist thou, whi*).

379 vnmesurable: Contrast Tobit 10: 4, *inremediabilibus* ('inconsolable').

386 the waye that he shold come: Contrast Tobit 10: 7, *vias omnes per quas spes remeandi videbatur.*

404–43 Tobit 11: 1–21.

405 thertenst: Contrast Tobit 11: 1, *undecimo. OED* accepts the form, citing only this passage. Compare Dutch *dertienste* and Caxton's *twentiest/twentyest* and *thyrttyest*, which *OED* identifies as West Germanic.

424–5 began, offendyng hys feet . . . hys honde: Contrast Tobit 11: 10, *coepit offendens pedibus currere / et data manu puero* [i.e. a servant], *occurrit in obviam filio suo*. The first two quotations in *MED*, *offenden* 4a, both from WB, provide parallels for this transitive use.

429 as it had be half an houre: Tobit 11: 14, *quasi dimidiam fere horam*; cf. *OED*, *as* adj. and conj. P2a, *as it were*, 'used to indicate that a word or phrase is perhaps not formally exact though practically right'.

441 thankyng God: Tobit 11: 20, *congratulationes ei.* WB (EV) has *thankende to hym.*

444–85 Tobit 12: 1–22.

471–2 thou beyng tempted, that he shold proue the: Cf. Tobit 12: 13, *ut temptatio probaret te.*

486–522 Tobit 13: 1–23.

489–90 Knowleche and confesse you to the Lord: Tobit 13: 3, *confitemini Domino*. Cf. *MED*, *confessen* 3, 'to acknowledge (a divinity, a divine attribute); avow one's faith in, worship'; several quotations under *OED*, *confess* 4 are comparable. Neither dictionary records the verb used reflexively or with *to* in this sense; *Confesse thou* in 504 below suggests that this is an early instance of post-verbal *you* as a nominative (see *Caxton's Blanchardyn and Eglantyne*, ed. Kellner, p. xiii), rather than a reflexive, and *to* may be prompted by the Latin dative. Cf. note to *Isaac* 241.

499 Confesse you: Contrast Tobit 13: 8, *convertimini*; perhaps mistaken for *confitemini*. Cf. 489–90 and 504 and notes.

504 Confesse thou to Our Lord in hys good thyngys: Tobit 13:12, *confitere Domino in bonis*. Cf. WB (EV and LV), *Knouleche thou to God in thi goodis.*

506 prysoners and them that ben in captyuyte: Tobit 13: 12, *captivos*.

510 shal haue thy londe into sanctificacion: Tobit 13: 14, *terram tuam in sanctificatione habebunt*; cf. *The Holy Bible*, ed. Knox, 'shall reckon thy soil holy ground'.

521 wayes: Contrast Tobit 13: 22, *vicos*.

523–59 Tobit 14: 1–17.

525 that is the sones of the sones of hys sone, yonge Thobye: Not in Tobit.

529 profyght: Tobit 14: 4, *profectu*.

533 passe: Tobit 14: 6, *excidit* ('fail, miss'). *MED* does not record a sense that precisely fits the source and context, but cf. 1a(e) 'of a spear or arrow: to miss', 6a 'to die', 10b 'to go unnoticed, . . . be ignored', and 10d 'to deviate'.

535 the londe therof shal be fulfyllid with deserte: Contrast Tobit 14: 7, *deserta terra eius replebitur* ('the wasteland shall be filled again').

the hows: Tobit 14: 7, *domus Dei*.

545 whansomeuer your moder shal deye, berye her by me, and: Contrast Tobit 14: 12, *quacumque die sepelieritis matrem vestram circa me in uno sepulchro*.

547 it: i.e. Nineveh; cf. 533 above.

552 and were with them vnto their deth: Not in Tobit.

555 he deyde: Not in Tobit.

556 cognacion: Tobit 14: 17, *cognatio*. The only *MED* citation in the relevant sense is from elsewhere in WB.

15. JUDITH

This translates sections of the Vulgate closely, with summary and linking passages; there are resemblances to *Bh* at several points and some notable agreements with WB.

The running head is *T(h)ystorye of Iudith*.

2 This line is followed by a woodcut depicting Judith, her handmaiden, and the beheaded Holofernes (Hodnett 256).

3–7 Arphaxat . . . cubytis hye: Judith 1: 1–2.

7–11 gloryfyed hymself . . . in the felde: Judith 1: 4–5.

11–13 Wherof Nabugodonosor . . . mountes of Ethyope: Cf. Judith 1: 7, 9.

13–14 for t'obeye and holde of hym: Cf. *Bh*, 227rb, *quilz se rendissent a lui du tout*.

14–18 Whyche all gaynsaid . . . on them all: Judith 1: 11–12.

19–29 callyd all hys . . . of the kynges: Judith 2: 2–10.

26 horsmen shoters: Judith 2: 7, *equites sagittarios.*

29–31 so wente . . . londe of Israhel: Cf. Judith 2: 11–3: 15.

32–3 whan the chyldren . . . the temple: Judith 4: 1–2.

34–6 Nabugodonosor had . . . shold subdue: Judith 3: 13.

36–9 Eliachym thenne . . . had ordeyned: Cf. Judith 4: 5–7.

39–51 Eliachym the preest . . . hys peple Israhel: Judith 4: 11–17.

43–5 trustyng . . . of holy prayers: *trustyng . . . horsmen* refers to Amalech, *not fyghtyng . . . prayers* to Moses.

44 helmes: Contrast Judith 4: 13, *clypeis* ('shields').

52–9 It was told . . . their knyghthode: Judith 5: 1–3.

55 furour: Judith 5: 2, *furore. MED* has only two citations, a1475 and a1500, and the earliest *OED* citation is from elsewhere in Caxton.

57 bisege: Judith 5: 3, *obsidet*, here 'inhabit'.

59–101 Thenne Achior . . . of thy power: Judith 5: 5–24.

66 whiche was in the multitude of many goddes: Judith 5: 8, *quae in multitudine deorum erant*, qualifying *caerimonias.*

73–4 the plaghe cessed fro them: Judith 5: 11, *cessasset plaga ab eis.*

79 Reed See: Following these words, the equivalent of *deserta Sina montis occupaverunt / in quibus nunquam homo habitare potuit, vel filius hominis requievit . . . de caelo consecuti sunt* (Judith 5: 14–15) is omitted at the end of the page.

80 gaf them water out of a stone: Not in Judith.

83 culture: Judith 5: 17, *cultura.* This is the only *OED* citation for the sense 'worship'; all the senses recorded by *MED* are agricultural.

89–90 Cananeum the kyng, Iebusee, Pheresee, Eueum, Etheum and Amorreum: A virgule follows *kyng.* Judith 5: 20, *Chananeum regem et Iebuseum et Ferezeum / et Hettheum et Eveum, et Amorreum.* These have apparently been treated as names of individuals rather than peoples.

95 late they be comen: *MED leten* 10a and *OED let* v.1 14b record hortative uses with the nominative, but none in the 3rd person.

102–120 And whan Achior . . . them and the: Judith 5: 26–6: 4.

105 Men cowardis: Judith 5: 27, *homines inermes*, suggests that *cowardis* is a postposed plural adjective rather than a noun.

120–31 And whan I haue . . . there bounden: Judith 6: 6–10.

132–3 And he told . . . them of Israhel: Cf. Judith 6: 12–13.

134–8 Thenne all . . . hys halowes: Judith 6: 14–15, but for the latter part, compare also WB (EV), *see the pride of hem, and beholde to oure meknesse, and to the face of thi halewis tac heede.*

138–40 and shewe . . . their enemyes: Cf. Judith 6: 15, 20.

141–3 And on that . . . horsmen: Judith 7: 1–2, though the number of horsemen is given as 22,000 (WB also has 12,000).

143–5 byseged the toun . . . penurye of water: Cf. Judith 7: 3–10. For *toke their water fro them*, compare *Hs*, Judith 1, *abstulit eis aquas.*

145–51 for in all the toun . . . hondes of them: Judith 7: 11–13. *Carmy and Gothoniel* are not mentioned here, but 6: 11 (Vulgate) states that the chieftains at the time were Ozias and Charmi, also called Gothoniel.

149 what: Contextually, the sense is approximately 'in that'. *MED*, *what* adv. and conj. 4, 5 records various uses as a subordinating conjunction, none precisely similar.

151–3 It is better . . . our eyen: Judith 7: 16.

153–7 And whan they . . . pyte on them: Cf. Judith 7: 18–20.

154 yollyng: This is the latest *OED* citation s.v. *yoll.* Cf. WB (EV), *ȝelling.*

157–60 Thenne at laste . . . ye haue said: Cf. Judith 7: 23–25.

161 And whan that Iudith . . . a wydowe: Judith 8: 1.

162 was left wydowe . . . monethis: Judith 8: 4.

163 Manasses her husbond deyde: Judith 8: 2.

163–92 she wente into . . . peple of God: Judith 8: 5–21.

172 the prestis of Cambre and of Carmy: Cf. Judith 8: 9, *presbyteros Chabri et Carmin.*

177 mercy-doyng: Judith 8: 13, *miserationis*; WB (EV), *mercy doing. MED* and *OED* combined record the compound three times from WB, translating plural forms of Latin *miseratio*, once in other Wycliffite writings and once a1425 in reference to the Works of Mercy.

187 into confusyon to theyr enemyes: Judith 8: 19, *in confusionem inimicis suis* ('to insult at the hands of their enemies'); WB (EV), *in to confusioun to ther enemys.*

190–1 shal make them without worship the Lord our God: Contrast Judith 8: 20, *faciet illas sine honore Dominus Deus noster*, in which God is the subject. *GoL* looks like a semantically plausible garbling of WB (EV), *and he shal make them with oute wrshipe, the Lord oure God*, in which *without* has been taken as an adverb meaning 'in other lands'.

192–6 praye ye . . . come agayn: Cf. Judith 8: 31–3. Contrast *my sowle* with *consilium meum* (8: 31).

197 And thenne Iudith . . . her oratorye: Judith 9: 1.

197–8 arayed her . . . and aournements: Cf. Judith 10: 3.

198–9 toke vnto her handmayde . . . lawfully ete: Cf. Judith 10: 5.

199–200 And whan she had . . . noble araye: An addition.

201–27 toward the gate . . . so comandyng: Judith 10: 6–20.

221 tiraunt knyghtis: Judith 10: 18, *satellites*; WB (EV), *tyraunt kny3tis*. *OED*, *tyrant* 6, cites sporadic adjectival uses in ME.

222–3 that not for hem of right we ought to fight ayenst hem: Judith 10: 18, *ut non pro his merito pugnare contra eos debeamus*, implying 'Who thought that the Jews were not worth fighting?'. Compare WB (EV), *that not for hem bi ri3t a3en hem wee owen to fi3ten*.

227–37 Thenne Holofernes . . . knowen ouerall: Judith 11: 1–6. For *my peple ne strengthe* (230) compare 11: 2, *lanceam*.

237–59 the chyldryn . . . hows of Nabugodonosor: Judith 11: 9–21, which has, however, nothing equivalent to *All thyse thynges God hath shewd to me* (241–2).

259–73 Thenne comanded . . . delyuer hys peple: Judith 12: 1–8. Contrast, however, *And she stratched her hondes vp to the God of Israhel* (271–2) with 12: 8, *ut ascendebat*.

270 baptysed: Judith 12: 7, *baptizabat*; cf. WB (EV), *baptiside*. *OED* does not record a precisely appropriate sense, but cf. *MED*, 2b, 'to cleanse', with one citation.

273–5 And thus . . . entrete Iudith: Judith 12: 10.

275–6 for to lye . . . wyn wyth hym: Cf. *Bh*, 230rb, *naies mye honte de venir a mon seigneur holofernes. et de mengier et boire en ioye auecques lui. et de faire toute sa voulente*. Contrast Judith 12: 10, *ut sponte consentiat habitare mecum*.

276–87 And Iudyth sayd . . . all his lyf: Judith 12: 13–20.

288–9 And at euen . . . closid the dore: Compare Judith 13: 1, *ut autem sero factum est / festinaverunt servi illius ad hospitia sua / et conclusit Bagao ostia cubiculi et abiit*. *Bh*, 230[rb], is in part closer: *Quant il fu temps de couschier. tous sen retournerent. Et holofernes sen ala couschier. et fist amener iudith en sa chambre pour gesir auecques lui.*

290–302 And whan Iudith . . . his heed: Judith 13: 3–10.

302–3 lefte the body . . . in the canape: Contrast Judith 13: 10, *et abstulit conopeum eius a columnis / et evolvit corpus eius truncum*. *Bh*, 230[va], is in part closer: *et sen issi de la chambre atout le chief holofernes auec le cincelier*.

303–31 delyueryd it . . . our enemyes: Judith 13: 11–24.

329–30 hath addressid the in the woundes of the heed: Judith 13: 24, *te* *direxit in vulnere capitis* ('sent you to wound the head'); WB (EV), *hath dressid thee in to the woundis of the hed.*

332–64 After this Iudith . . . in their tentis: Judith 14: 1–18.

352 his bawde: Not in Judith.

360 is deed: The omission of the pronoun subject, 'he', is unusually awkward and should perhaps be emended.

364–96 whan all th'oost . . . organs and harpes: Judith 15: 1–15.

384 worship-doyng: Judith 15: 10, *honorificentia*. The compound is not recorded in *MED* or *OED*. Cf. WB (EV), *the wrshipe doende.*

394 appertenancis to houshold: Judith 15: 14, *supellectile*; *Bh*, 231rb, *vaisellemen*; WB (EV), *purtenaunces to household.*

397–9 Thenne Iudith songe . . . newe psalme: Judith 16: 1–2.

398 manerly synge: Judith 16: 2, *modulamini*; WB (EV), *manerly singeth*. In both texts, the more general and common sense 'fittingly' is also possible.

399 Fully ioye ye and inwardly calle ye hys name: Judith 16: 2, *exaltate et invocate nomen eius*; WB (EV), *ful out ioȝeth, and inwardli clepeth his name. MED* s.v. *in-wardli* has 5a, 'As a rather vague equivalent of L *in-* in verbal composition', with eight citations from WB, not including the present passage.

400–3 And for this grete . . . behestis vnto God: Judith 16: 22.

403–9 the ioye . . . her husbond: Judith 16: 24–6.

409–15 duellyd in the hous . . . vnto this day: Judith 16: 28–31.

412 after this iourney: Not in Judith, but cf. *Bh*, 231va, *apres ceste victoire.*

GLOSSARY

The glossary is designed to include all obsolete words, senses, and forms as well as spellings that may be difficult to recognize. For words with a variety of meanings or forms, only those differing from modern English or likely to cause difficulty in context are recorded. References are usually given only to the first occurrence of a word, sense, or form within each legend and frequent items may not be entered for every legend in which they occur. Predictable spelling variants, and in particular forms within the one legend that differ only by variation between *i* and *y*, are not always recorded. Within an entry, a gloss is not repeated if it would be the same as that immediately preceding (with possible adjustment for number, tense, etc.). Cross-references are given only for words not easily referable to a headword. Emended forms are indicated by *; those which are discussed in explanatory notes are indicated by *N*.

In the alphabetical arrangement, both *i* and *y* are treated as *i* when they represent a vowel; *i* is treated as *j* when it represents a consonant; *y* representing a semi-vowel is treated as *y*; *v* representing a vowel is treated as *u*, and *u* representing a consonant as *v*.

Abbreviations: *acc*(usative), *adj*(ective), *adv*(erb), *comp*(arative), *conj*(unction), *dem*(onstrative), *gen*(itive), *imp*(erative), *inf*(initive), *interj*(ection), *intrans*(itive), *n*(oun), *nom*(inative), *num*(eral), *neut*(er), *ord*(inal), *p*(articiple), *pa*(st), *pl*(ural), *pr*(esent), *prep*(osition), *pron*(oun), *refl*(exive), *sg*. = *singular*, *subj*(unctive), *superl*(ative), *trans(itive)*, *v*(erb), *vbl. n.* = verbal noun

A

abasshed *v. pa. p.* dismayed 10.87; upset 5.121; perplexed 4.312; **abasshid** 4.98, 14.285; **abasshyd** 11.169

abide *v. inf.* remain, persist 2.19, 4.385; **abyde** 1.86; lodge 3.224, 14.242; *pr.* await 14.80; remain, persist 15.41; *imp.* 4.211; **abydest** *2 pr. sg.* 13.74; **abideth** *3 pr. sg.* 3.268; **abydyng** *pr. p.* 5.69, 10.202; awaiting 9.108; **abode** *pa.* 2.95, 15.201; remained 2.74, 3.350, 4.232, etc.; waited 10.236, 14.429; **abyden** *pa. p.* stayed 7.318, 10.246

abysmes *n. pl.* abysses 2.64

aboue *adv as n.* **at thyn** ~ in your prosperity, exalted rank 5.134

accombred *v. pa. p.* harassed 7.46

accompanyed *v. pa. p.* joined in a group 5.687

accomplyssheth *v. 3 pr. sg.* fulfils 7.42; **accomplysshyd** *pa.* 6.406; **accomplysshed** *pa. p.* completed 11.153, 14.113; **accomplisshid** 14.144; fulfilled 9.522

achyeuyd *v. pa. p.* brought to a successful conclusion 3.493

acompte *v. pr.* count 14.391

acordyng *v. pr. p.* ~ **to** in accordance with 9.510; **acorded** *pa. p.* in accord 11.75

adder-bolte *n.* dragon-fly 6.364 *N*

addresse *v. pr.* direct 14.117; **adresse** *pr. subj.* 14.166; **addressid** *pa. p.* 15.330 *N*; **adressyd** arranged 3.492

adherent *adj.* attached 1.86

adiured *v. pa.* entreated 14.344; *pa. p.* bound by oath 3.471

admytted *see* **amytteth**

admonesteth *v. 3 pr. sg.* charges, admonishes 7.72

adoo *n.* sexual intercourse 3.278

adowre *v. imp.* worship 14.417; **adowred** *pa.* 13.50, 14.14

adresse, adressyd *see* **addresse**

adulacion *n.* insincere praise 7.130

aduenture *n.* chance 10.21

aduoultrye *n.* adultery 1.250, 7.96, 10.189

aferd(e *adj.* afraid 1.98, 3.345, 4.397, etc.

aferre *adv.* in the distance 6.43, 14.414

afore *adv.* before, previously 9.337, 10.200

afore *prep.* in front of 4.305

afortymes *adv.* previously 9.472

after *adj.* rear 9.558 *N*

after *adv.* afterwards, later 1.259, 2.90, 3.117, etc.; in pursuit 10.9

after *prep.* behind 6.101; according to 1.255, 7.305; in compliance with 9.59; in pursuit of 9.167; in accordance with 5.330, 11.122; ~ **that** after 1.291, 2.3, 4.310, etc.
agayn *adv.* back 1.312, 2.85, 7.170, 9.350, 10.305, 12.7, 14.202, 14.448; back again 3.51, 5.292, 6.342; in return 13.94
agayn *prep.* against 2.16, 3.84, 7.117, 9.306, 15.11; in anticipation of 5.369
age *n.* **hath** ~ is of sufficient age 7.161
al-daye *adv.* all the time, again and again 11.242
almesse *n.* alms 14.147; **almesses** *pl.* 14.78
alonde *adv.* ashore 6.488
also *adv.* and so 5.248
alway(e *adv.* always 1.278, 5.74, 9.301, 11.16, 14.43; **alewaye** 14.196; **alleway(e** 2.124, 11.157, 12.13, 14.165
amyd-emong *prep.* in among 6.162 *N*
amytteth *v. 3 pr. sg.* allows, accepts 7.58; **admytted** *pa. p.* granted 14.261
an *prep.* on 9.23 (*see* **bere**), 9.233; *with vbl. n.* engaged in 4.23
angerly *adv.* angrily 4.344
anguyss(h)e *n.* distress 9.599, 10.94
anhungrid *v. pa. p.* hungry 4.23
anon(e *adv.* immediately 4.84, 5.44, 6.51, etc.
aourned *v. pa.* adorned 15.279
aournements *n. pl.* adornments 15.198
aparte *adv.* aside 14.455
aplye *v. pr.* attach (to) 1.101
appere *v. inf.* appear 5.40; **apperith** *3 pr. sg.* 9.592; **appiered** *v. pa.* appeared 2.82; **appered** 11.152; **apperyd** 7.299; **apperid** 3.102, 4.8, 5.440, etc.; *pa. p.* 6.147; **apperyd** 6.151
apperteynyng *v. pr. p.* belonging 15.391
appertenancis *n. pl.* ~ **to houshold** household items 15.394 *N*
arayed *v. pa. p.* arranged, drawn up 9.325
areyse *v. inf.* arouse 15.176
armee *n.* army 15.105
armylle *n.* armlet, bracelet 10.29 *N*; **armyllis** *pl.* 3.446
aromatykes *adj. pl.* aromatic 5.681 *N*
aromatikes *n. pl.* perfumes 5.723; **aromatykes** 11.189
aroos(e *v. pa.* rose, arose 3.263, 4.332, 5.523, etc.
assaylled *v. pa. p.* afflicted 14.76
asshy *adj.* baked in ashes 3.194
assoylle *v. pr. subj.* release 14.118
assotted *v. pa. p.* infatuated 4.471
astate *n.* state, condition 7.48
astoned *v. pa. p.* bewildered, astonished 4.99; **astonyed** 4.106, 5.120, 11.169, 14.285
aswage *v. inf.* subside 7.194
atte at the 1.71, 4.306, 6.395, 7.210, 15.194
attempered *v. pa.* moderated 3.510
attones *adv.* together 4.6
attouchyng *vbl. n.* touching 7.139 *N*
audyence *n.* hearing 5.423
avayled *v. pa. p.* prevailed, won 4.254
auerte *v. pr. intrans.* turn away 11.162
auys *n.* **by** ~ deliberately 7.27
auyse *v. imp. refl.* consider 10.328
auowed *v. pa.* promised solemnly 1.291; *pa. p.* 10.256
awayte *n.* **laye in** ~ lay in ambush 9.411
awayted *v. pa.* kept under surveillance 6.241
awerke *adv.* **sette** ~ put to work 6.15
awter *n.* altar 2.106, 3.383, 4.466, 10.340
axe *v. inf.* ask 5.555; **axest** *2 pr. sg.* 9.622; **axyng** *pr. p.* 5.233; **axid** *pa.* 3.205, 6.326, 9.90, 12.15; **axed** 5.32, 9.36; *pa. p.* 11.27
ayen *prep.* against 15.125
ayenst *prep.* against 1.126, 4.351, 6.480, etc.; towards, to meet 3.505, 4.202, 6.206, 7.238; in preparation for 5.193; facing, opposite 5.675, 7.364

B

bachows *n.* bakehouse 5.139
bad *v. pa.* bade, advised 12.16; commanded 2.45, 3.52, 4.391, etc.; **bad(d)e** 6.287, 6.648, 7.223, 7.328, 10.268; **boden** *pa. p.* 2.63, 14.237
baily *n.* steward 3.106
bayne *v. inf.* bathe 10.123; **bayned** *pa. p.* 5.171 *N*
baptysed *v. pa.* washed (ritually?) 15.270 *N*
bare *see* **bere**
batayll(e *n.* a body of troops in battle array 10.264; battle 6.13, 9.99, 10.18,

15.351; **batail** 9.317; **batailles** *pl.* 9.204; **bataillis** 9.519; **bataylles** 9.234; **batayllis** 8.3
bawde *n.* procurer 15.352
beaute *n.* beauty 3.41, 5.158, 6.64, 15.202; **beawte** 3.36
beautevous *adj.* beautiful 3.435
bedde *n.* bedroom 15.164
beelis *n. pl.* ulcers 6.354
be(e)ste *n.* animal, wild beast 1.93, 4.372, 5.64; **beestis** *pl.* 1.15, 2.46, 9.369, 11.96; cattle, livestock 3.56, 4.181, 5.30, etc.; **bestes** 4.299, 14.353; **beestes** 4.196
begonne *v. pa* began 14.455; *pa. p.* 15.47
behaue *v. inf. refl.* conduct (oneself in a certain manner) 7.238
beheld *v. pa.* looked 6.532
beheste *n.* **londe of** ~ Promised Land 8.2; **behestis** *n. pl.* promises 15.403
behoefful *adj.* requisite 5.242
belight *v. inf. intrans.* light 1.211
ben *v. inf.* be 5.635, 15.321; **by** 3.137, 11.161; *pr. subj.* 5.342, 6.598; **be** 5.29, 10.38, 11.204; *pr. pl.* 6.31; **ben** 1.31, 2.48, 3.41, 4.9, 5.34, 7.7, 9.120, 10.20, 11.205, 13.47, 14.96, 15.87; **been** 9.203; **be** *pa. p.* 14.31; **is** *3 pr. sg.* ~ **to** belongs to 7.149
benefaites *n. pl.* blessings, favours 7.54; **benefetes** 14.439
bere *n.* bier 10.84
bere *v. pa.* bore 1.184, 9.160; **bare** 2.71, 3.377, 5.139, etc.; gave birth to 1.240, 4.3, 6.104, 9.35; ~ **an hand** accused 9.23; **born** *pa. p.* **was** ~ moved 1.5
besaunt(e)s *n. pl.* coins, biblical 'talents' 11.181, 14.31
besought *v. pa.* begged, beseeched 4.4, 9.19, 11.150
beste(s *see* **beeste**
bete *v. inf.* beat 12.19[2]; *pa.* 11.271, 12.19[1]
betoke *v. pa.* bestowed, entrusted 5.77; **betaken** *pa. p.* taken 14.96; **bytaken** condemned, delivered 15.186
by *see* **ben**
bycause *conj.* so that 3.91; ~ **that** 3.252
bifore *prep.* beyond, more than 15.284
bylde *v. pa.* built 4.462; **bylded** 6.16, 11.121; *pa. p.* 11.195
bildyngis *vbl. n. pl.* building operations 15.71
byleue *n.* **out of** ~ unbelieving 7.329 *N*
byse *n.* 'a precious kind of linen or cotton cloth' (*MED*) 5.206
bysshop *n.* chief priest 7.342; **bisshop** 15.381
bytaken see **betoke**
bytymes *adv.* early 5.393
blaynes *n. pl.* sores 6.354, 13.71
blamed *v. pa.* rebuked 3.359, 5.21, 14.79
blereyed *adj.* having watery eyes, bleary-eyed 4.208
blew *adj.* dark-skinned 2.145
blewe *v. pa.* signalled (with a horn, etc.) 10.280; **blowen** *pa. p.* cast from molten metal 7.184
blyuen *v. pa. p.* remained 9.533 *N*
boden *see* **bad**
boyled *v. pa.* cooked 4.65
boystous *adj.* vigorous 6.259, 7.192
bonde *v. pa.* bound 5.14, 14.308, 15.127; **bounden** *pa. p.* 3.417, 5.273, 6.683, etc.
bondes *n. pl.* bundles, bunches 9.494
bondship *n.* bondage 5.595 *N*
borde *n.* table 5.382
botchis *n. pl.* boils, sores 6.354; **botchys** 13.71
bote *v. pa.* bit 6.332, 7.352
boteler *n.* chief servant in charge of wine or other drinks, cupbearer 5.117; **botelers** *gen.* 5.137; **botellers** *pl.* 11.197
botel(l *n.* bottle 3.338, 9.42; **botelles** *pl.* 9.493
botes *n. pl.* greaves? 9.313 *N*
bowe *v. inf.* bend, fall 1.99
bowhe *n.* bough 10.271
brake *v. pa.* broke 1.292, 6.546, 7.210, 9.122
brechis *n. pl.* underpants 1.130
brede *n.* food 5.47; bread 1.178, 3.96, 4.64, etc.; **breed** 7.350, 9.323
brede *n.* breadth 2.34, 3.79, 11.121, 15.6
brenne *v. inf.* burn 1.211; *imp.* 10.241; **brenneth** *3 pr. sg.* 6.119; **brennyng** *pr. p.* 1.191, 6.73, 11.255, 14.307; **brenned** *pa.* 6.75; was inflamed 15.282; **brente** burnt 7. 211, 9.663, 10.8; *pa. p.* 10.9, 13.38, 14.536; **brenned** inflamed 15.54
breres *n. pl.* briers, thorny bushes 1.173, 3.390; **breris** 2.130
brethern *see* **broder**
brynke *n.* shore 6.47; **brynkes** *pl.* 6.491
broder *n.* brother 1.219, 3.19, 4.22,

5.275; **broders** *gen.* 2.116, 4.15; **brother** first cousin 4.199; **brothern** *pl.* brothers 4.346, 5.21, 10.64; **brethern** 2.134, 3.232, 4.89, etc.; kinsmen 4.341, 14.271

brouht *v. pa.* brought 5.562, 9.534, 11.229; *pa. p.* 6.664, 9.252, 11.59, etc.

bubals *n. pl.* antelopes 11.79

burgenyng *v. pr. p.* burgeoning 3.266; **burgyng** 2.92; **burgeyned** *pa.* sprouted 7.243

burth(e *n.* birth 5.688, 6.24, 11.137

burthen *n.* burden 9.641, 12.6; **burthens** *pl.* burdens, carrying of loads 6.16, 11.111

but *conj.* unless 6.160; ~ **yf** if not, unless 2.42, 4.376, 5.322, 7.30, 9.416, 14.282

C

caytyf *n.* captive, prisoner 6.409

can *v. pr.* know 5.553, 6.30; **coude** *pa.* could 2.88, 5.162, 6.57, etc.

canape *n.* canopy 15.224

carayne *n.* carcass 2.86

cariacares *n. pl.* dried figs 9.495 *N*

cariage *n.* means of transportation 5.494

carre-men *n. pl.* men who drive carts or chariots 6.495 *N*

carres *n. pl.* chariots 6.482, 9.189; **carris** 9.185, 11.237

carters *n. pl.* charioteers 9.185

cartes *n. pl.* chariots 5.690, 6.463, 9.186, 11.85

cast *v. pa. p.* poured out? 9.26 *N*

castellis *n. pl.* encampments, encamped armies 4.389, 6.465, 7.276, 10.55

cat(h)aractes *n. pl.* floodgates (of heaven) 2.65, 2.78

causes *n. pl.* (legal) cases 6.630

centuriones *n. pl.* leaders of groups of one hundred 6.619; **centuryons** 9.187

cessed *v. pa.* disappeared 10.358; ended, stopped 2.77, 10.343; **cessyd of** 1.30; **cessed fro** departed from, left 15.74

cessyng *vbl. n.* stopping 2.83

chaas, chace *see* **chese**

chare *n.* chariot 5.208, 6.444; **chares** *pl.* 5.690, 6.445, 9.186, etc.; **charis** 11.236

charge *n.* obligation, task 5.399; importance 6.620; **gyue** ~ order 7.281

charged *v. pa. p.* loaded 11.189

chartre *n.* sheet of paper 14.299

chastyse *v. inf.* punish 15.235

chaungyng *vbl. n.* exchanging; **for** ~ **of** in exchange for 5.590

chere *n.* face, expression 1.101, 5.421, 10.292; **chyere** 11.233

chese *v. inf.* choose 3.62, 9.316, 10.323; *imp.* 6.571; **chace** *pa.* 1.101; **chase** 6.626, 9.363; **chees** 10.331; **chaas** ~ **out** selected 11.106

chest *n.* coffin 5.723

chyilde *n.* child 11.19; **chyld(e** young man 5.166, 9.594; **child** 5.4; young man in service 1.278, 3.194; **children** *pl.* 3.374

chyldesly *adv.* childishly 14.11

chyldhood *n.* immaturity, innocence 6.71

chyldyng *vbl. n.* childbirth 4.546

chymney *n.* fireplace 6.352

chyualrye *n.* a body of warriors 15.317

chores *n. pl.* a Hebrew dry measure 11.77

choris *n. pl.* dances 9.399 *N*

cycles *n. pl.* shekels, ancient units of weight 10.235

circuyte *n.* area 9.213; circumference 14.519; surroundings? 6.538 *N*

cisterne *n.* pit, cistern 5.39

clad *v. pa. p.* covered 11.221

claye *n.* clay used as mortar 6.21

cleer *adj.* illustrious 15.407; **clere** bright 6.661, 11.50

clene *adj.* pure, wholesome 1.113; bright 14.520

clere *adv.* brightly, sparklingly 1.211

clerenesse *n.* brightness 14.517

clerkys *n. pl.* scholars 11.127

clypped *v. pa.* trimmed 9.470

coarted *v. pa. p.* compelled, distressed 9.620

cognacion *n.* kindred 14.556 *N*

colestaf *n.* pole 7.286 *N*, 9.314

colyandre *n.* coriander 6.539

colompnes *n. pl.* columns 1.265

comanded *v. pa. p.* sentenced 14.63

comandement *n.* sentence 14.63; **Comandemens** *pl.* Commandments 7.1

comen *v. pr. pl.* issue 1.46; **cam** *pa.* came 1.66; **come** 1.312, 11.202; **camen** *pa. pl.* 5.702, 9.399, 13.80, 15.305; **comen** *pa. p.* 13.51, 15.95

comened *v. pa.* conversed 10.194

comestible *adj.* edible 2.48 *N*

comforte *n.* aid 15.189
comforte *v. inf.* strengthen, refresh 3.193; **comforted** *pa. p.* 15.385
comyn *see* **comune**
commyse *v. inf.* commit 3.233; **comysed** *pa.* 1.236; **commysed** *pa. p.* 7.62 *N*, 9.587, 10.152
commodytees *n. pl.* resources 7.288
comodyous *adj.* fertile 5.180 *N*
compared *v. pa. p.* matched, regarded as equal (to) 4.253
complayned *v. pa. refl.* made a complaint, appeal 10.217
complesshyd *v. pa. p.* attained 14.555
comune *adj.* unanimous 1.19; **comyn** ~ **woman/wymen** prostitute(s) 4.515, 11.40
conceyled *v. pa.* advised 6.72; **counceyllyd** taught, instructed 6.626, 10.365
conclude *v. imp.* decide 10.328
***concupyscence** *n.* (carnal) desire 14.121
condicion *n.* social status 1.161; stipulation 5.613, *5.673
confederyd *v. pa.* formed an alliance 11.105; **confederid** *pa. p.* allied, bound in friendship 9.393
confedersy *n.* alliance, covenant 4.383
conferme *v. pr. subj.* confirm, strengthen 10.363; *imp.* 15.295; **confermed** *pa. p.* securely established 11.3
confesse *v. imp.* ~ **to** avow one's faith in, worship 14.490 *N*, 14.504
confusyon *n.* destruction, ruin 9.134, 15.187
congrue *adj.* appropriate 1.146
coniectours *n. pl.* soothsayers 5.160 *N*
conioyne *v. pr. subj.* join 14.298
coniunctly *adv.* together 2.99
coniure *v. pr.* adjure, command 3.406
connyng *adj.* skilful 5.572
connynge *n.* skill 11.126
conscience *n.* knowledge 5.363
conscrypcion *n.* written agreement 14.299 *N*
consequently *adv.* accordingly 5.330
considere *v. inf.* examine 5.261, 7.282; **consyderyng** *pr. p.* observing 6.44; **consydered** *pa. p.* inspected 7.287
consonantes *n. pl.* consonance, harmony 1.260
constytued *v. pa. p.* appointed 9.523 *N*; **constytute** 10.332
constrayned *v. pa. p.* forced 10.329
consume *v. inf.* perish 5.242; **consumed** *pa. p.* enfeebled 4.556
contynaunce *n.* outward appearance; **makyng good** ~ appearing composed 5.382
contynue *v. inf.* remain 5.450
contradiction *n.* opposition, strife 7.338
contrarye *adv.* on the other hand 11.53
conueyed *v. pa.* escorted, accompanied 3.208
conueyeng *vbl. n.* escorting, guidance 10.10
conuenyent *adj.* appropriate 5.659
conuersacion *n.* manner of living, conduct 14.557
conuerte *v. pr.* turn 14.117
coostis *n. pl.* boundaries 15.375
coplement *n.* union 4.224 *N*
copulacion *n.* unity? 14.262 *N*
cordes *n. pl.* musical chords? stringed instruments? 6.498 *N*
cornes *n. pl.* grains 5.157
corrupt *adj.* polluted, fouled 6.311
cosyn *n.* relative 6.589
coude *see* **can**
couetyse *n.* covetousness 6.618, *7.153, 9.168
counceyllyd *see* **conceyled**
counseyl *n.* design, (secret) plan 14.126, 15.204; decision, plan 5.471; **counseilles** *pl.* 14.167
coure *v. inf.* cover 6.662
cryeng *v. pr. p.* ~ **wyth trumpes** sounding trumpets 15.370
cubycle *n.* small room, bedroom 11.42 *N*, 14.258; **cubicle** 14.110
cubyculyers *n. pl.* chamberlains 15.269
cubytes *n. pl.* a measure of length 2.34, 7.253, 9.310, 11.121; **cubitis** 15.6
culture *n.* worship 15.83 *N*
cure *n.* care 14.551; **haue the** ~ **of are** in charge of 7.76
curiosyte *n.* elaborate workmanship 11.124
curlews *n. pl.* quails 6.536, 7.251
curres *n. pl.* chariots 11.86 *N*
curs *n.* curse 1.165
cursid *adj.* wicked 3.6, 10.307
custumable *adj.* usual 6.249

D

dalf(e *see* **delue**

damoyselle *n.* maiden 4.472; handmaiden 15.410
dampnacion *n.* condemnation, perdition 1.282
dampned *v. pa.* condemned 1.226; *pa. p.* 1.238
dar *v. pr.* dare 5.437, 9.342; **durst(e** *pa.* 2.95, 4.527, 5.486, 6.125, 10.228
debonairly *adv.* courteously 5.373
deceyte *n.* trickery 7.111
deceyued *v. pa. p.* cheated 4.320
declyne *v. imp.* turn aside 10.66; **declyned** *pa.* 9.342; strayed (morally) 9.167
dede *n.* deed 6.88, 7.141, 10.320
deed *adj.* dead 1.116, 2.3, 3.292, etc.; **dede** 1.184, 2.86, 7.170, etc.
defaulte *n.* crime; **take with the** ~ detect in an offence 5.355
defended *v. pa. p.* forbidden 7.86
defowled *v. pa. p.* seduced, defiled 4.479, *5.51, 14.25, 15.322
defrauded *v. pa. p.* deprived 5.644
deyd(e *v. pa.* died 2.3, 3.20, 4.532, etc.; **deyed** 1.314, 2.140, 3.400, etc.
deiecte *v. pa. p.* cast thrown 1.95
deken *n.* deacon, Levite 6.191
delectacion *n.* delight 14.130
deled *v. pa.* dealt, divided 2.141
delyces *n. pl.* pleasures 1.35
delyte *n.* delight 1.191
delytyng *vbl. n.* pleasure, joy 1.51
delyuered *v. pa.* gave 4.217; **delyueryd** 15.303; entrusted, handed over 5.86, 9.325; **delyuerd** ~ **agayn** gave back 3.51; **delyuerd** *pa. p.* saved 14.128; surrendered 15.174; **be** ~ give birth 4.12; **was delyueryd of** gave birth to 3.141, 4.240, 11.42
deluuye *n.* deluge 1.285
delue *v. inf.* dig 14.326; **dalf(e** *pa.* 4.525; buried 10.196; **doluen** *pa. p.* 10.201; dug 6.316
demaundes *n. pl.* queries 11.187
demaundest *v. 2 pr. sg.* ask 14.275; **demaunded** *pa.* 10.42; *pa. p.* asked 15.131
deme *v. inf.* judge 6.629; *pr. subj.* 15.148; **demyng** *pr. p.* 6.630; **demed** *pa.* 6.604; ruled 8.10
demyng *vbl. n.* judging 11.70
denes *n. pl.* leaders of groups of ten 6.619
departe *v. inf.* separate 4.293; distribute 14.151; *pr.* branch 1.47; *imp.* divide 6.459; **departed** *pa.* 3.90, 7.239, 14.8; separated 1.254, 3.514; divided, distributed in tithing? 1.236 *N*; *pa. p.* shared out 2.142
depose *v. inf.* bring down 14.251
deserte *n.* wasteland 14.535
desperpled *v. pa. p.* scattered, dispersed 14.491; **disperplid** 15.95; **dysperplyd** 6.240; **dysperclyd** 14.98
despyse *v. inf.* disregard 14.358; **despysed** *pa.* 10.71
despyte *n.* contempt 3.128, 7.32
despoylled *v. pa.* stripped 7.341
destroye *v. inf.* remove 2.130
determynat *v. pa. p.* concluded 1.32
detraction *n.* slander 7.129
deuydeth *v. 3 pr. sg.* separates, makes a distinction between 6.400; **deuyded** *pa.* distributed 14.37
dighted *v. pa.* prepared 9.634
dylygently *adv.* carefully 11.50
dyme *v. inf.* impose a tithe 9.192 *N*
dyrepcyon *n.* deportation 14.97 *N*
discerne *v. inf.* determine 11.29
discoraged *v. pa. p.* disheartened 10.292
disiunctly *adv.* separately 2.100
dyspense *n.* expenditure 11.185
dysperclyd, disperplid, dysperplyd *see* **desperpled**
displeysyd *v. pa.* displeased 10.153
dysputed *v. pa.* debated, discussed 11.94
dissimylacion *n.* pretence 10.81
dyssimylyng *v. pr. p.* being hesitant, unheeding 3.251; **dissymilyng** pretending 4.489
distynctions *n. pl.* divisions 2.35
dyuynours *n. pl.* interpreters of dreams 5.160
docyle *adj.* willing to learn 11.22
do(o *v. inf.* cause (something to be done), have (something done) 1.264, 5.350, 6.413, 9.277, 10.84, 13.49, 14.342; **dyde** *pa.* put on 5.65; caused 9.12; **doo** *pa. p.* done 1.216, 5.413, 9.341, 10.165, 15.256; **doon** 3.507, 5.113, 6.361, 7.86, 9.328
doluen *see* **delue**
dome *n.* condemnation 15.177; judgement 6.608, 9.168, 11.29; **domes** *pl.* 11.70, 14.92
domyne *v. inf.* have lordship 1.68

dongehyll *n.* dunghill 13.73
doobted *v. pa.* feared, revered 11.257
double *adj.* **iiij** ~ four times, fourfold 10.166
douchtres *n. pl.* daughters 3.243
drawe *v. pa. p.* drawn, dragged 11.271
drede *v. pr. refl.* fear 4.55; *imp. refl.* 5.519; **dredyng** *pr. p.* fearing, revering 14.52; **dred(d)e** *pa.* feared 3.275, 4.354, 6.27, 11.8, 14.72, 15.32; **dredde** *pa. p.* 9.273
dredeful *adj.* frightening 6.668; dangerous 11.175
dredyngly *adv.* in awe 4.168 *N*
dreyde *see* **dryed**
dresse *v. imp.* direct 14.546
dryed *v. pa.* withered 4.430; **dreyde** dried 7.253; *pa. p.* 9.495
drye-foot *adv.* with dry feet 6.471, 15.76
dronke *v. pa. p.* drunk 2.131, 3.279, 7.61, 9.24, 10.142
dronkenhed *n.* drunkenness 15.318
droues *n. pl.* herds 15.168
duc *n.* guide, leader 6.436, 7.247, 8.1; **duke** 9.523, 15.59; **dukes** *pl.* commanders, leaders 6.446, 8.10, 10.296, 15.19; noblemen, chiefs 3.176, 11.138
duelle *v. inf.* remain, live 5.565; *imp.* 4.483; **duellyng** *pr. p.* 14.169; **duellid** *pa.* 3.273; **duellyd** 5.715, 6.263, 9.652, 15.409; *pa. p.* 6.516
dured *v. pa.* lasted 2.8
duryng *prep.* for the duration of 15.270
durst(e *see* **dar**

E

ease *v. inf. refl.* relieve oneself 9.444
edefye *v. inf.* construct, build 11.102; *pr.* exalt 14.513; **edefied** *pa.* 6.585; **edefy(e)ed** built 2.106, 4.529, 6.34, 15.4; *pa. p.* 11.155, 14.518
edefyeng *vbl. n.* construction 11.111
eere *n.* ear 13.107; **eeris** *pl.* 3.446, 4.524, 5.156, etc.; **eris** 5.179
effecte *n.* efficacy 2.126
eyen *n. pl.* eyes 1.270, 3.74, 4.36, etc.
eyres *see* **her**
elate *adj.* haughty 1.111
elegaunt *adj.* pleasing, graceful? 6.39 *N*
eleuate *v. pa. p.* elevated. lifted 2.66
ellis *adv.* otherwise 15.159
elthe *see* **helth**
emes *n. gen.* uncle's 4.197
emong(e *prep.* among 1.63, 3.92, 4.492, etc.
employe *v. pr.* make use of (time) 7.59
enbame *v. inf.* embalm 5.680; **enbamed** *pa. p.* 5.722
ende *n.* (vn)**to th'ende that/þat** in order that 1.184, 4.447, 5.195; **endes** *pl.* borders 5.600, 6.653, 11.74
enduced *v. pa.* induced 1.243
endurat *see* **indurat**
endure *v. inf.* resist, hold (against) 1.266; continue, last 1.233; **endured** *pa.* 1.235, 3.13, 6.317
enfamyned *v. pa. p.* starved, starving 5.195 *N*, 15.239
enflawme *v. inf.* become passionate 15.180
enforced *v. pa. p.* compelled, violated 5.100
Englysshe *v. inf.* translate into English 11.127
enharde *v. inf.* harden 6.278
enhaunsed *v. pa. refl.* was arrogant 15.12
enoynte *v. inf.* anoint 9.279; *imp.* 14.419; **enoynted** *pa.* 4.542, 9.210; *pa. p.* 10.36
enpayre *v. inf.* damage 7.126
ensample *n.* **take** ~ be warned 11.175
enseigneth *v. 3 pr. sg.* teaches 7.16
entende *v. inf.* ~ **to** attend to, devote oneself to 7.40
entre *n.* entrance, coming 4.290
entreted *v. pa.* treated, dealt with someone in a certain way 1.286
enuayhed *v. pa. p.* attacked 13.41 *N*
enuyroned *v. pa.* surrounded 3.228
equyte *n.* justice, righteousness 11.158
er *conj.* before 2.21, 3.227, 4.6, etc.
ere *v. inf.* plough 5.469; **erid** *pa.* 13.34
erers *n. pl.* ploughmen 9.187 *N*
erytage *see* **herytage**
erryng *v. pr. p.* wandering 5.32; **erryd** *pa.* wandered, got lost 3.340
eschewe *v. inf.* avoid, prevent 2.61, 5.238; **eschewed** *pa. p.* 7.102, 10.290
especyal *n.* **in** ~ in particular 8.4; **in especial** 15.22
espye *v. inf.* scout 5.256; **espyed** *pa.* saw, observed 3.504, 14.386; **espied** 2.133; *pa. p.* detected 1.98
espyes *n. pl.* spies 5.299; scouts 15.210
ete *v. pa.* ate 9.14, 13.32, 14.111

euen *adv.* exactly 6.670
euen *n.* evening 1.8, 2.91, 4.190, etc.; **euyn** 6.523
euentyde *n.* evening 3.222
euerich(e *pron.* each 2.101, 3.443, 5.500, etc.; **euerych(e** 1.16, 7.224
euyl *adv.* badly 1.286; wrongly 3.50
euyll *adj.* painful, hard 5.576
euyn *see* **euen**
exalted *v. pa. p.* empowered 15.12
exclude *v. pr.* shut out 14.255; **excluded** *pa. p.* 14.336
executed *v. pa.* performed, did 5.705
exequyes *n. pl.* funeral rites 5.692 *N*
exercise *v. imp.* cultivate 4.483; **excersised** *pa.* carried out, performed 14.372; **excercisid** *pa. p.* employed 6.235
expedyent *adj.* fitting 14.102
experyence *n.* knowledge from observation, test 5.265
experte *v. pa. p.* **were** ~ knew from experience 1.124
expowned *v. pa.* expounded 5.168, 6.642
***expresse** *adj.* clear, explicit 7.147
expressyd *v. pa.* manifested 4.77
extasi *n.* ecstatic state, trance 1.73
extimacion *n.* **without** ~ beyond calculation 11.144
extyncte *v. inf.* eliminate 15.34

F

fable *n.* subject of common talk 11.168; **fables** *pl.* 14.97
faculte *n.* property 4.311; **facultees** *pl.* possessions 14.38
failleth *v. 3 pr. sg.* runs short, runs out 7.350; **faylleth** 15.263; **fayllled** *pa. p.* run short, used up 5.592
fayn *adj.* eager 10.260
faynted *v. pa.* was afraid 9.611
fayr *adv.* graciously, kindly 10.81, 12.13
falle *v. inf.* happen, befall 6.44; **fill** *pa.* fell 9.504; **fyl(l** 3.146, 6.216, 7.244, 9.379, 14.475; **fylle** 3.484, 4.507, 5.678, etc.; happened, befell 3.37, 5.115, 10.301; **fallen** *pa. p.* 4.364, 5.279, 6.153, 7.218, 14.286
false *adv.* untruthfully 7.24
***falsely** *adv.* guilefully 1.237
famylye *n.* household 13.6 *N*, 14.407; kindred, clan 7.346; **famylyes** *pl.* 11.139 *N*
faste *adj.* firm 4.382
faste *adv.* securely 5.109
faste *v. pa. p.* caught, stuck 3.390
fatte *adj.* fertile 5.152[2]
fattenes *n.* fertility 4.87
fawte *n.* fault, blame 1.138; **faute** 1.142
felawshype *v. pr. subj.* be a companion 14.212; **felawshipeth** *3 pr. sg.* 14.221
fer *adj.* distant 11.187
fere *n.* fear 9.329, 11.83, 14.496
fere *v. inf.* frighten 1.117; *pr.* fear 3.40, 4.406; *imp.* 5.364; **fered** *pa. refl.* was afraid? 1.288 *N*; **ferd** *pa. p.* frightened, afraid 3.48
fer(re *adv.* far, afar 3.342, 4.190, 5.36, etc.
feruente *adj.* strong in effect 2.33
festful *adj.* ~ **dai/day** feast day 14.50, 15.414
fethers *n. pl.* fetters 5.267
fette *v. pa.* fetched 4.60, 6.49, 9.225
fyfte *ord.* fifth 5.606
fill, fyl(l, fylle *see* **falle**
fyllyd *v. pa. p.* defiled 2.25
fyndar *n.* finder, creator 1.260
fiscelle *n.* basket 6.48 *N*
fleyng *v. pr. p.* flying 11.79; **flewh(e** *pa.* 2.88, 7.252, 15.365
flesshe *n.* meat 6.517, 7.245
flexible *adj.* mentally pliable 1.107
flode *n.* river 3.69; **flood** 6.301; **flo(o)des** *pl.* 1.46, 14.316
flom *n.* river 3.68
floweth *v. 3 sg. pr.* abounds in, overflows with 6.131 *N*; abounds 7.296
folily *adv.* foolishly, wantonly 9.592; **folyly** 4.350, 7.271, 10.321, 13.55
folowe *v. inf.* strive for? 14.262 *N*
fonde *v. pa.* invented 1.253; found 1.312, 2.85, 3.36, etc.; **founden** *pa. p.* 4.285, 5.63, 10.315, 13.113, 15.283; formed, devised 15.217
fooles *n. pl.* colts 4.412
footmen *n. pl.* men travelling on foot 6.425, 9.239; footsoldiers 15.142; **fotemen** 9.104, 15.25
for *conj.* ~ **that** because 1.29, 9.30
for *prep.* instead of 4.56, 5.450; because of 4.286
forboden *v. pa. p.* forbidden 1.118, 2.79, 7.98, 15.240

fore *adv.* previously 7.204
forgate *v. pa.* forgot 1.166, 5.148
forgoo *v. inf.* part with 5.431[1]; *pr. subj.* 5.431[2]
formest *adj. superl.* first, original 5.132
fornfaders *n. pl.* forefathers, ancestors 5.622
forsoke *v. pa.* rejected 5.92, 12.14, 14.7; **forsoken** *pa. pl.* forsook 15.185; **forsake** *pa. p.*abandoned 7.183
forsomoche *conj.* ~ **as** because 6.666
forsothe *adv.* truly 4.318, 14.460, 15.188
forswere *v. pr. subj. refl.* lie under oath 7.124; **forsworn** *pa. p.* 7.25
forthynketh *v. 3 pr. sg.* **me** ~ I regret 9.246
forthon *adv.* henceforth 5.306 *N*
for-why *conj.* because 1.89
foryefnes *n.* forgiveness 1.227, 15.179
fosse *n.* ditch, pit 14.328
fotemen *see* **footmen**
foughten *v. pa. p.* fought 10.149
foundement *n.* foundation 11.116; **fundamente** 14.141
founden *see* **fonde**
frendely *adv.* in a friendly way 5.714
fro *prep.* from 1.7, 2.7, 3.4, etc.
frosshes *n. pl.* frogs 6.320
fruyt *n.* harvest 1.220; **fruytes** *pl.* fruit trees 1.13; produce 1.172
fulfyl *v. pr. subj.* accomplish, perform 14.298; **fulfylled** *pa. p.* filled 4.92; **fulfyllyd** 5.198; **fulfyllid** 14.535; ***fulfylled** finished, completed 4.93
fulle *n.* to ~ fully 14.337
fume *n.* smoke, exhalation 5.18 *N*, 14.239
fundamente *see* **foundement**
furour *n.* fury 15.55 *N*

G

gadre *v. inf.* collect 3.89, 4.513, 6.232; *pr.* 5.190; *imp.* 5.670, 6.150, 7.325; **gadred** *pa.* 5.67, 6.211, 7.171, etc.; *pa. p.* 3.371, 4.183, 5.161, etc.
gaf, gauest, gauyst *see* **yeue**
gayler *n.* jailer 5.113
garners *n. pl.* storehouses 5.190
gate *see* **gete**
gendre *n.* a class of individuals 1.16, 2.101
genelagye *n.* genealogy 12.40
generacion *n.* begetting 1.242; descendants, kindred, family 1.300, 2.7, 3.4, etc. **generacions** *pl.* descendants 3.152
gentyles *n. pl.* nations 5.664 *N*
germayn *adj.* of the same parents 4.107
gete *v. inf.* beget 3.123; **gate** *pa.* 1.247, 2.11, 5.531, 14.19; got, obtained 5.583, 9.412, 10.255, 13.115, 14.83; ~ **away** escaped 3.87; ~ **with chylde** made pregnant 3.125, 10.125
gheest *n.* guest 10.163
gheet *see* **ghoot**
ghelded *v. pa. p.* castrated 15.275
ghoostly *adj.* spiritual 7.53
ghoot *n.* goat 9.419; **ghotes** *gen.* (*pl.?*) 9.425; **gheet** *pl.* 1.255, 4.295; **ghotes** 11.79
gyle *n.* guile, treachery 11.6; **in** ~ deceitfully 4.488
gylefully *adv.* deceitfully 1.237
gyrde *v. inf. refl.* secure around one's waist, gird oneself 9.481; *pa.* 9.482; **gyrt** *pa. p.* girded, clothed and ready for action 14.183
gyue *see* **yeue**
glayue *n.* spear 9.314
glewe *n.* bitumen 2.32, 6.41
gobet *n.* a piece (of cloth) 9.449
gomor *n.* an ancient measure of weight or volume 6.543
goo *v. inf.* walk 6.57; **goon** go 6.164, 15.246; **goyng** *pr. p.* ~ **from** avoiding 13.4
goodes *n. pl.* good things 5.493; goods, possessions 7.84; benefits, blessings 14.442; **goodys** 14.346
gouerne *v. inf.* guide 15.272
grace *n.* good fortune 7.152
grauntsyre *n.* grandfather 4.142
grauel *n.* sand 3.395, 4.408, 5.221, 11.90
grauynges *n. pl.* carved works, engraved works 1.270
gree *n.* position 5.132; **grees** *pl.* steps 11.221
grete *adj.* large 11.115, 13.7; ~ **peple** many people 3.337; ~ **with** high in favour with 10.371; **gretter** *comp.* bigger, thicker 12.17
grette *v. pa.* greeted 9.471, 10.254
greue *v. inf.* harm, injure 4.322, 7.93, 9.448; *pr. subj.* 3.356; **greued** *pa.* caused discomfort 4.503; **greuyd** 10.234; oppressed, harassed; 6.21,

15.70; harmed, injured 15.228; *pa. p.* enraged, hardened 6.292
greuous *adj.* troublesome 5.92, 9.473
groflyng *adv.* face downward 14.476
grutche *n.* complaint 6.568
grutche *v. inf.* complain 13.27; *pr.* 6.557, 7.294; **grutchyng** *pr. p.* grumbling, indignant 4.365, 6.555, 7.255, 14.73; **grudchyd** *pa.* grumbled 7.246 *N*; **grutched** 6.502, 7.317; **grutchyd** 7.348
grutchyng *vbl. n.* grumbling, complaint 3.60; **grutchynges** *pl.* 6.533

H

habergeon *n.* coat of mail 9.311
habytacles *n. pl.* dwellings, rooms 11.196
habyte *n.* clothes 9.616
habondantly *adv.* abundantly 3.151
halowed *v. pa. p.* consecrated 11.135
halowes *n. pl.* saints 15.138
halted *v. pa.* limped 4.418
handle *v. inf.* touch with the hands, feel 4.73
handlynge *vbl n.* touching 7.139
happe *v. inf.* happen 5.315, 9.602, 14.250; **happid** *pa.* 10.267; **happed** 3.83, 4.260, 5.11, etc.; *pa. p.* 13.80, 14.327
happely *adv.* by chance 14.206; perhaps, probably 1.106, 4.377, 14.124; **happyly** 1.115
hardely *adv.* boldly 4.505
hardy *adj.* audacious, bold 5.421, 9.355, 15.347
hardnes *n.* hardship 6.128
harneys *n.* hunting gear 4.41; **harnoys** armour 9.188; equipment 10.67
hast *n.* haste 5.101
hauoyr *n.* property 7.111
heed *n.* individual, person 6.542
heer(e *n.* hair 10.234, 10.272, 15.300; **here** 5.442; **heres** *pl.* 5.316
heery *adj.* hairy 4.54
heyer *see* **hye**
heyr *n.* a garment of haircloth 15.165
heyres *see* **her**
helme *n.* helmet 9.311; **helmes** *pl.* 15.44
helth *n.* preservation 5.468; **elthe** health 5.265; **helth(e** welfare, safety 10.138, 14.29, 14.315
hem *pron. 3 pl. acc.* them 1.70, 2.42, 3.87, 4.63, 5.12, 6.578, 7.222, 9.131, 10.7, 11.135, 13.11, 14.213, 15.74
henge *v. pa.* hung 4.524, 9.658, 10.100, 15.343
her *n.* heir 3.333; **heyres** *pl.* 3.156, 9.667; **eyres** 3.33
her *pron. 3 pl. gen.* their 2.134, 5.245, 6.554; **herr** 6.659
herat *adv.* at this 15.17
herberowed *v. pa. p.* **be** ~ stay 3.191
herd *n.* affliction 6.361
here *pron. sg. fem. acc.* her 1.82, 2.90
here *v. inf.* hear, listen to 3.328, 5.281, 6.155, etc.; *pr.* 4.66, 6.181, 7.208, etc.; *imp.* 3.336, 4.58, 5.13, etc.; **herest** *2 pr. sg.* 6.507; **hereth** *3 pr. sg.* 9.76; **herd(e** *pa.* 1.131, 3.200, 4.5, etc.; *pa. p.* 3.174, 4.47, 5.21, etc.
here(s *see* **heer(e**
hereby *adv.* nearby 3.258; **herby** 14.243
herfor(e *adv.* because of this 6.32, 15.243
(h)erytage *n.* inherited property 13.114, 14.553
herkene *v. pr.* listen 7.130
herof *adv.* of this 9.416, 10.218, 15.32
hertes *n. pl.* harts 11.79
heuy *adj.* sad, sorrowful 5.122, 10.319, 14.357, 14.374; **heuyer** *comp.* 5.122
heuyly *adv.* indignantly 5.657
heuynes *n.* grief 9.28, 10.225, 14.252
hyd *v. pa. p.* hidden 9.224, 11.193, 14.57
hye *adj.* special, exalted 14.50; high, tall 3.7, 9.310, 15.7; **h(e)yer** *comp.* 2.68, 9.209; **hyest** *superl.* 2.72; **hiest** uppermost 5.139
hye *v. imp. refl.* make haste 3.260, 5.474; **hyed** *pa.* hurried 9.114; *pa. refl.* 4.200, 5.379, 9.493
hyer *adv.* here 5.1, 6.1
hyre *n.* wages 4.206, 11.101, 14.159
his *pron. 3 sg. gen.* its 1.16, 2.101, 6.484, etc.
historyal *adj.* historical, of historical importance 10.2
(h)ystorye *n.* story, history 2.1, 3.2–3, 4.34, etc.; **istorye** 4.1; **historyes** *pl.* 4.100
hit *pron. 3 sg. neut.* 2.135, 3.36, 4.30, 5.93, 6.671, 9.83, 10.132, 14.67; **hyt** 3.339, 4.468, 14.548, 15.5
hytherward *adv.* in this direction 6.122
holde *v. inf.* ~ **of** give allegiance to 15.14; **holden** *pa. p.* held, maintained

5.611, 7.90; detained 14.375; regarded 4.515
hond(e *n.* hand 3.347, 4.15, 5.609, etc.; **hondes** *pl.* 1.219, 3.377, 4.405, etc.
honderd *num.* hundred 3.325, 4.555, 5.616, etc.
honowrid *v. pa.* venerated, reverenced 15.225
hool *adj.* healthy, healed, unharmed 4.188, 14.397; **hole** 7.359, 10.199, 14.332
(h)oost *n.* army 3.354, 5.73, 6.440, etc.; **hoostes** *pl.* 6.446, 9.304, 13.41; **hoostis** 15.141
hopyng *v. pr. p.* ~ **in** trusting in 15.312
hore *adj.* grey 5.442
hostesse *n.* mistress of a household 6.165
hostyes *n. pl.* hosts, sacrificial victims 6.378 *N*
hound(e *n.* dog 6.398, 9.367, 14.224, 15.250
howbeit *conj.* ~ **that** although 7.100, 10.346, 14.10
hows *n.* clan 10.52

I

ydelly *adv.* without purpose 13.22
ydle *adj.* empty 1.4
yf *conj.* ~ **that** if 9.20
ylle *adj.* immoral, wicked 3.31, 7.28
imposicions *n. pl.* levies 12.4
incircumsiced *adj.* uncircumcised 4.491 *N*; **incircumcised** 9.335
indurat(e *adj.* hardened 6.314, 6.338; **endurat** 6.291
indurate *v. inf.* harden 6.461
infynyte *adj.* exceedingly abundant 11.21
innerest *adj. superl.* innermost 6.115
innocencye *n.* innocence 13.63; **innocensye** 1.92
inobedyent *adj.* disobedient 1.125, 7.80
ynough *adj.* enough 3.381, 4.263, 6.450, 14.218; **ynowgh** 15.145
ynough *adv.* sufficiently 9.487
inprenable *adj.* impregnable 7.290 *N*
instantly *adv.* fervently 14.315
inwardly *adv.* fervently? 15.399 *N*
irreprehensyble *adj.* beyond reproach, irreproachable 14.403
is *see* **ben**
ysope *n.* hyssop 11.95
yssue *v. inf.* be born 3.107; come out 15.61; **yssued** *pa.* 2.103, 4.13, 9.450; *pa. p.* born 5.540
ystorye *see* **hystorye**

J

ieopardye *n.* danger 10.145
iocunde *adj.* cheerful 9.539
iogelers *n. pl.* magicians 6.287
ioye *v. inf.* rejoice 14.421; *pr.* 14.515; *pr. subj.* 14.507; *imp.* 15.399; **ioyeng** *pr. p.* 14.441, 15.323; **ioyeden** *pa. pl.* 15.395
ioyned *v. pa. p.* united 14.293, 15.407
iourney *n.* undertaking, affair 15.412
iuged *v. pa.* ruled 8.10; *pa. p.* 7.167, 9.122

K

kalked *v. pa.* calculated (astrologically) 6.68
kepe *v. inf.* observe (a feast) 7.51; guard 15.38; **kepte** *pa.* 15.320
kyen *n. pl.* cows, cattle 4.412, 9.159, 14.343
kynred(e *n.* kindred, kinsmen, tribe 3.22, 4.133, 5.492, etc.; **kynredes** *pl.* 3.27
knewe *v. pa.* acknowledged 6.113
knyghtes *n. pl.* soldiers 5.71
knyghthode *n.* army, troops 15.22
know(e)leche *v. inf.* praise, honour, thank 14.461; ~ **to** 4.241 *N*, 14.498; *pr.* acknowledge 5.163; *imp.* praise, honour, thank 14.459, 14.489 *N*, 15.324; ~ **to** 14.496, 14.502; **knowlechyng** *pr. p.* acknowledging 15.155
knowleche *n.* divination 5.414 *N*; **had** ~ was informed, learnt 4.101; **haue gyue him in** ~ have informed him 9.83
kote *n.* garment 13.49
krybbe *n.* basket 6.41

L

labour *n.* distress of mind 1.232
laboure *v. inf.* till 1.220
lachet *n.* shoelace, thong used to fasten a shoe 3.100
ladde *see* **lede**
lade *v. imp.* 5.491 load; **laded** *pa.* 5.410; **laden** *pa. p.* 5.503, 15.27
layte *n.* flame, fire 3.270
langyng *see* **longe**

langours *n. pl.* diseases, tribulations 6.509
lasse *n.* younger person 4.11
lasse *v. imp.* lessen, diminish 6.233, 12.5
lassyng *vbl. n.* reducing 2.82
laste *adj. superl.* furthest 5.599
late *v. inf.* let, allow to 6.259; *imp.* 2.100, 3.63, 4.247, etc.; **laten** *pa. p.* 14.382
laton *n.* a metal alloy similar to brass 11.126
laude *n.* praise 7.336, 15.401
lawhe *v. inf.* laugh 3.328; **lawheth** *3 pr. sg.* laughs 3.203; **lawhed** *pa.* 1.313, 3.169; **lowhe** 2.133; **loughe** 3.200; **lawhedest** *2 pa. sg.* 3.207
lazar *n.* leper, diseased person 13.72
lede *v. imp.* carry 5.274; **ladde** *pa.* led 3.112, 10.50, 14.440, 15.219; *pa. p.* 9.139
leeful *adj.* permissible, right 14.87
lefte *v. pa.* lifted 7.331
lefte *see* **leue**
leghe *n.* pact 4.382 *N*
leye *v. inf.* put 6.166; *imp.* 4.368; **leyde** *pa.* cast (blame) on 1.138; **leyed** put 4.156; *pa. p.* 12.18; **leyde** laid away, stored 5.220
lendes *n. pl.* loins 4.539
lenger *adv. comp.* longer 3.275, 4.133, 5.459, 6.40, 7.71, 9.136; **lengre** 14.544
lepe *v. pa.* leapt, ran 14.55
lepre *adj.* afflicted with leprosy 7.268
lesynges *n. pl.* lies 6.236, 7.124
lette *n.* impediment 4.499
lette *v. imp.* hinder 3.492; **letted** *pa.* 6.75
lettyng *vbl. n.* hindrance, impairment 5.400, 6.186
leue *v. inf.* release 6.221; **lefte** *pa.* rejected 12.22; *pa. p.* **was** ~ remained 2.87
leuis *n. pl.* leaves 1.129
lyfelode *n.* necessities of life 2.129; **lyuelode** livelihood 14.84
lyght *adj.* bright; ~ **day** daylight, dawn 14.330
lyghter *adv. comp.* more easily 9.296
lyghtly *adv.* quickly 3.439; casually 7.29
lightnes *n.* frivolousness 14.122
lyke *adj.* similar ~ **to** like 1.62, 5.201, 6.539, 7.265, 11.34, 14.17
lyke *adv.* ~ **as** as though 3.270; just as 9.597, 14.76; ~ **as . . . so** since just as . . . then so 1.51
lyme *v. imp.* daub 2.31; **lymed** *pa.* 2.74
lyse *n. pl.* lice 6.336
lyste *v. pr.* desire 12.37
lytyl *adv.* **a** ~ for a little while 5.284
lytter *n.* bedding 4.361 *N*
lyuelode *see* **lyfelode**
locked *v. pa. p.* ~ **out** turned out of a place 7.193
lodged *v. pa. p.* stationed 11.238
loked *v. pa.* ~ **after** looked toward 14.414
lome *n.* clay 6.232
longe *v. pr.* belong 7.150; **longeth** *3 pr. sg.* 7.149; **longen** *pr. pl.* 4.441; **langyng** *pr. p.* 5.600; **longyng** 5.612; **longed** *pa.* 4.339
loose *v. inf.* release, let loose 1.234; **lo(o)sed** *pa.* untied 15.129, 15.299; *pa. p.* detached 2.33
lordeth *v. 3 pr. sg.* governs 5.508
lote *v. inf.* cast lots 9.221 *N*
loues *n. pl.* loaves 9.323, 11.132
lowhe, loughe *see* **lawheth**
lowtyng *v. pr. p.* bowing 3.146
luste *n.* desire 1.72

M

made *v. pa. p.* caused 10.184
magnefye *v. inf.* glorify, praise, exalt 3.24; **magnefied** *pa. p.* 6.495; **magnefy(e)ed** 3.468, 11.231, 15.284; **magnyfyed** 9.597
mayde *n.* maiden 3.427; handmaid 6.54, 14.107, 15.303
maist *v. 2 pr. sg.* may 6.612, 9.346, 14.171; **mayste** 14.200
maistres *n. pl.* commanders 15.24
maistresse *n.* mistress 3.126
maner *n.* 'with appositive noun: a kind of, sort of, etc.' (*MED*) 3.10, 4.9, 5.75, 6.335, 7.98, 11.94, 14.240; **in** ~ **of** after the fashion of 1.129; **by** ~ **of** in the guise of 7.130
manerly *adv.* 'in accord with good musical practice' (*MED*) 15.398 *N*
manly *adv.* like a man, valiantly 9.104, 15.385
mansion *n.* a stopping-place in a journey 14.225; **mansyons** *pl.* 6.554 *N*
mantel *n.* cloak, robe 2.136, 3.506, 5.95, 9.449

mary *n.* marrow; **the** ~ **of th'erthe** the fat of the land 5.494
markes *n. pl.* boundaries 6.652
masses *n. pl.* cakes 9.495 *N*
mawmetryee *n.* idol worship 3.13
meane *n.* help 10.309
mede *n.* recompense, gift 4.268; wages 4.321, 11.101; reward 3.104, 4.296, 6.56, 14.152
medlyd *v. pa. refl.* associated (with) 14.121
meyne *n.* household 3.30, 14.402; retinue, clan 6.4, 10.13; retinue of servants 15.168
meke *v. pr. subj.* make humble 15.180; **meked** *pa.* 1.159; **mekyd** *pa. p.* contrite 15.181
mekely *adv.* courteously, sweetly 5.547
mele *n.* meal made from grinding grain, flour 5.138, 6.419, 9.42, 11.77
meles *n. pl.* feasts 5.145
membres *n. pl.* organs of the body, limbs 1.125; **membris** 7.32, 11.63; *see also* **pryue**
mened *v. pa.* said, meant 9.113
mercenarye *n.* employee 14.160 *N*
mercy-doyng *vbl. n.* clemency 15.177 *N*
meruaylled *v. pa.* marvelled 4.99, 14.194, 15.202; **meruaylleden** *pa. pl.* 15.254
meruaylles *n. pl.* wonders, marvellous deeds 6.161, 7.307, 14.482; **meruaillis** 7.236; **meruayllys** 8.3
messager *n.* messenger 13.33, 14.423; **messagers** *pl.* 4.390, 9.299, 11.71, 14.389, 15.15
mesure *n.* ration, prescribed amount 15.146; ***out of** ~ exceedingly 4.308
mete *n.* food 1.169, 4.43, 5.139, etc.; **metes** *pl.* 2.48, 14.24
meuable *adj.* movable 3.514, 15.378
meue *v. inf.* move, stir (physically) 1.120, 5.211; **meuyd** *pa.* 2.62, 3.80, 9.23; *pa. p.* 5.380, 11.63, 13.63; dislodged? 7.374 *N*
meuyng *vbl. n.* (physical) stirring 1.91; moving, movement 15.294; **meuynges** *pl.* 1.121, 7.101; **mouynges** 7.156
myddelest *adj.* second oldest of three, middlemost 2.133
myddes *n.* middle, midst 1.38, 6.471
myes *n. pl.* mice 9.133, 15.351
mynde *n.* (the power of) thought 15.365; **in good** ~ in sound mind 3.517, 4.556, 10.376; **haue** ~ remember 7.36
mynystery *n.* service 5.450
mynystred *v. pa.* gave, provided 5.18, 14.16
mynystris *n. pl.* servants 5.196; **mynystres** officials 11.196
mynuysshe *v. imp.* reduce 12.5; **mynusshed** *pa. p.* 6.239
myssaye *v. inf.* slander 7.125
moche *adj.* great 3.24; numerous 6.228
moche *adv.* much 10.14
moyen *n.* mediation 10.229
molte *v. pa.* melted 7.176
mo(o *adj. comp.* more (in number) 4.460, 8.6, 9.284, etc.
more *adj. comp.* bigger, elder 3.285, 4.11, 4.77; greater 11.203, 14.463
morn *n.* morrow, the next day 6.327, 7.242; next morning 3.488, 5.393, 6.537, 9.88, 10.144
mortefyed *v. pa. p.* dead 9.542 *N*
mote *v. pr. subj.* may 14.211
motley *adj.* variegated in colour 5.8
mountes *n. pl.* mountains 15.13
mouynges *see* **meuyng**
multytude *n.* a large number of persons, throng 5.655, 7.327, 12.3; numerousness 3.137, 4.409, 11.21; (large) number, amount 9.28, 15.58; **multitude** 6.674
murmuracion *n.* grumbling 7.322
mused *v. pa. p.* grumbled 6.526 *N*

N

naylle *n.* hoof 6.380
named *v. pa. p.* renowned 11.93
nauye *n.* navy 11.228
ne *conj.* nor 1.192, 2.88, 3.48, etc.; ~ . . . ~ nor . . . and 3.64
necessaryes *n. pl.* utensils 11.125 *N*
necglygent *adj.* slothful, dilatory 5.240
nedely *adv.* of necessity 1.50
ner *conj.* nor 4.371, 7.125
ner *see* **nyhe**
nether *adj.* lower 9.142
neuew(e)s *n. pl.* grandsons 4.382, 14.532; **neuewis** 14.525
newe *adv.* newly 1.264
next *prep.* next to 5.477
nyhe *adv.* near, nearly 3.425, 6.424; **ner** *comp.* 5.421, 6.122

no *conj.* nor 6.509
noye *v. inf.* harm 7.94; **noyed** *pa.* 15.228
nombre *n.* amount 11.104; **without** ~ innumerable 11.144
none *adv.* not 6.521
noryce *n.* nursemaid 3.496, 4.532
norisshyd *v. pa. p.* brought up, raised 12.16
nothyng *adv.* not at all 6.10
notwythstondyng *adv.* nevertheless 9.103

O

obeye *v. pr. inf.* comply with 12.12
oblygacion *n.* bond, document recording obligation to repay 14.33
o(b)probrye *n.* disgrace 4.279 *N*, 9.354
occasyon *n.* opportunity 1.104
occupacion *n.* engagement in some activity; **in** ~ busy 4.475
of *adv.* off 9.128, 9.373, 10.100, 10.310[2]
of *prep.* by (with passive) 15.394; from 3.282; out of 6.617; during 9.632; *introducing partitive object* 1.121, 4.103, 14.409
offendyng *v. pr. p.* tripping over 14.424 *N*
offyce *n.* duty, task 6.25
offycers *n. pl.* servants, stewards 11.197
ofspryngyng *vbl. n.* descendants, lineage 3.110 *N*
oke *see* **ooke**
oldremen *n. pl.* elders 6.563 *N*
olyphauntes *n. pl.* elephants 11.230
on *prep.* towards 6.94; beside 10.27
ony *adj.* any 1.93, 3.47, 4.42, etc.
ony *pron.* any, anyone 5.200, 7.31, 9.226, etc.
onythyng(e *pron.* anything 5.441, 7.6, 14.87, 14.159
only *adj.* sole 14.339
o(o)ke *n.* oak 4.533, 10.271, 10.274
oost *see* **hoost.**
operacion *n.* labour 1.30, 7.38
opon *see* **vpon**
oppressyng *v. pr. p.* overcoming, overpowering, ravishing 4.471; **oppressyd** *pa.* crushed 13.47; **oppressid** smothered 11.46; *pa. p.* crushed 6.655
oprobrye *see* **o(b)probrye**
or *conj.* before 4.44
oracion *n.* prayer 11.154, 14.462
oracle *n.* inner sanctuary 11.145
ordeyne *v. inf.* arrange 14.341; appoint 5.189, 9.186; *imp.* 5.572; place 14.163; **ordeyned** *pa.* put in order 1.254; arranged, deployed 10.264; directed, commanded 2.128, 10.348; prepared, made ready 4.61, 5.368, 9.157; appointed, chose 15.21; *pa. p.* 3.150, 4.113, 5.204, 7.247, 14.290, 15.178; prepared 3.461; commanded 15.39; arranged 15.286
ordre *n.* temporal sequence 5.511
ornacion *n.* decoration, ornamenting 1.28
ouerall *adv.* everywhere 15.237
ouercomen *v. pa. p.* overcome 9.317, 15.85
ouerest *adj.* uppermost 15.163
ouerlaboured *v. pa. trans.* overworked 4.455 *N*
ouermoche *adj.* excessive 15.55
ouermoche *adv.* excessively 7.9, 11.249
ouerpartyes *n. pl.* upper parts 14.4 *N*
ouerpassed *v. pa. p.* past, finished 4.128
ouerthrewest *v. 2 pa. sg.* destroyed 13.23
oultrages *n.* offences 7.61 *N*
our *pron.* ours 9.488
outrageous *adj.* wicked, excessive 7.103
owe *v. inf.* possess, own 4.141, 14.245; *pr.* 7.109; **owest** *2 pr. sg.* 5.481; ought 14.142; **oweth** *3 pr. sg.* owns 5.604, 7.118, 13.28

P

payne *n.* punishment 1.59
paynems *n. pl.* pagans 14.24
palays *n.* palace 11.130
palle *n.* covering, cloak 3.506
palme *n.* a handbreadth 9.310
palpable *adj.* tangible; (of darkness) intense, thick 6.373
pappe *n.* breast 3.329, 9.40
parablis *n. pl.* proverbs 11.93; **Parables** 11.246
parauenture *adv.* by chance, perhaps *2.85, 6.224
parfyght *adj.* perfect 1.26, 3.145; **perfight** 2.10, 15.233
parfyghtly *adv.* perfectly 2.45; **perfightly** fully 11.153
parte *n.* side, party 7.221, 9.307
parted *v. pa. p.* apportioned 6.622

parteyne *v. pr.* pertain 6.197; **perteyned** *pa.* belonged 9.501
party *adj.* variegated, mixed 4.322 *N*
partye *n.* group of people 10.57; **partyes** *pl.* 3.91, 9.132; parts, sections 1.42, 10.266, 11.60
pask(e *adj.* paschal, of the Passover 6.404, 9.633
passe *v. inf.* fail, miss? 14.533 *N*; **passed** *pa.* surpassed 11.91
passyng *adv.* exceedingly 4.479, 13.7
pauillons *n. pl.* tents 9.385; **pauylions** 10.135
pecis *n. pl.* pieces, coins 5.54
pees *n.* peace 3.119, 4.384, 5.364, etc.; **helde his** ~ remained silent 14.288
penurye *n.* lack, scarcity 6.558, 15.144
percyd *v. pa. p.* pierced 15.281
perdicion *n.* destruction, ruin 14.130, 15.117
perfight *see* **parfyght**
perfightly *see* **parfyghtly**
persecucion *n.* affliction 9.134
perteyned *see* **parteyne**
pesyble *adj.* friendly 5.10; peacemaking, peaceable 10.374; **pesible** 4.499; untroubled 11.4
pesybly *adv.* peacefully 5.259, 15.150; **pesibly** 9.535
phisik *n.* medicine 5.679
phiton *n.* the spirit possessing a soothsayer 9.614 *N*
phytonesse *n.* a female medium 9.614
pyetous *adj.* pitiable 15.154
pylgremage *n.* sojourn, wandering abroad 3.153, 4.142; man's sojourn in the world 5.575; journey 14.380
pyllage *n.* plunder, booty 9.249
pylle *v. inf.* rob 9.653
piscene *n.* pool 10.56; **pyscene** 10.101
pitchid *v. pa.* covered with pitch 6.41
pyt(te *n.* well, pool 3.349, 4.180, 5.515, 6.90
plag(h)e *n.* slaughter, calamity 14.40; plague 6.317, 6.371, 7.256, etc.; **plaghes** *pl.* 15.73
players *n. pl.* revellers 14.121
plaisaunt *adj.* gracious 5.343; **playsaunt** pleasant 3.68
playsir *n.* pleasure 1.270, 9.190; **playsyr** 3.53, 15.269; **pleasir** 10.216
plancte *n.* lamentation 5.693
plante *n.* the sole of the foot 4.15, 13.71
platte *adj.* flat 5.412
pleased, pleysid *see* **plese**
pleasir *see* **playsir**
plenteuosnes *n.* fertility 5.218
plenteuous *adj.* fertile, plentiful, copious 5.154
plentyuously *adv.* plentifully 1.172
plese *v. inf.* please 4.415, 9.197, 11.260, 15.278; *pr.* 15.92; *pr. subj.* 4.456, 14.407; **pleseth** *3 pr. sg.* 3.130, 9.79; **plesed** *pa.* 1.210, 5.76; ~ **to** 4.495, 14.408, 15.253; **pleysid to** 5.196; **pleysid** *pa. p.* appeased, placated 7.195
plyaunt *adj.* turning, revolving 1.191
poynettis *n. pl.* ornamental wrist bands, armlets 3.458
poruyde *v. imp.* provide 6.617 *N*
possede *v. inf.* possess, hold, occupy 3.115, 7.199, 15.95
possession *n.* worldly goods, property 4.288
postes *n. pl.* door-posts 9.18
potage *n.* thick soup or stew 4.22, 9.323
pouldre *n.* dust of the earth 3.77; powder, dust 7.212
pourchaceth *v. 3 pr. sg.* brings about, contrives 7.92
poursiewed, poursyewyd, poursyewyng *see* **pursiewe**
pourueyed *v. pa.* purveyed 3.47
pray(e *n.* booty, spoil 3.99, 15.376
praty *adj.* fine, good-looking 6.60
preef *n.* test 6.72
prefectes *n. pl.* overseers 6.230; officers 11.86
preue *v. inf.* test, try 4.73, 5.275; **proue** 6.520, 14.472; **prouyng** *pr. p.* realizing 4.150; **prouyd** *pa. p.* discovered 5.268, 11.203
preuy, prevy *see* **pryue**
prynce *n.* governor 5.248; **prynces** *pl.* rulers 6.627
pryue *adj.* private 15.164; **preuy** 15.292; ~ **membre** sexual organ 3.158, 15.341; ~ **membres** *pl.* 1.127; **prevy membres** 2.132
pryued *v. pa. p.* deprived, taken away 4.246 *N*
pryuely *adv.* confidentially, discreetly, secretly 1.142, 5.701, 10.90, 14.56; **pryuyly** 11.47
pryuetees *n. pl.* secrets 15.213
probacion *n.* testing 14.127

prodyges *n. pl.* portents 5.166 *N*
profyght *n.* increase 14.529 *N*
progenye *n.* kindred 5.328
promyssyon *n.* **londe of** ~ Promised Land 7.366
proposicion *n.* **loues of** ~ the shewbread of ancient Judaism 11.132
propre *adj.* own 5.446; belonging to an individual 15.391
propretees *n. pl.* nature, characteristics 11.96
proue, prouyd, prouyng *see* **preue**
prouerbe *n.* object of general reproach, byword 11.168
prouffitable *adj.* useful 14.232
prouydence *n.* bounty, provision 14.352
prouoste *n.* officer 5.209; **prouostis** *pl.* 5.189; **prouostes** overseers 6.14
Psawter *n.* Psalter 10.367
puyssance *n.* power 15.8
pulmente *n.* thick vegetable soup, food 4.65
punicion *n.* (divine) punishment 1.233
purpose *v. pr.* intend 3.209, 9.490, 15.242; **purposed** *pa.* proposed 11.191; *pa. p.* resolved upon 15.194
purpure *n.* purple fabric 15.224
pursyewe *v. inf.* pursue 6.439; persecute, attack 10.281; **pursiewe** 9.521; pursue 15.374; **pursyewe** *pr.* 9.586; **poursyewyng** *pr. p.* 6.473, 14.336, 15.77; **poursiewed** *pa.* 4.342; **poursyewyd** 6.447; **pursyewed** 9.218, 10.9; **pursyewid** 10.263; **pursiewed** *pa. p.* 4.367
put *v. pa.* ~ **to** added to 15.341; ~ **vnder** conquered 10.119; **putte** pushed, shoved 6.95

Q

quinquagenaries *n. pl.* leaders of groups of fifty 6.628

R

rackes *n. pl.* mangers 11.85
raught *v. pa.* reached, took 7.211
rauayne *n.* robbery, rapine 7.110; **ravayne** plundering 15.187
rauyss(h)ed *v. pa.* took away, carried away 4.470, 4.474
rauysshement *n.* deflowering, rape 4.489
rebelle *adj.* rebellious, disobedient 7.296
recreacyng *vbl. n.* refreshing 1.51
red(de *v. pa. p.* read 1.2, 1.27, 3.2, etc.
redy *adj.* prudent 5.74
reduce *v. inf.* lead back 5.667
re-edyfye *v. inf.* rebuild 14.505; **re-edefyed** *pa. p.* 14.536
refrayne *v. inf.* suppress, restrain 7.102; *refl.* 1.91
regne *n.* kingdom 6.640 *N*; sovereignty 11.162
reherceth *v. 3 pr. sg.* narrates 5.455; **rehersed** *pa. p.* recounted 6.682
reyse *v. inf.* stir up 10.178; erect, set up 3.34; **reysed** *pa.* 4.171; *pa. p.* stirred up 15.230
reysyns *n. pl.* raisins 5.48 *N*
remembrid *v. pa. refl.* remembered 5.144
remenaunt *n.* remainder 9.48, 14.234
remeuyd *v. pa.* moved, departed 7.278; removed 4.198
rendyng *v. pr. p.* tearing 15.356; **rente** *pa.* 5.65, 10.31, 15.362; **rented** 5.409
rendre *v. inf.* give back 5.44, 7.114, 14.210
renyed *v. pa.* refused 5.661
rennar *n.* runner 10.65
renne *v. inf.* run 9.324, 14.424, 15.335; **renneth** *3 pr. sg.* 1.44; **ronne** *pa.* ~ **to** pursued 9.260; **ronnen** *pa. pl.* ran 15.345
repleness(h)yd *v. pa. p.* filled 2.28–9, 7.376, 14.452
repreef *n.* insult 9.12; condemnation 14.97
repreuest *v. 2 pr. sg.* reproach, rebuke 4.355; **repreuyd** *pa.* 4.379, 7.266, 10.77, 14.62
repugne *v. inf.* rebel 9.268
repute *v. inf.* regard 4.329; *imp.* 9.27; **reputed** *pa.* 6.62; *pa. p.* reckoned, credited 3.111 *N*; ascribed 5.636
requyre *v. pr.* petition, request 9.509, 14.118; *imp.* ask for 5.333; **requyred** *pa. p.* requested 11.27
requyryng *vbl. n.* demanding, exaction 7.22
rescowe *n.* rescue 15.158
rescowed *v. pa.* rescued 3.92, 10.13
reserue *v. pr.* preserve 6.29; **reseruyd** *pa.* 6.28; *pa. p.* 5.470

residue *n.* remainder 9.253; **resydue** 14.528
resonable *adj.* possessing the power of reason 4.17
resseyue *v. inf.* look after 5.333
resten *v. pr. pl.* remain 5.479
restore *v. inf.* pay 14.201 *N*
reteyned *v. pa.* held back, restrained 10.280
retrayt *n.* retreat 10.280
rewlid *v. pa. p.* directed 10.129
rychesses *n. pl.* riches 11.28, 15.391; **rychessis** 9.333, 11.232
ryght *adj.* direct 6.429
right *adv.* very 10.157
right *n.* **of** ~ rightly, lawfully 4.340
rightful *adj.* just, virtuous 2.52, 3.294, 6.508, etc.; **ryghtful** 13.62; appropriate, satisfactory 14.398; **rightfuller** *comp.* more virtuous 9.458
rightfully *adv.* rightly, virtuously 5.415; **ryghtfully** 13.96
rightwys *adj.* righteous 2.10; **rightwis** 3.214; **ryghtwys** 15.205
rightwysnes *n.* justice, righteousness 11.209; **ryghtwisnes** 14.93; **rightwisnessis** *pl.* virtuous actions 14.542
rysshes *n. pl.* rushes 6.41
roddes *n. pl.* sticks 4.297
royam(e *n.* realm, kingdom 2.148, 3.304, 5.190, etc.; **royames** *pl.* 11.73
rome *n.* room, space 3.448
rood *v. pa.* rode 9.552
roof *v. pa.* thrust 10.61 *N*
rosted *v. pa.* roasted, cooked with dry heat 14.233
rote *n.* foothills 4.533; base 6.664
roted *v. pa.* ~ **of** rotted off 9.143
rough *adj.* shaggy 4.13, 9.287 *N*; **rowhe** 4.54, 9.419
ruyne *n.* devastation 9.119, 15.116; downfall 10.28
rumour *n.* outcry of protest 3.59

S

Sabottis *n. pl.* Sabbaths 15.166
sacramente *n.* secret information, confidence 14.460
sacrefyed *v. pa.* sacrificed 9.43; *pa. p.* 11.12
saefte *n.* safety 5.344
saynctes *n. pl.* holy people 14.313
salewed *v. pa.* greeted 5.373, 14.185; **salued** 10.254
sanctefyed *v. pa.* blessed, dedicated to God's service, rendered holy 13.12 *N*
sapyence *n.* wisdom 11.28
satysfye *v. inf.* recompense 14.352; **satisfye** *imp.* appease 10.298
sauf *adj.* saved, preserved 4.428; safe 14.332
sauf *conj.* except that 9.241
sauf *prep.* except 5.461, 9.284, 14.156, 15.166
sauely *adv.* safely 14.209; **saufly** 14.210
sauour *n.* smell 4.84
sawest *v. 2 pa. sg.* had (something) in mind, envisaged 3.305
scarmusshe *v. inf.* skirmish, play roughly 10.58
scarse *adj.* characterised by scarcity, famine 5.194
science *n.* (branch of) knowledge 1.108, 5.414
scylence *n.* silence 15.311
scorgest *v. 2 pr. sg.* scourge, punish 14.488
scorgys *n. pl.* whips 11.272; **scorgis** 12.19
scryppe *n.* bag 15.304
scripture *n.* writing, inscription 7.203
scropule *n.* pang of conscience 9.524
seche *v. inf.* seek 5.59, 9.606; *pr.* 5.33; *imp.* 4.356, 14.181; **sechest** *2 pr. sg.* 9.454; **secheth** *3 pr. sg.* 9.441; **souht** *pa.* 9.223
sechyng *vbl. n.* seeking 1.169
secondly *adv.* for the second time 4.111 *N*
sectes *n. pl.* faiths 11.250
seeason *n.* season 1.257
seelyng *n.* ceiling 11.226
seke *adj.* sick 5.627, 9.421, 10.11
sekenes *n.* sickness 4.364; **sekenesses** *pl.* 9.131
seld *adv.* seldom 1.172
semblable *adj.* similar 5.90
semblaunt *n.* outward show, manner 10.80
semeth *v. 3 pr. sg.* **me** ~ it seems to me 4.450
sempyternal *adj.* everlasting 5.633
senyors *n. pl.* elders 6.150, 10.107, 12.9

sentence *n.* pronouncement 5.405; text, passage 7.144
sepulcre *n.* grave 7.372, 10.102, 14.326
sepulture *n.* land for burials 6.450; **sepultures** *pl.* burials 14.78
serche *v. imp.* investigate 15.98; **serched** *pa. p.* 4.367
seruyse *n.* liturgical service 7.60; the dishes served at a meal 11.195
sete *n.* throne 10.354, 11.162; **setes** *pl.* seats 9.143
settyst *v. 2 pr. sg.* ~ **lityl by** care nothing for 10.295; **settyng** *pr. p.* ~ **nothyng therby** not caring 4.32; **setted** *pa.* ~ **nought by** scorned 15.15; **sette** *pa. p.* appointed 14.378
seurete *n.* safety 1.245
shadowe *n.* umbrella covering, shelter 3.236
share *v. pa.* shore 9.470
shette *v. inf.* shut 3.241; *pa.* 3.231; **shitte** 2.73; **shytte** 7.241; *pa. p.* 7.277; **shette** 4.182
shewe *v. inf..* announce, make known 5.544, 6.195, 9.90, 13.37, 14.253; *imp.* 5.482; **sheweth** *3 pr. sg.* demonstrates 1.241; **shew(e)d** *pa.* manifested 8.3, 9.130; made known 6.262; *pa. p.* 5.172, 6.645, 9.71, 11.164
shold *pa.* should, would 1.52, 2.42, 3.45, etc.; **sholdest** *2 pa. sg.* 3.305
shone *n. pl.* shoes 6.123
shote *v. inf.* shoot 1.274
shoter *n.* shooter, archer 1.274; **shoters** *pl.* 15.26
sichomours *n. pl.* sycamores 11.240
sicles *n. pl.* shekels, ancient units of weight 9.312; **sycles** 3.447
syege *n.* **lyeng at a** ~ lying in siege 10.121
sykernesse *n.* security 14.154
symylacre *n.* effigy 9.424
symple *adj.* blameless, innocent 3.296, 13.4; quiet, meek 4.19
symplenes *n.* innocence, guilelessness 3.295; integrity?, foolish behaviour? 13.74 *N*
symplycyte *n.* meekness 11.158
synguler *adj.* ~ **batail** single combat 9.316
singulerly *adv.* one by one 5.673
synnar *n.* sinner 3.214
sith *conj.* since 4.330, 5.443, 6.255, 9.177; **syth** 3.128
sythes *n. pl.* times 1.231
sixt(e *ord.* sixth 6.352, 6.521
slear *n.* slayer 14.108
sle(e *v. inf.* kill 1.225, 2.115, 3.41, etc.; *pr.* 7.64; *imp.* 5.312, 6.26, 9.258, 10.26, 11.65; **sleeth** *3 pr. sg.* 1.230, 14.250; **slewe** *pa.* struck 10.13
slyde *v. inf.* fall 1.99
smale *adj.* few in number 5.576
smaragdes *n. pl.* emeralds 15.224
smote *v. pa.* beat 7.212; struck 6.82, 7.255, 9.131, 13.46, 15.72; ~ **in** attacked 3.91, 9.639; ~ **on** 10.12; **smotest** *2 pa. sg.* struck 6.564; **smeten** *pa. p.* 13.35; **smeton** 6.675, 7.268, 10.310, 15.319; ravaged 5.158
socoure *n.* refuge 15.366
soden *v. pa. p.* boiled, cooked 3.195; **sothen** 9.494
softe *adv.* comfortably 9.144
softly *adv.* without haste 14.408
solempne *adj.* solemn 7.55; **solompne** 9.37
solempnysed *v. pa. p.* celebrated 15.403
sollycyte *v. pr.* disturb 6.225
sonde *n.* sand 6.83
sone *adv.* immediately 1.230, 7.183, 13.24
songe *v. pa.* sang 6.493, 15.397
sore *adj.* severe 6.20
sore *adv.* profusely, in great numbers 3.58; cruelly 15.131; extremely, grievously 2.83, 3.40, 4.23, 5.107, 6.449, 9.320, 10.87, 15.32; **sorer** *comp.* 1.289
sorowyng *v. pr. p.* mourning 5.682
sothen *see* **soden**
sothly *adv.* truly 5.522, 14.312, 15.229
souht *see* **seche**
souke *v. inf.* **gyue** ~ suckle 3.326
souped *v. pa. p.* dined 14.305
sourde *v. inf.* arise 3.60
sowne *n.* sound 1.271; **soun** 6.668
sowne *v. inf.* resound 9.81
spack *v. pa.* spoke, composed 11.93; said, spoke 1.18, 4.542, 5.37, etc.; **spake** 1.102, 13.86; **spakest** *2 pa. sg.* 15.149; **spa(c)ken** *pa. pl.* 5.276, 5.700
spelunke *n.* sepulchre, cave 3.403, 5.674
spende *v. inf.* use, consume 5.288, 15.265
spyre *v. imp.* enquire 14.170
spyte *n.* contempt 5.559

spoylled *v. pa.* despoiled 3.86, 6.422
sportes *n. pl.* amusement, entertainment 1.261
spryngyng *vbl. n.* dawning 15.209
stablisshe *v. inf.* establish 3.151; **stablysshid** *pa. p.* 7.49; **stablysshed** sustained? 4.114 *N*
***stacten** *n.* myrrh 5.340
stale *v. pa.* stole 4.337, 5.419
steppes *n. pl.* 'a unit of linear measure, approximately equal to two and a half feet' (*MED*) 3.12 *N*
sterte *v. pa.* woke suddenly 5.155; rushed 15.358
stylle *adj.* quiet, calm 6.457, 14.223
stole *n.* robe 5.206
stopple *n.* stalks of grain, stubble 6.232
storax *n.* gum from the storax tree 5.340
store *n.* livestock 3.56
storye *n.* historical/biblical narrative 1.1, 13.119
straynyng *v. pr. p.* embracing, clasping 4.438
strayte *adj.* narrow 15.38
straitly *adv.* strictly 7.48
stratche *v. inf.* stretch 6.160; *imp.* 6.304, 13.26; **stratched** *pa.* 6.174, 15.271
stra(u)nge *adj.* foreign 4.211, 6.105, 11.250; alien 4.520, 7.3, 9.179, 11.165, 15.85
straungers *n. pl.* guests 3.179
strenger *adj. comp.* stronger 6.12, 7.290; **strengest** *superl.* 4.467, 5.518, 6.626
strength *n.* fighting force 15.25
stroof *v. pa.* strove, contended 11.54
strowed *v. pa.* provided with straw 3.462
studye *v. imp.* strive 14.150
subdued *v. pa.* made subservient, subjugated 5.598, 15.3; *pa. p.* 4.113, 15.100
subgette *adj.* subservient 5.16
substa(u)nce *n.* property, riches, possessions 2.57, 3.30, 4.325, etc.
subuerte *v. inf.* raze, destroy 3.260
sue *v. inf.* petition 5.134
suffre *v. inf.* allow 4.515, 5.453, 6.160, 9.628, 10.371; *pr. subj.* 3.407, 6.277; *imp.* 6.219, 7.188, 9.512, 14.156; **suffreth** *3 pr. sg.* 14.153; **suffred** *pa.* 14.70, 15.94; *pa. p.* 4.321, 5.393, 10.355, 11.149, *15.321
summa *n.* total 5.542
supplanted *v. pa.* dispossessed 4.110
***supplantyng** *vbl. n.* usurping 4.121
surer *adj. comp.* more secure 9.466
surplys *n.* surplice, a Hebrew priestly vestment 9.60
susteyne *v. inf.* endure 6.613, 13.77
sware *v. pa.* made an oath, swore 4.31, 6.102, 9.464; **swarest** *2 pa. sg.* 7.197
swerd *n.* sword 3.377, 4.119, 5.669, etc.
sweuene *n.* dream 5.11; **sweuenes** *pl.* 9.612

T

tabernacle *n.* portable shrine 6.552, 7.234, 14.505; tent 3.80, 4.345, 9.387, 11.8, 15.219; **tabernacles** *pl.* 7.254, 10.305; shrines 11.260
table *n.* inscribed tablet 7.69; **tablys** *pl.* 11.146; **tables** 6.691; decorative panels, paintings 11.125
takles *n. pl.* arrows 4.41
tare *v. pa.* tore 5.57, 13.84
tarye *v. inf.* wait 3.192; *pr.* 6.606; *imp.* 14.192
taske *v. inf.* impose tax 9.192
taste *v. pr. subj.* feel, examine by touching 4.55
teenth *adj.* tenth 4.179
teliar *n.* tiller, cultivator 1.204; **telyar** 4.18; **tylyers** *pl.* 9.187
Temporal *n.* 'the list of Biblical passages to be recited during mass for the seasons of the church year [as opposed to those for saints' days]' (*MED*) 8.20 *N*
tempryd *v. pa. p.* moistened 2.124
temptacion *n.* trial, testing 6.567, 14.70
tempte *v. inf.* test, try 11.187; *pr.* 6.557, 15.175; **temptyd** *pa.* 3.365; **tempted** 6.506; *pa. p.* 7.308, 14.471
termes *n. pl.* limits, borders 5.599, 6.652
texture *n.* weaving 1.273 *N*
than *adv.* then 14.545
that *conj.* so that 4.5, 5.558, 9.379[2]
that *pron.* that which, what 3.209, 3.305, 4.58, 4.292[2], 5.253, 5.330, 6.508, 11.192, 14.541[1]
theder *adv.* thither 3.412, 4.346, 5.241, etc.; **thedre** 5.334; **thether** 9.326, 14.178
themself *pron. 3 pl.* themselves 1.255
then *conj.* than 9.265
therafter *adv.* according to that 6.613

therebinthe *n.* 'The turpentine tree, Pistacia terebinthus' (*MED*) 5.340
therfore *adv.* for that 4.373; as a result 5.342
theron *adv.* on top of it 9.314
thertenst *adj.* thirteenth 14.405 *N*
therwhiles *adv.* meanwhile 5.346
thether *see* **theder**
thye *n.* thigh 4.418
thilke *dem. adj.* that 14.217
this *dem. adj. pl.* these 10.327; **thyse** 10.338; **thys xlv dayes** the next forty-five days 14.46
tho *dem. adj. pl.* those 1.121, 4.298, 5.268, etc.
thral *adj.* in a state of servitude 9.197 *N*
thraldom *n.* slavery 6.680
thurgh *adv.* through 9.564, 15.76
thurgh *prep.* through 6.460, 8.20, 10.313, etc.
thurghout *prep.* throughout 6.408
thurghwalked *v. pa. p.* walked through 13.19 *N*
tyde *n.* time 9.114
tyle *n.* brick 6.21
tylyers *see* **teliar**
tymbres *n. pl.* small drums 15.398
tympane *n.* small drum, tambourine 6.496; **tympanes** *pl.* 6.497, 9.399
tiraunt *adj.* villainous, cruel? 15.221 *N*
tytle *n.* stone memorial 4.551
to *prep.* as 3.509; for 6.571[2]
tofore *adv.* ahead, in front 4.434, 6.498, 9.496; before, previously 1.162, 4.152, 5.176, etc.; in advance 9.180, 14.407
tofore *conj.* before 5.36; ~ **that** 1.121
tofor(e *prep.* in front of 3.65, 4.298, 5.203, etc.; in/into the presence of 1.66, 4.356, 5.172, etc.; within the purview of 2.28; before (in time) 1.198, 3.9, 4.103, etc.; ~ **Our Lord** taking Our Lord to witness 4.49
tokest *v. 2 pa. sg.* took 3.229; **token** *pa. pl.* 9.104, 9.349
tomorn(e *adv.* tomorrow 6.293, 9.417
torne *v. inf.* turn 6.301, 7.30, 11.253; *pr.* 3.14, 11.162; *pr. subj.* 5.596, 10.339, 14.148; *imp.* 14.147; **torned** *pa.* 6.172, 11.256, 15.126; *pa. refl.* 3.267, 5.284; *pa. p.* 3.268, 5.711, 9.641, 10.289, 14.60
***toslen** *v. pa. p.* struck down dead 6.656
tour *n.* tower 3.7
tourbe *n.* band 5.691; **tourbes** *pl.* crowds, multitudes 4.139 *N*, 5.632
towched *v. pa. p.* modified? 10.3 *N*
trade *v. pa.* trod 6.66
trauaylled *v. pa.* was in labour 4.545
tree *n.* wood, timber 2.30
treen *adj.* wooden 6.307
tresory(e *n.* treasury 5.584, 11.136, 15.29
treso(u)r *n.* treasure, stored riches, coins 5.365, 7.321, 14.151, 15.260; **tresours** *pl.* 7.9, 14.463
trespaced *v. pa.* offended 5.115; *pa. p.* done wrong 1.119, 3.304, 7.225
trewe *adj.* loyal 14.384
tribunes *n. pl.* leaders of groups of a thousand 6.627; **trybunes** 6.619, 9.186
tribus *n. pl.* tribes 7.239, 10.103, 12.30; **trybus** 4.89, 8.9, 9.256, 11.138, 12.24
troble *v. imp. refl.* become upset 14.383
trompe *n.* trumpet 6.657, 10.352; **trumpes** *pl.* trumpets 15.371
tromped *v. pa.* sounded a trumpet 10.280
trone *n.* throne 6.394, 10.354, 15.18
trouthe *n.* fidelity, faithfulness 3.453, 7.22, 9.518, 14.540
trow(e *v. pr.* think 6.561, 7.62, 7.330, 9.478; **trowest** *2 pr. sg.* 5.23, 9.264, 14.374; **trowed** *pa.* believed 14.349
trumpes *see* **trompe**
turmes *n. pl.* bands, groups (of people) 4.398 *N*
tweyne *num.* two 1.89, 4.6, 5.542, 11.44

U

vnbonde *v. pa.* unbound 15.129
vndefowled *v. pa. p.* undefiled 5.43
vndernome *v. pa. p.* took by stealth 4.111 *N*
vnderstande(n *v. pa. p.* understood 1.65, 7.74; **vnderstonden** 6.625
vnguentaryes *n. pl.* perfumers 9.190 *N*
vnyuersal *adj.* entire 5.476, 6.336, 7.198, 14.339
vnyuersyte *n.* totality 14.338
vnkynde *adj.* rebellious 7.250
vnmesurable *adj.* immeasurable 14.379
vnmeuable *adj.* steadfast 14.74
vnneth(e *adv.* hardly, barely 3.58, 4.93, 14.63, 15.390
vnto *prep.* until 15.120

vpon *prep.* over 10.26; **opon** concerning 9.82
vpperist *adj. superl.* highest in rank 3.405, 5.77, 6.245 *N*, 7.342, 9.257; uppermost 14.110; **vpperyst** 14.308
vp-so-doun *adv.* upside-down 6.477–8
vse *v. inf.* have sexual intercourse with 3.42; **vsid** *pa. p.* accustomed 9.362
vsure *n.* usury 7.110
vtterist *adj. superl.* outermost, most remote 5.600
vttermest *adj. superl.* furthest 15.374

V

vacabunde *adj.* wandering 1.221
variable *adj.* diverse 4.304
veer *n.* as *adj.* spring 4.544
veneson *n.* game, wild animals hunted for food 11.78; **venyson** 4.20
vengea(u)nce *n.* tribulation, punishment 6.306, 6.319; **vengeange** 6.330
veray *adj.* true 1.318
veryly *adv.* truly 11.68
vertue *n.* valour 15.58; power 11.94, 15.88; **virtue** 15.326
vessellis *n. pl.* luggage 5.339
vestement *n.* garment 10.31
victymes *n. pl.* animals offered in sacrifice 11.38 *N*
vynne *n.* gill 14.229 *N*
virtue *see* **vertue**
vysage *n.* face 4.450, 5.82, 13.99 *N*, etc.; **visage** 4.208
visite *v. inf.* come to someone in order to comfort 15.50; **vysytyng** *pr. p.* observing 6.152
vytayll *n.* food, provisions 5.504, 15.28; **vytayllis** *pl.* 5.239; **vytaylles** 5.258; **vytayllys** 15.199
voyd(e *adj.* destitute, empty-handed 1.221, 6.164, 15.15; empty 1.4, 5.158; **uoyde** 9.155
uoyded *v. pa.* were removed, withdrew 6.328; **voyded** 6.343; **voided** *pa. p.* removed 6.326
voys *n.* statement 14.109

W

wayes *n. pl.* roads 15.38
waylled *v. pa.* mourned 5.682, 7.345, 9.248, 10.151
wayllyng *vbl. n.* lamentation, mourning 5.683, 6.111, 9.112, 10.290; **waillyng** 14.58
wayn(e *n.* wagon 9.159, 9.161; **waynes** *pl.* battle chariots 6.446
wayte *v. inf.* ~ **aboute** keep watch 15.293; *pr.* be concerned about, pay attention to 14.255
walke *v. inf.* travel 14.184
walled *v. pa.* constructed walls around a city 1.244
ward *adv.* **to hym** ~ towards him 4.313, 10.23; **fro them** ~ from them 5.379
warderops *n. pl.* storage rooms, cellars 2.36
ware *adj.* **be** ~ beware, guard against 7.72
wast *v. inf.* consume 15.242; **wastyng** *pr. p.* slaughtering 4.509
waxe *see* **wexe**
weder *n.* wether, ram 9.349, 14.280; **weders** *pl.* 9.268, 13.97, 14.343
weel *adj.* satisfactory 14.398
weyker *adj. comp.* weaker 2.127; **weykest** *superl.* 5.256; most vulnerable 10.145
weyward *adj.* contumacious 9.486
wele *n.* prosperity, property 7.151
welfare *n.* good fortune 7.152
welle *adv.* truly, fully 3.105; **wel(l** 6.62, 11.202, 13.68, 14.420; surely, certainly 1.241, 9.357; **as** ~ as well as 3.183; **as** ~ . . . **as** both . . . and, not only . . . but also 4.295, 5.80, 6.353, 14.558, 15.393
welle *n.* spring 1.40 **welles** *pl.* 2.64, 14.316
wene *v. pr.* think 5.710; **wenest** *2 pr. sg.* 4.245, 9.367; **wenyng** *pr. p.* 1.280, 4.218, 15.353
wened *v. pa. p.* weaned 3.328, 6.57, 9.40
wenyng *vbl. n.* weaning 3.329
wente *v. pa.* ~ **tofore** was superior to 11.91; ~ **fro** turned away from 15.93
were *adv.* where 5.33
werke *v. pr. subj.* perform a job 14.158; **wrought** *pa.* acted 1.237; worked 11.114
werkis *n. pl.* acts, deeds 1.32, 3.6, 5.114, 9.95, 11.204; physical labours 6.21
wesshe *v. inf.* wash 3.224, 6.649; *pa.* 3.191, 5.367
wesshed *v. pa.* wished 7.318; **wesshyng** *pr. p.* 1.228, 9.198

wete *v. inf.* know 11.101; **that is to ~** that is to say 2.32, 14.432; **wote** *pr. 1 sg.* know 1.215, 5.661, 14.177; **wotest** *2 pr. sg.* 3.105; **wete** *pr. pl.* 5.363; **wist(e** *pa.* 4.168, 5.330
wethes *n.* weeds, undesirable plants 1.208
wetyngly *adv.* knowingly, consciously 7.24
wexe *v. inf.* become, grow 4.36, 5.231, 7.348, 14.322; *pa.* 6.60; **waxe** 6.470; **wexed** 6.661; **wexid** 14.341; **woxen** *pa. p.* 9.115
whan-so *conj.* when, whenever 6.24
whansomeuer *conj.* whenever 14.545
what *adj.* whatever 3.183; **~ tyme** when 3.271, 5.458
what *adv.* why 6.457, 6.526[1], 9.622; how 11.242
what *pron.* whatever 9.93; **~ that** 5.306
whatsomeuer *adj.* whatever 1.60, 4.459, 6.318
whatsom(m)euer *pron.* whatever 3.335, 4.485, 5.234, etc.
where *conj.* whereas 9.255
whereas *conj.* where 1.189, 3.457, 4.316, etc.
wheresom(m)euer *adv.* wheresoever 3.310, 15.81
wherto *adv.* to what end 14.237
whiche *pron.* whichever 3.65; ***wich** which 5.178
whyles *conj.* while 3.515, 13.37, 14.373; **whylis** 12.9, 14.18; **whylys** 13.40
who *pron. nom.* whoever 7.219; **~ that** 2.121, 3.78, 4.91, 7.5, 14.465; who 3.504; **as ~ said(e** as if to say 1.134, 2.20; **as wo saith** 1.175; **whom** *acc.* whomever 5.403
whoso *pron.* whoever 1.227, 7.120, 9.81
whosomeuer *pron.* whoever 1.230, 2.116, 4.90, etc.
wykers *n. pl.* thin plant stalks 6.41
***wich** *see* **whiche**
wil *v. pr.* accede, consent 3.105, 6.341; ordains, requires 7.83; wish, want 1.289, 15.278; **wyl(l** 4.292, 13.68; **wille** 4.499; **wilt** *2 pr. sg.* 3.63, 4.264, 5.324, etc.; **willyng** *pr. p.* 1.111, 5.43; **wold(e** *pa.* 1.108, 2.135, 3.42, etc.; **woldest** *2 pa. sg.* 4.348; **wolde** *pa. p.* 9.452
will(e *n.* desire 3.481, 6.298, 9.190; **wylle** 7.149
wynne *v. inf.* take possession of 7.295, 15.214
wyse *n.* way, manner 1.107, 3.9, 4.135, etc.; **in lyke ~** in a similar way 3.283, 4.300, 5.177, etc.
wysedom *n.* skill, expertise 15.106
wist *see* **wete**
wythalle *adv.* with it 9.482
within *adv.* inside 15.225
within-forth *adv.* internally 7.142
without *adv.* outside 2.32, 3.241
without *prep.* outside 3.421; apart from 11.78
without-forth *adv.* from the outside 2.73–4; out in the open 3.503; externally 7.137; outside 15.292
withstande *v. inf.* disobey 9.268
wytte *n.* mind 14.157; **witte** skill, ability 15.256; understanding 7.160; **wittes** *pl.* minds 15.363
wytty *adj.* discerning 5.188
wo *see* **who**
wodenes *n.* anger 15.176
wold(e *see* **wil**
wonder *adj.* miraculous, extraordinary 6.347
woned *v. pa. p.* accustomed 4.43, 5.123
woo *adj.* grieved 7.248
woo-begoon *adj.* deeply grieved 4.121, 6.322
worship-doyng *vbl. n.* honour 15.384 *N*
worshype *n.* respect, honour 15.15
worshipe *v. inf.* show respect to 14.401
worshypful *adj.* honourable 14.462
wote(st) *see* **wete**
woxen *see* **wexe**
wrange *v. pa.* wrung 5.129
wreke *v. inf.* **~ on** vent (anger, etc.) on 7.188; **wroken** *pa. p.* avenged 5.281
wreton *v. pa. p.* written 1.25, 5.176, 6.682, 7.68, 10.147
wroth *adj.* angry 1.287, 4.245, 5.107, etc.
wrought *see* **werke**

Y

yaf *see* **yeue**
yate *n.* gate, doorway 4.170, 5.356, 10.131, 15.207; **yates** *pl.* 14.517, 15.307; gateways, strongholds 3.396
ye *interj.* yea, yes 5.417, 10.240
yefte *n.* gift 3.486, 4.449; **yeftes** *pl.* 1.202, 3.487, 4.410, etc.; **yeftys** 14.31

yeld(e *v. inf.* pay 10.166, 11.100; ~ **agayn** repay 7.113; *imp.* give back 3.298; ~ **agayn** restore 14.86; **yelded** *pa. p.* repaid 9.501; **yolden** 9.548; handed over 15.237

yet *adv.* furthermore 1.222, 3.155; still 4.274; once again 4.272, 10.68

yeue *v. pr. subj.* give 15.203; **gaf** *pa.* 1.23, 2.43, 3.51, etc.; **yaf** 14.27; **gauest** *2 pa. sg.* 14.78; **gauyst** 1.139, 14.318; **gyue** *pa. p.* 9.83, 11.179; **yeuen** 14.105; *see also* **knowleche**

yock *n.* yoke 15.100

yollyng *vbl. n.* howling 15.154 *N*

yonglyng *n.* young man 14.198

yongthe *n.* youth 2.110, 5.652

INDEX OF PROPER NAMES

Conventions for alphabetical arrangement and abbreviations are the same as for the glossary; *N* refers to a discussion in the Notes. If a name occurs with the same spelling more than once in an episode, only the first line number is cited. The name of the central figure in each legend is cited only once, unless there are variant spellings. Names of biblical books and their authors are not included. For clarity, in this index modern spellings of Old Testament names have been taken from *The New Oxford Annotated Bible*, 3rd edn. (Oxford: Oxford University Press, 2001), as being generally more familiar to present-day readers. Forms from the Vulgate or Douay-Reims are occasionally added in parentheses where they cast light on the form in *GoL*.

L

M